of England and Wales

LIBRARY SERVICES

The College of Law, Braboeuf Manor, St. Catherines, Portsmouth Road, Guildford, GU3 1HA
Telephone: 01483 216788   E-mail: library.gld@lawcol.co.uk

**This book MUST be returned on or before the last date stamped below.
Failure to do so will result in a fine.**

Birmingham · Chester · Guildford · London · Manchester · York

Structure and Effects in EU Competition Law

International Competition Law Series

VOLUME 47

Editor-in-Chief

Alastair Sutton,

Visiting Fellow at the Centre of European Law at King's College,
London

The titles published in this series are listed at the end of this volume.

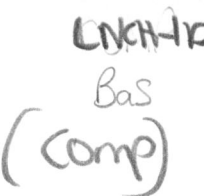

Structure and Effects in EU Competition Law

Studies on Exclusionary Conduct and State Aid

Edited by

Jürgen Basedow

Wolfgang Wurmnest

Wolters Kluwer
Law & Business

Published by:
Kluwer Law International
PO Box 316
2400 AH Alphen aan den Rijn
The Netherlands
Website: www.kluwerlaw.com

Sold and distributed in North, Central and South America by:
Aspen Publishers, Inc.
7201 McKinney Circle
Frederick, MD 21704
United States of America
Email: customer.service@aspenpublishers.com

Sold and distributed in all other countries by:
Turpin Distribution Services Ltd.
Stratton Business Park
Pegasus Drive, Biggleswade
Bedfordshire SG18 8TQ
United Kingdom
Email: kluwerlaw@turpin-distribution.com

Printed on acid-free paper.

ISBN 978-90-411-3174-4

© 2011 Kluwer Law International BV, The Netherlands

Printed in Great Britain.

PREFACE

Ever since the establishment of the European Economic Community the evolution and application of European competition law has strongly been influenced by the German ordo-liberal philosophy underpinning the Freiburg School focusing on the balance of powers of undertakings and economic liberties. It is only in the last decade that the European Commission has progressively abandoned that approach in favor of what is called a more economic approach concentrating on efficiency gains generated by, or expected from transactions with possible anti-competitive effects. In order to stimulate the debate on this basic reorientation, the Max Planck Institute for Comparative and International Private Law at Hamburg organized a conference on 23 and 24 January 2009. It convened economists, legal scholars and practitioners for an exchange of views on the methodological foundations of competition policy and competition law with the focus on two special areas: The prohibition of abuses of dominant positions and the review of State aid. The collected papers of this conference are hereby presented to the public.

While the abuse of market dominance has repeatedly been the object of academic discussion, the review of State aid by the European Commission has for a long time been in the shadow of academic interest. That is why the German Monopolies Commission devoted a special chapter of its XVIIth Biennial Opinion on the state of German and European competition policy, to the review of State aid (Monopolkommission, XVII. Hauptgutachten 2006/2007, Baden-Baden 2008, nos. 886 ff.). It explores the use of economic arguments in that sector and provides the background to the discussions conducted at the Hamburg conference on that matter. Its publication in this book is the more important as the present chairman of the German Monopolies Commission, Professor Dr. *Justus Haucap*, who presented a paper and the views of the Monopolies Commission at the Hamburg conference, despite repeated assurances, did not deliver a manuscript and thereby delayed the publication of the whole book.

The editors gratefully acknowledge the help of *Ann-Christin Maak* and *Julian Sanner* in the preparation of the various papers for the printing process, of Dr. *Jan Jacob* who drew up the index and of *Ingeborg Stahl* who produced the printer's copy. Their assistance has provided great help in the publication process.

Hamburg, January 2011   *Jürgen Basedow, Wolfgang Wurmnest*

SUMMARY OF CONTENTS

TABLE OF CONTENTS

CONTRIBUTORS

Svend Albæk, Member of the Chief Economist Team, European Commission, DG Competition, Brussels

Prof. Dr. Mag. Josef Azizi, Judge at the General Court of the European Union, Luxembourg

Prof. Dr. Dr. h.c. Jürgen Basedow, Max Planck Institute for Comparative and International Private Law, Hamburg; former Chairman of the German Monopolies Commission

Prof. Dr. Philippe Choné, ENSAE-CREST, Paris; former Chef économiste de l'Autorité de la concurrence

Carles Esteva Mosso, Director, European Commission, DG Competition, Brussels

Christian Ewald, Head of Unit 'Economic Issues in Competition Policy' (Chief Economist), Bonn

Prof. Dr. Wolfgang Kerber, Philipps-Universität Marburg

Prof. Dr. Jürgen Kühling, Universität Regensburg

Dr. Dominik Massing, Max Planck Institute for Comparative and International Private Law, Hamburg

Prof. Giorgio Monti, European University Institute, Florence

Dr. Lukas Repa, Case Officer, European Commission, DG Competition, Brussels

Prof. Dr. Ulrich Schwalbe, Universität Hohenheim

Prof. Dr. Piet Jan Slot, Universiteit Leiden

Prof. Dr. Wolfgang Wurmnest, Gottfried Wilhelm Leibniz Universität Hannover

Prof. Dr. Daniel Zimmer, Rheinische Friedrich-Wilhelms-Universität Bonn; Member of the German Monopolies Commission

PART I: THE MORE ECONOMIC APPROACH IN EU COMPETITION LAW

INTRODUCTION

Jürgen Basedow

I. Four stages of competition law development

The history of the law against restrictions of competition in Europe which started soon after World War II can be divided into four stages. The first stage, running up to the foundation of the European Economic Community in 1957 may be called the *post-war period* because political action in those years was still very much influenced by the experience of World War II and the strong desire to avoid the resurrection of Germany's economic and political power. The transfer of sovereign power over the coal and steel sectors, by the European Coal and Steel Treaty, to a supranational High Authority, was essentially motivated by these post-war sentiments, and it took some time before economic and political leaders acknowledged that the integration of markets into a European market and the implementation of competition rules in that market were important goals as such.

As a consequence, the competition provisions of the EEC Treaty were adopted with a general purview. They gave rise to the second stage, which may be called the *pioneer phase*. The Community had to conceive devices for the effective implementation of competition law: In the 1960s the direct applicability and the priority principles were stated by the Court of Justice, and the Commission and Council instituted the notification system, block exemption

3

regulations and comfort letters. The third stage of the 1970s and 1980s is the *stage of expansion*: Community competition law conquered new horizons, defeating the idea of exempted markets, particularly in the regulated industries, and gradually developed merger control.

The collapse of the socialist regimes in Eastern Europe in 1991 gave rise to the fourth stage of European competition law, which may be called the *post-socialist stage*. It is characterised by three major developments:[1] The decentralisation of public enforcement by Regulation 1/2003[2], the quest for private enforcement,[3] and the growing impact of economic thought in the implementation of competition law, the so-called more economic approach, which is the focus of this symposium.

II. The more economic approach

The more economic approach endorsed by the European Commission ever since the mid-1990s draws from antecedents in American antitrust that became dominant in the US under the *Reagan* administration. The insight that competition helps to increase welfare and the efficient use of scarce economic resources was not novel, but it generated normative consequences which have led to far reaching changes in the application of the US antitrust laws. These consequences may be summarised in three points: First, the purpose of competition law is neither the protection of competitors nor the preservation of a competitive structure of the market as a safeguard for future competitive processes, but the *maximisation of welfare*; there is some debate about whether total welfare or simply consumer welfare is the main goal. Second, what matters in the light of this objective is not a well-defined type of behaviour which can be ascertained in the antitrust enforcement procedure, but rather the *effects* that this behaviour is likely to have. As a consequence, the prognostic element which has always played a certain role, in particular in competition legislation, acquires increased significance in the application of competition law. Third, *efficiency gains* caused

---

[1] J. Basedow, 'The modernisation of European competition law: A story of unfinished concepts' (2007) 42 *Texas International Law Journal*, 429-439.

[2] Council Regulation (EC) No. 1/2003 (16 December 2002) on the implementation of the rules on competition laid down in Articles 81 and 82 of the Treaty [2003] OJ L 1/1.

[3] White Paper on damages actions for breach of the EC antitrust rules (2 April 2008), COM(2008) 165 final.

by restrictive practices have to be taken into account in the overall competition analysis.

The simplification inherent in this summary may help understanding the intellectual attraction of the approach which has had more and more impact on the European side of the Atlantic. Beginning in the late 1990s the rule-making activities of the European Commission have increasingly been inspired by the more economic approach. An early example relates to the block exemption regulation for vertical agreements which exempts agreements and practices irrespective of their anti-competitive character and purpose, if the market share of the companies involved is below 30%.[4] As to horizontal agreements the guidelines of the Commission on horizontal cooperation agreements equally give evidence of the effort for a thorough investigation into competitive effects. Not even traditional *per se* prohibitions are unequivocally affirmed; thus, price fixing or market sharing agreements are only said to be 'almost always prohibited'.[5] The new Merger Control Regulation of 2004 has substituted the traditional market dominance test[6] by the SIEC test[7]: Where a concentration would 'significantly impede effective competition..., [it] shall be declared incompatible with the common market'. The creation or strengthening of a dominant position is now only an example for a significant impediment to effective competition ('SIEC') and is no longer the decisive test. Moreover, efficiency gains brought about by the concentration are said to possibly counteract the effects on competition, in which case the concentration would not significantly impede effective competition.[8] These developments have been the object of broad comment since the turn of the century.

---

[4]   Commission Regulation (EC) No. 2790/1999 (22 December 1999) on the application of Article 81(3) of the Treaty on categories of vertical agreements and concerted practices [1999] OJ L 336/21.

[5]   Guidelines on the applicability of Article 81 of the EC Treaty to horizontal cooperation agreements [2001] OJ C 3/2 para. 25.

[6]   See Article 3(3) of Council Regulation (EEC) No. 4064/89 (21 December 1989) on the control of concentrations between undertakings [1989] OJ L 395/1.

[7]   See Article 3(3) of Council Regulation (EC) No. 139/2004 (20 January 2004) on the control of concentrations between undertakings (the EC Merger Regulation) [2004] OJ L 24/1.

[8]   See Recital 29 of Regulation 139/2004 (*supra* n. 7).

III. Programme and issues of the symposium

Less attention has been focused on two areas of competition law which have been targeted by the more economic approach only in recent years. These areas are the unilateral conduct of dominant undertakings and its regulation by Article 102 TFEU, and State aid. As to the former, the Commission has published a communication on its own enforcement policy only in December 2008. This document does not deal with abusive practices of dominant firms at large, but only with exclusionary conduct.[9] Compared to the draft published in 2005[10] the final version of the Communication has been streamlined considerably. But it emerges quite clearly from this paper that the Commission considers efficiencies as the main justification of anti-competitive conduct. The second part of this symposium sheds some light on this new document, in particular on the dominance threshold and predatory pricing.

The control of State aid has received a second-class treatment by most competition scholars for a long time. This may be due to the fact that the substance of State aid is very much a matter of political discretion. In fact, the recent European wave of apparently unlimited overspending gives evidence of the psychological and political factors inherent in the democratic process which determine the granting of State aid. Nonetheless, any aid granted by a Member State that distorts competition and affects trade between Member States is basically prohibited under Article 107 TFEU as being incompatible with the common Market. It is difficult to explain the large number of heterogeneous exceptions to this prohibition in a consistent way. The Commission has embarked on the road to that goal by publishing, in 2005, a State Aid Action Plan which focuses on economic justifications for State aid, in particular market failure.[11] The last part of this symposium focuses on that action plan and its critical assessment by the German Monopolies Commission.[12]

---

[9] Communication from the Commission – Guidance on the Commission's enforcement priorities in applying Article 82 EC Treaty to abusive exclusionary conduct by dominant undertakings (3 December 2008), COM(2008) 832.

[10] DG Competition Discussion Paper on the application of Article 82 of the Treaty to exclusionary abuses – public consultation (Brussels, December 2005) <ec.europa.eu/comm/competition/antitrust/art82/discpaper2005.pdf>, 11 October 2010.

[11] State Aid Action Plan: Less and better targeted state aid: a roadmap for state aid reform 2005-2009 (7 June 2005), COM(2005) 107 final.

[12] Monopolkommission, *Weniger Staat, mehr Wettbewerb. XVII. Hauptgutachten 2006/ 2007* (Baden-Baden, 2008) para. 886 *et seq*. An English translation of the German Monopolies Commission's chapter on State aid can be found in the Annex to this book.

As shown above, the more economic approach has had a considerable impact on various sectors of competition law. This does not necessarily mean that the ideas reflected in the sectorial developments are the same. But our observation gives rise to horizontal questions, for example, in respect of the welfare standard applied: Is it consumer welfare or general welfare, or do we adhere to different standards in different areas? Other horizontal questions may arise in respect of the 'effects-forecast' required in the various parts of competition law and the procedural possibilities and framework for such prognostic investigations. A general issue that is both of theoretical interest and practical relevance concerns the relation between efficiency gains and the downgrading of the competitive structure of the market. It is the first part of the symposium that focuses on such general matters.

IV. Interdisciplinary research in economics and law

Competition law is one of the traditional areas of common interest of economics and law. Their respective views can be compared to the studies in perspective carried out by Renaissance painters. Artists like the Italian *Andrea Mantegna* used to draw one and the same individual from various different points: From the front, from the left, from the right, from above and even, while that individual was lying on a bed, from his feet upwards. The resulting drawings reflect very different appearances. Yet, they are all correct in the sense that it is not possible to fix one single point of view as the only one possible.

In a similar vein, economic and legal considerations relating to competition and markets may produce very diverse accounts of one and the same course of events. While this may trigger disputes about who is right and wrong, there cannot be any doubt that both are justified and necessary. What differs is their place and point in time in the competition analysis. In this respect, the symposium provides some important clarification. It is for example undisputed that economic theory has a significant role to play when it comes to the demarcation of the relevant market, to the assessment of entry-barriers or to the evaluation of the competitive risks inherent in predatory pricing. In these areas the legal rules either refer to economic insight and experience, or they are drafted in such a wide manner that recourse to all kinds of theories on economic behaviour and its effects is at least not excluded.

What appears to be more controversial is the *supreme objective* of competition law. Again, the significance of a welfare standard and the consequential importance of efficiency gains are generally approved and there are no objections as far as their implementation in competition *legislation* is concerned. The symposium shows, however, that there may be good reasons for some qualifications to the welfare standard, in particular the limited prognostic abilities of competition authorities and courts. But there is no doubt that the European legislator is empowered, within the limits laid down in the Treaty, to grant high priority to considerations of welfare maximisation and efficiency gains.

It has to be acknowledged, however, that the European Treaty has not placed the maximisation of welfare and efficiency at the top rank of its objectives. Quite to the contrary, the former Article 3(1)(g) EC which has been transformed into Protocol No. 27 by the Treaty of Lisbon puts the Community under an obligation to establish 'a system ensuring that competition is not distorted'. Thus, the Treaty awards the highest rank to a competitive structure of the market and of the market process.[13] While it is agreed that this structure generally serves the maximisation of welfare, the latter goal cannot be substituted for the system of undistorted competition where it does not. The competition analysis carried out by competition authorities and by the courts must comply with the binding authority of the Treaty. The Treaty has opened some gateways to economic thought, in particular to efficiency considerations, in Article 101(3) TFEU, and to a certain extent by using the concept of abusiveness, in Article 102 TFEU. But these provisions do not permit the authorities and the courts to displace the structural aim of undistorted competition in favour of the maximisation of welfare. This would require an amendment to the Treaty.

Such amendment has not been adopted by the Treaty of Lisbon. While the Treaty of Lisbon has removed the goal of the establishment of a system of undistorted competition from the list of Community objectives, Article 2(3) TEU will still provide for the establishment of an internal market, and a special protocol (No. 27) unequivocally sets out that the internal market 'includes a system ensuring that competition is not distorted'.[14] Thus, undistorted competition in the internal market is still to be considered as the ultimate goal of European competition law.

The practical significance of my preceding remarks and of the many debates taking centre stage at this symposium is rather low. In fact, in my experience of

---

[13] See for the particular significance of the protection of the market structure, *British Airways v. Commission*, Case No. C-95/04 P [2007] ECR I-2331 paras 86, 106 in respect of Article 82 EC/102 TFEU; *T-Mobile Netherlands v. Raad van Bestuur*, Case No. C-8/08 [2009] ECR I-4529 para. 38 (concerning Article 81 EC/101 TFEU).

[14] See the Treaty of Lisbon amending the Treaty on European Union and the Treaty establishing the European Community (13 December 2007) [2007] OJ C 306/1 and the Protocol on the internal market and competition at p. 156.

eight years as a member of the German Monopolies Commission, my assessment of individual cases has nearly always been the same as that of my colleague members who were economists. Rather, what I said before was meant to elaborate on the legal framework in order to show the peculiar properties of the legal analysis. It does not change on the sole ground that a new school of economic thought defines new objectives for existing law. This does not exclude that elements of such new analysis penetrate the interpretation of existing provisions where that is possible given the constraints of legal method.

In the interdisciplinary discourse it would appear necessary that both sides take notice of, and respect the characteristics of the other discipline. This is true for legal scholarship which should try to accommodate new insights of economic theory where the law in force so permits, and that will often be the case; it is also true for economics which has to take account of the limitations and sometimes the petrifying effect of the law which although occasionally appearing as an impediment, makes an important contribution to the stability of society.

THE MORE ECONOMIC APPROACH PARADIGM – AN EFFECTS-BASED APPROACH TO EU COMPETITION POLICY

Carles Esteva Mosso[*]

I.   Introduction

Good morning Ladies and gentlemen,

I would like to start my presentation by congratulating the Max Planck Institute for organizing this conference on a more economic approach to Article

---

[*] Transcript of a speech delivered and recorded at the Max Planck Institute for Comparative and Private International Law. The speech was complemented by footnotes and was later updated to reflect recent legislative amendments.

82 EC/102 TFEU and to the field of State aids. I think this is the first major academic event taking place after the approval by the European Commission ('the Commission') of the 'Guidance on the Commission's enforcement priorities in applying Article 82 of the EC Treaty to abusive exclusionary conduct by dominant undertakings' of December 2008 ('the Enforcement Communication').[1] The Enforcement Communication concludes a long process of moving the enforcement and the interpretation of competition law towards a more economic, a more effects-based approach. I will not be talking abut the Enforcement Communication in detail even though I was very much involved in its conclusion. It will be *Svend Albaek* from our Chief Economist Team who will present this issue[2] as he has been involved in this project for much longer than I was. I will focus on what I have been asked to do and present some general thoughts on the economic approach. I think a lot has already been said in this area but I will try to focus on four different issues.

First of all, I will try to review with you briefly the major steps in the adoption of this more economic and more effects-based approach, a process that has taken more than eleven years, which started with the Green Paper on vertical restraints in 1997 (II.). Then I will present the main features of the more economic approach which applies across all the instruments of competition law (III.). I will then briefly touch upon the relation between the effects-based approach and the approach to protect the competitive process (IV.). In this respect let me already say in advance that I do not see a contradiction at all between these two approaches. And finally, I would like to discuss with you, what the next policy development steps are in the area of antitrust and merger law planned at the European Commission (V.). I will not deal with the subject of State aid, as *Lukas Repa* from our State Aid Unit will be here tomorrow and will be able to say more about this issue.[3]

---

[1] Communication from the Commission – Guidance on the Commission's enforcement priorities in applying Article 82 of the EC Treaty to abusive exclusionary conduct by dominant undertakings [2009] OJ C 45/7.
[2] See pp. 41 *et seq.* in this book.
[3] See pp. 231 *et seq.* in this book.

II. The progressive adoption of an effects-based approach to EU competition law

A. *Reform of vertical restraints policy*

Let me start with a brief historical evolution. As *Jürgen Basedow* has already indicated, the first step towards a more economics based approach was the reform of our old approach to vertical restraints. At the beginning of the 1990s, it was becoming obvious that our tight control of vertical restraints in the past contained a significant number of shortcomings. The Commission in 1997 therefore published, as you all know, a Green Paper presenting a number of options to ameliorate the law. After a public consultation, the Commission adopted a Communication on the follow up of the Green Paper on vertical restraints in which it already mentions the necessity and the basic components of a more economic approach to competition law. Indeed, this Communication points out that the result of a legalistic form-based approach is often a 'straight-jacket' for undertakings and continues to state that 'to better protect competition a more economics based approach is required' which 'should be based on the effects of the practices on the market'.[4]

This basic statement summarises all what happened afterwards. Two years later, the Block Exemption Regulation and Guidelines on Vertical Restraints were adopted to shape the new approach to EU competition policy.[5] The novel features introduced by this reform were meant to ensure that only those vertical agreements having a detrimental effect on consumers are prohibited: For this purpose a wide-ranging block exemption covering all types of distribution agreements was adopted and not, as in the past, a detailed regulation for certain distribution formats only. Moreover, the new Regulation contained only very few black clauses and set forth a safe harbour based on a market share threshold of 30%. This was a clear signal to undertakings that without market power

---

[4] Communication from the Commission on the application of the Community competition rules to vertical restraints (Follow-up to the Green Paper on Vertical Restraints) [1998] OJ C 365/3.

[5] Council Regulation (EC) No. 1215/1999 (10 June 1999) amending Regulation No. 19/65/EEC on the application of Article 81(3) of the Treaty to certain categories of agreements and concerted practices [1999] OJ L 148/1; Commission Regulation (EC) No. 2790/1999 (22 December 1999) on the application of Article 81(3) of the Treaty to categories of vertical agreements and concerted practices [1999] OJ L 336/21; Commission Notice – Guidelines on Vertical Restraints [2000] OJ C 291/1.

vertical restraints in general pose no problems for competition and therefore for competition law, except when the agreement contains one or more hardcore restrictions. Finally, it is also important to note, that above this safe harbour of 30% market share, there is no presumption of illegality at all. Vertical agreements must be analysed in light of the market circumstances in each individual case to compare possible negative effects with potential positive effects on markets and competition.

The approach to vertical restraints was later extended to horizontal agreements amongst competitors, with the adoption of the block exemption regulations on horizontal cooperation agreements and the corresponding guidelines of 2000[6] and the block exemption and guidelines on transfer of technology adopted in 2004.[7]

B. Guidelines on the application of Article 81(3) EC/101(3) TFEU

The second major step in the extension of a more effects-based approach to EU competition law was the adoption of the Guidelines on the application of Article 81(3) EC/101(3) TFEU by the European Commission in 2004.[8] And not so much because what the guidelines said about Article 81(3) EC/101(3) TFEU but what they say about Article 81(1) EC/101(1) TFEU. In the guidelines for the first time the Commission presented in a general manner the interpretation of the notion of restriction of competition of Article 81(1) EC/101(1) TFEU with a truly effects-based approach. And with regard to Article 81(3) EC/101(3) TFEU, these guidelines clearly imply that Article 81(3) EC/101(3) TFEU is about an efficiency assessment. There was at the time a debate whether under Article 81(1) EC/101(1) TFEU, the European Commission had to do the competition

---

[6]   Commission Regulation (EC) No. 2658/2000 (29 November 2000) on the application of Article 81(3) of the Treaty to categories of specialisation agreements [2000] OJ L 304/3; Commission Regulation (EC) No. 2659/2000 (29 November 2000) on the application of Article 81(3) of the Treaty to categories of research and development agreements [2000] OJ L 304/7; Commission Notice – Guidelines on the applicability of Article 81 of the Treaty to horizontal cooperation agreements [2001] OJ C 3/2.

[7]   Commission Regulation (EC) No. 772/2004 (27 April 2004) on the application of Article 81(3) of the Treaty to categories of technology transfer agreements [2004] OJ L 123/11; Commission Notice – Guidelines on the application of Article 81 of the EC Treaty to technology transfer agreements [2004] OJ C 101/2.

[8]   Communication from the Commission – Notice – Guidelines on the application of Article 81(3) of the Treaty [2004] OJ C 101/97.

analysis and then pursuant to Article 81(3) EC/101(3) TFEU take into account other goals and do a balancing of the different goals or, whether Article 81(3) EC/101(3) TFEU is only about an analysis of economic efficiencies and that in the end what you have to do in applying the whole Article 81 EC/101 TFEU is the balancing of anti-competitive and pro-competitive effects of the conduct in question. The latter position was taken by the Commission in its guidelines on Article 81(3) EC/101(3) TFEU. And here you see a bit of a difference in the area of State aids in Article 87 EC/107 TFEU where, under the balancing test, one compares the anti-competitive effects prohibited by Article 87(1) EC/107(1) TFEU with a number of policy goals (economic efficiency but also equity related goals), in accordance with Article 87(3) EC/107(3) TFEU.

Why was this change so relevant? I think it was relevant because it results in a limited discretionary power of the enforcement agencies. An independent enforcer or a judge must only look at the effects in a given market and does not have to make a trade-off between different policy goals. These guidelines were being adopted at the same time that the Commission was starting a decentralisation process of the application of competition law by national authorities and courts, and I think it is important to keep in mind the impact of the effects-based approach not only on the substantive analysis but also on the institutional context. Indeed, by introducing an effects-based approach, and correspondingly a narrow (economic) goal of consumer welfare, the application of competition law by independent competition authorities and courts is facilitated.

C. The new merger control regime

The third major step, I think, was linked to the merger area. In mergers, the economic approach had always been more prevalent but some argued that there were, nevertheless, some gaps between the legal tools and economic theory. The replacement of the dominance test by the significant impact of competition test laid down in the Regulation 139/2004 ('Merger Regulation')[9] and its implementing legislation[10] eliminated these possible gaps. It removed the vestiges of a structural approach in merger control and moved to a full effects-based analysis focused on the impact a merger has on consumer welfare. In particular in the area of horizontal mergers these changes ensure that the Commission can look at

---

[9] Council Regulation (EC) No. 139/2004 (20 January 2004) on the control of concentrations between undertakings [2004] OJ L 24/1.

[10] Commission Regulation (EC) No. 802/2004 implementing Council Regulation (EC) No. 139/2004 [2004] OJ L 133/1.

unilateral effects arising from mergers that would not lead to dominance. It was doubtful whether such anti-competitive effects could be caught with the old merger control test. However, under the new significant impediment to effective competition standard such effects are now certainly covered by the Merger Regulation.

Also in merger control, guidelines on horizontal mergers were adopted that introduce safe harbours based on market shares and concentration indexes, detail how the Commission would assess non-coordinated and co-ordinated theories of harm and very importantly, explain under which circumstances efficiencies have to be taken into account positively in merger control.[11]

At that moment, in 2004, it was considered still too early to develop these guidelines in the area of non-horizontal mergers, in particular because there were important cases still pending before the European courts, for instance *Tetra Laval*[12] and *GE/Honeywell*[13].The Commission decided to wait until there was clear jurisprudence in this area. And in fact this jurisprudence happened to become truly effects-based. The Court of First Instance – which has been renamed into General Court after the Treaty of Lisbon became effective – in *GE/Honeywell* told very clearly that in order to identify a problem in a non-horizontal merger you had to prove likely effects and this is the approach that was then incorporated into the merger guidelines for non-horizontal mergers subsequently in 2008.[14]

For the first time in these guidelines, the Commission makes a distinction between foreclosure, that is the exclusion of competitors, and anti-competitive foreclosure, that is exclusion of competitors that leads to consumer harm. This distinction is very important because if you only focus on the first type of foreclosure you may end up protecting competitors which is clearly not what our goal in competition policy is. But if you only focus on anti-competitive foreclosure then you only care about competitors where these competitors have an importance in order to ensure consumer welfare. And as we will see, this distinction is also now included in the guidance paper on Article 82 EC/102 TFEU.

As in previous reforms, the non-horizontal merger guidelines also include a safe harbour based on market shares and concentration indexes. It is also recog-

---

[11] Guidelines on the assessment of horizontal mergers under the Council Regulation on the control of concentrations between undertakings [2004] OJ C 31/5.

[12] *Tetra Laval BV v. Commission*, Case No. T-5/02 [2002] ECR II-4381; *Commission v. Tetra Laval BV*, Case No. C-12/03 P [2005] ECR I-987.

[13] *General Electric Company v. Commission*, Case No. T-210/01 [2005] ECR II-5575.

[14] Guidelines on the assessment of non-horizontal mergers under the Council Regulation on the control of concentrations between undertakings [2008] OJ C 265/6.

nised that non-horizontal mergers have substantial scope for efficiencies and, in particular in this case, pricing efficiencies such as the elimination of the double mark-up.

D. Turning towards an effects-based approach in abuse control

1. What is the Enforcement Communication about?

The sketched reforms paved the way for moving toward a more effects-based approach in abuse matters. As in most races, the last mile is the most difficult to run. Also our efforts to reconcile the application and interpretation of Article 82 EC/102 TFEU with an effects-based approach were rather exhausting. The Commission issued a discussion paper in 2005.[15] Yet it took three years to adopt the Enforcement Communication.[16] Let me say only a few general things about this Communication.

First of all, unlike all the other guidelines I have been talking about, the Enforcement Communication is not an interpretative notice but an enforcement priorities paper. Why? Because apparently in abuse control, the European courts have not yet fully embraced the effects-based approach as in other areas. There are some judgments of the courts that can clearly be read with this perspective but there are some others that are still too much form-based. Therefore, the Commission could not rely on judgments rendered by the European courts calling for a more effects-based analysis in abuse control cases as it was the case in non-horizontal mergers, for instance. There has not been an equivalent to the *GE/Honeywell* or a *Tetra* judgment that would allow us to move clearly towards a more effects-based approach. Against this background, the Commission took the position that, among all the potential cases involving practices that the European courts had condemned as exclusionary abuses pursuant to Article 82 EC/102 TFEU, it will choose to focus its scarce enforcement resources on only some of them. Which ones? The ones that result in anti-competitive effects and really harm the consumer. This is what is meant by enforcement priorities. The Enforcement Communication sets forth guidelines on which cases the Commission will focus its enforcement efforts in future. The basic rule is that only those cases shall be taken up that will likely end up harming the consumer. Com-

---

[15] DG Competition discussion paper on the application of Article 82 of the Treaty to exclusionary abuses (Brussels, December 2005) <ec.europa.eu/competition/antitrust/art82/discpaper2005.pdf>, 27 September 2010.

[16] See *supra* n. 1.

plaints on cases not fulfilling the assessment criteria in the Enforcement Communication will therefore normally be rejected for lack of Community interest.

Of course, this approach has some drawbacks in terms of coherence. An enforcement priority notice does not have the same impact on coherence across the network of competition authorities or the network of judges as interpretative guidelines would have. But, nevertheless, this Notice has been discussed with all national competition authorities in Europe. A large number of them seem to share the approach and we hope that this approach will also largely ensure coherence. In the end, we thought it was better to put forth a Communication that outlines which are the criteria that the Commission thinks have to be used for the enforcement of Article 82 EC/102 TFEU rather than to wait with giving clarity and predictability to companies until the Court would really issue these more effects-based judgments that would allow us to turn to interpretative guidelines.

2.   What is the focus of the Enforcement Communication?

The Enforcement Communication aims to ensure that companies in a dominant position do not exclude rivals by means other than competition on the merits. This also implies that dominant companies have the right to compete aggressively. To ensure this goal the Commission wants to focus on those practices that will harm consumer welfare and, again, here the distinction between foreclose and anti-competitive foreclosure leading to consumer harm happens to be a useful instrument to distinguish between the practices that are anti-competitive and which are not. The Enforcement Communication thus follows a full effects-based approach. The Commission will focus on those cases where it can prove likely negative effects on consumers. These likely negative effects on consumer welfare will also have to be balanced with possible pro-competitive efficiencies raised by the practice by the dominant undertaking. This general approach is specified in the Enforcement Communication for four categories of practices: exclusive dealing, tying and bundling, predation, and refusal to supply. I will let *Svend Albaek* develop these in more detail and will now turn to an analysis of the general features of the more economic approach paradigm.

III. The effects-based approach

With the Enforcement Communication infusing the effects-based analysis into the application of Article 82 EC/102 TFEU, the Commission has developed a coherent approach across all instruments of antitrust and merger control. This effects-based approach has various important implications that apply equally across instruments.

The first implication is that the Commission will focus on detrimental effects on consumer welfare to see whether an agreement, merger or unilateral conduct should be prohibited. Consumers can usually only be harmed by undertakings with a certain degree of market power. Therefore the Commission has introduced safe harbours in all the instruments. I have already mentioned the safe harbours based on market shares and/or concentration indexes in the context of the assessment of agreements or concerted practices and in the field of merger control.[17] The safe harbour in dominance cases is built on the notion of dominance.

A second point to be mentioned is that under the new approach the theory of harm now comes at the forefront of enforcement of competition law. In every case the Commission needs to explain how an individual practice, an individual agreement or an individual merger will end up harming the consumer. There needs to be a story, a coherent narrative that explains such negative effects on consumer welfare and the theory of harm advanced has to be backed by facts and evidence. It is not enough to say that there might be a possibility that certain practice will have negative effects on competition. We will need to prove that it is likely that negative effects on competition will arise. Let me be clear that when the Enforcement Communication or other guidelines are talking about likely effects, they do not mean actual effects. It is not as if the Commission needs to have the 'dead body on the table'. Further it is important to stress that the Commission does not intent to simply focus on immediate or short-term effects on prices. Rather, the Commission wants also to take into account effects on other parameters of competition, such as long-term effects on quality, innovation or diversity. The Enforcement Communication on Article 82 EC/102 TFEU is, for instance, very explicit about such long term effects in its section on refusals to deal. It is thus not sufficient to prove that there will be an immediate impact on the consumer by an increase of prices but that, before identifying a problem of refusal to deal, the Commission will have to be convinced that we are not affecting the incentives for a long-term innovation or development of infrastructure in prosecuting a refusal to deal.

A third distinctive feature of the effects-based approach is the balancing test to be applied across all our instruments. One has to assess positive effects and efficiencies and to balance them against possible anti-competitive effects. The conditions under which efficiencies can be taken into account are essentially the

---

[17] See *supra* II.

same under all instruments. Thus, the efficiencies must (i.) be realised or likely to be realised as a result of the conduct, agreement or merger concerned. The conduct, agreement or merger must (ii.) also be indispensable or merger specific to realise these efficiencies. Moreover, (iii.) the efficiencies generated by a given conduct, agreement or merger must be passed onto consumers and finally (iv.) it needs to be ensured that the competitive process in respect of a substantial part of the products or services concerned will not entirely be eliminated. In merger control the last condition is presented as a sliding scale. The higher the market share or the market power of the merged company, the less likely it will be that the efficiency defence will be accepted by the Commission, which is similar than the last condition of Article 81(3) EC/101(3) TFEU.

A fourth improvement coming with the effects-based approach is that different types of behaviour are dealt with by the same approach, an approach which focuses on effects and not on form. It is important to avoid forcing companies to stick to certain business practices for legal reasons even though there are more efficient ways to conduct business which would bring benefits to consumers. Focusing on effects will allow companies to choose the business practice they consider best for competition. Let me give you two examples: First, the new approach has lead to a convergent approach in the assessment of horizontal mergers and horizontal agreements. In the past, we had the dominance test in merger control which, in a certain way, involved an implicit efficiency consideration. We assumed that mergers involve efficiencies and, therefore, we would only intervene when the merger would create a problem of dominance; we would not intervene at lower levels of market power. I do not think this implicit efficiency was backed at all by empirical analysis. On the contrary, for horizontal agreements, Article 81(1) EC/101(1) TFEU would be infringed by companies with joint market power well below dominance levels, but efficiencies could be explicitly taken into account under Article 81(3) EC/101(3) TFEU. Under the new approach we have a coherent and much more refined analysis as we look, both in merger control and in the assessment of horizontal agreements, at any level of anti-competitive effects and we balance these with efficiencies.

A second example showing the necessity of a coherent approach is when one looks at anti-competitive foreclosure. What is the difference between an anti-competitive foreclosure resulting from a company with market power upstream, merging with another company downstream as opposed to a dominant company already integrated using the power upstream to foreclose some competitor downstream? The form is different but the effect in the market is the same. The only difference could be in the area of efficiencies where the vertical integration could lead more clearly to the elimination of double mark-ups. But leaving efficiencies aside, the type of effects that we are examining in a vertical merger or in, let's say, a refusal to deal case, are the same from an economic point of view and we will be treating them in the same way in the future.

IV. Effects-based approach vs. protecting competition

Let me now come to the debate on the effects-based approach vs. the competition based approach. I think all these changes I have explained do not mean that EU Competition policy no longer cares about the competition process. It is rather the contrary: The European approach cares very much about ensuring the competition process as a means to protect consumer welfare. And I think this is clearly seen by looking at the last condition of Article 81(3) EC/101(3) TFEU which essentially states that one cannot take into account efficiencies when this would lead to the complete elimination of the competitive process. And this is very clearly spelt out in the Guidelines on Article 81(3) EC/101(3) TFEU. Let me quote '[that] the protection of rivalry and the competitive process is given priority of a potentially pro-competitive efficiency gains which could result from restrictive agreements. In other words, the ultimate aim of Article 81 of the EC Treaty is to protect the competitive process.'[18] In other words, if we are in this extreme situation where a practice could lead to efficiencies but would eliminate the competitive process, EU competition law chooses in favour of the competitive process, not in favour of the efficiencies.

However, if we agree that our goal is consumer welfare, that the competition process in itself is not a goal, but merely a means, then we need to establish an economically sound distinction between practices that will harm consumer welfare and practices that will enhance consumer welfare. Such a distinction cannot be established by simply examining how the competitive process will be affected. For example, a conditional rebate by a dominant company could lead to exclusion of competitors, affecting the competitive process, but even leading to exclusion of competitors it could be pro-competitive or anti-competitive. By only looking at the effects on the competition process, we will not be able to discriminate in which cases the rebate is good for competition. We therefore need to analysis the impact of the rebate scheme on consumer welfare to make a sound separation. And to do this, we will need to examine whether the rebates would likely exclude a competitor as effective as the dominant undertaking.

---

[18] Communication from the Commission – Notice – Guidelines on the application of Article 81(3) of the Treaty [2004] OJ C 101/97 para. 105.

V. What next?

The EU has now concluded a major cycle of reform of its antitrust and merger rules. I see it as the most important substantive change in the approach of competition law since the coming into force of the EC Treaty. This cycle is over but immediately now a new cycle starts. This new cycle requires the revision of documents that already incorporate a more economic based approach. In this context, we will have to revise our rules on vertical and horizontal agreements. A new Block Exemption Regulation was adopted in April 2010,[19] and the two Horizontal Block Exemption Regulations should be renewed before the end of 2010.

Generally speaking, these revisions will be much more facts-based. We are not any longer in the political cycle of moving to an effects-based approach, which is a more conceptual type of revision. We need now a better understanding of the actual impact of our rules. Only by learning how our previous practice was really operating in the market we can move to a better enforcement policy. And the current reforms in the sectors of vertical restrains and horizontal agreements will hopefully be examples proving that such a facts-based approach can make competition law better.

Thank you very much for your attention.

---

[19] Commission Regulation (EU) No. 330/2010 (20 April 2010) on the application of Article 101(3) of the Treaty on the Functioning of the European Union to categories of vertical agreements and concerted practices [2010] OJ L 102/1.

PROTECTION OF COMPETITION
v. MAXIMIZING (CONSUMER) WELFARE

Daniel Zimmer

I.   Legislative objectives

Under the EC Treaty, the Community was obliged to set up 'a system ensuring that competition in the internal market is not distorted' (Article 3(1)(g) EC). This holds still true after the Treaty of Lisbon has entered into force. Even though the reference in Article 3 EC was extinguished by the Lisbon Treaty, a so-called competition protocol to this Treaty states in a legally binding manner that the system of undistorted competition is part of the *internal market* – which remains, in any case, among the central goals of the Treaty. The pivotal importance of competition policy is also confirmed by other Treaty provisions: According to Article 119(1) TFEU (hereinafter: 'Treaty'; ex-Article 4(1) EC) the activities of the Member States and the Union include the adoption of an economic policy based on the close coordination of Member States' economic policies, on the internal market and on the definition of common objectives, and conducted in accordance with the principle of an 'open market economy with free competition'. The competition rules laid down in Articles 101 to 109 TFEU contain more detailed provisions: agreements, decisions and concerted practices 'which may affect trade between Member States and which have as their object or effect the prevention, restriction or distortion of competition within the internal market' are incompatible with Union law. This general prohibition on

23

cartels reflects the dual objective of the competition rules. First of all, under-takings may not distort competition by way of their private autonomous conduct (agreements, decisions, concerted practices). This goal, related specifically to the policy on the market economy and competition, is accompanied by a second aim of market integration: practices which impair trade between the Member States and thus partition the national markets are incompatible with Union law. In addition to the prohibition on cartels outlined here, the competition rules also prohibit the abusive exploitation of a dominant position on the common market or a substantial part of that market and contain special provisions for public or equivalent undertakings and detailed rules on the granting of State subsidies. Moreover, on the basis of an enabling clause in the Treaty, the Council has adopted a Regulation on the control of mergers between undertakings (the 'Merger Regulation').

However, the competition policy outlined so far is not without rivals. The EU is active in a number of other fields, including a common policy in the areas of agriculture, fisheries and transport; the co-ordination of the Member States' employment policy, social and environmental policy; the promotion of research and technological progress; the encouragement of the development of trans-European networks; and measures to achieve a high level of health protection and to strengthen consumer protection. The institutions of the Union, in par-ticular the Court of Justice, the Court of First Instance (now the General Court) and the Commission, have usually settled the issue of conflict under Article 101(3) TFEU. Under that article, the prohibition on restrictive practices may be declared 'inapplicable' to any agreement 'which contributes to improving the production or distribution of goods or to promoting technical or economic pro-gress, while allowing consumers a fair share of the resulting benefit'. In prac-tice, this exception has been interpreted very broadly. Not only efficiency gains but also, for example, the provision of employment,[1] promotion of infrastructure (and employment) in one of the poorest regions in the Community[2] and environmental protection[3] have been recognised as 'improving the production or distribution of goods'. Agreements on securing the provision of energy,[4] on the

---

[1] *Metro v. Commission*, Case No. 26/76 [1977] ECR 1875 para. 43.

[2] Commission Decision, *Ford/Volkswagen*, Case No. IV/33.814 [1993] OJ L 20/14, 20.

[3] Commission Decision, *Bayerische Motoren Werke*, Case No. IV/14.650 [1975] OJ L 29/1, 7.

[4] Commission Decision, *International Energy Agency*, Case No. IV/30.525 [1994] OJ L 68/35, 37 *et seq.*

improvement of road traffic safety[5] and on the creation of cross-border railway infrastructures such as the Eurotunnel[6] have likewise been excluded from the scope of the cartel prohibition as measures promoting technical or economic progress. The fact that such cases have been dealt with under Article 101(3) TFEU reflects an important decision of general principle. The exemption may only be used to override the principle of competition in certain special circumstances: the statutory requirements for qualification for exemption are that no restrictions 'which are not indispensable to the attainment of these objectives' are imposed on the undertakings concerned and that the undertakings are not afforded 'the possibility of eliminating competition in respect of a substantial part of the products in question'. Whilst the first restrictive condition gives expression to a strict principle of proportionality, the second is an absolute limit. In no circumstances may competition be eliminated entirely. Thus, a core of competitive activity is protected even in the face of the aims of conflicting policies.

This makes clear how fundamental the concept of competition is to the system of Union law. The fact that the Treaty provisions require the establishment of an undistorted system of competition and impose on the Member States and the Union a duty to observe the principle of an 'open market economy with free competition' and that Article 101(3) TFEU declares a core of competitive activity to be inviolable highlights the need for careful study of the Treaty definition of 'competition'. The highest and definitive authority on interpretation of the Treaty provisions is the Court of Justice of the European Union. An analysis of the Court's comprehensive decision-making practice in the field of competition law shows that its understanding of 'competition' has both 'process' (competition as a process) and 'structural' (competition as the result of particular structural market circumstances) aspects. Its process-orientated interpretation of competition has been expressed in a series of decisions in which the Court has developed a 'requirement of independence': in its famous *wood pulp* judgment of 1993, the Court summarised its case-law, holding that undertakings are prohibited from substituting practical co-operation for the 'risks of competition between them'. Each undertaking must determine independently the policy which it intends to adopt.[7] As ruled by the Court as early as 1975 in a case concerning the division of the European market for sugar, the case-law

---

[5] Commission Decision, *Asahi/Saint Gobain*, Case No. IV/33.863 [1994] OJ L 354/87, 92.
[6] Commission Decision, *Eurotunnel*, Case No. IV/32.490 [1994] OJ L 354/66, 72.
[7] *Ahlström Osakeyhtiö and others v. Commission*, Case No. C-89/85 [1994] ECR I-1307 para. 63.

prohibits not only the conclusion of explicit cartel agreements but even any 'contact' between competitors whose object or effect is to influence the market conduct of one of those competitors or to 'disclose' to the competitor an undertaking's own future market conduct.[8]

The structural components of the Court's competition concept were likewise established in an early decision: in its *Continental Can* judgment of 1973, the Court ruled that the acquisition of a majority share in an undertaking by the competitor and market leader may constitute an abuse of a dominant position within the meaning of the Treaty. The reasons for the judgment state that the prohibition on cartels and the prohibition on abuse by dominant firms serve the same purpose of maintaining effective competition in the common market. It cannot be assumed that the Treaty, which in its prohibition on cartels precludes certain decisions restricting competition, permits the same conduct where undertakings, by way of a merger, obtain such a dominant position that any serious chance of competition is practically rendered impossible. The reservation laid down in the Treaty with respect to exemptions from the prohibition on cartels, to the effect that at no time may competition be eliminated entirely and that, rather, real or potential competition must be maintained at all times, must therefore apply in this context also, i.e. to the supervision of abuse by dominant undertakings.[9] Elaborating on the definition of the competitive core to be protected, the Court stated that the prohibition on abuse is aimed not only at practices which may cause damage to the consumers directly but also at practices which are detrimental to them through their 'impact on an effective competition structure'.[10] The Court went on to hold that an – impermissible – complete elimination of competition may be established at least where competition 'was so essentially affected that the remaining competitors could no longer provide a sufficient counterweight'.[11]

What is remarkable about the last-mentioned judgment is that, long before the adoption of a special merger-control procedure in a regulation of 1989, the Court already took the view that a control of changes in market structure was permissible: the Commission was entitled to review the acquisition by a dominant firm of a share in a competitor undertaking on the basis of the Treaty rules on competition.[12]

---

[8] *Suiker Unie v. Commission*, Case No. 40/73 [1975] ECR 1663 para. 173 *et seq.*
[9] *Continental Can v. Commission*, Case No. 6/72 [1973] ECR 495 para. 25.
[10] *Ibid.* para. 26.
[11] *Ibid.* para. 29.
[12] See also *Philip Morris/Rothmans* judgment of the Court holding that a share acquisition may fall under the cartel prohibition of Article 81 EC/101 TFEU, as
cont.

The judgments cited show that the Court's interpretation of competition is open at the outset: whilst it specifies the conditions necessary for competition to exist, it does not define competition in terms of a specific outcome. The Court clearly regards the existence of several independent undertakings as one of the structural conditions, whilst the absence of 'contact' between those undertakings is a 'process' requirement. The legal system must protect those fundamental functional conditions for the competitive process and need not investigate in each individual case whether the competition as so defined leads to a desirable outcome. The decision to opt for an open definition is a corollary of the principle that, *as a rule*, competition leads to an acceptable or even desirable result. However, as shown, the Treaty provides for an *exceptional* disapplication of the principle of competition where it is demonstrated that a restriction of competition, for example by way of a cartel, is necessary to improve the production or distribution of goods or to promote technical or economic progress, while allowing consumers a fair share of the resulting benefit. Another condition is that residual effective competition is guaranteed by, for example, those undertakings not participating in the cartel. Such a restriction of competition, which in recent times has often been described as an efficiency defence or justification, has largely been accepted since the law was amended to a similar effect in the 2004 Merger Regulation.[13] However, both under the Treaty rules on competition and in the specific context of merger control, it is crucial to such an interpretation that the relationship between the rule and the exception be borne in mind: in principle, the law favours competition, which means that it precludes restrictions of competition without requiring that it be established in each individual case that those restrictions will be prejudicial to, for example, consumers. The principle of competition may be overridden only *in exceptional cases* in which it can be shown that a restriction of competition is *necessary* in order to achieve certain specified advantages which will also be enjoyed by consumers.

---

well: *BAT/Reynolds v. Commission*, joined Cases No. 142 and 156/84 [1987] ECR 4487 para. 37.

[13] See, for a discussion of the new criterion in Regulation No. 139/2004, D. Zimmer, 'Significant impediment to effective competition' [2004] (2) *Zeitschrift für Wettbewerbsrecht/Journal of Competition Law*, 250 *et seq*. However, a prominent scholar has expressed doubts as to the conformity of an efficiency defence with the European competition rules, U. Immenga, 'Der SIEC-Test der europäischen Fusionskontrolle als Kompetenzfrage', in *Recht und spontane Ordnung, Festschrift für Ernst-Joachim Mestmäcker*, C. Engel and W. Möschel (eds) (Baden-Baden, 2006), 269 *et seq*.

Does the commission's so-called more economic approach fit into this system? First of all we must know what we mean when we talk about a more economic approach. My perception is that the approach consists basically of two elements: One element is the use of modern economic methods when applying competition law. The other concerns the *normative* question of the guiding objectives of competition policy and law. With respect to the *first* issue – methods – there seems to be wide spread, if not full, agreement about the usefulness of modern economics. We would be insane, in my opinion, if we rejected the expertise of the discipline which can contribute most to the analysis of economic occurrences.

In practice, account has been taken of the findings of micro-economics in the drawing up of abstract general rules such as, for example, the new parameters described above for assessing vertical competitive restraints and the Commission's revision of its practice in supervising abuse by dominant undertakings. However, the 'economisation' of competition law has not only had an impact on the rule-making process but is also increasingly encroaching on the practice adopted in assessing specific cases. In that regard, the Commission's recent merger-control practice is impressive. Whilst, previously, the competitive assessment under merger law was essentially limited to defining the relevant market, calculating the merging parties' market shares and conducting a detailed 'qualitative' analysis of aspects such as financial strength, cross-links between the merging parties and other undertakings and the existence of barriers to market entry, the Commission now also frequently conducts comprehensive econometric studies. Such analyses can provide information on whether the merging parties are close or distant competitors. Data suitable for use in such econometric studies is available particularly often on those markets on which customers meet their needs by way of invitations to tender. In such a context, analyses of the bids submitted in response to past invitations to tender can provide information as to the nature of the competitive relationship between the merging parties.[14] On other markets too, it may be possible to draw similar inferences from studies of the market outcome: by analysing the scanner data of payment systems of traders, it can be established whether prices in the areas in

---

[14] Commission Decision, *GE/Instrumentarium*, Case No. COMP/M.3083 [2004] OJ L 109/1; on that decision, A. Lofaro and S. Bishop, 'Assessing Unilateral Effects in Practice: Lessons from *GE/Instrumentarium*' [2005] *European Competition Law Review*, 205 *et seq.*; see also the earlier Commission Decision, *Philips Agilent Health Care Solutions*, Case No. COMP/M. 2256 [2001] OJ C 292/10, Recital 33 *et seq.*

which particular competitors operate are significantly different from those in the areas in which they do not operate.[15]

The quantitative economic approach is taken to extremes where economists process data in simulation models and, on that basis, draw conclusions as to what impact a merger will have on quantities and prices.[16] Such a study was of central relevance to the Commission's 2004 decision in *Lagardère/Natexis/ VUP*.[17] In that procedure, which concerned the French book market, the Commission obtained a study conducted by external experts. Crucial to the conclusion reached in the experts' analysis was the finding that one of the merging parties had so far been able to attract a significant share of those customers who the other lost in the event of a price increase; as a result of the merger, the new entity would recuperate that customer segment itself, leading to a reduced competitive restraint. The experts concluded that the net retail prices for general literature could rise by an average of more than four per cent.[18] However, the Commission did not base its decision primarily on the results of their econometric study but rather on a conventional line of argument based on the merging parties' market shares, the wide gap between them and the nearest competitor as well as 'qualitative' criteria, this line of argument merely being confirmed by the results of the simulation.

The limits on the ability to reach findings on the basis of a quantitative economic analysis became apparent in the case concerning the merger between the software companies *Oracle* and *PeopleSoft*. In the merger-control procedure conducted in 2003/2004, the Commission for the first time refrained from presenting its evidence in the traditional form of a calculation of the market shares and a subsequent discussion of 'qualitative' aspects. Instead, its investi-

---

[15] See, with respect to such an approach, the US case *FTC v. Staples*, 970 F. Supp. 1066, 1075 *et seq.* (DDC. 1997); in that respect, see also J.B. Baker, 'Econometric Analysis in FTC v. Staples', Federal Trade Commission Working Paper (1997); P. Florian and M. Walker, 'The Correct Approach to the Use of Empirical Analysis in Competition Policy' [2005] *European Competition Law Review*, 320 *et seq.*

[16] For a discussion of the basic principles relating to such an approach, see R. Epstein and D.L. Rubinfeld, 'Merger Simulation: A Simplified Approach with New Applications' (2002) 70 *Antitrust Law Journal*, 882 *et seq.*; G.J. Werden and L.M. Froeb, 'Simulation as an Alternative to Structural Merger Policy in Differentiated Products Industries', in *The Economics of the Antitrust Process*, M.B. Coate and A.N. Kleit (eds) (1996), p. 65 *et seq.*

[17] Commission Decision, *Lagardère/Natexis/VUP*, COMP/M. 2978 Recital 700 *et seq.*

[18] *Ibid.* Recital 702.

gation was based essentially on econometric analyses. The data available to the Commission first of all suggested a connection between the number of bidders responding to a particular invitation to tender and the amount of discount ultimately offered. That observation would have supported a prognosis to the effect that a reduction in the number of market operators as a result of the merger would lead to a decrease in discounts and thus to anti-competitive effects. However, on closer examination, the Commission noted that the amount of the discount offered depended greatly on the relevant contract volume. In other words, whilst there was a correlation between the number of bidders and the discount amount, that connection could also be interpreted as meaning that a larger contract volume attracted a higher number of bidders, so that a direct connection between the number of bidders and the discounts, attributable to the contract volume, could not be established.[19] The case indicates the limited relevance of 'regression analyses': such studies can provide information on the relationship between certain values actually observed, but not certainty as to the *cause* of those relationships.

The Commission also based its *initial* finding that the merger between Oracle and PeopleSoft would have an anti-competitive effect on a complex simulation model. It later rejected that finding, declaring that its own simulation could no longer be considered meaningful because it was based on inaccurate assumptions. The simulation had been based on the assumption that, apart from Oracle and PeopleSoft, the only other supplier on the market for high functional needs business software was the German undertaking SAP. Once it became apparent that that assumption could not be sustained in light of the presence of other suppliers, the Commission authorised the merger.[20]

II. Assessment of the 'more economic approach'

The last-mentioned merger control procedure in *Oracle/PeopleSoft* shows that, in the context of competition policy and the application of law to specific cases, quantitative economic reasoning is only as good as the *assumptions* on which it is based. Since such assumptions are inevitably simplifications of the complex reality, econometric methods are just as incapable of supplying definitive evidence for a decision on a specific case as the wording of abstract general legislation. That is not intended to call into question the value of economic evidence:

---

[19] Commission Decision, *Oracle/PeopleSoft*, Case No. COMP/M. 3216 Recitals 197-202.

[20] *Ibid.* Recitals 196, 219.

in contrast with the more intuitive reasoning predominately given for decisions in the past, a mathematical formulation has the considerable advantage of compelling a greater degree of rationality. Where certain correlations are identified in economically recognised models, the legal practice must concentrate on ascertaining whether and in what circumstances it can be concluded that the model assumptions reflect reality.

Now I turn to the second element of the commission's more economic approach, i.e. the focus on efficiency and consumer welfare. Whether competition law is to serve such goals as efficiency and consumer welfare is – obviously – a normative question and, as such, a policy question. Economics, as a positive discipline, can provide no answer to policy questions. Economists can, of course, make propositions to rule makers and rule makers may decide for or against the adoption of such a proposition.

Many industrial economists are in favour of an exclusive orientation of competition law on the aims of efficiency and welfare – be it total welfare, be it consumer welfare. Such a concept has the charm of making things apparently unambiguous. If you have only one value – such as consumer welfare – which you would like to maximize, you can formulate your problem relatively easily in mathematical terms and find a microeconomic formula how to achieve that end. This aspect – that a concentration on just one aim makes things seemingly clear and unambiguous – may explain to a certain degree the success of the economic approach in the recent debate. However, things become less definite if we take a closer look at them.

There is not just one dimension to efficiency, but three: productive, allocative and dynamic efficiency. The effects of a certain arrangement – a contractual agreement or a merger – on productive and allocative efficiency may often be prognosticated. With respect to dynamic efficiency, in contrast, economic theory is much more uncertain. If we recognize that dynamic effects – effects on innovation, for example – are of particular importance for society, we discover that the apparent advantage of having just one unambiguous directive vanishes: When deciding whether to prohibit or to clear a merger, a competition authority may – even if it adheres to a consumer welfare standard – still have to take a tough decision: Let us assume that a particular merger between competitors leads to a considerable gain in productive efficiency, and let us assume further that the merged entity will pass the advantage on to consumers, there might still be a *negative* impact on *dynamic* efficiency: If prior to the merger two independent firms A and B competed in the field of research and development, this element of competition will cease to exist. The competition authority may find itself in the tricky situation of deciding either in favour of a short-term price advantage or in favour of a potential of long-term research and development advantages. Both would benefit consumers, so a decision has still to be taken. I mentioned this example only to demonstrate that even under a consumer benefit approach a competition authority may face situations of ambiguity.[21]

Now I turn to the question *whether* a one-dimensional approach – in particular a consumer-welfare approach – would be in accordance with the existing law. This is not an easy question.

The heading of Articles 101 to 109 TFEU is 'Rules on Competition' – not 'Efficiency Rules' or 'Rules for Consumers'. If we look at the plain text of Article 101 TFEU and of the merger regulation, the central term is again 'competition', not 'efficiency' or 'consumers'. The consumers come only into play in third paragraph of Article 101 TFEU.

Is it then admissible to interpret the legal term 'competition' in a very narrow sense, taking it as a synonym of 'efficiency' or 'consumer welfare'? If we follow legal methodology – which we are used to in order to determine the sense of a legal rule – we start from the literal meaning. Can 'competition' be defined by an efficient outcome, can we say – as some economists suggest – that an efficient outcome is the same as a competitive market result?

Lawyers, and in particular judges, have to take the wording serious – because legal rules are laid down in words, and it is these words upon which the members of a legislative body or the persons signing an international treaty have agreed. Now, arguing with the wording of Article 101 TFEU, I must conclude that the term cannot mean precisely the same as an efficient outcome. Imagine a natural monopoly, for example an electricity distribution network. Here the monopoly is the efficient solution – but you will not convince anyone that a monopoly is the same as competition.

What about 'consumer welfare'? Can we argue that competition means the same as an outcome which benefits consumers? The concept of the competition rules seems to exclude also this reasoning. Look at Article 101(1)(a) TFEU: The cartel prohibition is directed against agreements which 'directly or indirectly fix purchase or selling prices or any other trading conditions'. If agreements not only on selling prices but also on purchase prices are covered by the prohibition, it appears evident that buyer cartels – cartels fixing purchase prices – are in

---

[21] See, in this respect, W. Kerber, 'Should competition law promote efficiency? Some reflections of an economist on the normative foundations of competition law', in *Economic Theory and Competition Law*, J. Drexl, L. Idot and J. Monéger (eds) (Cheltenham, 2009), pp. 93-120 (98 *et seq.*), who also raises concerns over the neglect of long-term effects on dynamic efficiency in the 'more economic approach' of EU competition policy in favour of short-term static-efficiency effects.

principle in the same way under the prohibition as seller cartels. Buyer cartels, however, will in the first instance harm sellers – not necessarily consumers.

We can make a similar observation when we go on to Article 102 TFEU: According to Article 102(a) TFEU, an abuse may consist in 'directly or indirectly imposing unfair purchase or selling prices or other unfair trading conditions'. Again both sides of a market are addressed: An abuse of buyer power ('unfair purchase prices') may in the same way constitute a violation as an abuse of market power by a seller.

I do not want to enter the intricate discussion on economic effects – in particular welfare effects – of buyer power.[22] All I want to say here is: It seems obvious that competition *law* is designed not to serve just consumer needs but has – relying on 'competition' as the core term – a broader basis.

Now, finally: Could the Commission narrow the concept and redefine the law by saying: For us – the Commission – competition law is *just* about consumer welfare or consumer benefit, and we will apply it only to that end?

Let me say *at the outset*: I do *not* think that the Commission would go so far. In its recent 'Guidance' on Article 82 EC/102 TFEU, the Commission explicitly refers to *competition as a process*. In paragraph 6, the Commission states: 'The emphasis of the Commission's enforcement activity in relation to exclusionary conduct is on safeguarding the competitive process in the internal market ... In doing so the Commission is mindful that what really matters is to protect an effective competitive process and not simply protecting competitors'.

This reads different than some communications dating from previous years, communications which seemed to focus entirely and directly on efficiency and consumer benefit. Maybe the recent ECJ-Judgment in *British Airways* has given some *guidance* to the Commission – in this case a guidance not by, but for the Commission – causing it to state that the competitive process is at the heart of the competition rules, not a particular outcome.

British Airways, by far the leading airline on the UK market – with a market share seven times as large as that of the second largest airline – had concluded agreements with a large number of travel agencies which provided for entitlement to commissions tied to sales.[23] The agreements enabled the travel agencies

---

[22] See on this issue R. Inderst, 'Die ökonomische Analyse von Nachfragemacht in der Wettbewerbspolitik' [2008] *Wirtschaft und Wettbewerb*, 1261 *et seq.*; see also W. Kerber (*supra* n. 21) p. 113 *et seq.*, who argues for the protection against buyer power using an approach based on constitutional economics.

[23] In 1998, British Airways obtained a share of 39.7% by way of sales made via travel agencies in the United Kingdom, whilst the nearest competitor – Virgin –

cont.

to obtain *additional commissions* by increasing their sales of British Airways tickets. A special feature of the scheme was that the additional commissions were payable not only for sales made *after* reaching the sales target but – retrospectively, so to speak – for all sales of British Airways tickets made by the agency during the relevant period. Thus, if the target was exceeded, the agency's commission rose exponentially.[24] The Commission itself had found the bonus scheme applied by the dominant British Airways to have the effect of excluding competitors. The progressive scale entailed by the system was detrimental to the competitive chances of smaller airlines and thus to competition in general.[25] The decision, which was adopted before the Commission began to contemplate 'revising' its system of supervising abuse, was fully upheld by the Court of First Instance.[26] After British Airways lodged an appeal against that court's judgment, specialists' attention was drawn to the final ruling to be given by the Court of Justice.

The Court of Justice's judgment of 15 March 2007 has something for everyone. Those are not my words but those of the Chairman of the UK Competition Commission, *Peter Freeman*, when analysing the *British Airways* judgment at the International Competition Conference in Munich on 26 and 27 March 2007.

It is my view that the judgment first of all confirms the position taken by those advocating an open approach orientated to competition as a process.[27] The airline had challenged the first-instance judgment on the ground, *inter alia*, that the Court of First Instance had erred in law by failing to examine whether the conduct complained of had prejudiced consumers within the meaning of Article 82(b) EC Treaty/102(b) TFEU. The Court of Justice rejected that ground of appeal. It expressly reiterated the frequently repeated ruling made in its 1973 *Continental Can* judgment that not only practices which may cause prejudice to consumers directly, but also those which are detrimental to them through their impact 'on an effective competition structure' fall within the scope of the

---

achieved 5.5%. See Commission Decision, *Virgin/British Airways*, Case No. IV/D-2/34.780 [2000] OJ L 30/1, Recital 88.
[24] *Ibid.* Recital 17.
[25] *Ibid.* Recitals 97-106.
[26] *British Airways v. Commission*, Case No. T-219/99 [2003] ECR II-5197.
[27] Similarly, W. Wurmnest, 'The Reform of Article 82 EC in the Light of the "Economic Approach"', in *Abuse of Dominant Position: New Interpretation, New Enforcement Mechanisms?*, M.-O. Mackenrodt, B. Conde Gallego and S. Enchelmaier (eds) (Berlin, 2008), pp. 1-20 (15 *et seq.*).

prohibition.[28] In *British Airways*, the Court added that, accordingly, the Court of First Instance had not erred in law by examining not whether the conduct in question had caused prejudice to consumers, but rather whether the bonus schemes had a *restrictive effect on competition.*[29]

The Court of Justice went on to make clear how evidence of such a restrictive effect on competition can be adduced. The Commission had argued that the increased bonuses offered by British Airways once the sales targets had been exceeded were much more than a reward for the profit made by British Airways as a result of the targets' being met. The exponential rise in the commission paid for all sales already made was not mere consideration but also a special loyalty bonus which was liable to oust British Airways' smaller competitors from the market.[30] British Airways had contested the Commission's line of argument, which the Court of First Instance had likewise regarded as conclusive, on the ground that it was superficial. It submitted that it ought to have been thoroughly examined whether and to what extent competing airlines had been prevented from making counter-offers to the travel agencies. According to British Airways, the Court ought to have examined the overall and relative amounts of profit obtained on reaching the threshold, whether the threshold was close to the agencies' total needs, whether the market was capable of evolving, the length of the period concerned and the percentage of the overall market which was subject to the price reduction. The Court of Justice rejected that challenge. In its view, the findings made by the Commission and the Court of First Instance in relation to the exponential effect of changes in sales on the amounts of the commission were sufficient. Moreover, the Commission had demonstrated that effect by way of a fictitious example and provided figures to show that smaller competitors would have to have offered a significantly higher percentage bonus than British Airways in order for their counter-offer to be accepted.[31]

The Commission also based its decision on the *discriminatory effect* of the bonus scheme: the calculation of the bonus which was dependent not on absolute sales of British Airways tickets but on changes in sales distorted the travel agencies' competitive prospects. Since the income from commissions had an

---

[28] *British Airways v. Commission*, Case No. C-95/04 P [2007] ECR I-2331 para. 106 (with reference to *Continental Can v. Commission*, Case No. 6/72 [1973] ECR 495 para. 26).

[29] *Ibid.* para. 107.

[30] Commission Decision, *Virgin/British Airways*, Case No. IV/D-2/34.780 [2000] OJ L 30/1, Recitals 97-107.

[31] *Ibid.* Recital 30.

effect on sales competition, the bonus scheme linked not to actual objective performance but to changes in sales distorted the agencies' sales chances. The substance of this part of the decision was likewise upheld by the Court of Justice.

Much can be gathered from the Court's findings with regard to evidence of a *discriminatory effect* of the bonus scheme: the Court comments only briefly on this point. There is, according to the Court, nothing to preclude a finding that discrimination between business partners is abusive if the dominant undertaking's conduct is *aimed* at distorting competition between them. In those circumstances, it cannot be required *in addition* that proof be adduced of an actual *quantifiable* deterioration in the competitive position of the business partners *taken individually*. The fact that the travel agencies' *competitive chances* depended on the amount of income from commissions and that it was shown that the bonus scheme operated by British Airways was liable to lead to 'exponential' and appreciable changes in income from commissions which were not solely related to performance therefore provided the Court with sufficient grounds for ruling that there was a discriminatory effect within the meaning of – then – Article 82 EC.[32] It can be inferred that quantitative economic evidence is not required where the same conclusion can otherwise be drawn in accordance with principles of logic, possibly in combination with accepted empirical findings as to causal links.

All of this confirms the view taken by those advocating an interpretation of merger law which is *orientated to competition as a process*. In particular, the reiteration of the *Continental Can* finding of 1973 that the Commission and Court of Justice were right to consider the *structural conditions for competition* instead of basing the application of the prohibition directly on the prejudice to consumers appears to endorse the outdated open approach.

But, as stated above, *British Airways* has something for everyone, including those in favour of orientation towards efficiency and consumer welfare. The good news from this perspective is to be found in paragraphs 69 and 84 et seq. of the judgment: here, the Court for the first time clearly concedes that an efficiency defence is permissible *even* in the context of the supervision of abuse under Article 82 EC/102 TFEU. The relevant passage reads: 'It has to be determined whether the exclusionary effect arising from such a system, which is disadvantageous for competition, may be counterbalanced, or outweighed, by

---

[32] *British Airways v. Commission*, Case No. C-95/04 P [2007] ECR I-2331 paras 145-149.

advantages in terms of efficiency which also benefit the consumer'.[33] However, the Court of First Instance did not err in law by rejecting British Airways' argument that increased aircraft occupancy rates justified the exclusion of competitors.[34]

III. Conclusion

The Court of Justice's judgment in *British Airways* has outlined the European system of competition law more clearly than ever. At the initial examination stage, the applicable law follows an open approach. This applies generally to all three areas – prohibition on anti-competitive agreements, prohibition on abuse and merger control. In all three areas, therefore, it is *unnecessary* to prove that the restriction on competition causes prejudice to consumers. The applicable law – including the requirement of independence and the protection of the structural conditions for competition – deems the various anti-competitive measures to be unlawful in principle. However, again in all three areas, an efficiency defence may be considered at a second stage: if it is *unnecessary* even for the application of the prohibition provisions to prove that, in the specific case, the measure is *detrimental* to efficiency and consumers, it remains possible in all three contexts to justify a restriction of competition exceptionally on the grounds that efficiency gains which will, in any event, also benefit consumers outweigh the detriment. With respect to the prohibition on cartels, this has been enshrined since 1958 in the form of the exemption provided for in Article 81(3) EC/101 (3) TFEU. With regard to merger control, the Council opted for the admissibility of an efficiency defence in the 2004 Merger Regulation. The process has now been completed by the Court of Justice in the *British Airways* judgment. Following a similar ruling by the (then) Court of First Instance, it has made clear that, even in the context of Article 102 TFEU, efficiency defences may be admitted and that the requirements are basically no different from those in Article 101(3) TFEU: firstly, efficiency gains benefiting the 'consumer' may constitute an 'objective economic justification'; secondly, Article 102 TFEU – which does not contain an express provision similar to that in Article 101(3) TFEU – naturally *likewise* requires a stringent examination of necessity. In the words of the Court: 'If the exclusionary effect of that system bears no relation to advantages for the market and consumers, or if it goes beyond what is necessary

---

[33] *Ibid.* para. 86.

[34] *Ibid.* paras 87-90.

in order to attain those advantages, that system must be regarded as an abuse'.[35] The Court has thus added the finishing touch to a structure of competition law which – I find – is on the whole convincing. After all, why should the substantive assessment criteria applied in the context of competition law differ depending on the form of the restriction on competition?

IV. Prospects

In light of the above, it remains likely that Union law will continue to protect competition as such. The decision enshrined in the TFEU is based on a fundamental, perhaps even primeval, confidence in the blessings of a market operating on the basis of freedom of conduct and protected against structural threats. It is incompatible with this understanding of the applicable law to restrict it to the pursuit of just one single aim protected by the principle of competition. Instead, competition automatically promotes a number of protective aims which cannot be determined precisely. In the past, these have been considered to include individual freedom of action, the protection of market operators against the exercise of economic power by others, the consumer interest in the guarantee of a cheap supply of the goods desired by them and a collective interest in promoting technical innovation. The existing law does not make application of the principle of competition dependent on evidence that even one of those aims is achieved. Competition must be protected as such because – in accordance with the binding decision made by the drafters of the Treaty – it is deemed, *by way of presumption*, to have the favourable effects described above or of some other kind. Only in exceptional cases may a deviation from the principle of competition be contemplated, where it can be shown that a restriction of competition, such as a cartel agreement, is necessary to improve the production or distribution of goods or to promote technical or economic progress while allowing consumers a fair share of the resulting benefit. Following the clarification provided in the *British Airways* judgment, such an economic justification is conceivable not only in the case of cartel agreements but also in the context of the supervision of dominant behaviour.

This legal framework offers various opportunities for co-operation between economists and lawyers: rather than conducting a fruitless discussion as to whether consumer welfare ought to be the ultimate goal of competition policy, future co-operation will have to aim at developing a more concrete definition of the *legal concept of competition* (in the German version of the Treaty *Wett-*

---

[35] *Ibid.* para. 86.

bewerb, in the French *concurrence*). Whilst, as already indicated, the Treaty and the case-law of the Court of Justice have established certain rules and principles in this regard, the legal concept needs to be developed in more detail in a number of respects. This requires co-operation between the field of economics dealing with theoretical research into economic inter-relationships and the field of legal study aiming at providing legal institutions with the means to reach findings and interpret the law in line with appropriate methodology and to train in such methods. Improved co-operation between those two fields may contribute to establishing decision-making principles which provide legal certainty and thus to promoting general welfare.

THE EUROPEAN COMMISSION'S PRIORITIES FOR ENFORCEMENT OF ARTICLE 102 TFEU

Svend Albæk[*]

I. Introduction

Ladies and gentlemen,

you will understand that I can only provide a sort of sweeping overview in my presentation on the European Commission's ('the Commission') Communication 'Guidance on the Commission's enforcement priorities in applying Article 82 of the EC Treaty to abusive exclusionary conduct by dominant undertakings' ('Guidance paper') that was adopted on 3 December 2008.[1] This Guidance paper on Article 82 EC – or as we have to say after the Treaty of Lisbon entered into force: on Article 102 TFEU – is a fairly densely written document with lots of ideas, and we will discuss some of them in the afternoon. The general aim of the Guidance paper, which focuses on single dominance and

---

[*] Transcript of a speech delivered and recorded at the Max Planck Institute for Comparative and Private International Law. The speech was complemented by footnotes and was later updated to reflect recent legislative amendments.

[1] [2009] OJ C 45/7.

thus leaves out the issue of collective dominance, has been aptly described by
Carles Esteva Mosso: The Commission wants to ensure that the application of
the EC Competition rules safeguards the competitive process and not the
protection of competitors. To ensure that dominant firms do not impair effective
competition by foreclosing rivals in an anti-competitive way, the Commission
wants to investigate the effects of single firm conduct on consumers. This also
implies that efficiencies flowing from the conduct in question need to be taken
into account. But as *Carles Esteva Mosso* has discussed this general approach in
detail, I will not readdress this issue. Thus, my presentation will be structured as
follows: I will briefly address the issues of dominance and market power (II.),
before highlighting the Commission's foreclosure analysis (III.). Finally, I will
explain the Commission's approach towards analysing certain abusive practices
(IV.).

II. Market power and dominance

I am not sharing a secret here when I say that dominance according to the
definition given by the European Court of Justice is a position of economic
strength enjoyed by an undertaking which enables it to prevent effective competition from being maintained on the relevant market by affording it the power
to behave to an appreciable extent independently of its competitors, customers
and ultimately of its consumers.[2] The Guidance paper interprets this definition
as being equivalent to the economic concept of having substantial market power.
We say that this type of market power has to be over a significant period of time
– which as a rule of thumb means two years.

To assess such a strong market position we will take a close look at the
competitive constraints a firm is facing. Such constraints can be imposed by
actual competitors but also by threats of expansion or entry and by the bar-
gaining strength of customers. Then the Guidance paper – and this is perhaps of
greatest interest here – says what market shares mean for the finding of dominant positions. Market shares provide a useful first indication of the market
structure and of the relative importance of the various competitors active on the
market. And the higher the market share is and the longer the time it has been
high, the stronger the indication. Still, one cannot, or at least we will not, on the
basis of market share alone find a dominant position. However, the Commission

---

[2] See *United Brands Company and United Brands Continentaal v. Commission*,
Case No. 27/76 [1978] ECR 207 para. 65; *Hoffmann-La Roche & Co. v. Commission*, Case No. 85/76 [1979] ECR 461 para. 38.

is of the opinion that a low market share, i.e. a market share below 40%, is actually a fairly good proxy for determining the absence of substantial market power. So that means that only in rare situations will we feel that we can find dominance at a level under 40%. This rule can be labelled a 'soft safe harbour'. It is not a true safe harbour but it is a fairly good indication for firms.

III. Anti-competitive foreclosure

The Commission only wants to intervene when the conduct in question is likely to result in anti-competitive foreclosure. Thus we have to 'measure' the impact of the exclusionary behaviour on consumer welfare. In other words, there must be a balancing of anti-competitive effects with possible efficiencies. But how should this analysis be conducted in practice? In the last several years many different tests have been discussed in Europe and the US. And as many in the audience might be aware, the so-called 'no economic sense' test has gained much support in the US Department of Justice. The European Commission however is of the opinion that there is no single test that yields satisfactory results for all exclusionary abuses. So we approach the issue by looking at possible anti-competitive foreclosure effects that the conduct in question can result in. By foreclosure we talk about access to the market which is hampered or eliminated for competitors. So it may be that some firms or some of the competitors find it hard to gain access to the market. We would say that is foreclosure. But is that foreclosure anti-competitive? This depends on whether consumers are harmed by this foreclosure. Whether this is the case must be tested against an appropriate counterfactual hypothesis. One has to think about what would happen if this behaviour was not taking place. To understand the effects of the alleged exclusionary behaviour a close look at the conditions of the market is necessary: We have to understand the conditions of entry in that market and identify the existence of economies of scale or scope that could make it difficult for smaller firms to operate. We have to know well whether there are network effects that would perhaps tip the market in favour of the dominant firm, and one also has to think about what counter-strategies the competitors could adopt in order to reply to this presumably foreclosing be-haviour by the dominant firm. Thus, the simple fact that a certain percentage of the market is seemingly closed off for competitors is hardly in itself proof that it has resulted from anti-competitive conduct. In each and every case the Commission has to delve into the details.

With regard to pricing abuses, however, the situation is slightly different as with regard to these abuses the Commission finds a particular test useful as a first screen when checking for anti-competitive behaviour. The Guidance paper builds upon the so-called 'as efficient competitor' test, which famously has been advocated by *Richard Posner* in his classic book 'Antitrust Law'.[3] The Commission will normally only intervene where the conduct concerned has already been hampering or would be likely to hamper competition from competitors which were as efficient as the dominant undertaking. This test provides a very useful benchmark. It does not look at whether the actual competitors in the market are as efficient; it looks at whether a hypothetical as efficient competitor could survive faced with the behaviour deployed by the dominant firm. A hypothetical as efficient competitor would have a similarly cost structure as does the dominant firm. Therefore one can apply a price/cost-test based on the cost data provided by the dominant undertaking. This test has the advantage that the dominant firm itself can look at its pricing behaviour and its cost structure and see whether its behaviour fulfils this test. The exact cost-benchmark that would be used depends on the various types of behaviour one is considering. I will come back to that issue in a moment when discussing typical pricing abuses in more detail.

IV. Specific forms of abuses

A. Exclusive dealing

The Guidance paper contains sections on specific forms of abuses and outlines the circumstances which are most likely to prompt an intervention by the Commission. The first of these sections is concerned with exclusive dealing arrangements entered into by dominant undertakings. Economists tend to think – at least in principle – that a producer proposing an exclusive dealing contract is probably reasonably happy with it and that the other side to the contract, the dealer, is happy too. Both parties to the contract will compare their deal to a contractual arrangement without an exclusivity clause. To make the contract attractive for its dealers the dominant producer usually has to provide a little bit extra on top of a normal sales contract. He has to offer a better price or make some marketing contribution. So, in principle, individual dealers will benefit from exclusive dealing contracts. But there may be spill-over effects which can cause anti-competitive effects on the market. In such cases, an intervention of the Commission may be warranted.

In distinguishing between pro- and anti-competitive exclusive dealing agreements it is not very helpful to ask whether the dealer's options to choose the

---

[3]   R. Posner, *Antitrust Law* 2nd ed (Chicago, 2001), pp. 195 *et seq.*

market products of other producers are constrained because he obtains the products under the exclusive dealing contract at a lower price or some other advantage. Therefore, one has to focus on what happens in the market to demonstrate a credible theory of harm to competition. For example, anti-competitive foreclosure resulting from exclusive dealing arrangements entered into by dominant undertakings may be likely when there is an entrant who is not yet present in the market at the moment when the exclusive dealing contracts are concluded by the dominant firm. In such a scenario, the competitor cannot convince the dealers to contract with him instead of the dominant undertaking. Economic theory has shown that such an exclusionary scenario can happen. Another scenario in which anti-competitive exclusion may happen is when the dominant firm provides 'must-stock items'. In this case each dealer simply has to deal with the dominant firm in order to satisfy the demand of its downstream customers. In other words, competitors can only compete for a small percentage of the overall demand in a market. In turn, if the downstream demand does not reflect such a strong preference for the dominant firm's products, each competitor can try to convince dealers to contract with him and not with the dominant firm. In this case it is not really that much of a problem if a smaller newcomer has only a small percentage of the market even if the dominant firm has a much larger share and binds, for instance, 60% of the market by exclusive dealing agreements as long as the smaller competitors could enlarge their market share by offering better prices or better products. Thus, the Commission has to assess the market conditions very carefully to understand how exclusive dealing agreements affect a particular market. In this regard one should also be aware of the fact that exclusive dealing can have efficiencies. Such contracts may especially be necessary to protect relationship-specific investments. A producer wants his dealers to work efficiently for him. He therefore, for instance, may have to train them to sell the product well. Such training does not come for free, so the dominant firm has to invest in the training of the dealers. Against this background, it is understandable that the dominant firm wants to prevent its dealers from stocking competing products on their shelves if that would allow free-riding on the training that he is providing. Otherwise, he would not undertake any relationship-specific investment.

B.   Rebates having similar effects as exclusive dealing

Related to exclusive dealing arrangements are so-called conditional rebate schemes. Under such schemes the buyers are not contractually bound by an exclusive dealing clause but the dominant undertaking gives those who purchase certain quantities over a given amount of time an attractive discount to prevent buyers from switching to other suppliers. In the past, the Commission has struggled to deal with such pricing schemes and there was a considerable discussion on cases like *Michelin II*[4] or *British Airways*[5]. In the US as well there is much debate as to how to deal with rebates and it seems that in this field of law there is a difference in minds of how to approach the issue, at least for the moment. Most cases decided by the Commission concerned retroactive rebates, i.e. rebates where once you surpass a certain threshold you receive a rebate not only on the products that you are buying (which is an incremental rebate), but a rebate calculated on the entire sales during the threshold period, i.e. even on items that you have already bought. And of course this can create great problems, especially if the product in question is a must-stock item. Again, if retailers basically divide the dealers between them, then it is not clear that this is a problem at all. If one retailer is giving some rebates at the margin to make his dealer sell more, this should not be a problem for his competitors because in principle they can offer similar rebates. So the real problem is when the dealer of the smaller firm can only compete for sales 'on the margin' because the dominant firm is an unavoidable trading partner. In this case rebates can make it unattractive to switch small amounts of demand. So these are the cases in which the Commission wants to become active to check whether the rebate structure that is being offered is in fact a way of inducing exclusive dealing without having it written down as a contract. You cannot say across the board that all retroactive rebates will induce exclusive dealing. Rather, one has to carefully look at the circumstances in the case at hand to understand how the rebate scheme affects competition. In this respect the Commission wants to conduct a price/cost-analysis. I do not wish to go into the details, but we are basically saying: 'Calculate the effective price over that part of demand for which rivals can compete and dealers are willing to switch and compare it to the relevant cost benchmark'. Thus the analysis follows a similar pattern as in predation cases: If customers have to forego a high rebate while switching a small (but realistic) amount of their total demand, the effective price will be low. If the effective price is below average avoidable cost ('AAC'), then the Commission will assume that the rebate is capable of foreclosing as efficient rivals. If the effective price is however in between AAC and the long-run average incremental cost ('LRAIC'), one should not assume anti-competitive foreclosure. Rather, the

---

[4] *Michelin v. Commission (Michelin II)*, Case No. T-203/01 [2003] ECR II-4071.
[5] *British Airways v. Commission*, Case No. T-219/99 [2003] ECR II-591; *British Airways v. Commission*, Case No. C-95/04 P [2007] ECR I-2331.

Commission will have to present additional evidence to conclude that (as efficient) competitors would be prevented from expanding or entering the relevant market.

C. *Tying and bundling*

'Tying' usually refers to situations where customers that purchase one product (the tying product) are required also to purchase another product from the dominant undertaking (the tied product). Tying can take place on a contractual basis (when the producer only sells the two products together) or on a technical basis (when the producer designs the products in a way that the tying product only works properly with the producer's own tied product and not with the alternatives offered by competitors). 'Bundling' usually refers to the way products are offered and priced by the dominant undertaking. In the case of pure bundling the products are only sold jointly in fixed proportions. In the case of mixed bundling, often referred to as a multi-product rebate, the products are also made available separately, but the sum of the prices when sold separately is higher than the bundled price.

Tying and bundling are common business practices often intended to provide customers with better products or offerings in more cost effective ways. But that does not mean the dominant firm should have a free hand in doing it. However, to the extent that many non-dominant firms are doing this, perhaps we should consider why dominant firms are doing it as well. In such a case the business rationale behind this policy of the dominant firm may be non-abusive because non-dominant firms are apparently using the same business strategy to a large extent also. So in the end we have to think about the efficiencies of it. At the end of the process, as *Daniel Zimmer* said in his presentation, there should be room for discussion on efficiencies here as well.

For those of you who know the *Microsoft* case[6], the Commission is basically using the framework that is well-known for tying in the US and which can be labelled the 'distinct products' test. In reality, this distinct-product test is actually an efficiency test although this may not be apparent. The test was developed in the US as a tool to circumvent the *per se* prohibition of contractual tying arrangements. It basically asks the question whether customers would purchase the tying product without the tied product from the same supplier if they were not forced to take the two products together. Evidently the customer would not try to shop for the tied product elsewhere if it is either an extreme

---

[6] *Microsoft v. Commission*, Case No. T-201/04 [2007] ECR II-3601.

hassle to do so or if it is obviously too costly from a production point to sell the products separately. The classic but useful example is the sale of a left and a right shoe as a pair of shoes. Nobody would argue that a dealer offering pairs of shoes abuses its market power. But why not? Because consumers usually do not want to buy their shoes in different styles and colours. They want two shoes that match. Thus, consumers would waste a lot of time if they would go to one shop to buy a left shoe and to another shop to buy a right shoe of a similar style and colour. Moreover, from the production point of view the producer can realise cost savings by producing shoes that match exactly. Therefore, in the end we are talking about efficiencies when we conclude that left and rights shoes are not distinct products.

Let me further say some words on the theories of harm that economists have developed to demonstrate that tying may have anti-competitive effects. There are two favourite 'narratives' on which most economists today would agree and which I would like to highlight here.

The first theory of harm goes basically back to a paper by *Michael Whinston*[7] who described what has later been called the 'restaurant on the island' paradigm. It shows that the famous Chicago School theorem that tying cannot create anti-competitive effects because there is only a single monopoly profit is not entirely correct. Tying can cause anti-competitive effects in the tied market if it drives out competitors that only want to serve this market. Imagine an exotic island with one hotel and various small local restaurants. The hotel guests can go to a small restaurant or dine in the expensive hotel. The local people only go to the small restaurants. If the hotel suddenly starts selling only full room and board, then all tourists on the island would have basically paid for their meals before coming to the island. As a consequence most of the hotel guests, unless they were very rich, would probably not go out and eat in the small local restaurants anymore. So what happens then? As the small local restaurants cannot open hotels and offer similar package deals as does the monopolist, these restaurants may be forced to exit the market. If they do not survive, then where can the locals on the island go to eat if they want to go to a restaurant? They have to go to the hotel restaurant, thus increasing the profit of the hotel. Thus, by tying, a dominant player on one market (the hotel) can drive out some of the competitors who only want to serve the tied market (restaurant services) and thereby extract more from this market than without the tying policy.

---

[7]   M. Whinston, 'Tying, foreclosure, and exclusion' (1990) 80 *American Economic Review*, 837-859.

That tying can cause harm to the tied market is, however, not what most economists nowadays worry most about. More important is a second theory of harm which was relevant in the *Microsoft* case. This theory of harm builds upon the narrative that the tying of complements is used to make entry in the tying market more difficult. Why was Microsoft tying its Internet Explorer and the Media Player to the Windows operating system? Because this policy protected the market for operating systems on which Microsoft enjoyed a very strong position. If people want the tying good and the tied good together – here we can talk of complements – the tying policy of the dominant undertaking can by eliminating competition in the tied market make it much harder for competitors to enter the tying market because a newcomer would now have to enter into both the tying market and the tied market. Microsoft was not really worried about its market share in the browser market (tied market) or the possibility of raising its revenue in the tied market by leveraging. Microsoft was worried about the scenario that somebody could use Internet Explorer to jump into the Windows market, i.e. the tying market, a fear which was clearly shown in internal e-mail communications.

The last issue related to tying and bundling that I want to address briefly is the problem of multi-product rebates or mixed bundling as the economists call it. In this scenario you have two products: You have the dominant product and you have another product but they are not contractually tied. However, if you buy them separately each product has – for instance – a price of 10 Euro. If you buy the two products together the seller offers you a better deal and sells them for the price of 18 Euro. How do we deal with that? Is this anti-competitive or not? To answer the question one should have in mind that such a multi-product rebate may be anti-competitive if it is so large that equally efficient competitors offering only some of the components cannot compete against the discounted bundle. But how can we find out whether equally efficient competitors can compete? In theory we would have to investigate whether the incremental revenue covers the incremental costs for each product in the dominant undertaking's bundle. Such a test is however difficult to assess in real life antitrust cases. Therefore, the Commission wants to make recourse to the incremental price as a good proxy. To put it simply, in my example we would say that in reality when you buy the bundle you are only paying 8 Euro for the tied product because you would have to pay 10 Euro for the tying product anyway. So in reality the real incremental price you are paying is only 8 Euro. Thus the question is whether the price of 8 Euro covers the cost of making this product if it would be sold on a stand alone basis. If the incremental price that customers pay for that product in the bundle remains above the long-run average incremental cost ('LRAIC') of the dominant undertaking, the Commission will normally not intervene since an equally efficient competitor with only one product should in principle be able to compete profitably against the bundle. Things are different if the incremental price is below the LRAIC of the dominant undertaking, because in such a case even an equally efficient competitor may be driven from the market. Then we have to look at the market conditions to see whether such a scenario is likely. Matters are different when everybody in the market is selling these bundles. Then it is not necessary to distinguish between the two products. One can just look at the figure of 18 Euro and check whether this bundle price is covering the cost of producing the bundle.

D. Predation

Let me now turn to predation. The Commission's Guidance paper basically follows the sacrifice-test. Moreover, the Commission only intervenes when it can demonstrate that the predation campaign is likely to cause harm to competition. As we will hear in the afternoon, economists have developed various predation scenarios which show that predation can cause smaller competitors to exit the market. In practice we have to show that the market in which the low pricing strategy is pursued has the features which make predation an economically rational business strategy. We need to think about the mechanism which is applied to force competitors out of the market or to compete less aggressively, and we also have to think about the issue whether consumers in the end are going to be harmed. That does not mean that the Commission advocates a recoupment test as is known from US law. Our standard is less strict, as under the Commission's approach it suffices to show that prices may actually increase in the end. For instance, the Commission will not intervene when market entry is easy as potential competition will make it unlikely that prices can go up. Thus the Commission does not want to do a spread sheet exercise with hours spent discussing discount factors, but wants to make sure that a predation scenario is not implausible from an economic point of view. In other words, we need to come up with a reliable narrative which explains why consumers in the end would be harmed by the low pricing policy of the dominant undertaking.

E. Refusal to deal

Let me conclude my presentation with some brief thoughts on refusal to deal cases as I will not have the time to go into details. The most important point I want to stress here is that the Commission has tried to assemble many scenarios under one heading and to develop a coherent analytical framework for assessing such abuses. We have spent a great deal of time discussing what the main lines of this type of abuse are, how to divide them and how to integrate them in our general framework of thinking about the issue. The Commission is, to a large extent, very concerned with not hampering the incentives of the dominant undertaking to invest in both tangible and intangible assets. However, each case has to be assessed on its own facts and you will see that the analytical framework laid down in the Guidance paper is based on well known cases like *Bronner*[8], *IMS-Health*[9] and *Microsoft*[10]. Thus I do not think I need to go into details. Instead, I will simply focus on the consumer harm here which is really the dynamic perspective that *Carles Esteva Mosso* mentioned in his opening talk. The Commission will examine whether, for consumers, the likely negative consequences of the refusal to supply in the relevant market outweigh over time the negative consequences of imposing an obligation to supply. In this respect, as I have said, the circumstances of the case matter. Consumer harm is, for example, likely when the refusal to supply prevents competitors from furnishing the market with new or better products. On the other hand, it may be that the dominant firm responds: If you pursue these measures to supply, my incentives to invest would be considerably harmed. Thus, in the end you may come to a situation where you have balance efficiencies and incentives to invest as was done in our *Microsoft*-decision.

I see my time is up and therefore I will stop here. Thank you for your attention.

---

[8] *Oscar Bronner v. Mediaprint Zeitungs- und Zeitschriftenverlag, Mediaprint Zeitungsvertriebsgesellschaft and Mediaprint Anzeigengesellschaft*, Case No. 7/97 [1998] ECR I-7791.

[9] *IMS Health v. NDC Health*, Case No. C-418/01 [2004] ECR I-5039.

[10] *Microsoft v. Commission*, Case No. T-201/04 [2007] ECR II-3601.

DISCUSSION

At the outset *Thomas Ackermann* asked whether there can be a unified concept of a more economic approach as EU competition law contains different rules with different formulations. *Carles Esteva Mosso* replied that the EU Competition rules do indeed contain different articles with different wordings but this does not seem to be an obstacle to formulating a common approach. A unified approach is also desired by the undertakings operating in the common market as it ensures predictability. In addition there is another advantage in transforming Article 81(3) EC/101(3) TFEU into a pure efficiency defence, which can be applied in a more formal and technical way. It should be noted that under the regime of Regulation 1/2003 the enforcement of the EU competition rules has entered a new area. With the abolishment of the centralised notification and authorisation system for Article 81(3) EC/101(3) TFEU and the introduction of a directly applicable exception system, the Regulation raised the danger of an incoherent enforcement of EU competition law across the common market. Different goals would therefore form an additional obstacle for an effective and coherent enforcement of the EU competition rules. Thus, the way of the Commission is to look to the objectives of EU competition law in order to abstract common goals for formulating a unified approach applicable to all fields of competition law.

Daniel Zimmer remarked that the general concept of having a kind of prohibition of restraints of competition at the outset and an efficiency objection on a second level does indeed fit in the concept of the European competition rules even though there is no explicit paragraph relating to such an efficiency exemption in Article 82 EC/102 TFEU. However, he added, putting the main focus on consumer welfare may have the effect of increasing the protection of the suppliers.

Wolfgang Kerber first pointed out that from the economist's point of view it may be – in part – very difficult to agree with the interpretation of the law as described by *Daniel Zimmer*. As economic concepts relating to competition policy do change, the question is if it is possible to adapt the legal objectives of a given legal framework correspondingly. His second remark was dedicated to the problematic goal of consumer welfare. As there is no economic theory of competition as a dynamic process, from an economic point of view it seems problematic to establish consumer welfare as the main goal of Competition policy. Finally, he emphasised that there is a need for some kind of a coherent

53

concept of what the notion of consumer really means. *Daniel Zimmer* answered that it is obvious that to a certain degree the law is open to changes, but the room is limited to the explicit wording of the provisions.

Carles Esteva Mosso then stepped in to explain that the Commission uses the term consumer in respect to the relevant market which is affected by the questionable anticompetitive behaviour and looks at the effects on the welfare of the market participants receiving the goods or services. Against this background *Peter Behrens* remarked that to him it is not clear what the Commission really wants to protect with the so-called effects based approach: Effects on the market or on consumer welfare? *Carles Esteva Mosso* replied that focusing on consumer welfare is the most important element of the more economic approach as it is implemented by the Commission. The reason for focusing on consumer welfare is to provide a clear standard for deciding whether a given behaviour is anticompetitive or not. Moreover, the guidance paper is not a restatement of the law itself. It sketches the enforcement priorities of the Commission. For a public enforcement policy the desire to implement a common concept seems to be correct.

Replying to this *Ulrich Immenga* insisted that from a legal point of view it is not possible to change the legal objectives of the Treaty by guidelines of the Commission. *Carles Esteva Mosso* reiterated that the Commission does not want to change the law in a fundamental fashion by the guidance paper, although he admitted that the Commission hopes that the new ideas of the guidance paper will influence the decision practice of the European and national courts as well as national enforcement authorities.

Most participants shared the view that a coherent enforcement policy is needed but pointed out that the under the law as it stands it is not possible to argue that the only goal of EU Competition policy is consumer welfare. In this context *Jürgen Basedow* drew the attention to the fact that the discretion the Commission has to enforce EU competition law is limited. The Commission is primarily responsible to enforcing the European competition rules. Admittedly, it has to set priorities if its capacities are not sufficient to investigate every case, but it seems doubtful if it does so by introducing guidelines which require many more investigation resources. In practise the more economic approach bears the danger that fewer cases can be investigated. Especially in the field of merger control one should bear in mind that the periods in which decisions have to be taken are very short and the investigations require so much man power that the more economic approach may lead to less enforcement. In addition, he illustrated on the example of the *Airtours*-case that the effects on the consumers may differ from market to market. Thus, the importance of defining a coherent concept of the goal of consumer welfare becomes crucial.

Dominik Massing

PART II: STUDIES ON ARTICLE 102 TFEU

THE DOMINANCE THRESHOLD
IN ARTICLE 102 TFEU

Giorgio Monti[*]

I.   Introduction

Two issues arise when exploring the implementation of a dominance threshold. The first is whether one wishes to deploy a threshold at all. For the purposes of this paper, a threshold is defined as a marker, normally based upon the determination of the firm's market share, which triggers the application or non-application of a rule. The second is what dominance means. The two questions are interlinked in that what we mean by dominance determines how we design the threshold; nevertheless, in this essay I consider the two questions separately while commenting on how they are addressed in the Commission's 2009 *Guidance Paper on Enforcement Priorities in Applying Article 82 EC (now:*

---

[*]   I am grateful to *Christian Ewald* who commented on the paper.

Article 102 TFEU) to exclusionary Conduct by Dominant Undertakings.[1] Attention is also paid to the US Department of Justice's 2008 report on single-firm conduct under Section 2 of the Sherman Act, while noting that it is unlikely that it will inform US antitrust policy significantly, if at all.[2]

I argue that in the Guidance Paper, the Commission has distanced itself from a presumptive threshold, established by the case law of the European Court of Justice, and favoured a safe harbour threshold; and it has narrowed the definition of dominance, again departing from the wider definition set out by the ECJ. These two moves are coherent and consistent with the general policy that informs the Guidance Paper: a wish to reduce enforcement efforts through the use of a 'more economics-based approach.'[3]

Some prefatory notes:[4] First, all firms (except those where the conditions of perfect competition obtain, a rare occurrence indeed) possess some market power when this is defined as the ability to set prices above marginal cost, but not every firm has a dominant position as a result. Second, proof of market power of some degree is normally a pre-requisite for any competition law intervention, whether under Articles 101 and 102 TFEU or the EU Merger Regulation. Two implications arise from this: (1) that competition law is not designed

---

[1]   Guidance Paper on the Commission's Enforcement priorities in Applying Article 82 EC Treaty to Abusive Exclusionary Conduct by Dominant Undertakings (9 February 2009), C(2009) 864 final (hereinafter 'GP'). This document is based on the Discussion Paper on the Application of Article 82 EC Treaty to Exclusionary Abuses (December 2005) <ec.europa.eu/competition/antitrust/art82/discpaper 2005.pdf>, 15 October 2010 (hereinafter 'DP').

[2]   US Department of Justice, *Competition and Monopoly: Single-Firm Conduct Under Section 2 of the Sherman Act* (2008) <www.usdoj.gov/atr/public/reports/ 236681.htm>, 15 October 2010 (hereinafter 'DOJ Report'). The FTC did not endorse the report, see <www.ftc.gov/opa/2008/09/section2.shtm>, 15 October 2010 and the incoming administration has withdrawn the report suggesting a more aggressive attitude will be taken by the Department of Justice, 'Justice Department Withdraws Report on Antitrust Monopoly Law' (11 May 2009) <www.usdoj.gov>, 15 October 2010.

[3]   This is the oft-repeated phrase used in many speeches by members of DG Competition. For a critical assessment, see G. Monti, 'EC Competition Law: The Dominance of Economic Analysis?', in *The development of competition law: global perspectives*, R. Zäch, A. Heinemann and A. Kellerhals (eds) (Cheltenham, 2010).

[4]   See generally L. Kaplow and C. Shapiro, 'Antitrust', in *Harvard John M. Olin Discussion Paper Series, Discussion Paper No. 575* (Cambridge, January 2007), pp. 2-22 <www.law.harvard.edu/programs/olin_center/>, 15 October 2010, for a helpful discussion of market power.

to tackle every manifestation of market power (either because it is not its role, or because even if it were it would be administratively impossible to regulate every firm, or because applying antitrust to low manifestations of market power risks chilling pro-competitive conduct), and (2) that, as a result, 'screens' for intervention based on a given degree of market power are in place to trigger the application of each substantive competition law provision. The highest market power screen is reserved for the application of Article 102 TFEU, and this is so in particular since the reform of the EU Merger Regulation where under which the Commission can intervene even when a merger does not create or strengthen a dominant position.[5]

Recognising that market power is a matter of degree is significant because it indicates that the choice of a dominance screen is ultimately a rough estimate of when it is thought it would be most appropriate for Article 102 TFEU to apply. It is not true that below the dominance screen, for example, predatory pricing cannot take place – on the contrary it can occur but a policy decision has been taken that the likelihood of that practice taking place is low enough not to warrant scrutiny.[6] In this example, the dominance screen indicates a desire to under-enforce the law because the cost of finding predatory pricing below the dominance level outweighs any potential benefit in pursuing such cases. On the other hand, one might wish to design a screen that purposively over-enforces Article 102 TFEU, perhaps as a means of deterring undertakings from disrupting the competitive process. Thus, the concept of dominance ultimately reflects a policy choice (rather than a scientifically precise measure) of when Article 102 TFEU should apply. This policy choice is informed by economic analysis, but it is not determined by economics but rather by the enforcement strategy of the competition authority or by the legal framework in question.

---

[5] See generally J. Vickers, 'How Does the Prohibition of Abuse of Dominance Fit with the Rest of Competition Policy?', in *European Competition Law Annual 2003*, C.-D. Ehlermann and I. Atanasiu (eds) (Oxford, 2006); cf. G. Monti, 'The New Substantive Test in the EC Merger Regulation Bridging the Gap Between Economics and Law?', *LSE Law, Society and Economy Working Papers*, WPS 10-2008 <www.lse.ac.uk/collections/law/wps/wps1.htm>, 15 October 2010.

[6] M. Motta, *Competition Policy* (Cambridge, 2004), p. 444 noting that in exceptional circumstances there might be a non-dominant predator but suggesting that leaving it unpunished is better than the costs of widening the scope of the prohibition against predatory pricing.

II. Thresholds

A. What kind of threshold for abuse of dominance cases?

It is possible to identify certain characteristics of thresholds that are currently in use. Some are in the form of presumptions, indicating at what degree of market power a rule will apply (these tend to favour plaintiffs and competition authorities), while some are in the form of safe harbours, indicating that a rule will not apply below a given threshold (these tend to favour defendants). Some thresholds serve to create stronger indicators than others. From this we can derive the following taxonomy of four different types of thresholds, an example of each is provided in the table below:

Thresholds Table

	Presumption	**Safe harbour**
Strong indicator	Dominance presumed at 50% market share	De minimis rule
Weak indicator	Merger inquiry proceeds when certain concentration levels are reached	Benefit of Vertical Restraints Block Exemption Regulation applies below 30% market share

The strong-weak division is more fluid than the matrix suggests: there are relatively stronger and weaker indicators. For example, the Vertical Restraints Block Exemption Regulation is weaker than the de minimis rule set out in the *Volk* case because the latter appears to be unconditional,[7] while the benefit of the Block Exemption may be removed by the Commission in certain circumstances.[8]

---

[7] *Volk v. Vervaecke*, Case No. 5/69 [1969] ECR 295. For discussion, see A. Nikpay and J. Faull, 'Article 81', in *The EC Law of Competition* 2nd ed, J. Faull and A. Nikpay (eds) (Oxford, 2007), pp. 250-251.

[8] Article 6 Commission Regulation (EU) No. 303/2010 (20 April 2010) on the application of Article 101(3) of the Treaty on the Functioning of the European Union to categories of vertical agreements and concerted practices [2010] OJ L 102/1. The powers to withdraw the benefit of the exemption were broader, and were also vested to National Competition Authorities in the earlier block exemption, but they were exercised rarely. See Commission Regulation (EC) No.

cont.

Presently, the European Court of Justice has set out a strong presumptive threshold. In *Hoffmann La Roche* the Court opined that when a firm has enjoyed a very high market share for a significant period, this may be sufficient to establish dominance, absent exceptional circumstances.[9] Applied to the facts, in a range of markets where the firm held market shares of 80% or above (vitamins B, B3 and B6) the Court found these were 'so large as to be in themselves evidence of a dominant position.'[10] Even in the market for vitamin C, market shares between 63-66% during the infringement period appeared sufficient evidence of dominance.[11] In the market for Vitamin A the firm's 47% market share which was equal to the aggregate of the shares of the two largest competitors, 'proves that it is entirely free to decide what attitude to adopt when confronted by competition.'[12] Additional factors, such as the firm's technical lead were a further indication of dominance, but probably unnecessary given the conclusions reached when assessing the market shares of the players. The findings indicated that the Court might be willing to presume dominance from market shares, but no precise threshold was set.

Subsequently in *AKZO* it was more explicit: a market share of 50%, which on the facts the defendant had held for three years, would (save in exceptional circumstances) lead to a presumption of dominance.[13] Some appear to minimise the impact of the presumption in *AKZO*,[14] but I believe the Court made a deliberate statement to set out a strong presumptive threshold. While the Court noted in the paragraph immediately after articulating the presumption that the Commission had confirmed AKZO's predominance on the market by considering other factors,[15] it did not say that it was necessary for the Commission

---

2790/99 (22 December 1999) on the application of Article 81(3) of the Treaty to categories of vertical agreements and concerted practices [1999] OJ L 336/21.

[9] *Hoffmann-La Roche & Co. AG v. Commission*, Case No. 85/76 [1979] ECR 461 para. 41.

[10] *Ibid.* para. 56.

[11] *Ibid.* para. 63.

[12] *Ibid.* para. 51.

[13] *AKZO v. Commission*, Case No. C-62/86 [1991] ECR I-3359 para. 60.

[14] E.g. R. Thompson and J. O'Flaherty, 'Article 82', in *Bellamy & Child European Community Law of Competition* 6th ed, P. Roth and V. Rose (eds) (Oxford, 2008), para. 10.029 suggest that only percentages significantly and consistently above 50% are strong dominance indicators.

[15] *AKZO v. Commission*, Case No. C-62/86 [1991] ECR I-3359 para. 61.

to review these other factors once the market share threshold had been met.[16] The Court's statement also departs from the Opinion of the Advocate General in the case who suggested that market shares were significant evidence of dominance but not sufficient. This divergence between the ECJ on the one hand and the views expressed by the Commission and Advocate General on the other suggest that the Court wished to distance itself from that position taken and establish a strong threshold. The General Court has ratified the *AKZO* presumption in two recent judgments, indicating that this approach retains judicial support.[17]

It appears that the effect of the Commission proving that a firm has a market share of 50% or more is to shift the burden of proof to the defendant to rebut the presumption of dominance.[18] In administrative proceedings the defendant bears the evidential burden of pleading facts that negate dominance, but it remains for the Commission to establish that the evidence relied on by the defendant does not negate the finding of dominance.[19] However, in practice the Commission and the Courts always take into consideration other evidence to establish dominance on their own initiative.[20] For instance in *Hilti*, while the General Court applied the above case law to conclude that a market share of between 70-80% was, 'in itself, a clear indication of the existence of a dominant position in the relevant market',[21] it also noted that intellectual property rights protected Hilti's position and that the firm's own practices were evidence of dominance, i.e. a non-dominant firm carrying out similar acts would be punished by market forces.[22] Accordingly, the Commission has not taken advantage of the *AKZO* presumption and instead has relied on additional evidence to confirm the finding of dominance.

In private litigation, however, the plaintiff could rest its case upon the presumption of dominance when market shares are at 50% or more, and in private

---

[16] Contra R. O'Donoghue and A.J. Padilla, *The Law and Economics of Article 82 EC* (Oxford, 2006), p. 114 who appear to place more value on the Commission's decision (where market shares were found to be only one indicator) than on the basis for the ruling of the Court.

[17] See e.g. *easyJet Airline Co. Ltd. v. Commission*, Case No. T-177/04 [2006] ECR II-1931 para. 174; *General Electric v. Commission*, Case No. T-210/01 [2005] ECR II-5575 para. 115.

[18] R. Whish, *Competition Law* 6th ed (Oxford, 2008), pp. 176-177.

[19] R. Thompson and J. O'Flaherty (*supra* n. 14) para. 10.063, citing *Microsoft v. Commission*, Case No. T-201/04 [2007] ECR II-3601 para. 688.

[20] R. Whish (*supra* n. 18) pp. 176-177.

[21] *Hilti AG v. Commission*, Case No. T-30/89 [1991] ECR II-1439 para. 92.

[22] *Ibid.* para. 93.

proceedings the legal burden of proof (or the burden of persuasion) shifts to the defendant. In a time when the Commission seeks to encourage private litigation, the *AKZO* presumption seems a helpful means of reducing plaintiff's litigation costs. So in principle there could be a divergence developing between the Commission's practice and the approach taken in national courts.

A pertinent question is whether a strong presumption is the best type of threshold (irrespective of the market share level). Most commentators fear that market shares are too imprecise to serve as presumptions: first, because of the complexity of market definition (both the general problem about getting sound enough data to carry out the hypothetical monopolist test and about the limits of performing this test when there is already a dominant player so that the test underestimates market power, the so-called cellophane fallacy) market shares are in their nature an imperfect indicator so that using them to generate pre-sumptions or safe harbours is undesirable. Second, even if the markets are defined satisfactorily, they say nothing about the competitive dynamics and the pressures upon firms; they do not show whether the market shares are sus-tainable; they do not inform us about potential entrants (traditionally market definition is only about making inquiries into demand substitution, not supply substitution);[23] nor about buyer power.[24] So a firm with a market share of 90% in a contestable market has less market power than a firm with a market share of 50% in a market with high entry barriers populated by weak firms. These defects suggest that a presumption based upon market shares tends to overestimate dominance. Thus, those convinced that the supreme evil of competition law en-forcement is false positives would reject the *AKZO* test.[25]

Those same people might prefer a safe harbour which immunises firms within it and at the same time raises the burden of proof for the plaintiff. Two noted US scholars, *Louis Kaplow* and *Carl Shapiro*, made the case for safe harbours in these terms:

> substantial costs of administration, mistaken prohibition, and inhibition of com-petitive vigor can be avoided by in essence granting immunity. To give a concrete example, imposing a monopoly power screen in the area of predatory pricing avoids

---

[23] For discussion of this point see J.B. Baker, 'Market Definition: An Analytical Overview' (2007) 74 *Antitrust Law Journal*, 129, 131-138.

[24] R. Thompson and J. O'Flaherty (*supra* n. 14) para. 10.022.

[25] E.g. Justice Scalia's fears of false positives in the context of Section 2 of the Sherman Act in *Verizon Communications Inc. v. Law Offices of Curtis Trinko*, 540 U.S. 398 (2004).

potentially enormous costs that could arise if every firm contemplating an aggressive low-price strategy had to fear a possible predatory pricing challenge from its rivals.[26]

In this spirit, the US Department of Justice had taken the view that courts should consider developing such a safe harbour, suggesting that no firm with a market share below 50% has ever been found liable under Section 2 Sherman Act and this could thus serve as a helpful threshold where the costs of seeking out monopolisation conduct below this level outweigh the gains of any lawsuit.[27] The criticisms of market share measures noted above apply less strongly here because the tendency of market shares to overestimate dominance means that the safe harbour is possibly too low and that a higher safe harbour would work as well, but at least an imperfectly low safe harbour does not create risks of over-enforcement and does not even create significant risks of under-enforcement. While there is some risk of under-enforcement if the safe harbour is pitched at a high level, the supporters of safe harbours would argue that false negatives are less harmful than false positives.[28]

Others might say that market shares should only provide a weak indication of dominance, as in merger cases. There is some merit to this suggestion because, as noted above, market shares by themselves are a poor indicator of market power in that one needs to also look at the market elasticity of demand and the elasticity of supply of rivals. So deriving a weak presumption from market shares is preferable because a given level will trigger a more complete market power analysis by the competition authority. Thus, even if one gets the market definition wrong, this can be corrected by including excluded firms through analysis of potential entry. Usually a weak presumptive approach is reserved for merger cases where the competition authority has to review each notified transaction and filters are used systematically for every case and are designed to save resources, but it could equally apply to other Commission investigations. However, the weak presumptive approach is of no help in private litigation where the legal process does not provide for the plaintiff to have one trial where market shares are established by the court that then allows plaintiff to start a second trial to see if market shares tell the whole story.

In sum: a strong, presumptive threshold risks over-enforcing the law, and the lower the threshold is, the more over-enforcement is risked. In contrast, by

---

[26] L. Kaplow and C. Shapiro (*supra* n. 4) p.101.

[27] DOJ Report (*supra* n. 2) ch. 2.

[28] This discussion assumes that we know, *ex ante*, what constitutes over- or under-enforcement, but one may legitimately question whether there is enough information to determine in each instance whether the law will be (or has been) over- or under-enforced.

opting for a strong safe harbour one reduces the number of lawsuits. The nature of competition law enforcement may influence a jurisdiction's choice between safe harbours and presumptions. Safe harbours seem more attractive in the United States where juries are said to be overly eager to condemn ruthless conduct by competitors.[29] A paradox in the US is that as courts continue to rein in the substantive law to avoid the defendant's over-exposure to the risks of jury trials, the same case law is also making it more difficult for the US antitrust agencies to enforce the law.[30] In the EU, instead, over-enforcement by courts is not as great a concern as cases are argued either by the Commission or in front of judges more likely to filter out unmeritorious claims when examining whether the behaviour in question is an abuse, although some would even contest the ability of the judiciary to sift the wheat from the chaff.[31]

Which of the approaches canvassed above should be selected is a question on which there seems to be no international consensus. In one document by the International Competition Network's Unilateral Conduct Working Group setting out 'Recommended Practices' on dominance analysis, three views are taken: that a firm should not be found dominant absent a full analysis of all economic factors and that market shares should serve as a starting point (a weak, presumptive threshold); but that it can be beneficial to have market share based safe harbours (without detailing what level would be desirable); but that it can also be beneficial to use market shares as an indicator of dominance (a stronger presumptive threshold, again with no indication of what level might be desirable).[32] This is not particularly helpful because it restates the question without answering it, but it does allow for a final reflection: whether one should contemplate both a safe harbour *and* a presumptive threshold. There seems to be no logical or legal argument against this; in fact in the context of vertical restraints one finds a safe harbour in the Block Exemption Regulation and some fairly

---

[29] L. Kaplow and C. Shapiro (*supra* n. 4) *passim*.
[30] Statement of Federal Trade Commission Chairman W.E. Kovacic, 'Modern U.S. Competition Law and the Treatment of Dominant Firms: Comments on the Department of Justice and Federal Trade Commission Proceedings Relating to Section 2 of the Sherman Act' (8 September 2008), p. 8 <www.ftc.gov/opa/2008/09/section2.shtm>, 15 October 2010.
[31] F.H. Easterbrook, 'The Limits of Antitrust' (1984) 63 *Texas Law Review*, 1.
[32] ICN Unilateral Conduct Working Group, 'Dominance/Substantial Market Power Analysis Pursuant to Unilateral Conduct Laws, Recommended Practices' (May 2007) <www.internationalcompetitionnetwork.org/>, 15 October 2010.

strong presumptions in the accompanying Guidelines that certain types of vertical restraint cannot be exempted when practised by dominant firms.[33]

B. *Threshold-scepticism*

For the most part, thresholds are based on a single variable: market share, although in some instances readily observable contractual conduct also contributes to the threshold (e.g. in the Vertical Restraints Block Exemption Regulation there is a double threshold: market share plus a lack of black listed clauses). The advantage of a single variable is that the plaintiff saves resources; however, one criticism of using market shares as the single variable (in addition to its imprecision noted above) is that because interminable disputes over market definition ensue in almost every case, the avowed cost savings of such a threshold can be nullified. Moreover, some commentators say that market shares have an 'undue sway' over the assessment of dominance in the EU.[34] The challenge then is to consider if there is any other way of measuring market power directly, but so far these methods have only had limited practical effect and most often have been applied in merger cases.[35] A selection of alternatives is discussed below.

An economically sound way to measure dominance is to look for excess profits, but this is difficult to implement in practice.[36] As an alternative, some competition authorities have examined whether the consumer price for the goods in question is higher than it ought to be. This approach was taken in the *Staples*

---

[33] E.g. 'Where a company is dominant on the downstream market, any obligation to supply the products only or mainly to the dominant buyer may easily have significant anti-competitive effects.', Guidelines on Vertical Restraints [2010] OJ C 291/1 para.194.

[34] J. Vickers, 'Market Power in Competition Cases' (2006) 2 (Special Issue) *European Competition Journal*, 3, 4; G. Werden, 'Assigning Market Shares' (2002) 70 *Antitrust Law Journal*, 67.

[35] M. Motta (*supra* n. 6) ch. 3; G. Monti, *EC Competition Law* (Cambridge, 2007), pp. 150-153; J.B. Baker and T. Bresnahan, 'Economic Evidence in Antitrust: Defining Markets and Measuring Market Power' *Stanford Law and Economics Olin Working Paper No. 328* (2006), p. 5.

[36] For discussion, see J.A. Kay, 'Assessing Market Dominance Using Accounting Rates of Profit', in *The Economics of Market Dominance*, D. Hay and J. Vickers (eds) (Oxford, 1987); G.K. Ottosen, *Monopoly Power* (Salt Lake City, 1990), ch. 3; R. Schmalensee, 'Another Look at Market Power' (1981-1982) 95 *Harvard Law Review*, 1789.

merger in the US where, in considering a merger between two of the three office supply superstores, the evidence showed that in geographical areas with fewer competing office supply superstores prices were higher and that in markets where only Staples was present prices were 13% higher than in markets where Staples competed with the other two superstores; in addition, the evidence established that when one of the three entered an area where only the other two had been present, prices fell. The evidence indicated that there was market power in those areas with few superstores so that a merger of two of the three superstores would harm competition.[37] And a recent paper makes a similar observation showing how retail mobile phone tariffs were lower in a Member State where the market was very highly concentrated and higher in a Member State where the market was effectively competitive, showing the irrelevance of market shares in estimating market power and the importance of price comparisons.[38] Applied to Article 102 TFEU cases, the approach could be to compare the prices in the region where one suspects a firm holds a dominant position with prices in a region where the market is known to be competitive and to exclude other reasons for the price differences, e.g. cost differences in operating in the two regions.[39] If prices are substantially higher in the suspected zone, this indicates dominance. Obviously this approach requires one to identify a competitive market (and also to agree on a geographical market definition), but arguably US courts have some experience in this regard since this method is used in damages actions to decide if a cartel has overcharged the plaintiff and, if so, by what amount. Here the courts compare the price in the cartelised territory with the price in a non-cartelised territory (the so-called yardstick approach). So it may be plausible to rely on this method also for the purposes of determining dominance. The upshot is that there is no role for product market definition or market shares because monopoly power can be shown directly through supra-competitive prices or proven not to exist when prices are competitive.

A related suggestion is to examine whether the behaviour of the defendant yields anticompetitive effects proscribed by the relevant rule. This was suggested in the EU by the Economic Advisory Group for Competition Policy and also by some commentators at the DOJ hearings on Section 2 Sherman Act.[40]

---

[37] *Federal Trade Commission v. Staples, Inc.*, 970 F. Supp. 1066 (D.D.C. 1997).

[38] J.A. Hausman and J.G. Sidak, 'Evaluating Market Power Using Competitive Benchmark Prices instead of the Herfindahl-Hirschman Index' (2007) 74 *Antitrust Law Journal*, 387.

[39] J.B. Baker and T. Bresnahan (*supra* n. 35) p. 5.

[40] A. Perrot, M. Polo, P. Rey, K. Schmidt and R. Stenbacka, 'An Economic Approach to Article 82' (2006) 2 *Competition Policy International*, 111.

Under this approach, rather than litigating on market definition, a finding of dominance is made when we see undesired effects (e.g. exclusion/elimination of efficient rivals), regardless of market shares. Some might say that this approach should be embraced by the EU, in particular because of the current approach which appears to penalise firms under Article 102 TFEU when there is little likelihood (or at least little evidence) of anticompetitive harm – the Commission finding abuse by 'object', as it were.[41] However, evidence of anticompetitive effects is just as contentious as evidence about relevant markets, so this would not obviate the costs inherent in a market share based threshold. Moreover this approach presupposes (if it is to remain lawful for the purposes of Article 102 TFEU, which requires a finding of dominance and a finding of abuse) that one is able to identify a list of anticompetitive conduct that can only be carried out by firms with dominance, so that only those anticompetitive effects resulting from that kind of behaviour fall within Article 102 TFEU, a task which seems close to impossible to carry out across the board given that vertical restraints may cause anticompetitive foreclosure whether they are carried out by dominant or non-dominant firms.[42] And so, as one commentator has suggested, this approach creates a risk of over-enforcement.[43] But this suggestion could be used episodically when the conditions are right. Consider the decision of the 6th Circuit where (albeit in ruling merely that the plaintiff survived summary judgment, reading the evidence accordingly in the light most favourable to him) the court accepted evidence that the defendant's practices had an adverse effect on competition in the relevant geographic markets as proof of monopoly power. The principle articulated by the Court is as follows: 'an antitrust plaintiff is not required to rely on indirect evidence of a defendant's monopoly power, such as high market share within a defined market, when there is direct evidence that the defendant has actually set prices or excluded competition.'[44] On the facts, the case concerned the commissions that estate agents could earn: the plaintiff, a new entrant estate agent franchisor, granted very generous commissions to agents with a view to attracting the best agents; in response the incumbent competitors instituted a policy whereby any agent who was associated with the

---

[41] An instance of this is *British Airways v. Commission*, Case No. C-95/04 P [2007] ECR I-2331.

[42] For similar doubts, see J. Vickers and D. Hay, 'The Economics of Market Dominance', in *The Economics of Market Dominance*, D. Hay and J. Vickers (eds) (Oxford, 1987), p. 38.

[43] A. Majumdar, 'Whither Dominance?' [2006] *European Competition Law Review*, 161, 163.

[44] *Re Max Ltd. v. Realty One*, 173 F.3d 995, 1018 (6th Cir. 1999).

plaintiff and who brought defendants a customer would receive a lower commission than other agents. The impact of this was deterring agents from entering into franchise agreements with the plaintiff, and the Court accepted as evidence of monopoly power that several agents refused to switch to the plaintiff, that some who did went out of business, and also, perhaps most tellingly, that when defendant tried a similar exclusionary strategy in a market where it patently did not have dominance, it failed. The latter finding is in my view crucial because it serves to establish that dominance was a necessary condition for the resulting harm and so is consistent with the requirement that the monopolisation offence requires monopoly power in addition to the exclusion of rivals. Indeed, if this method were to be utilised it would be necessary to show that the practice in question would be economically irrational without dominance because in those instances the behaviour is self-correcting.[45] Again, with this approach we do not use thresholds but find dominance directly, this time by noting exclusionary conduct that can only be successful if the defendant has monopoly power.

A related argument against the use of thresholds is that considering the dominance question without thinking about the abuse fails to yield helpful formulations of any threshold. This has been set out most clearly by *Thomas Eilmansberger.*[46] In brief, the argument boils down to suggesting that a 'one size fits all' concept of dominance is unworkable and that dominance should be defined as the ability to bring about a certain distortion of competition. He then argues that as a result of this, a different standard of dominance analysis should be carried out depending on whether the abuse is exclusionary or exploitative. Focusing on exploitative abuses, he suggests that bilateral practices (e.g. contracts with single branding obligations) should fall to being regulated under Article 101 TFEU, thus obviating the need for a dominance test. For unilateral foreclosure practices (an example of which appears to be rebates that are not agreed upon by the buyer) he suggests a market share threshold can be used (of 40-50% upwards) given that this level allows the dominant firm to foreclose the market single-handedly; while a 'superdominance' threshold should apply to above-cost discounts because only firms that are extremely powerful are able to use above-cost price cuts to achieve the exclusion of rivals; and in refusal to deal cases, establishing dominance is unnecessary because the finding of an abuse

---

[45] See generally G.A. Hay, 'The Interaction of Market Structure and Conduct', in *The Economics of Market Dominance*, D. Hay and J. Vickers (eds) (Oxford, 1987), pp. 120-122.

[46] T. Eilmansberger, 'Dominance – The Lost Child? How Effects-Based Rules Could and Should Change Dominance Analysis' (2006) 2 (Special Issue) *European Competition Journal*, 15.

requires that the facility in question is indispensable, so there is no need for a threshold based on market shares here. To a large extent this approach already reflects the way the Commission and the Court handle abuse cases (save that for certain other abuses that disrupt the competitive process, which he calls structural abuses – e.g. perhaps below cost pricing – the author seeks a higher threshold of dominance than is applied currently). *Eilmansberger*'s approach does cast doubt on the usefulness of a presumptive threshold because if the ultimate finding entirely depends on what the abuse at stake is, then we gain nothing with a presumptive approach. On the other hand the presumption still aids plaintiffs in satisfying the first step in the application of Article 102 TFEU, and the degree of dominance necessary to carry out the abuse in question can be considered at a second stage in deciding whether the abuse has anticompetitive effects. And while the critique is valid for presumptive thresholds, it does not undermine the usefulness of a safe harbour threshold.

Perhaps as a result of the limits of using market shares alone as a strong presumptive indicator of monopoly, and the absence of a workable, generally applicable alternative, the US Department of Justice ('DOJ') had taken the view that a rebuttable presumption of monopoly power for the purposes of Section 2 Sherman Act arises when three conditions are met: (1) a firm has a market share in excess of two thirds; (2) it has maintained that market share for a significant period; (3) other market conditions like entry barriers suggest that the position is durable.[47] This is a significantly more detailed market analysis than that suggested by a market share threshold, so much so that this approach does not merit the name 'threshold' at all, given the amount of variables involved. But recall the DOJ, while sceptical of presumptive thresholds, was in favour of a safe harbour.[48]

C. The Commission's approach

In the Guidance Paper the Commission sets a soft safe harbour, whereby dominance is unlikely when the firm's market share is below 40% but the Commission reserves the right to intervene if competitors cannot constrain the dominant firm, citing capacity constraints as an example, which seems to draw on a similar approach taken in the Horizontal Merger Guidelines and is identical to

---

[47]   DOJ Report (*supra* n. 2) p. 30.
[48]   DOJ Report (*supra* n. 2) p. 24.

that taken by the UK's Office of Fair Trading in 2004.[49] For cases above this threshold the Commission undertakes to examine all relevant factors to determine whether the firm in question faces sufficient competitive constraints.[50] This is different from the Court's strong presumption of dominance at 50% if held for a long period of time. Thus, after the Commission's Guidance Paper we have two thresholds, but it seems as if they will work in two different contexts: the safe harbour will be used by the Commission, and the Commission will not take advantage of the *AKZO* presumption; while private litigants may well be tempted to rely on the strong presumption to help them litigate. In this context the comment of a member of DG Competition written when the 2005 Discussion Paper was issued is worth recalling. *Michael Albers* said that the aim was to 'remove the dominance presumption that the courts have created for a firm with a 50% market share.'[51] This removal cannot occur through soft law but the intention of the Commission is to remove it from its mind as a basis for intervention. A question that arises in this context is whether National Competition Authorities will follow the Commission's line and revise their thresholds for intervention when these differ. There is no obligation on them to do so as the Guidance Paper intends to steer the Commission's approach, not to restate the law. So we may well have multiple thresholds which emerge.

Significantly, the Commission's approach differs from that which had been canvassed in the Discussion Paper in 2005. There, it suggested dominance was very likely when market shares were above 50%, more likely when market shares were between 40-50% than when below 40%, and not likely with market shares below 25%.[52] The Guidance Paper is more explicit in removing any sense that 50% is a relevant market share at all, and it also revises upwards the safe harbour, as a 25% safe harbour is so low as to provide no safeguard at all as hardly any firm would fear the application of Article 102 TFEU with such low market presence. These amendments between the 2005 discussion paper and the 2009 guidance paper indicate that the Commission finds the risk of over-enforcement increasingly convincing.

---

[49] GP (*supra* n. 1) para. 14; Guidelines on the assessment of horizontal mergers under the Council Regulation on the control of concentrations between undertakings [2004] OJ C 31/5 para. 17; Office of Fair Trading (OFT), *Abuse of a Dominant Position* (December 2004) para. 4.18.

[50] GP (*supra* n. 1) para. 15.

[51] M. Albers, quoted in 'Article 82 Exclusionary Conduct Discussion Paper: An Interview with Michael Albers and Luc Peeperkorn' <ec.europa.eu/competition/index_en.html>, 15 October 2010.

[52] DP (*supra* n. 1) para. 31.

III. Dominance

A. The power to exclude versus the power to exploit

The concept of dominance in EU competition law is complex. Merely being the largest firm by reference to market shares is insufficient to trigger the application of Article 102 TFEU, although in every case taken by the Commission so far the dominant firm has been the largest player in the relevant market. The Court's definition of dominance has received much criticism:

> a position of economic strength enjoyed by an undertaking which *enables* it to hinder the maintenance of effective competition on the relevant market *by allowing* it to behave *to an appreciable extent* independently of its competitors and customers and ultimately of consumers.[53]

The most common criticism is that no firm acts independently of competitors and customers, because there is always a limit to how high the profit-maximising monopoly price can be.[54] This critique misses out on the key qualification that the Court made (italicised in the passage above): the dominant firm can only behave independently of competitors and customers to an appreciable extent; it is not absolute power that the dominant firm has.[55] The Commission is correct in its Guidance Paper to interpret this passage as meaning that the dominant firm faces ineffective competitive constraints and so 'enjoys substantial market power over a period of time.'[56] This is sound in economic terms in that, as noted in the introduction, market power is a matter of degree and also a matter of being able to sustain power over a long time (usually considering a period of 2-3 years).

---

[53] *Michelin v. Commission*, Case No. 322/81 [1983] ECR 3461 para. 30, first devised in *United Brands v. Commission*, Case No. 27/76 [1978] ECR 207 (my emphasis).

[54] L. Kaplow and C. Shapiro (*supra* n. 4) p. 20; L. Coppi and M. Walker 'Substantial Convergence or Parallel Paths? Similarities and differences in the economic analysis of horizontal mergers in US and EC Competition Law' (2004) 49 *Antitrust Bulletin*, 101, 121.

[55] G. Monti, 'The Concept of Dominance in Article 82 EC' (2006) 2 (Special Issue) *European Competition Journal*, 31, 38; in a similar vein E. Arezzo, 'Is there a role for market definition and dominance in an effects-based approach?', in *Abuse of Dominant Position: New Interpretation, New Enforcement Mechanisms?*, M.-O. Mackenrodt, B. Conde Gallego and S. Enchelmaier (eds) (Berlin, 2008), p. 25.

[56] GP (*supra* n. 1) para. 10.

A more pertinent criticism is that made by *Richard Whish* and concerns the underlined passages above. He notes that the definition has two elements: the ability to prevent competition and the ability to behave independently, but that it does not explain how they relate to each other. It could be that both elements must be proven or that one depends on the other, but then it is not clear which is the fundamental concept. His view is that the essential issue is the ability to act independently on the market.[57] This opinion is reflected in the subtle alteration to this definition found in the Framework Directive for electronic communications, which avoids reference to the hindrance of effective competition and retains merely the reference to the ability to act independently.[58] And the Commission believes that this abridged test means that 'the definition used in this Directive is *equivalent* to the concept of dominance as defined in the case law of the Court of Justice and the Court of First Instance of the European Communities.'[59]

A different criticism of the same issue is made by *Eilmansberger*.[60] In his view the definition is sound because both categories of abuse, exploitative (the latter part of the passage above) and exclusionary (the former), are included. His problem is with the connecting phrase 'by giving it the power' which assumes that the ability to exclude results from the ability to exploit. In his view the unfortunate consequence of this is that in all cases dominance is tested as if the abuse were exploitative, and so a one size fits all approach to dominance has prevailed, which as noted above (section II.B) he deems inappropriate.

With respect, both authors seem to read the passage above as if it were a statutory text and ignore any further explanations that the ECJ might offer in its judgments. Admittedly the Court does at times speak as if its sentences ought to be read as statutes, but this is not the way judgments are intended to be read unless the court makes it clear that a single paragraph provides a synthesis of its legal approach. Instead one should look at the judgment as a whole. I say this

---

[57] R. Whish (*supra* n. 18) pp. 174-175.

[58] Article 14(2): 'An undertaking shall be deemed to have significant market power if, either individually or jointly with others, it enjoys a position equivalent to dominance, that is to say a position of economic strength affording it the power to behave to an appreciable extent independently of competitors, customers and ultimately consumers.', Directive 2002/21/EC of the European Parliament and of the Council (7 March 2002) on a common regulatory framework for electronic communications networks and services (Framework Directive) [2002] OJ L 108/33.

[59] *Ibid.* Recital 25.

[60] T. Eilmansberger (*supra* n. 46).

because in *Hoffmann La Roche* (where the criticised definition appears again) the Court developed its definition. At one point the ECJ observes that Hoffmann La Roche enjoyed 'that freedom of action which is the special feature of a dominant position.'[61] This would support *Whish's* interpretation because it focuses on the freedom to exploit (and as we shall see below, also the Commission's new approach). But another passage offers I think a clearer elaboration. Dominance

> does not preclude some competition, which it does where there is a monopoly or a quasi-monopoly, but enables the undertaking which profits by it, if not to determine, at least to have an appreciable influence on the conditions under which that competition will develop, and in any case to act largely in disregard of it so long as such conduct does not operate to its detriment.[62]

As with *Eilmansberger's* interpretation, this passage embodies both exploitative abuses (acting largely in disregard of competitors) and exclusionary ones (the power to determine or influence the conditions of competition). But this passage removes the problematic linking clauses that bothered both critics and identifies two different manifestations of market power: the power to exploit and the power to exclude. This in my view is important because it clashes directly with the economists' general definition of dominance which they identify exclusively with the power to exploit.

An important attribute of the core identity of EU competition law is the commitment to the competitive process, of seeing competition as an institution, and of the recognition that the economic freedom of market participants merits protection from the private power of dominant firms. Accordingly *Giuliano Amato* has noted that the 'special responsibility' that dominant firms have to not harm the competitive process resembles a principle of public law.[63] And he goes on to observe that 'the formation of private power is opposed in Europe very often at the stage before antitrust intervention would be legitimate in the USA, not just according to the most extreme followers of the Chicago School but also according to those who fear the consolidation of that power more than the obstructive interventions of public power.'[64] So that in Europe weak competition is protected against the strongest competitors. This then leads US critics and economists to claim that EU competition law protects competitors, and not com-

---

[61] *Hoffmann-La Roche & Co. AG v. Commission*, Case No. 85/76 [1979] ECR 461 para. 41.
[62] *Ibid.* para. 39.
[63] G. Amato, *Antitrust and the Bounds of Power* (Oxford, 1997), p. 66.
[64] *Ibid.* p. 68.

petition. But this misunderstands the intellectual force of the Community's position: private power is seen as a danger in particular when it excludes those market players that would challenge it. The European ideology does not believe that by under-enforcing competition law markets will somehow discipline dominant players and that over-enforcing the law has a chilling effect. The political commitment is about restraining market power. It is a political commitment which requires a lower dominance screen because the adverse effects of economic power that the EU is worried about manifest themselves with less than monopoly power. Of course we can give this political commitment an economic spin. For example we can say that innovation is more likely in markets where mavericks are allowed to thrive than in markets dominated by a single firm, and that consumers are better served when the dynamics of markets are allowed to thrive.[65] Likewise it is plausible to ask whether over-enforcement is always worse than under-enforcement: if a dominant firm deters new entrants but one does not act against it because the firm does not have power over price, this seems to hinder the possibility of consumer welfare gains to a significant extent.[66] But these kinds of economic rationalisations are unnecessary if the political commitment is to competition and not to efficiency or consumer welfare.

To elaborate on this further, it is important also to determine what the power to exclude entails. Some would like to see this defined in a narrow way as the power to damage the structure of competition (see especially *Eilmansberger*),[67] some economists might want to see this concept developed in a strategic manner by suggesting that the power to exclude must entail, in the period after exclusion, that the dominant firm gains (or re-gains) the power to exploit. This approach is consistent with the economic analysis of predation as a two-step process: exclusion and recoupment. On the other hand, the Court's case law in my view has, to date, espoused a looser definition of the power to exclude which does not require such severe harm to the market – almost any harm to the economic freedom of market participants suffices to trigger the application of Article 102 TFEU. In an earlier paper I characterised the Court's approach to dominance as one that focuses on commercial power, drawing on an earlier assessment by John Temple Lang where he suggested dominance meant the ability to react when confronted by competition and the power to contain

---

[65] See e.g. E.M. Fox, 'The Efficiency Paradox', in *How the Chicago School Overshot the Mark*, R. Pitofsy (ed.) (Oxford, 2008), p. 80.

[66] I.M. Selzer, 'Some Practical Thoughts About Entry', in *How the Chicago School Overshot the Mark*, R. Pitofsy (ed.) (Oxford, 2008), p.24.

[67] T. Eilmansberger (*supra* n. 46).

competition.[68] Commercial power is a much wider concept than the power to exploit one's market power, but it tallies with the commitment of safeguarding the competitive process.

B. A shift in policy

The above remarks are significant because in its 2005 Discussion Paper and again in the 2009 Guidance Paper the Commission gives a definition of dominance that is more in line with that of economists:

> an undertaking which is capable of profitably increasing prices above the competitive level for a significant period of time [normally two years] does not face sufficiently effective competitive constraints and can thus generally be regarded as dominant.[69]

Comparing this with the Court's definition, a subtle but significant difference emerges: the Court placed emphasis on the power of the dominant firm to harm rivals or its power to exploit clients, while this definition places emphasis only on the firm's ability to exploit its dominant position. The upshot is that some undertakings found dominant under the Court's definition would not be found dominant under the Commission's new approach.

The question is whether this is a deliberate shift in policy to restrict the ambit of Article 102 TFEU. On the one hand, the Guidance Paper also retains the classical definition of dominance from the case law.[70] As the two are not consistent this might indicate some division inside the Commission as to which approach should be followed, or that the Commission reserves the power to intervene even in cases where the dominant firm does not have the power to exploit. On the other hand, the tenor of the Guidance Paper as a whole appears to demonstrate a commitment to the narrower conception of dominance. The section explaining the purpose of the document, for example, states that the Commission's priority is on those cases that are most harmful for consumers and that the protection of the competitive process does not entail the mere protection of competitors.[71] Furthermore, in using the concept of anticompetitive foreclosure the Guidance Paper (which is crucial for determining if there has been an abuse of dominance) suggests that the Commission will have to prove not

---

[68] G. Monti (*supra* n. 55) 31; J. Temple Lang, 'Some Aspects of Abuse of a Dominant Position in EC Antitrust Law' (1979) 3 *Fordham International Law Journal*, 1, 12.

[69] GP (*supra* n. 1) para. 11.

[70] *Ibid.* para. 10.

[71] *Ibid.* paras 5 and 6.

only that the abuse hampers effective access of actual or potential competitors, but also that consumer harm results.[72] These passages are responses to the criticisms of the current approach: that it protects small firms, that there are per se abuses and that the economic impact of the behaviour is ignored. The general impact of these statements is that the enforcement of Article 102 TFEU is to be scaled down. Narrowing the concept of dominance would seem consistent with this policy. Moreover, if the concept of abuse requires economic analysis of the effects, it appears to follow that an economic analysis of dominance is preferable to a concept of dominance premised upon finding commercial power.

C. Implications for the measurement of dominance and for enforcement

1. For the measurement of dominance

If there is a deliberate change of policy, the practical consequence is fewer Article 102 TFEU decisions given that the competition authority will determine, at the first hurdle, that defendants lack significant market power. That said, it is unlikely that the basic methodology for testing for dominance will change in a significant manner: markets will continue to be defined using the hypothetical monopolist test (the transition away from unstructured market definitions towards more systematic economic appraisal occurred in the early days of the European Merger Regulation, fifteen years before the 2005 Discussion Paper), and the Commission will check for entry barriers and buyer power as it has done in the past. As I noted in an earlier work, the Commission and Courts appear to have blended a definition of dominance premised upon commercial power with a methodology for measuring dominance which is drawn from economic studies that define dominance as significant market power.[73] The reform aligns the definition with the methods.

However, one commentator, *Emanuela Arezzo,* suggests that there is a possible significant shift of focus by the Commission: onto the efficiency of rivals rather than on the conduct of the dominant firm. She argues that the effects-based analysis of dominance will require a direct measurement of economic power based on the actual conduct of the firm on the market and so the dominance and abuse tests will be one and the same. And three consequences result: (1) competition authorities focus on the efficiency levels of competitors to see if they offer an effective competitive constraint; (2) the anticompetitive

---

[72] *Ibid.* para. 19.
[73] G. Monti (*supra* n. 35) ch. 5.

character of a practice depends upon how rivals can respond; (3) competition authorities are over-stretched by having to test the efficiency of competitors.[74] This could be a significant set of effects, but the examination of rivals' efficiency is only necessary if it is found that entry barriers are sufficiently low to allow for theoretical entry of rivals. Only once this finding is made will there be a need to examine the capacities of rivals. This resolves the risk of an over-stretched competition authority. And the Commission appears to have been up to the task in some merger cases where it examined whether rivals had sufficient production capacity to constrain the merged entity.[75] Nor is this analysis completely alien to Article 102 TFEU litigation: rivals' lack of an efficient distribution network was noted in *United Brands* to help establish the dominance of the leading banana seller. Accordingly, one should not be worried if the Commission starts to explore the real ability of rivals to expand; on the contrary it is a sensible step in Article 102 TFEU litigation. Granted, it imposes greater costs in some instances, but this merely reinforces the need for a threshold type approach to save resources and focus enforcement towards the most relevant cases.

One aspect that remains unclear is what degree of market power is 'significant' under this new approach? I am not certain that economists have yet contributed enough to this question, for instance *Kaplow* and *Shapiro* merely suggest that the question is difficult to answer but that the degree of power should be in sync with the relevant practice under scrutiny and that a lower level of power is required when the practice is clearly anticompetitive, while a higher level should apply when the practice is potentially efficient.[76] Accordingly their criticism that the US courts have failed to explain what level of power indicates monopoly is not entirely fair since there is no apparent answer from economists. A possible solution (which they do mention but do not seem to endorse) might be to draw on the Commission Notice on market definition or the US guidelines on Horizontal Mergers and see what definition they provide of the hypothetical monopolist. The Commission's Guidelines provide that the SSNIP test is carried out by examining a permanent price increase of 5-10%;[77] in the US the agencies use a price increase of 5% for the foreseeable future. Drawing on the nature of

---

[74] E. Arezzo (*supra* n. 55) pp. 36-40.

[75] See Guidelines on the assessment of horizontal mergers under the Council Regulation on the control of concentrations between undertakings [2004] OJ C 31/5 paras 32-35.

[76] L. Kaplow and C. Shapiro (*supra* n. 4) p. 102.

[77] Commission Notice on the definition of the relevant market for the purposes of Community competition law [1997] OJ C 372/5 para. 17.

the hypothetical monopolist test, if a firm were actually able to exercise such power over price, that ought to constitute significant market power and hence dominance. Proving this can be done in two ways: one can, as in the *Staples* case, compare prices in different zones and determine whether prices are 5-10% higher in certain zones where dominance is suspected.[78] Alternatively one can infer that high market shares held in a market with high entry barriers and low buyer power indicate significant market power, and this inference is sound because in defining the market with the hypothetical monopolist test, the market so defined reflects price elasticity of demand. Although this method still fails to offer much precision on the question of how much market power is enough.

On perhaps a lighter note, the million dollar question is to pinpoint which past cases where the ECJ ruled the defendant was dominant would today result in a finding that there is no dominance. Without complete data on the firms' power over price, this is a difficult question to answer, but two cases strike me as prima facie instances of a lack of significant market power: *United Brands* and *British Airways*.[79] In each the dominant firm was facing strong competition from a new entrant (a price war in some instances) and its market shares were falling during the period of the abuse, suggesting that the firms had no power to raise prices by 5-10%. A third perhaps being *Hugin* but for different reasons.[80] Here the Commission found dominance in the after market of spare parts for Hugin's cash register; however, it ignored the fact that the market for cash registers was highly competitive and that if Hugin's activities made owners of their machines worse off, they would switch to alternative supplies, so any abuse by Hugin would be self-correcting.[81] The Commission here was protecting small repairers but the approach in the Guidance Paper requires a focus on the impact on consumers.

2. For enforcement

The impact of the policy change entails reduced enforcement and also a loss of the commitment to protecting the competitive process and the economic free-dom of market participants as an end in itself. Aligning dominance with signi-

---

[78] *Federal Trade Commission v. Staples, Inc.*, 970 F. Supp. 1066 (D.D.C. 1997).
[79] *United Brands v. Commission*, Case No. 27/76 [1978] ECR 207; *British Airways v. Commission*, Case No. C-95/04 P [2007] ECR I-2331.
[80] Commission Decision, *Hugin/Liptons*, Case No. IV/29.132 [1978] OJ L 22/23, annulled by the ECJ on other grounds: *Hugin Kassaregister AB and Hugin Cash Registers Ltd. v. Commission*, Case No. 22/78 [1979] ECR 1869.
[81] D. Hay (*supra* n. 45) pp. 120-121.

ficant market power, as in the US, ignores the presence in the US (and the absence in the EC) of a doctrine of attempted monopolisation. In a nutshell, attempted monopolisation is a Section 2 Sherman Act offence that requires proof '(1) that the defendant has engaged in predatory or anticompetitive conduct with (2) a specific intent to monopolize and (3) a dangerous probability of achieving monopoly power.'[82] No monopoly power need be shown although a degree of market power is required to trigger the application of this rule in order to demonstrate that there is a dangerous probability that the practice will lead the defendant to hold monopoly power.[83] In trying to bring in some certainty, the Fourth Circuit suggested that claims where the firm has market shares less than 30% should be rejected, claims involving firms with market shares greater than 50% should be treated as attempts, and those in between should normally be rejected unless there is a likelihood that the firm will achieve monopoly.[84] The implication, as *Herbert Hovenkamp* noted, is that the European concept of dominance covers all firms capable of committing either the mono-polisation offence or the attempt to monopolise.[85] In comparative law terms, 'dominance' is the functional equivalent of the market power screen for both monopolisation and attempted monopolisation.

The upshot is that while I suggested above that *United Brands* and *BA* are cases where the firms probably lacked significant market power (defined as the power to exploit), it may well be desirable to bring their conduct within the scope of Article 102 TFEU given the risk they pose to the competitive process (although in both the Court may still be criticised for not coming anywhere near showing that the defendants had a real chance to secure monopoly power through their tactics). Accordingly one might legitimately argue for a preference for the old style approach towards defining dominance because it ensures that the law can capture not only behaviour by firms already capable of exercising market power to harm consumers, but also the behaviour of firms capable of destroying the competitive process with the result of subsequently harming consumers.

---

[82] *Spectrum Sports, Inc. v. McQuillan*, 506 U.S. 447, 456 (1993).

[83] *Ibid.*

[84] *M&M Medical Supplies & Serv Inc. v. Pleasant Valley Hosp. Inc.*, 981 F.2d 160, 168 (4th Cir. 1992).

[85] H. Hovenkamp, 'The Legal Periphery of Dominant Firm Conduct', *University of Iowa Legal Studies Research Paper No.07-21* (September 2007), p. 10.

IV. Conclusions

The main points in this essay are the following. First, the Guidance Paper suggests a shift away from a definition of dominance premised upon the power to exploit or the power to exclude and towards one that defines dominance only as the power to exploit. Dominant then are those firms which can raise prices by 5-10% for a sustained period and still make a profit. This is a policy shift, not an objective/scientific change of paradigm. It is a change that is in line with the 'more economics based approach' to competition law in that it backs away from the concerns over private power.

Second, this shift does not necessarily require an alteration in the methods by which dominance is determined because the market share/entry barriers/buyer power approach is the most common means of determining market power. The problem however is that this approach does not help us determine when market power is significant. We have two options: to establish an arbitrary market share when, provided entry barriers are high and buyer power is low, we assume that the firm has significant market power; or we test for the power to raise prices directly, although this direct approach depends on data being available.

Third, there is a risk that this policy shift eliminates an important component of competition law enforcement, which the US courts label attempted monopolisation. The conventional approach to dominance instead allowed the Commission to pursue those firms which threatened the competitive process without already being able to raise prices by 5-10%.

Finally, the Commission's decision to opt for a narrower definition of dominance and for a safe harbour while rejecting the strong presumptive approach of the case law is in line with the concerns about over-enforcement and the wish to free enterprises from the clutches of Article 102 TFEU (i.e. that the costs of false negatives are less than the costs of discovering those cases and the risks of over-deterrence).

More generally, it is remarkable how the segment of the Guidance Paper on dominance tallies with the now withdrawn DOJ Report.[86] Granted the latter thought the safe harbour should be at 50% and the Commission went for 40%, but this is a small difference. More important is the commitment of both agencies to a thorough market analysis before concluding there is significant market power, a fear of false positives, a comparatively smaller concern about

---

[86] Which should not be taken as representing a consensus among US commentators. For an approach closer to the standards set out by the ECJ, see S. Salop, 'Exclusionary Conduct, Effect on Consumers, and the Flawed Profit-Sacrifice Standard' (2006) 73 *Antitrust Law Journal*, 311.

false negatives, a commitment to using the law for protecting consumers and not for containing private power. This creates a coherent policy framework insofar as one believes in the assumptions that underpin it: that a competition law designed to safeguard consumer welfare is just, that consumer welfare is best protected by a less severe enforcement of the laws because markets work to discipline those excesses that the law fails to regulate, and that the elimination of rivals is not inherently unproblematic. These are controversial assumptions. And these assumptions have very little to do with the Court's doctrine on Article 102 TFEU as it stands at present nor with the constitutional basis of EU competition law,[87] although at least some Advocates General and probably some members of the judiciary are increasingly attracted to such a policy framework.[88] Accordingly, we are seeing an evolution in EU competition law in that the economic approach is premised upon a political commitment to a style of enforcement that has little in common with that associated with those who are concerned about private power and the economic freedom of those who lack such power. What is worrying about the Commission's approach is that in making this shift it is merely reorganising its enforcement priorities so as to avoid taking those cases which would be taken under the traditional approach, such that the changes will happen implicitly, not through judicial approval. That the Guidance Paper merely applies to the Commission does, however, allow national courts and competition authorities to continue under the old paradigm. And it may also create greater urgency in some Member States to strengthen the enforcement of national laws that prohibit unilateral conduct, especially as they remain free to address such conduct in ways that are more robust than Article 102 TFEU.[89]

---

[87] On a defence of the traditional approach, see J. Drexl, 'Competition Law as Part of the European Constitution', in *Principles of European Constitutional Law*, A. v. Bogdandy and J. Blast (eds) (Oxford, 2006), p. 659.

[88] See, for instance, the differences between the Court and Advocate general in *France Télécom v. Commission*, Case No. C-202/07 P [2009] ECR I-2369.

[89] Article 3(2) Council Regulation (EC) No. 1/2003 (16 December 2002) on the implementation of the rules on competition laid down in Articles 81 and 82 of the Treaty [2003] OJ L 1/1.

THE DOMINANCE THRESHOLD: A COMMENT

Christian Ewald

I.   Introduction

The luminous paper by *Giorgio Monti* on the dominance threshold in Article 102 TFEU invites to some thoughts on a more general issue which – like a golden thread – also pervades the paper's convincing line of arguments: the interaction between economic analysis, policy discretion and legal principles in the field of antitrust. Due to its vital importance for any intervention under Article 102 TFEU, the dominance threshold is particularly well suited to carve out some core elements of this suspense-packed interplay. To this effect this comment will provide some considerations on (II.) how economics can but also should inform policy and law on the dominance threshold, (III.) the scope of policy discretion concerning the definition of respective enforcement standards, and (IV.) the legal regulating screws in the context of implementing the dominance threshold in single cases. Based on these considerations, I want to conclude with an elementary rule which in my view should be observed in contemporary competition policy debate for the sake of clarity and bilateral intelligibility in particular between economists and lawyers.

II. Economics as the route-map

Each economist has to acknowledge that there is no direct line from textbook theory to accurate competition law enforcement practice. This assertion is persuasively evidenced by the fact that the dominance threshold is no clear-cut concept derived from or consistently defined in economic theory. The pertinent gradual concept of *market power* is decidedly related to but by no means coincident with the concept of *dominance*. Thus economic theory does not provide a precise standard to determine whether or not a specific firm should be subject to special scrutiny under single firm conduct provisions.

To elucidate the consequences of this conceptual gap it is rewarding to refer to one of the best-known economic indicators of market power, the so-called Lerner-Index. This index relates the degree of market power (defined as the ability to raise price P above its competitive level, i.e. marginal cost, MC) to the individual market share of company i (m_i) or the concentration level prevailing in the market (covered by the Herfindahl-Hirshman-Index, 'HHI'), taking into account the elasticity of demand (ε) for the products concerned. Since economists are – in particular due to its conciseness – very fond of using the algebraic language, the relevant relationship is very often depicted with the following mathematical representation:[1]

$$L_i = \frac{P - MC}{P} = \frac{m_i}{\varepsilon}$$

$$L = \sum_i (m_i^2 / \varepsilon) = HHI / \varepsilon$$

These two laconic equations essentially provide the core economic underpinning for the prominent role of market shares and concentration levels in the assessment of whether the company under scrutiny meets the dominance threshold or not. The limitations of these equations and the corresponding very strong advice against hasty judgements based on market share levels become obvious when taking a closer look at the underlying theoretical model:

Like any relationship deduced in economic theory, also the Lerner-Index is contingent upon several side conditions specified in the respective theoretical model which intentionally abstracts from some details of market reality to focus

---

[1] See M. Motta, *Competition Policy, Theory and Practice* (Cambridge, 2004), pp. 123 *et seq.*

on the issue of interest. The model which yields the Lerner-Index inter alia is based on the assumptions (1.) of a well-defined relevant market, (2.) that firms compete in quantities of a perfectly homogeneous product (Cournot-type competition; no product differentiation, linear demand, linear pricing/no price discrimination), and (3.) that the marginal cost of production are constant. Relaxing these assumptions bring in a lot of additional factors (such as barriers to entry, product differentiation/closeness of competition, economies of scale, network effects or other cost-related particularities, etc.) which would in addition have to be considered and assessed properly to end up with a robust conclusion on the prevailing degree of market power.

The conceptual foundation of the Lerner-Index, i.e. the stipulation that market power is equivalent to the ability to raise price above the perfectly-competitive benchmark of marginal cost, furthermore implies that a direct measurement of market power may be possible and – provided that the necessary data base is available – probably even desirable. In this context, however, the question whether and to which extent the structure and assumptions of the respective quantitative model 'fit in' sufficiently with the relevant market under scrutiny provides significant room for discussion and probably even insurmountable differences of opinion in single cases.

The limitations of competition economics just described however do not provide any viable justification for something like a *less economic approach* in competition law enforcement. The contingency of theoretical and empirical economic inferences in fact is common to any economic analysis and represents to a certain extent the essence of the methodological paradigm of economic science in general. This however does not reduce the merits of sound economic analysis in competition law enforcement but only implies the inevitable need for a high degree of transparency and replicability regarding their deduction and depiction. Accordingly, while it is true that economics does not definitely or conclusively define the threshold where market power becomes dominance, economics can and also should inform policymakers and law enforcers about the different aspects of market reality which must be considered and assessed properly in this context. Economics in addition holds available some very useful quantitative tools which can help to collect probative evidence and arrive at a better informed conclusion on the degree of market power prevailing in a market. In other words, economic theory provides the route-map for the definition of the dominance threshold and also offers useful quantitative instruments to apply this map in single cases.

III. The scalier between economics and law: policy discretion

Eventually it is the gradual character of market power together with the multiplicity of factors to be considered for its proper assessment which throws open the door for policy discretion in the field of defining the dominance threshold. To sketch the relevant scope of policy discretion in this context, the decision-theoretic framework of an optimal competition enforcement regime provides the most suitable starting point. According to this framework, competition enforcement looks like a quite simple optimization task. The optimal enforcement regime minimizes the sum of the expected cost of erroneous decisions (error cost) and its implementation cost. The concept of implementation cost encompasses all the cost defrayed by the relevant players involved in enforcement action (administrative bodies, courts, parties etc.). The level of error cost is affected by two different types of errors. The direct and indirect error cost associated with false-positive (type-I) errors (over-enforcement) mainly result from chilling competition on the merits (unilateral conduct cases) or welfare reducing effects (inefficiencies) of erroneously vetoing a pro-competitive mergers or agreements. The welfare reducing cost associated with false negative (type-II) errors (under-enforcement) stem from short-run allocative effects (deadweight loss) as well as productive and dynamic inefficiencies associated with the exercise of fortified market power.

Economists very much like such compelling optimization problems. But considering the optimization problem at hand, each economist – while being emphatic about its theoretical consistency – in all honesty would have to concede that it is not at all operational. Any empirical implementation would require not less than a consistent *ex post* evaluation of the decision practice of very different enforcement regimes. But robust data on whether specific enforcement regimes are characterized by significant over- or under-enforcement is not (yet) available. In the area of *ex post* evaluation economic science is on the contrary still in its infancy.[2] The first careful steps forward in addition are much more focused on measuring the beneficial effects of particular enforcement action (primarily cartel enforcement) for consumers than assessing whether overall (the lack of) enforcement action has to be considered as systematic over- or under-enforcement.[3] But even if economic science would make significant progress in

---

[2] See e.g. OECD Roundtable, *Evaluation of the Actions and Resources of the Competition Authorities* (Paris, 2005) <www.oecd.org/dataoecd/7/15/35910995. pdf>, 11 October 2010.

[3] In its Annual Report on Competition Policy 2008 the European Commission for example tried to assess the positive effects of its cartel enforcement practice,

cont.

this regard, it seems very unlikely that any empirical results on the error rate of a specific enforcement regime could be gathered in an indisputable way.[4] And here again basically the contingency of any economic analysis is the prime reasons.

Despite this lack of operationality the theory of optional decision making nevertheless provides a useful framework to sketch the scope of policy discretion in competition law enforcement in general and in the context of the dominance specifically. For even if no exact level of 'error cost' can be measured, different policy approaches and enforcement regimes at least can be assessed and compared according to the *relative weight assigned to the risk enforcement errors*, i.e. of over- and under-enforcement. In this respect, competition policy very much resembles the challenge of the ancient hero *Ulysses* who once upon a time was forced to find his way through the narrow Strait of Messina which bounding rocks were closely guarded by the terrible sea-monsters Scylla (type-II error) and Charybdis (type-I error).[5] Like *Ulysses*,

---

Report from the Commission – Report on Competition Policy 2008 (23 July 2009), COM(2009) 374 final, pp. 3 *et seq.* and pp. 16 *et seq.*; other competition authorities even regularly publish key indicators to assess the effectiveness of their competition law enforcement practice, see e.g. G. Werden, 'Assessing the Effects of Antitrust Enforcement in the United States' [2008] *De Economist*, 433-451; for the approach of the British Office of Fair Trading ('OFT') which regularly publishes an 'impact analysis' of its enforcement practice, OFT, *Positive Impact 2008/09* (July 2009) <www.oft.gov.uk/shared_oft/reports/Evaluating-OFTs-work/oft1102.pdf>, 11 October 2010.

4 For quite a telling example in this regard one can refer to the discussion between the US General Accounting Office ('GAO') and the US Federal Trade Commission ('FTC') whether the enforcement practice of the FTC in the field of merger control in the US gasoline market has – as the GAO concluded – to be considered as 'under-enforcement' or not; for some details of this very intense and resource swallowing debate see e.g.: GAO, *Energy Markets: Effects of Mergers and Market Concentration in the US Petroleum Industry* (Washington/DC, 2004) <www.gao.gov/new.items/d0496.pdf>, 11 October 2010; FTC (Bureau of Economics), *The Petroleum Industry: Mergers, Structural Change, and Antitrust Enforcement* (Washington/DC, 2004) <www.ftc.gov/os/2004/08/040813mergers inpetrolberpt.pdf>, 11 October 2010.

5 The decision-theorist is represented in this ancient myth by *Ulysses'* advisor *Circe* who gave the perfect (but very hard and most likely impossible to head) advice to avoid both monsters, the one because of the risk of losing the ship (Charybdis), the other because of the risk of losing comrades (Scylla).

competition policy thus ultimately has to take a decision whether over- or under-enforcement is considered the more dreadful monster.[6]

A policy approach which puts significantly more weight on the risk of type-I errors (over-enforcement) than the risk of type-II errors (under-enforcement) would inevitably establish an enforcement regime with significantly higher thresholds for intervention than an approach putting more or even preponderant weight on the potential direct and indirect economic detriments of connived anticompetitive behavior. Since the dominance threshold is the first hurdle to be cleared by any intervention in unilateral conduct cases its enforcement standards crucially determine the positioning of competition policy and enforcement regimes between the poles of over- and under-enforcement.

IV. Legal 'regulating screws': standard of proof and the role of legal institutions

The question of how the (relative) weighting of the risk of type-I and type-II errors translates into law enforcement practice brings into focus the standard of proof as the most relevant 'regulating screw'. It is specified by the level of proof, i.e. the required scope and probative force of the factual evidence to be presented, on the one hand and the assignment of the burden of proof on the other hand. In the context of the dominance threshold the debate very often finds its focal point in the relevance and binding force to be assigned to (rebuttable) presumptions or safe harbours based on market share levels.[7] Enforcement regimes emphasising the risk of over-enforcement tend to refrain from using strong presumptions based on market share levels but, on the contrary, would be in favour of stipulating immunity by defining stringent safe harbours; enforcement regimes putting more emphasis on the risk of under-enforcement on the other hand may by tendency be reluctant to define binding safe harbours but use (rebuttable) presumptions.

---

[6]   According to *Homer*, the 'policy maker' *Ulysses* decided to focus exclusively on Charybdis (type-I errors), not even telling his comrades anything about the existence of Scylla (type-II errors). *Ulysses* finally came through but lost a lot of his best men. Whether a more balanced strategy would have been the better one (i.e. 'welfare enhancing') is not delivered to posterity by *Homer*.

[7]   For an overview see e.g. OECD Roundtable, *Evidentiary Issues in Proving Dominance* (Paris 2006) <www.oecd.org/dataoecd/42/8/41651328.pdf>, 11 October 2010.

In fact, most enforcement regimes lie in between the conceivable extremes of binding presumptions or categorical safe harbours based on market share levels. In line with the economic route-map outlined above, neither for establishing nor for rejecting dominance a certain market share threshold in most jurisdictions is considered to be definitively conclusive. Accordingly, the issue of the standard of proof in the context of the dominance threshold is less a matter of black and white than much an issue of the right shade of grey. This is also evidenced by the Recommended Practices ('RP') of the International Competition Network ('ICN') on the analysis of dominance pursuant to unilateral conduct laws which were adopted in 2008.[8] The need to strike a compromise between very different enforcement regimes worldwide finally did not allow for the RP to make a clear-cut recommendation of whether presumptions or safe harbours *should* be used or not. The RP just states that presumptions and safe harbours *can* be useful. They furthermore describe several features of their legal design and point to the risk of over- and under-enforcement which may inevitably stem from putting too much emphasis on such legal screens.[9]

It is beyond doubt that changes or adjustments of the 'regulating screw' of the prevailing standard of proof can be done by the legislator. Like e.g. in the German Act against Restraints of Competition, he may stipulate statutory presumptions or explicit rules on the assignment or the shift of the substantive burden of proof. Furthermore, at least absent any legally binding thresholds or presumptions, competition authorities and courts play a significant role in defining the relevant standards of proof; as *Giorgio Monti*'s paper carves out convincingly for the very recent European decision practice, a changing interpretation of an totally unchanged legal framework can indeed lead to quite significant variations in the relevant standards of proof and thus in the positioning of the enforcement regime between the poles of potential over- and under-enforcement.

But also the general institutional framework of an enforcement regime can have a significant impact on how and in which direction the relevant standards of proof develops over time. In this context, the experience in the US provides a good example. In the US, private enforcement traditionally plays a much more prominent role in competition law enforcement than in Europe. Some very

---

[8] <www.internationalcompetitionnetwork.org/uploads/library/doc317.pdf>, 11 October 2010.

[9] For further details see K. Hooghoff and M. Lange, *The ICN Recommended Practices on Dominance Analysis in Unilateral Conduct, Concurrence No. 1-2010;* <www.concurrences.com/article_revue_web.php3?idarticle=30156&lang=en>.

specific elements of the legal framework such as the aspiration of treble damages for successful plaintiffs in addition set very strong incentives for going after even less than convincing claims. This tendency most likely has animated courts to increase the standard and burden of proof for private plaintiffs in general hereby also impeding not only justified private claims but public enforcement by competition authorities. This problem was very recently highlighted by *William Kovacic*, the then chairman of the US Federal Trade Commission, in the course of the quite intense debate on the US Department of Justice's report on the standards to be applied for cases under Section 2 Sherman Act.[10]

> Judicial concerns about over-deterrence also appear to stem from perceptions that the existing system of private rights of action is unduly expansive. Fears about unduly expansive private enforcement are driving doctrine in an increasingly non-intervention minded direction that encumbers public agencies as well. In their efforts to correct what they believe to be overreaching by private litigants, courts are embracing liability standards that inevitably curb public enforcement bodies.[11]

But in the same breath he also emphasizes the strong need for a deeper empirical examination of the impact of the legal institutional set-up on prevailing enforcement standards.[12]

V. Conclusion

The main conclusions to be drawn from the foregoing arguments must be that the prevailing commonalities and differences between enforcement standards

---

[10] US Department of Justice, *Competition and Monopoly: Single Firm Conduct under Section 2 of the Sherman Act* (Washington, September 2008) <www.justice.gov/atr/public/reports/236681.htm>, 12 October 2010; the FTC did not endorse main elements of this report; the statement of the FTC is available at <www.ftc.gov/opa/2008/09/section2.shtm>, 12 October 2010; in the meantime, the report has officially been revoked by the new administration, see Press Release *Justice Department Withdraws Report on Antitrust Monopoly Law* (11 May 2009) <www.justice.gov/atr/public/press_releases/2009/245710.htm>, 12 October 2010.

[11] Statement of FTC Chairman W.E. Kovacic, 'Modern Competition Law and the Treatment of Dominant Firms: Comments on the Department of Justice and Federal Trade Commission Proceedings Relating to Section 2 of the Sherman Act' (8 September 2008), p. 4 <www.ftc.gov/os/2008/09/080908section2stmt kovacic.pdf>, 12 October 2010.

[12] *Ibid.* p. 8.

applied in different jurisdictions can only be assessed and discussed properly if all three paradigms of competition enforcement – economics, policy and law – are envisaged. But at the same time it is equally or even more important to clearly identify and address the relevant paradigm underlying different opinions on which direction competition law enforcement should follow. In my view, contemporary policy debate in this area at least sometimes seems to be trapped in catch-phrases like *more economic approach, effects-based approach*, or *protection of the competitive process*. Against the background of the complex interplay between economics, policy and law these very abstract terms are not very useful to mark the differences between alternative enforcement approaches.

The notion that competition law finally should protect *competition as a process* in this regard may serve as an example: going through some very recent documents on enforcement standards for unilateral conduct cases in the US, the EU and Germany reveals that in all these documents the protection of *competition as a process* is marked as the relevant benchmark.[13] It needs no further elucidations to conclude that nevertheless the enforcement practice in these three jurisdictions differs quite significantly. Accordingly, the notion that competition law should protect *competition as a process* seems not to be a suitable one in the discussion of the pros and cons of different enforcement approaches in unilateral conduct cases.

Contemporary competition policy debate in my view would already gain a lot of clarity and would also improve bilateral intelligibility between economists and lawyers if the elementary rule would be observed to clearly address the

---

[13] For the US: 'Section 2 of the Sherman Act plays a unique role in U.S. antitrust law by prohibiting single-firm conduct that undermines the competitive process [...]', US Department of Justice (*supra* n. 10) p. vii; for the EU: 'The emphasis of the Commission's enforcement activity in relation to exclusionary conduct is on safeguarding the competitive process in the internal market [...]', Communication from the Commission – Guidance on the Commission's enforcement priorities in applying Article 82 of the EC Treaty to abusive exclusionary conduct by dominant undertakings [2009] OJ C 45/7 para. 6; for Germany: 'Article 82, like the other competition rules of the Treaty, is not designed only or primarily to protect the immediate interests of individual competitors or the consumers, but to protect the structure of the market and thus competition as such [...]', Bundeskartellamt, *Statement of the Bundeskartellamt and the German Ministry of Economics and Technology on the DG Competition discussion paper on the Application of Article 82 of the Treaty* (Bonn, 2006), p. 4 <cms.bundeskartellamt.de/w Englisch/Publications/statements.php>, 12 October 2010.

relevant level of argument: Does the differences in opinion stem from a different understanding of the underlying economic route-map or does the controversy mainly bear on a different appraisal of the risk of over- and under-enforcement and a respectively different assessment of appropriate standard of proof? It is one of the numerous merits of *Giorgio Monti*'s paper to follow this rule consistently and thus to be able to provide convincing insights into the key challenges of defining the dominance threshold and the adjustments taken by the European Commission recently.

DISCUSSION

Carl Christian von Weizsäcker opened the debate by questioning whether it is still appropriate to say that the Lerner-index is an indication of market power as *Giorgio Monti* had said at the very outset of his presentation. It may have provided a theoretical framework which has been useful for decades; but its point of reference is perfect competition which never exists in any real market. Thus, it might be that the concept of market power today represents a pure theoretical artefact and may provide little to shape the concept of dominance in real-life competition cases. *Christian Ewald* agreed that no one should use the concept of perfect competition as the theoretical benchmark for practical enforcement of competition law.

Jürgen Basedow pointed out that undertakings in practice need clear guidelines to assess whether they fall within the scope of Article 82 EC/102 TFEU or not. Therefore certain indicators such as fixed market shares are good proxies to measure dominance. However, if one agrees on a certain market share threshold, it only amounts to a presumption. Therefore, the investigation is not complete once a certain market share has been established as the defendant can rebut the presumption by showing that under the existing conditions of the market it faces sufficient competitive pressure from actual or prospective rivals. Compared to German law, European law seems not very well developed on this point. § 19 of the German Law against Restraints of Competition (*Gesetz gegen Wettbewerbsbeschränkungen*) contains a detailed list of factors which have to been taken into account before one can come to the conclusion that a firm is dominant whereas the test of Article 82 EC/102 TFEU does not contain such a list.

Jürgen Basedow asked *Christian Ewald* to explain the practical significance of this long list of factors in the decision making process of the Bundeskartellamt. *Christian Ewald* made clear that no decision of the Bundeskartellamt relies merely on the market share threshold. It is a much more complex analysis, where many factors are taken into account. *Giorgio Monti* added that it may be seen as a great advantage of the Commission's Guidance Paper that it tries to codify the relevant factors in the decision making process. Moreover, he agreed with *Jürgen Basedow* that any presumption based on market share or other factors should indeed be rebuttable and criticised the *AKZO*-ruling of the ECJ. The ECJ considers a stable market share above a certain threshold as conclusive

93

evidence for a dominant position 'unless there are exceptional circumstances'. This implies that the Court seems to construe exceptional circumstances in a very narrow manner.

Jürgen Basedow then touched upon the significance of comparative studies in the field of dominance law. He stressed that even though recent developments in European competition law have been considerably influenced by U.S. anti-trust law, the respective enforcement systems in the U.S. and Europe are still completely different. Thus, private enforcement plays a much more important role in the U.S. system. The U.S. antitrust law has for many years put emphasis on incentives which encourage private plaintiffs to claim compensation for losses suffered as a result of anticompetitive conduct. In more recent years, the American courts have however tried to restrict the position of plaintiffs to ensure that private litigation in this field does not counteract public interests. In Europe, *Jürgen Basedow* noted, the relation between the more economic approach and private enforcement, which also forms an objective of the European Com-mission is not entirely settled. The Commission has to understand that it may be a difficult task for judges in national courts as well as for private plaintiffs to deal with the more economic approach. A plaintiff who suffered losses as a result of anticompetitive behaviour wants to see a certain likelihood of winning the case before going to court. In the U.S. this likelihood can be lower as the antitrust law provides a strong financial incentive in the form of treble damages. *Christian Ewald* replied that the economic discussion takes place at a very international level. Economists are, from a comparative perspective, trying to find out why competition law systems really differ in certain aspects of the enforcement issue. Thus, it is of high relevance to ascertain whether the respec-tive differences are due to different understandings of economic principles or to other factors inherent to the distinct legal systems.

Thomas Ackermann then turned to the question whether it is appropriate to differentiate between the issues of market definition on the one hand and dominance and market power on the other as from an economic standpoint these issues are closely interrelated. *Christian Ewald* replied that from the economic point of view there is certainly no need for a distinct market definition at all but from a legal point a proper market definition is essential to convince the courts that market power can be assumed. *Jürgen Basedow* added that in his experience enforcers are often dealing with the same problem under the headings of the relevant market and the assessment of dominance. But as Article 82 EC/102 TFEU prohibits any abuse of a dominant position within the internal market or in a substantial part of it, courts and national authorities are facing the challenge of applying the proper economic thinking in a setting prescribed by law.

Christian Ewald agreed and stressed that often economic and legal thinking only differ in their way of putting the same things together.

As to the relation between dominance and abuse, *Peter Behrens* mentioned that there are judgments where the European Court of Justice (ECJ) has inferred dominance from abuse, for example in *Michelin II* and also to a certain extent in *AKZO*. Thus the *AKZO*-judgment must probably be read differently as it does not clearly establish that a threshold of fifty percent indicates dominance in all cases. *Giorgio Monti* replied that in *Michelin II*, the ECJ indeed made use of the assessment of abusive behaviour in the way described. In *AKZO*, however, the Court explicitly decided to focus on the market share, whereas both the Advocate General and the Commission had deemed the market share insufficient for the inference of a dominant position.

Dominik Massing

PREDATORY PRICING: FROM PRICE/COST-COMPARISONS TO POST-CHICAGO THINKING

Wolfgang Wurmnest[*]

[*] With exception of the changes brought by the Treaty of Lisbon, this chapter reflects the law of August 2009. I am grateful to *Philippe Choné* who commented on an earlier version of this paper.

97

I. Introduction

Price cutting strategies undertaken by dominant firms to exclude or discipline actual rivals or to deter prospective ones are the type of abusive behaviour which has attracted the most attention in the economic and legal literature.[1]

---

[1]   Recent publications are, e.g., H. Fleischer, 'Gezielte Kampfpreisunterbietung im Recht der Vereinigten Staaten: Der Supreme Court zwischen Chicago School und Post-Chicago Economics' [1995] *Wirtschaft und Wettbewerb*, 796 *et seq.*; J.A. Ordover, 'Predatory Pricing', in *The New Palgrave Dictionary of Economics and the Law*, vol. III, P. Newman (ed.) (London, 1998), pp. 77 *et seq.*; P. Bolton, J.F. Brodley and M.H. Riordan, 'Predatory Pricing: Strategic Theory and Legal Policy' (2000) 88 *Georgetown Law Journal*, 2239 *et seq.*; A. Eckert, 'Predatory Pricing and the Speed of Antitrust Enforcement' (2002) 20 *Review of Industrial Organization*, 375 *et seq.*; A.S. Edlin, 'Stopping Above-Cost Predatory Pricing' (2002) 111 *Yale Law Journal*, 941 *et seq.*; E. Elhauge, 'Why Above-Cost Price Cuts to Drive out Entrants Are Not Predatory – and the Implications for Defining Costs and Market Power' (2003) 112 *Yale Law Journal*, 681 *et seq.*; W.J. Baumol, 'Principles relevant to predatory pricing', in *The Pros and Cons of Low Prices*, Konkurrensverket (ed.) (Stockholm, 2003), pp. 15 *et seq.*; C. Ewald, 'Predatory Pricing als Problem der Missbrauchsaufsicht: Eine Bewertung der aktuellen Entscheidungspraxis in den USA und in Deutschland im Luftverkehrs-sektor' [2003] *Wirtschaft und Wettbewerb*, 1165 *et seq.*; T. Campbell and N. Sandman, 'A New Test for Predation: Targeting' (2004) 52 *University of California at Los Angeles Law Review*, 365 *et seq.*; J. Haucap and J. Kruse, 'Predatory Pricing in Liberalized Telecommunications Markets', in *Trends in Infrastructure Regulation and Financing*, C. von Hirschhausen, T. Beckers and K. Mitusch (eds) (Cheltenham, 2004), pp. 43 *et seq.*; D. Crane, 'The Paradox of

cont.

Even though the first reported cases of such predatory strategies are (nearly) a century old,[2] today there is still no broad consensus as to which strategies involving low pricing should be deemed anti-competitive. Although it is generally accepted that predatory pricing is not usually an irrational practice employed to dampen competition – as argued not long ago by some Chicago Scholars[3] – there is a heated debate on which analytical framework should be applied by enforcement agencies and courts to test for predatory pricing. This debate is rooted to a large extent in opposing views on the accurateness of the various economic tests and models proposed and their benefits in relation to enforcement costs and minimisation of decision errors.

Despite this lack of an economic *cantus firmus*, the European Commission's decision practice and, even more so, the case law of the European courts has been repeatedly criticised as being economically unsound. The European approach is often viewed as placing neither sufficient weight on the anti-competitive effects of low pricing strategies[4] nor on the economic reasons why firms

Predatory Pricing' (2005) 91 *Cornell Law Review*, 1 *et seq.*; K.W. Lange, 'Kampfpreisstrategien (predatory pricing) im europäischen Kartellrecht' (2005) 169 *Zeitschrift für das gesamte Handelsrecht und Wirtschaftsrecht*, 495 *et seq.*; E.M. Iacobucci, 'Predatory pricing, the theory of the firm, and the recoupment test: An examination of recent developments in Canadian predatory pricing law' (2006) 51 *Antitrust Bulletin*, 281 *et seq.*; K. Hüschelrath, 'Pushing Predators with Pecuniary Fines' [2008] *European Competition Law Review*, 383 *et seq.*; J.B. Kirkwood, 'Controlling above-cost predation: An alternative to Weyerhaeuser and Brooke Group' (2008) 53 *Antitrust Bulletin*, 369 *et seq.*; M. Moura e Silva, 'Predatory Pricing under Article 82 and the Recoupment Test: Do Not Go Gentle into that Good Night' [2009] *European Competition Law Review*, 61 *et seq.*; K.W. Lange and T. Pries, 'Die Neuorientierung der europäischen Missbrauchsaufsicht in dem Bereich von Kampfpreisstrategien (predatory pricing)' [2009] *Zeitschrift für Europäisches Wirtschafts- und Steuerrecht*, 57 *et seq.*

2   See *Mogul Steamship Co. v. McGregor, Gow & Co.*, [1892] A.C. 25 (HL); *Standard Oil Co. of New Jersey v. United States*, 221 U.S. 1 (1911); RG 18.12.1931, RGZ 134, 342 – *Benrather Tankstelle*.

3   See J. McGee, 'Predatory Price Cutting: The Standard Oil (N.J.) Case' (1958) 1 *Journal of Law and Economics*, 137-169; R.H. Koller, 'The Myth of Predatory Pricing: An Empirical Study' [1971] *Antitrust Law and Economics Review*, 105-123; J. McGee, 'Predatory Pricing Revisited' (1980) 23 *Journal of Law and Economics*, 289-330; F.H. Easterbrook, 'Predatory Strategies and Counterstrategies' (1981) 48 *University of Chicago Law Review*, 263, 337.

4   See R.J. Van den Bergh and P.D. Camesasca, *European Competition Law and Economics: A Comparative Perspective* 2nd ed (London, 2006), pp. 294-299; V. Korah, *An Introductory Guide to EC Competition Law and Practice* 9th ed

cont.

need to price their products below cost.[5] The legal rules, it is often argued, lead to the interdiction of aggressive pricing strategies that are painful for rivals but benevolent for consumers. In other words: The law as it stands in Europe chills vigorous price competition. It thus violates the basic tenet of competition policy which should encourage firms to compete on price and sell their products as closely as possible to the minimum profitable price. To overcome this supposed shortcoming, some commentators have urged the European Commission ('the Commission') to align the interpretation and application of Article 82 EC – which became Article 102 TFEU when the Treaty of Lisbon entered into force on 1 December 2009 – with US predatory pricing law. Those voices favouring such an alignment point out that US law better reflects modern economic insights on predatory pricing.[6]

The Commission has, in principle, agreed that a more nuanced approach for assessing pricing abuses is necessary,[7] but seems divided as to what extent its prior decision practice and – more important – the case law of the European courts needs to be refined. The Communication on 'Guidance on the Commission's enforcement priorities in applying Article 82 of the EC Treaty to abusive exclusionary conduct by dominant undertakings' of December 2008 ('the Enforcement Communication')[8] supports essentially a more effects based approach. It is however much shorter than its 'informal predecessor', the DG Competition discussion paper 'on the application of Article 82 of the Treaty to

---

(Oxford, 2007), pp. 194-197; A. Ezrachi, *EC Competition Law: An Analytical Guide to the Leading Cases* (Oxford, 2008), p. 140.

5   See V. Korah, 'The Paucity of Economic Analysis in the EEC Decisions on Competition – Tetra Pak II', (1993) 46 (2) *Current Legal Problems*, 149, 185; G. Goeteyn, S. Mavroghenis, M. Piergiovanni, E. Reed and D. Ridyard, 'Predatory Pricing', in *GCLC Research Papers on Article 82 EC* (Bruges, 2005), p. 65, 78; M. Hellwig, 'Wirtschaftspolitik als Rechtsanwendung: Zum Verhältnis von Jurisprudenz und Ökonomie in der Wettbewerbspolitik', in *Volkswirtschaftliche Beiträge der Forschungsgemeinschaft für Nationalökonomie* (St. Gallen, 2007), pp. 6-8.

6   See R.J. Van den Bergh and P.D. Camesasca (*supra* n. 4) p. 299; C. Ahlborn and B. Allan, 'The Napp Case: A Study of Predation?' (2003) 26 *World Competition*, 233, 262; see also A. Ezrachi (*supra* n. 4) p. 140 (criticising the 'form-based approach' of European courts to predatory pricing).

7   See N. Kroes, 'Tackling Exclusionary Practices to Avoid Exploitation of Market Power: Some Preliminary Thoughts on the Policy Review of Article 82', in *Fordham Corporate Law Institute, International Antitrust Law & Policy 2005*, B.E. Hawk (ed.) (Huntington/NY, 2006), p. 381, 383.

8   [2009] OJ C 45/7.

exclusionary abuses' of December 2005 ('the Discussion Paper').[9] The Enforcement Communication focuses only on very severe forms of abuses and provides far fewer details as to how the more effects based approach should be implemented. The brevity of the Enforcement Communication appears to be a compromise reached between those forces within the Commission centred around the Chief Economist, who pushed for a strong effects based approach under which only practices to the detriment of the welfare of consumers[10] should be deemed abusive and those who, like the Legal Service, argued that such a radical shift is contrary to the case law of the European courts which have recently approved the traditional approach to abuse control.[11]

The analytical framework for analysing predatory pricing described in the Enforcement Communication deviates in part from the settled case law of the European courts. The Enforcement Communication is however not intended to constitute a statement of law.[12] It merely sketches the priorities that determine which future abuse cases are to be taken up by the Commission.[13] The Enforcement Communication does therefore not bind national authorities or courts. The analytical framework introduced by the Enforcement Communication could however, by influencing the decision practice of the European (or the national) Courts, one day become law. To better understand the changes that the Enforcement Communication might bring, this chapter will first highlight the traditional approach to predatory pricing (II.). As the current move towards a more economic approach is strongly influenced by the debate in the United States (US), parts of the first section will also analyse the US standards to test

---

[9]   <ec.europa.eu/competition/antitrust/art82/discpaper2005.pdf>, 12 October 2010.

[10] Unlike the Chicago School, the Commission does not seem to understand the notion of consumer welfare as total welfare standard but in the sense that such conduct shall be prohibited which in the long run lowers the welfare of (end-) consumers, cf. Enforcement Communication (*supra* n. 8) para. 19 with note 2. For an overview of the different meanings of the term consumer welfare, see S. Möller, *Verbraucherbegriff und Verbraucherwohlfahrt im europäischen und amerikanischen Kartellrecht* (Baden-Baden, 2008), pp. 39-56 and pp. 221-236.

[11] See, e.g., *British Airways v. Commission*, Case No. C-95/04 P [2007] ECR I-2331 para. 107; for further examples see H. Schweitzer, 'Recent developments in EU competition law (2006-2008): Single-firm dominance and the interpretation of Article 82' [2009] *European Review of Contract Law*, 175, 182-185.

[12] Cf. Enforcement Communication (*supra* n. 8) para. 2.

[13] The Commission's guidelines generally do not bind national competition authorities and courts. *De facto* however they have a strong persuasive authority as they are considered to restate the law. It remains to be seen what kind of effects the Enforcement Communication will have in practice.

for predatory pricing. Against this background, the new approach of the European Commission will be explained (III.) and assessed (IV.).

II. Brief outline of the case law on predatory pricing

A. The AKZO-rules

1. Basic concept

The basic rules of EU law on predatory pricing were laid down in *AKZO v. Commission*. AKZO was the dominant supplier of various organic peroxides used in the manufacture of certain plastics and also as a whitening agent for flour. The complainant, ECS, was a small company initially serving the flour bleaching sub-market which subsequently tried to enter the lucrative plastics sector. In response, AKZO made various directs threats to ECS in meetings in an attempt to persuade its competitor to withdraw from the plastics market. Further, it sold organic peroxides to ECS's clients at very low prices whilst maintaining higher prices for its other customers. AKZO argued for the application of a price/cost-test which had been developed by *Phillip Areeda and Donald Turner*, two distinguished academics affiliated with the so-called Harvard School of antitrust analysis.[14] According to the *Areeda/Turner*-test, only prices below average variable cost ('AVC'), i.e. those costs which vary depending on the quantities produced, must be regarded as predatory.[15] The

---

[14] On the basic concepts of the Harvard School and its gradual convergence with other (economic) schools of thought, see W.E. Kovacic, 'The Intellectual DNA of Modern US Competition Law for Dominant Firm Conduct: The Chicago/Harvard Double Helix' (2007) 1 *Columbia Business Law Review*, 17-52.

[15] This rule is based on insights derived from neoclassical price theory. According to the models of perfect competition and monopoly a firm cannot maximise its profits in the short run by pricing its products below its marginal costs, irrespective of whether it is a monopolist or whether it operates in a competitive market. On these models and their interpretation see L. Pepall, D.J. Richards and G. Norman, *Industrial Organization: Contemporary Theory and Empirical Applications* 4th ed (Oxford, 2008), pp. 20-34; U. Schwalbe and D. Zimmer, *Kartellrecht und Ökonomie: Moderne Ökonomische Ansätze in der europäischen und deutschen Zusammenschlusskontrolle* (Frankfurt am Main, 2006), pp. 12-26. Thus a price below marginal cost is at risk of being exclusionary as the targeted firms cannot survive even if they are as efficient as the dominant predator. As marginal cost is a theoretical cost concept which cannot be measured in practice with accurate precision, *Areeda* and *Turner* proposed using the average variable

cont.

Commission rejected the idea that a mechanically applied price/cost-test could give solid guidance in the legal assessment of predation cases[16] and argued that price cutting strategies shall be deemed predatory when they are pursued with the intention of eliminating a competitor.[17]

On appeal, the European Court of Justice ('ECJ') agreed that AKZO's low price strategy was predatory but grounded its finding on a rationale different to that of the Commission. The Court noted that Article 82 EC (now: Article 102 TFEU) prohibits a dominant undertaking from eliminating a competitor and thereby strengthening its position by using methods other than those which come within the scope of competition on the basis of quality.[18] From that point of view not all price competition can be regarded as legitimate as price cuts below certain cost benchmarks may drive competitors, which are otherwise as efficient as the dominant undertaking, from the market.[19] To separate legitimate yet aggressive price competition from anti-competitive predatory conduct, the Court relied on an assessment of pricing criteria based on the costs incurred by the dominant undertaking and on an assessment of its strategy.

According to the first *AKZO*-rule prices below AVC 'by means of which a dominant undertaking seeks to eliminate a competitor must be regarded as abusive'.[20] Since under such a pricing policy 'each sale generates a loss', the Court was convinced that a dominant undertaking has no interest in applying such prices except for the purpose of eliminating competitors so as to enable 'it subsequently to raise its prices by taking advantage of its monopolistic position'.[21]

The AVC-benchmark proposed by *Areeda/Turner* is, however, merely a proxy for the theoretical concept of marginal costs which many economists consider as a relevant cost-benchmark – but which cannot be measured in real-life cases with precision.[22] This proxy, as many critiques of the *Areeda/Turner*-

---

cost, i.e. those costs that vary with any change in output, as a reasonable proxy for marginal cost, see P. Areeda and D. Turner, 'Predatory Pricing and Related Practices under Section 2 of the Sherman Act' (1957) 88 *Harvard Law Review*, 697, 716-718.

[16] Commission Decision, *ECS/AKZO*, Case No. IV/30.698 [1985] OJ L 374/1 para. 77.

[17] *Ibid.* para. 80.

[18] *AKZO v. Commission*, Case No. C-62/86 [1991] ECR I-3359 para. 70.

[19] *Ibid.* para. 72.

[20] *Ibid.* para. 71.

[21] *Ibid.*

[22] See M.A. Salinger, 'The Legacy of Matsushita: Has this Thing Called Economics Gotten Way out of Hand?', Paper presented at the Loyola University School of

cont.

rule were quick to point out, does not necessarily reflect the economic realities that make a low price strategy an abusive weapon in the hand of dominant undertakings.[23] Influenced by this critique, the European Court of Justice did not fully adhere to the *Areeda/Turner*-rule and rejected a safe harbour for prices above AVC. Under the second *AKZO*-rule formulated by the ECJ, prices above average variable costs but below average total costs ('ATC') may also be found abusive in the sense of (now) Article 102 TFEU 'if they are determined as part of a plan for eliminating a competitor'.[24]

By endorsing two cost-benchmarks as a basic framework to test for predatory pricing, the ECJ went further than the US Supreme Court. To date, that Court has not decided which cost standard is appropriate to determine whether an incumbent has priced its product or services 'below cost' and therefore might be held liable for predatory pricing.[25] The Courts of Appeals are divided on the appropriate cost-benchmark. Some have embraced the *Areeda/Turner*-test and therefore consider AVC as the appropriate measure of cost.[26] Yet, others have

---

Law (Chicago, 29 September 2006), p. 7 <www.ftc.gov>, 12 October 2010 (noting that 'in Industrial Economics, the distinguishing feature of the so-called "new empirical industrial organization" is the presumption that marginal cost is essentially impossible to measure. As a consequence, one might paraphrase Oscar Wilde's definition of a cynic to define a "new" industrial economist as someone who knows the price of everything but the marginal cost of nothing').

[23] See F.M. Scherer, 'Predatory Pricing and the Sherman Act: A Comment' (1976) 89 *Harvard Law Review*, 869, 890; O.E. Williamson, 'Predatory Pricing: A Strategic and Welfare Analysis' (1977) 87 *Yale Law Journal*, 284-340; P.L. Joskow and A.K. Klevorick, 'A Framework for Analyzing Predatory Pricing Policy' (1979) 89 *Yale Law Journal*, 206, 213-270; E.-J. Mestmäcker, *Der verwaltete Wettbewerb: Eine vergleichende Untersuchung über den Schutz von Freiheit und Lauterkeit im Wettbewerbsrecht* (Tübingen, 1984), p. 195; W. Möschel, 'Preis- und Konditionendifferenzierung durch marktbeherrschende Unternehmen nach EG-Recht' [1988] *Recht der Internationalen Wirtschaft*, 501, 506-08; J. Haucap and J. Kruse (*supra* n. 1) pp. 58 *et seq.*; R. Posner, *Antitrust Law* 2nd ed (Chicago, 2001), p. 218; E.-J. Mestmäcker and H. Schweitzer, *Europäisches Wettbewerbsrecht* 2nd ed (München, 2004), p. 438; D. Howarth, 'Pricing Abuses – Unfair and Predatory Pricing under Article 82 EC: From Cost-price Comparisons to the Search for Strategic Standards', in *EC Competition Law: A Critical Assessment*, G. Amato and C.-D. Ehlermann (eds) (Oxford, 2007), p. 249, 260.

[24] *AKZO v. Commission*, Case No. C-62/86 [1991] ECR I-3359 para. 72.

[25] See *Brooke Group Ltd. v. Brown & Williamson Tobacco Corp.*, 509 U.S. 209, 222 (1993).

[26] See *Clamp-All Corp. v. Cast Iron Soil Pipe Institute*, 851 F.2d 478, 483 (1st Cir. 1988); *Irvin Industries, Inc. v. Goodyear Aerospace Corp.*, 974 F.2d 241, 245

cont.

accepted different proxies for marginal cost[27] and some have even argued that prices below ATC but above AVC can be deemed predatory.[28] It seems, however, that the early enthusiasm voiced by US courts for the application of a simple one-size-fits-all-price/cost-rule to test for predatory prices has gone astray. In a recent decision, the Tenth Circuit noted that 'marginal cost, an economic abstraction, is notoriously difficult to measure and cannot be determined from conventional accounting methods.'[29] Therefore 'courts need the flexibility to examine both AVC as well as other proxies for marginal cost in order to evaluate an alleged predatory pricing scheme', as '[s]ole reliance on AVC ... may obscure the nature of a particular predatory scheme.'[30]

2. Refinements

The two basic rules of analysis, developed by the ECJ in *AKZO* were refined by subsequent case law and the decision practice of the Commission.

a) Adjustments of the price/cost-comparisons

In *Tetra Pak II* the Court amended the first *AKZO*-rule by stating that prices below AVC must *always* be regarded as abusive, as such prices may have 'no conceivable economic purpose other than the elimination of a competitor'.[31] Accordingly, prices below AVC must be regarded as a violation of Article 82 EC/102 TFEU.[32] Dominant undertakings, it seems, are not given the possibility to justify their pricing behaviour.

Another modification of the first *AKZO*-rule has been put forward by the Commission. Emphasising that looking at AVC in industries characterised by high fixed costs and variable costs close to zero (telecommunication, energy,

---

[27] (2d Cir. 1992); *Taylor Pub. Co. v. Jostens, Inc.*, 216 F.3d 465, 478 with note 6 (5th Cir. 2000).

[27] See *MCI Communications Corp. v. American Tel. & Tel. Co.*, 708 F.2d 1081, 1120 (7th Cir. 1981); *United States v. AMR Corp.*, 335 F.3d 1109, 1116 (10th Cir. 2003).

[28] See *International Travel Arrangers v. NWA, Inc.*, 991 F.2d 1389, 1396 (8th Cir. 1993); *Spirit Airlines, Inc. v. Northwest Airlines, Inc.*, 431 F.3d 917, 938 (6th Cir. 2005).

[29] *United States v. AMR Corp.*, 335 F.3d 1109, 1116 (10th Cir. 2003).

[30] *Ibid.*

[31] Cf. *Tetra Pak v. Commission*, Case No. C-333/94 P [1996] ECR I-5951 para. 41.

[32] In its latest jurisprudence the ECJ seems to have departed from this overbroad holding; see infra III C.

postal services) is economically unreliable as the dominant undertaking's prices may never be below AVC even if they are close to zero, the Commission wants to base its analysis in such industries on the long-run average incremental cost ('LRAIC').[33] LRAIC is the incremental cost for a defined amount of production, measured over the time-frame in which fixed costs can be varied, and so it includes all the fixed and variable costs incurred specific to the good or service being considered.[34] In other words, LRAIC measures total cost of supplying a product or service, i.e. all costs that are causally related to a specific product, rather than a larger category of sales (as AVC does).[35] LRAIC and ATC are good proxies for each other. Both cost standards are the same in the case of single-product firms. In cases of multi-product firms, LRAIC will however be regularly lower as ATC, because common costs are usually not fully taken into account.[36] For multi-product firms operating on markets with a high share of common costs, the Commission however wants to make an exception. In such circumstances an adequate amount of these costs should be considered in the price/cost-comparison to reflect the economic realities of such industries.[37]

b) Proving predatory intent

To prove the intention to eliminate a competitor, the Commission and the European courts have always relied on a combination of direct evidence (such as internal memoranda, reports or statements by business executives),[38] and indirect evidence (such as the scale, duration and continuity of the low pricing).[39] As stated by the CFI (now: the General Court) in *Tetra Pak II*, it is necessary to look at a 'whole series of important and convergent factors' to find a strong

---

[33] Cf. Notice on the application of competition rules to access agreements in the telecommunications sector [1998] OJ C 265/2 paras 110-115.

[34] See D. Howarth (*supra* n. 23) p. 254.

[35] See R. O'Donoghue and A.J. Padilla, *The Law and Economics of Article 82 EC* (Oxford, 2006), p. 269.

[36] See D. Howarth (*supra* n. 23) p. 254.

[37] Cf. Notice on the application of competition rules to access agreements in the telecommunications sector [1998] OJ C 265/2 para. 114.

[38] See *AKZO v. Commission*, Case No. C-62/86 [1991] ECR I-3359 para. 78; *Tetra Pak v. Commission*, Case No. T-83/91 [1994] ECR II-755 para. 171; *France Télécom v. Commission*, Case No. T-340/03 [2007] ECR II-107 paras 199-217.

[39] See *AKZO v. Commission*, Case No. C-62/86 [1991] ECR I-3359 paras 140 and 146; *Tetra Pak v. Commission*, Case No. T-83/91 [1994] ECR II-755 paras 151 and 190.

evidentiary basis that the price cutting has no legitimate explanation other than predation.[40]

B. *Above-cost predation*

Unlike in US law, where the Supreme Court has stated – albeit in *dicta* – that prices above the appropriate measure of cost are considered legal *per se*,[41] predatory pricing under Article 102 TFEU is not limited to situations in which the dominant firm prices below its average total costs. Under exceptional circumstances selective price reductions by dominant undertakings that undercut the prices of the targeted rival but which are above the dominant undertakings' ATC can be regarded as abusive conduct. The cases in which such above-cost price cuts were found to be exclusionary concerned situations in which (collectively) dominant undertakings held a very high degree of market power, practiced their price cuts essentially against the last remaining competitor in the market and coupled their low pricing strategy with a range of other exclusionary practices.[42] In these cases, the overall evidence presented by the Commission convinced the European courts that the sole purpose of these strategies was to eliminate a rival by sacrificing short-term profits and to strengthen their position with the result that the degree of dominance reached would substantially fetter competition.

The leading case on above-cost predation is *Compagnie maritime belge.* It concerned 'fighting ship' practices by a dominant shipping liner conference for the avowed purpose of 'getting rid' of a newcomer. The use of 'fighting ships' was a common practice in maritime transport at times when this industry was predominantly organised by large shipping liner conferences, i.e. price fixing and market sharing cartels exempted from the application of Article 101(1)

---

[40] Cf. *Tetra Pak v. Commission*, Case No. T-83/91 [1994] ECR II-755 paras 140 and 146; see further *France Télécom v. Commission*, Case No. T-340/03 [2007] ECR II-107 para. 197.

[41] See *Brooke Group Ltd. v. Brown & Williamson Tobacco Corp.*, 509 U.S. 209, 222-23 (1993).

[42] For an overview of the case law see J. Temple Lang and R. O'Donoghue, 'Defining Legitimate Competition: How to Clarify Pricing Abuses under Article 82 EC' (2002) 26 *Fordham International Law Journal*, 83, 127-145; R. O'Donoghue and A.J. Padilla (*supra* n. 35) pp. 274-283; T. Eilmansberger, in *Münchener Kommentar zum Europäischen Wettbewerbsrecht*, G. Hirsch, F. Montag and F.J. Säcker (eds) (München, 2007), Art. 82 EG paras 528-532.

TFEU.[43] In response to a new entrant not belonging to the conference, the members of the liner conference designed special ships to fight entry. These 'fighting ships' sailed on the same routes and essentially at the same time as the ships of the targeted competitor and offered special discounted freight rates that matched or undercut the rates of the competitor. In *Compagnie maritime belge* such practices were carried out by the dominant shipping liner conference, CEWAL, to exclude a newcomer which had started to offer transport services on certain routes between African and European ports on which CEWAL held a *de facto* monopoly.[44] The ECJ found the selective price cuts coupled with the use of 'fighting ships' to be abusive as this strategy eliminated 'the principal, and possibly the only, means of competition open to the competing undertaking'[45]. In reaching this finding, the Court pointed to the unusual circumstances of the case at hand, namely that the fighting ship practices were carried out for the express purpose of eliminating CEWAL's only competitor on the relevant routes on which the shipping liner conference enjoyed a market share over 90%, and that price competition was already weakened in the maritime transport sector because the applicable legislation at that time allowed tariff setting agreements between shipping liner companies.[46]

---

[43] Cf. Article 3 Council Regulation (EEC) No. 4056/86 (22 December 1986) laying down detailed rules for the application of Articles 85 and 86 of the Treaty to maritime transport [1986] OJ L 378/4.

[44] See Commission Decision, *CEWAL*, Case No. IV/32.448 and IV/32.450 [1993] OJ L 34/20 paras 57-60.

[45] *Compagnie maritime belge transports v. Commission*, joined Cases No. C-395/96 P and C-396/96 P [2000] ECR I-1365 para. 117. The 2006 reform of the application of the EC competition rules to the maritime sector has abolished the rules laid down in Council Regulation No. 4056/86 and limited the exemption of agreements between shipping companies according to Article 81(3) EC/101(3) TFEU; for a detailed overview of the application of the EU competition law rules to the maritime industry see J. Basedow, in *EG-Wettbewerbsrecht* 4th ed, U. Immenga and E.-J. Mestmäcker (eds) (München, 2007), Seeverkehr: VO 4056/86 paras 12-14.

[46] Cf. *Compagnie maritime belge transports v. Commission*, joined Cases No. C-395/96 P and C-396/96 P [2000] ECR I-1365 paras 116-119.

C. Recoupment

1. Basic economic concept

From a neoclassical point of view, predation is an investment in a future monopoly, a sacrifice of today's profits for tomorrow's: The predator starts a price war to eliminate or discipline an actual rival or deter a potential one. Once he has achieved his goal, he will raise prices to make good the losses sustained during the price war. Thus, for analytical reasons predatory pricing can be split into two periods: The predation period in which the predator incurs losses and the post-predation (recoupment) period in which he recovers his costs by monopoly pricing.[47] Without the possibility of economically recouping the investment sacrificed in the predation period phase during in the post-predation phase, predatory pricing is not profitable for the predator and thus – from a neoclassical point of view – not a business strategy which a rational profit-maximising firm would adopt. From this point of view unsuccessful predation is seen as a boon to consumers: the predator inflicts a loss onto himself without being able to damage competition in the long run.[48]

Against this background many commentators argue that low prices may only be regarded as abusive if it can be shown that prospective future gains stemming from the fortified position in the market outweigh the losses of the predation phase considerably. There is however no consensus as to which factors should be taken into account to show the possibility of recoupment. Essentially two basic concepts can be distinguished.

The *structural recoupment-test* intends to assess the chances of success of the predatory pricing strategy (and therefore its plausibility) by a closer inspection of the structural factors of the market, such as the strong market position of the predator vis-à-vis its prey, excess capacity, high barriers to entry

---

[47] See P.L. Joskow and A.K. Klevorick (*supra* n. 23) 219-20; H. Fleischer, *Behinderungsmißbrauch durch Produktinnovation: Eine ökonomische Analyse zum deutschen, europäischen und amerikanischen Kartellrecht* (Baden-Baden, 1997), p. 52; H. Hovenkamp, *Federal Antitrust Policy: The Law of Competition and its Practice* 3rd ed (St. Paul/Minn., 2005), p. 350.

[48] See K.G. Elzinga and D.E. Mills, 'Testing for predation: Is recoupment feasible?' (1989) 34 *Antitrust Bulletin*, 869, 873-875; J. Gual, M. Hellwig, A. Perrot, M. Polo, P. Rey, K. Schmidt and R. Stenbacka, 'An Economic Approach to Article 82' (2006) 2 *Competition Policy International*, 111, 153-154 (so called 'EAGCP-Report').

and the development of market shares during the predation campaign.[49] The modern version of this understanding of the recoupment criterion demands, in addition, a closer look at strategic decisions and the chances of success of the pricing policy to show that the pricing can cause social harm.[50]

In contrast, the *strict recoupment-test* puts a higher evidentiary burden on the competition authority or a private plaintiff. According to this approach the analysis of the market setting serves merely as starting point and the economic success of the predatory pricing strategy has to be shown by a quantification of losses and (prospective) gains. Only if estimated gains in the post-predation phase show that the predator can, on balance recoup each cent of his predatory investment, including an adequate interest rate, should an incumbent be held liable for a low pricing strategy.[51]

2. US antitrust law

The current discussion in Europe on the incorporation of a recoupment-test into the EU predatory pricing law has been strongly influenced by the US debate. Therefore a closer look at the functions of the recoupment requirement under US law seems in order.

a) Background of the debate

The debate as to what extent the economic recoupment concept shall be made part of the law was opened by *Areeda/Turner*. They argued that predation in any

---

[49] See P.L. Joskow and A.K. Klevorick (*supra* n. 23) 245-249; H. Hovenkamp (*supra* n. 47) pp. 350-356.

[50] See C.S. Hemphill, 'The Role of Recoupment in Predatory Pricing Analyses' (2001) 53 *Stanford Law Review*, 1581-1612; see further E.M. Iacobucci (*supra* n. 1) 288-318. A forerunner of this analysis was proposed by P.L. Joskow and A.K. Klevorick (*supra* n. 23) 245-249 (arguing for a thorough structural analysis as a first screen to distinguish monopoly problems from pro-competitive price cutting).

[51] See K.G. Elzinga and D.E. Mills (*supra* n. 48) 869-893. The EAGCP takes some form of middle ground as it argues that in cases in which a competition authority intervenes when the intended disciplinary or exclusionary effect has not yet been achieved, a closer look at structural or strategic factors suffices; conversely, in cases in which the incumbent is in the recoupment phase, possible gains must be quantified on the basis of post-predation prices in the market, see J. Gual, M. Hellwig, A. Perrot, M. Polo, P. Rey, K. Schmidt and R. Stenbacka (*supra* n. 48) 111, 127.

meaningful sense cannot exist unless the predator can recoup sustained losses in the post-predation phase through higher profits to be earned after his rivals have been destroyed.[52] This line of thought was later taken up and refined by commentators affiliated with the Chicago School. The findings of the Chicago economists indicated that predatory pricing is a cost-intensive strategy which is never or hardly ever successful as potential competition severely restricts the chances of the incumbent reaping the fruits of his predation campaign.[53] Therefore many Chicagoans favoured either a strict recoupment test[54] or recommended '[to forget] the antitrust offense of predation'.[55]

In the 1980s, the Chicago-doctrine that predation is essentially not worth dealing with gained more and more support in the case law. The Supreme Court subscribed to the view that 'predatory pricing schemes are rarely tried and even more rarely successful'.[56] This sceptical view strongly influences the Court's view today even though post-Chicago models and tests have debunked the comfortable position that predatory pricing is always an irrational business practice.[57]

The Supreme Court's sceptical view has to be seen against the background that under US law, predatory pricing claims were traditionally either judged as a violation of the prohibition against any attempt to monopolise as laid down in Section 2 Sherman Act or – in case of selective price cuts – as a violation of the price discrimination law enshrined in Section 2(a) (Clayton Act as amended by the) Robinson-Patman Act. From their wording, both prohibitions also apply to non-dominant firms. The missing dominance threshold combined with an enforcement system relying on private plaintiffs who in case of success are awarded treble damages[58] creates a large risk of false positives, i.e. judicial

---

[52] See P. Areeda and D. Turner (*supra* n. 15) 698.

[53] See J. McGee (*supra* n. 3) 137-169; R.H. Koller (*supra* n. 3) 105-123; J. McGee (*supra* n. 3) 289-330.

[54] See R.H. Bork, *The Antitrust Paradox: A Policy at war with itself* (New York, 1978), p. 145.

[55] See F.H. Easterbrook (*supra* n. 3) 337.

[56] Cf. *Matsushita Elec. Indus. Co. v. Zenith Radio Corp.*, 475 U.S. 574, 589 (1986); see further *Weyerhaeuser Co. v. Ross-Simmons Hardwood Lumber Co.*, 127 S. Ct. 1069, 1077 (2007).

[57] See R. Selten, 'The Chain Store Paradox' (1978) 9 *Theory and Decision*, 127-159; D.M. Kreps and R. Wilson, 'Reputation and Imperfect Information' (1982) 27 *Journal of Economic Theory*, 253-279; P. Milgrom and J. Roberts, 'Predation, Reputation, and Entry Deterrence' (1982) 27 *Journal of Economic Theory*, 280-312.

[58] Cf. Section 4(a) Clayton Act.

prohibition of benevolent price competition.[59] Plaintiffs are habitually competitors.[60] The plaintiff-friendly litigation system appears to create incentives to 'abuse' antitrust law to subvert competition.[61]

The Supreme Court therefore has searched for ways to interpret the prohibitions of the Sherman and Robinson-Patman Acts narrowly and to limit the powers of the jury in antitrust proceedings. The latter seemed necessary as juries often struggle to grasp the economic complexities involved in antitrust litigation[62] and tend to decide in favour of smaller firms suing 'big business'.[63] Both goals could be achieved by the endorsement of a strict recoupment-test, as can be aptly demonstrated by a closer look at the recent cases decided by the Supreme Court.

b) Stringent liability standards to avoid false positives

The aim of avoiding overcompensation of plaintiffs who use antitrust law as a tool to chill vigorous price competition lies at the core of *Brooke Group*, the leading case on modern US predatory pricing law. It concerned an action for damages brought by a producer of generic cigarettes against a competitor active in both the market for generic and branded cigarettes.[64] The plaintiff began to sell a generic brand in 1980 at prices well below those of the major brands. When consumers responded favourably to the introduction of these cheap

---

[59] It seems that especially the fear of excessive compensation as a result of mandatory treble damages is a very strong factor in favour of designing antitrust liability standards which primarily aim at diminishing the private litigant's prospects for success; see W.E. Kovacic (*supra* n. 14) 61; a similar point is made by H. Hovenkamp, *The Antitrust Enterprise: Principle and Execution* (Cambridge/Mass., 2005), p. 76.

[60] Cf. the statistical data provided by S.C. Salop and L.J. White, 'Private Antitrust Litigation: An Introduction and Framework', in *Private Antitrust Litigation: New Evidence, New Learning*, L.J. White (ed.) (Cambridge/Mass., 1988), p. 3, 9.

[61] See, e.g., W.J. Baumol and J.A. Ordover, 'Use of Antitrust to Subvert Competition' (1985) 28 *Journal of Law and Economics*, 247-265; E.A. Snyder and T.E. Kauper, 'Misuse of Antitrust Laws: The Competitor Plaintiff' (1990) 90 *Michigan Law Review*, 551-598.

[62] See generally T.M. Jorde, 'The Seventh Amendment to Jury Trial of Antitrust Issues' (1981) 69 *California Law Review*, 1-79.

[63] See J. Lande, 'Failing Faith in Litigation? A Survey of Business Lawyers' and Executives' Opinions' (1998) 3 *Harvard Negotiation Law Review*, 1, 33; H. Hovenkamp, 'The Law of Exclusionary Pricing' (2006) 2 *Competition Policy International*, 21, 39.

[64] *Brooke Group Ltd. v. Brown & Williamson Tobacco Corp.*, 509 U.S. 209 (1993).

cigarettes, the defendant (as well as other large tobacco companies) responded with vigorous price cuts, thereby incurring losses. The plaintiff complained that the defendant had engaged in a below-cost campaign to hamper competition. As the defendant's market share in the oligopolistic market for cigarettes was only slightly over 10%, the plaintiff argued that the purpose of the predation strategy was not to drive him out of business – which the defendant obviously could not have achieved given its small market share – but rather to discipline him into raising retail prices for generic cigarettes, thus narrowing the price gap between generic and branded cigarettes to protect the higher revenue margins in the market for branded cigarettes. At the end of a lengthy trial, the jury accepted the plaintiff's theory of harm to competition and awarded treble damages of almost 150 million USD.[65] The District Court judge, however, was not convinced and held that a reasonable jury could come to but one conclusion about the existence of injury to competition – that it did not exist. Therefore, the judge set aside the verdict of the jury and dismissed the action as a matter of law.[66] The Fourth Circuit affirmed this judgment notwithstanding the verdict.[67]

Certiorari was granted and the Supreme Court's majority opinion took the opportunity to tighten predation law by 'distinguishing to death' its elder *Utah Pie*-decision under which price cuts were found predatory if they were executed with predatory intent.[68] The majority of the Supreme Court subscribed to the

---

[65] The jury awarded Liggett 49,6 million USD in damages, which the District Court trebled to 148,8 million USD.

[66] See *Liggett Group, Inc. v. Brown & Williamson Tobacco Corp.*, 748 F.Supp. 344 (MDNC 1990).

[67] See *Liggett Group, Inc. v. Brown & Williamson Tobacco Corp.*, 964 F.2d 335 (4th Cir. 1992).

[68] See *Utah Pie Co. v. Continental Baking Co.*, 386 U.S. 685 (1967). The decision was widely criticised by commentators as it stood antitrust principles on their head. In this case, the plaintiff was a (family owned) local monopolist enjoying a quasi-monopolistic 66,5% of the market for frozen pies who argued that the price war started by three national bakeries was predatory. Despite the fact that the defendants had a much smaller market share in the relevant geographic market than the plaintiff, the Supreme Court ruled in favour of the latter, thereby protecting a local monopolist's attempt to defend its market position against growing competition; for a critical assessment of the Supreme Court's reasoning see W.S. Bowman, 'Restraint of Trade by the Supreme Court: The Utah Pie Case' (1967) 77 *Yale Law Journal*, 70, 84 (concluding that *Utah Pie* must rank 'as the most anticompetitive decision of the decade'). In *Brooke Group*, the Supreme Court did not expressly overrule *Utah Pie*. But if it were again decided today, the Court would dismiss the action. Given the rather small market share of the defendants, the plaintiff would struggle to demonstrate that there was a

cont.

view that predatory pricing claims need to be judged according to the same two-prong test irrespective of whether they are brought under Section 2 Sherman Act or Section 2(a) Robinson-Patman Act. Under this test, holding a firm liable for charging low prices requires:

– first, showing pricing below 'an adequate measure of cost'[69], and
– second, demonstrating that the alleged predator had a 'reasonable prospect', or, under Section 2 Sherman Act, a 'dangerous probability', of recouping its investment in below-cost prices.[70]

Determining whether recoupment of predatory losses is sufficiently likely requires demonstrating that, after the below-cost price predatory campaign, the predator will be able to set supra-competitive prices so as to recover the losses sustained during the predatory pricing campaign, 'including the time value of the money invested in it'.[71] The majority opinion conceded that a recoupment threshold defined this strictly is not easy to overcome but was convinced that the narrow construction of the law was necessary to avoid false positives: 'It would be ironic indeed', wrote Justice *Kennedy* for the majority of the Supreme Court, 'if the standards for predatory pricing liability were so low that antitrust suits themselves became a tool for keeping prices high.'[72]

The recoupment test's function of impeding anti-competitive suits by private plaintiffs was reiterated in the recent *Weyerhaeuser*-case which concerned allegations of a predatory bidding strategy in a monopsonist market.[73] The jury had ruled in favour of the plaintiff who was awarded approximately 80 million USD as damages and the Ninth Circuit affirmed the Districts Courts decision.[74] The Supreme Court vacated the judgment as the likelihood of recoupment was not demonstrated. Justice *Clarence Thomas* writing for a unanimous Court

---

dangerous probability that the defendants could recoup their investment in below-cost prices.
[69] Cf. *Brooke Group Ltd. v. Brown & Williamson Tobacco Corp.*, 509 U.S. 209, 225 (1993).
[70] *Ibid.* 226.
[71] *Ibid.* 225.
[72] *Ibid.* 226.
[73] See *Weyerhaeuser Co. v. Ross-Simmons Hardwood Lumber Co.*, 127 S. Ct. 1069 (2007).
[74] The jury returned a 26 million USD verdict against the defendant which was then trebled to approximately 79 million USD. The District Court entered judgment in favour of the plaintiff based on this jury verdict and the Court of Appeals for the Ninth Circuit affirmed; cf. *Confederated Tribes of Siletz Indians of Ore. v. Weyerhaeuser Co.*, 411 F.3d 1030 (9th Cir. 2005).

stated that 'the costs of erroneous findings of predatory-pricing liability were quite high' because the mechanism by which a firm engages in predatory price cutting is the same mechanism by which a firm stimulates competition, and therefore, 'mistaken findings of liability would chill the very conduct the anti-trust laws are designed to protect'.[75]

c) Recoupment as a tool for cutting back the powers of the jury

Besides being a barrier against abusive competitor suits facilitated by the lack of a strict dominance threshold and the economic incentives given to private attorney generals to sue their rivals, the recoupment requirement serves as a tool to curtail the traditional fact-finding role of the jury. The VII. Amendment of the US Constitution preserves the right of trial by jury in suits at common law where the value in controversy shall exceed twenty dollars. Yet, to preserve the integrity of law, the Federal Rules of Civil Procedure gives the judge some form of control over the jury.[76] In all stages of the proceeding he can decide the issues before him 'as a matter of law', i.e. without referring the case to the jury or without accepting its verdict. Upon a motion to dismiss, the judge can enter such a judgment provided that a reasonable jury would not judge in favour of the non-moving party in light of the presented evidence. The procedural particularity of the *Brooke Group* case lies in the fact that the Supreme Court allowed judges to dismiss predatory pricing actions *as a matter of law* for lack of the likelihood of recoupment. Thus the Supreme Court has strengthened the judge's power vis-à-vis the jury by allowing judges to review and assess the complex economic evidence presented on the recoupment issue against the market's realities and – if they do not find the evidence sufficient to establish the high recoupment threshold – to dismiss the action without the involvement of the jury. Today judges exercise this power on a large scale. Most predation cases are therefore dismissed as a matter of law.[77]

---

[75] Cf. *Weyerhaeuser Co. v. Ross-Simmons Hardwood Lumber Co.*, 127 S. Ct. 1069, 1075 (2007).

[76] Cf. Rules 50 and 56 Federal Rules of Civil Procedure; for a comprehensive overview of the powers of the judge to dismiss an action as a matter of law, see J.H. Friedenthal, M.K. Kane and A.R. Miller, *Civil Procedure* 4th ed (St. Paul/Minn., 2005), pp. 465-479 and pp. 578-617.

[77] See, e.g., *R.W. Intern. Corp. v. Welch Food, Inc.*, 13 F.3d 478 (1st Cir. 1994); *Rebel Oil Co. v. Atlantic Richfield Co.*, 51 F.3d 1421 (9th Cir. 1995); *AD/SAT, Div. of Skylight, Inc. v. Associated Press*, 181 F.3d 216 (2d Cir. 1999); *Stearns Airport Equipment Co. v. FMC Corp.*, 170 F.3d 518 (5th Cir. 1999); *Taylor Pub.*

cont.

3. European Competition law

In the wake of the *Brooke Group*-decision, the discussion on the necessity of a recoupment requirement in EU competition law intensified considerably. Defendants in predatory pricing proceedings argued that their price cuts were not anti-competitive for lack of the possibility of recoupment. Their push towards an alignment of European predatory pricing standards with US law did not fall on receptive ears.

a) Tetra Pak II: rejection of the recoupment requirement

The first case in which the ECJ addressed the recoupment issue expressly was *Tetra Pak II*. According to the Commission's findings, Tetra Pak was dominant in the markets for both the aseptic cartons used in packaging liquid food as well as the machines used to fill these cartons, and they had a strong, albeit not dominant, position on the markets for non-aseptic cartons and machines.[78] It sold its machines to packagers on various restrictive terms, including a tying condition under which packers could only use Tetra Pak cartons with Tetra Pak machines. The Commission found various infringements of (then) Article 82 EC, including pricing of non-aseptic cartons and machines below AVC.[79] By limiting its price cuts to particular geographic markets, Tetra Pak was able to reduce its losses. In addition, the tying requirement facilitated the elimination of competitors as it forced purchasers of non-aseptic machines to use Tetra Pak's cartons over the life cycle of the machine.[80] The Commission further concluded after investigation that Tetra Pak's profits in the aseptic markets covered its losses in the non-aseptic markets and that Tetra Pak could expand its activities in the non-aseptic markets. These facts combined with the 'associative links' between the two markets – purchasers using aseptic machines and cartons very often needed non-aseptic machines as well[81] – convinced the Commission that

---

Co. v. Jostens, Inc., 216 F.3d 465 (5th Cir. 2000); *United States v. AMR Corp.*, 335 F.3d 1109, 1116 (10th Cir. 2003).

[78] See Commission Decision, *Tetra Pak II*, Case No. IV/31.043 [1992] OJ L 72/1 para. 101.

[79] Although the Commission found below-cost pricing of cartons in various Member States, it focused on Italy, as for this State it had uncovered 'clear and unequivocal data', cf. Commission Decision, *Tetra Pak II*, Case No. IV/31.043 [1992] OJ L 72/1 para. 147.

[80] *Ibid.* para. 158.

[81] *Ibid.* para. 104.

the pricing policy was a rational tool for eliminating competition in the non-aseptic markets and fined the defendant.

Tetra Pak argued that its prices were not predatory as it had no reasonable probability of fully recouping its losses by charging supra-competitive prices in the non-aseptic markets once the targeted rival was destroyed given its lack of market power in these (predation) markets. Upon appeal, the ECJ rejected this argument straightforwardly. It found that there could be no economic reason for the below-cost pricing strategy other than predation. In this context the Court reasoned that it 'must be possible to penalize predatory pricing whenever there is a risk that competitors will be eliminated' because 'the aim pursued, which is to maintain undistorted competition, rules out waiting until such a strategy leads to the actual elimination of competitors.'[82] Accordingly, the Court did not find it 'appropriate, in the circumstances of the present case, to require in addition [to the *AKZO*-rules] proof that the predator had a realistic chance of recouping its losses.'[83] This sweeping statement is questionable. Tetra Pak pursued its exclusionary strategy on an adjacent market in which it held no dominant position. Such a scenario would appear to lack the structural factors which usually make a predation strategy pursued by a dominant undertaking successful, namely a high market share held by the predator, high barriers to entry and excess capacity, are not obvious.[84] Therefore a closer look at the chances of recoupment would have been warranted.[85]

---

[82] Cf. *Tetra Pak v. Commission*, Case No. C-333/94 P [1996] ECR I-5951 para. 44. The Advocate was even more categorical. He recommended that the Court 'should not lay down the prospect of recouping losses as a new prerequisite for establishing the existence of predatory pricing contrary to Article [82 EC, now: Article 102 TFEU]', because, inter alia, 'recouping losses is the result sought by the dominant undertaking, but predatory pricing is in itself anti-competitive, regardless of whether it achieves that aim.'; cf. opinion of AG D. Ruiz-Jarabo Colomer, *Tetra Pak v. Commission*, Case No. C-333/94 P [1996] ECR I-5954 para. 78.

[83] *Ibid.* para. 44.

[84] On the structural factors making a predatory pricing strategy plausible, see *supra* section II.C.1.

[85] This does not mean that given Tetra Pak's conduct, the outcome of the case would have changed. The Commission had uncovered that Tetra Pak's market share in the non-dominant market was around 50% and that its competitors were much smaller and that Tetra Pak could constantly raise its sales at the expense of its rivals, cf. Commission Decision, *Tetra Pak II*, Case No. IV/31.043 [1992] OJ L 72/1, 34 paras 101 and 151. Thus, the overall evidence presented indicates that a recoupment would have been likely: Tetra Pak priced low in one market to earn economic profits by establishing a dominant position in an adjacent market. Such

cont.

b) France Télécom: recoupment as one factor to show predatory intent

More recently the ECJ slightly softened its rejection of the recoupment requirement in a judgment that was handed down after the adoption of the Enforcement Communication. In *France Télécom*, the Commission found that the prices charged by WIN (a company of the France Telecom group) for high speed internet access services were predatory.[86] The anti-competitive nature of the defendant's pricing strategy was inferred from the fact that the prices charged to customers in France (i.) did not enable WIN to cover its variable costs for a shorter, nor its full costs for a longer period of time and (ii.) were part of a plan to pre-empt the market for high-speed internet access services in France during a key phase in its development by eliminating existing competitors and deterring prospective rivals from entering the market.[87] Although expressly subscribing to the view that 'recoupment is not a precondition before a finding can be made of abuse through predatory pricing', the Commission – for the first time – expressly reviewed the likelihood of recoupment and found that such a recoupment of losses is rendered plausible 'by the structure of the market and the associated revenue prospects'.[88]

The Court of First Instance – which has recently been renamed as the General Court – upheld the Commission's decision. Referring to *Tetra Pak II* it found that recoupment is generally not a precondition for finding low prices predatory.[89] On appeal, Advocate General *Jan Mazák*, criticized this absence of need to prove recoupment. In a rather weak opinion, he argued that the ECJ in *Tetra Pak II* used the qualifying words 'in the circumstances of the present case', to avoid making a general statement that would render it unnecessary to prove the possibility of recoupment in future predatory pricing cases.[90] The Advocate General thus read *Tetra Pak II* as the exception to the general rule that prices can only be regarded as predatory when the possibility of recoupment can be shown – a general rule that according to *Mazák's* view is also inherent in cases like *AKZO* and *Hoffmann-La Roche*.[91] This reasoning is not very con-

---

form of recoupment is sometimes referred to as 'leverage recoupment', see
D. Howarth (*supra* n. 23) p. 287.
[86] See Commission Decision, *Wanadoo Interactive*, Case No. COMP/38.233.
[87] *Ibid.* paras 255-331.
[88] *Ibid.* paras 335 and 336.
[89] See *France Télécom v. Commission*, Case No. T-340/03 [2007] ECR II-107 paras 224-230.
[90] See opinion of AG J. Mazák, *France Télécom v. Commission*, Case No. C-202/07 P [2009] ECR I-2369 para. 70.
[91] *Ibid.* para. 75.

vincing. First, in *AKZO* the Court did not address the issue of recoupment explicitly but appeared to assume that a dominant undertaking will be able to recoup its losses when predatory intent or pricing below AVC can be proven. Second, the passage of *Hoffmann-La Roche* in which the ECJ defined abusive conduct as behaviour influencing 'the structure of the market' by anti-competitive means[92] stands rather for the general rule that the ECJ supports a finding of abuse whenever the degree of competition in the market is hindered. This occurs once the rival leaves, irrespective of whether later consumers will be hurt by supra-competitive prices or not.

Against this background, the Advocate General would have been better advised to more frankly build his opinion on the argument that the law as it stands might be over-inclusive from a consumer welfare perspective as – once the requirements set out in *AKZO* are met – the risk of elimination can essentially be presumed so that a closer look at the recoupment issue is never compulsory.[93]

Given the clear indications in prior case law, it was no surprise that the ECJ did not follow *Mazák's* call to make the demonstration of the likelihood of recoupment a necessary precondition for a finding of predatory pricing. Rather, the Court declared that in *Tetra Pak II* it 'has taken the opportunity to dispense with such proof in circumstances where the eliminatory intent of the undertaking at issue could be presumed in view of that undertaking's application of prices lower than average variable costs'.[94] Yet, the Court did not go as far as saying that a closer look at the plausibility that the predator has a chance to recoup its losses is entirely irrelevant when assessing predatory pricing allegations. It found that a closer look at the predator's chances to profit from its price cutting strategy may help in ruling out economic justifications for prices below AVC or in establishing that a plan to eliminate a competitor exists in a case where prices were set below ATC but above AVC,[95] without however giving a clear indi-

---

[92] See *Hoffmann-La Roche v. Commission*, Case No. 85/76 [1979] ECR 461 para. 91.

[93] That the desire to bring European competition law in line with the consumer welfare approach was the main reason for *Mazák's* attempt to change the law, can be inferred from his referrals to economic literature such as the EAGCP-report on Article 82 EC (*supra* n. 48) which called for a closer look at recoupment, cf. opinion of AG J. Mazák, *France Télécom v. Commission*, Case No. C-202/07 P [2009] ECR I-2369 para. 75.

[94] Cf. *France Télécom v. Commission*, Case No. C-202/07 P [2009] ECR I-2369 para. 110.

[95] *Ibid.* para. 111.

cation how such an analysis should be carried out. Rather, the ECJ closed its line of reasoning with the statement that the lack of any possibility to recoup sustained losses is not sufficient to prevent an undertaking from reinforcing its dominant position by eliminating a rival which causes harm to competition as the degree of competition is further reduced and customers suffer loss as a result of the limitation of the choices available to them.[96] This could be interpreted as if the ECJ rejected the strict recoupment test which is based on a quantification of gains and losses. As the Court did not condemn the recoupment requirement in its entirety, it seems that it left the door open for the structural recoupment test which explains the rationality of a price predation campaign by looking at the market setting and strategic considerations behind the pricing policy. Moreover, by admitting that a recoupment analyses may help to weed out economic justifications for pricing below AVC, the Court seems to have silently corrected its overbroad statement in *Tetra Pak II* that prices below AVC are always abusive if set by an undertaking in a dominant position.

To summarise, under the law as it stands, a strict recoupment analysis is not a prerequisite for finding a low price strategy abusive. A structural recoupment test can however be included in the analysis to prove that the low price strategy did not make economic sense, except for exclusionary means, so that predatory intent can be assumed.

III. The Enforcement Communication

The older case law of the European courts has attracted considerable economic criticism over the last years. The main critique was essentially directed against the scope and content of the cost measures in force,[97] the strong reliance on the fuzzy criterion of predatory intent[98] and the ECJ's reluctance to make recoupment a precondition for finding low prices abusive.[99] Further, it was argued

---

[96] *Ibid.* para. 112.

[97] See W.J. Baumol, 'Predation and the Logic of the Average Variable Cost Test' (1996) 39 *Journal of Law and Economics*, 49, 57; K.W. Lange (*supra* n. 1) 505; M. Kling and S. Thomas, *Kartellrecht* (München, 2007), p. 233.

[98] See R. O'Donoghue and A.J. Padilla (*supra* n. 35) p. 250; G. Monti, *EC Competition Law* (Cambridge, 2008), p. 180.

[99] See E.P. Mastromanolis, 'Predatory Pricing Strategies in the European Union: A Case for Reform' [1998] *European Competition Law Review*, 211, 224; G. Niels and A. ten Kate, 'Predatory pricing standards: Is there a growing consensus?' (2000) 45 *Antitrust Bulletin*, 787, 808-809; C. Ahlborn and B. Allan (*supra* n. 6) 246; R.J. Van den Bergh and P.D. Camesasca (*supra* n. 4) p. 299; but see C. cont.

that the overbroad rules in force chill price competition. In this regard, it was pointed out that the ECJ does not accept a safe harbour for above-cost pricing (*Compagnie maritime belge*), although such prices rarely lead to anti-competitive exclusion,[100] but rather seems to find all prices below AVC abusive (*Tetra Pak II*), although there are good commercial reasons why dominant firms price below this cost-benchmark.[101]

The Enforcement Communication acknowledges some of the aforementioned criticisms. Consequently the general analytical framework proposed by the Commission departs from the case law on Article 82 EC/102 TFEU. The rather short section on predation[102] of the Enforcement Communication has to be read in conjunction with the more general sections on anti-competitive foreclosure,[103] price-based exclusionary conduct[104] and objective justifications[105] to understand how the Commission intends to restructure and refine the *AKZO*-rules and the complementary case law.

Generally speaking, the Commission wants to intervene when a dominant undertaking engages in predatory conduct by deliberately incurring losses or foregoing profits in the short term ('sacrifice'), so as to foreclose or be likely to foreclose one or more of its actual or potential competitors with a view to strengthening or maintaining its market power, thereby causing consumer harm ('anti-competitive foreclosure'). There are, however, instances in which sacrificed profits capable of foreclosing competitors are not abusive. If the low pricing strategy serves a legitimate business goal, it can be justified and does not infringe Article 102 TFEU.

A.   Sacrifice

According to the Enforcement Communication, conduct will be viewed by the Commission as entailing a sacrifice if the dominant undertaking, by charging a

---

Ritter, 'Does the Law of Predatory Pricing and Cross-Subsidisation Need a Radical Rethink?' (2004) 27 *World Competition*, 613, 647 (contesting the use of recoupment as such a requirement would be based on 'bad economics').

[100] See E. Elhauge (*supra* n. 1) 681-827.

[101] See V. Korah (*supra* n. 5) 185; R. O'Donoghue and A.J. Padilla (*supra* n. 35) p. 283; M. Hellwig (*supra* n. 5) p. 8; G. Monti (*supra* n. 98) pp. 179-182; K.W. Lange and T. Pries (*supra* n. 1) 63.

[102] See Enforcement Communication (*supra* n. 8) paras 63-74.

[103] *Ibid.* paras 19-22.

[104] *Ibid.* paras 23-27.

[105] *Ibid.* paras 28-31.

lower price for all or a particular part of its output over the relevant time period, or by expanding its output over the relevant time period, incurred or is incurring losses that could have been avoided.[106] Thus, the Commission refines the first *AKZO*-rule by taking the AAC-benchmark as the starting point for assessing whether prices are predatory.

This move does not come as a surprise. The Discussion Paper already opted for this cost-benchmark as the starting point instead of AVC,[107] and the Commission applied the AAC-benchmark *de facto* in its recent *Wanadoo*-decision.[108] In *Wanadoo*, the Commission regarded certain product-specific fixed costs, in the case at hand general marketing costs, as variable costs. Usually, marketing costs are regarded as fixed costs. The Commission however justified their classification as variable costs with the particularities of the sale of internet services in a growing market which allowed an attribution of certain marketing costs to single sales.[109] Such a calculation is essentially an application of the AAC-benchmark as the marketing costs could have been avoided if the dominant undertaking would not have offered its services.[110] As AAC in comparison to AVC includes certain product-specific fixed costs, it can be predicted that in the future more cases will infringe the sacrifice-criterion than would have been caught by the AVC-benchmark set forth in the first *AKZO*-rule.

The AAC-standard is, however, not seen as a bright line test, functioning to separate between aggressive price competition from predatory conduct. Rather, it serves as the starting point of the analysis. Thus price cuts above AAC (and even above ATC) can also be viewed as a sacrifice.[111] It seems that the Commission shares the critique that there is no price/cost-test which catches all anti-competitive conduct without overshooting the mark and that the transposition of any theoretical cost concept into practice is often more guesswork than hard science.[112] Therefore it resisted calls to consider pricing above a so-called marginal cost standard (AVC, AAC or LRAIC which are all proxy measures for

---

[106] *Ibid.* para. 64.
[107] See Discussion Paper (*supra* n. 9) para. 108.
[108] See Commission Decision, *Wanadoo Interactive*, Case No. COMP/38.233.
[109] *Ibid.* para. 64.
[110] See F. Schuhmacher, 'Altes und Neues zur Kampfpreisunterbietung: Gleichzeitig eine Besprechung des Urteils des EuG v. 30.01.2007 – Rs T-340/03 – France Télécom SA/Kommission' [2007] *Zeitschrift für Wettbewerbsrecht*, 352, 363.
[111] Cf. Enforcement Communication (*supra* n. 8) para. 65.
[112] See D. Howarth (*supra* n. 23) p. 259.

the theoretical concept of marginal cost)[113] or at least above ATC[114] as legal *per se*.

To assess whether above-cost prices can be viewed as a sacrifice, the Commission wants to investigate whether a pricing strategy led in the short term to net revenues lower than could have been expected from a reasonable alternative conduct, that is to say whether the dominant undertaking incurred a loss that it could have avoided.[115] As dominant undertakings often have alternative possibilities for pricing their products or spending profits, an overly wide perception of sacrifice would send competition authorities and courts on ill-defined fishing expeditions in search of hypothetical, more profitable pricing or investment policies the dominant firm could have applied. This could easily lead to over-enforcement as from an *ex post* view it is easy to detect many business decisions which turned out not to be profit-maximising and therefore led to lower net-revenues that a rational actor could have avoided.[116]

To overcome this problem, the Commission will only consider economically rational and practicable alternatives which, taking into account the market conditions and business realities facing the dominant undertaking, can realistically be expected to be more profitable.[117] In this regard, it shall be possible to rely on direct evidence consisting of documents from the dominant undertaking which clearly show a predatory strategy such as a detailed plan to sacrifice in order to exclude a competitor, to prevent entry or to pre-empt the emergence of a market, or evidence of concrete threats of predation.[118]

---

[113] This view is predominant in the US-literature, see, e.g., W.J. Baumol (*supra* n. 1) p. 23; H. Hovenkamp (*supra* n. 59) pp. 162-165; G.J. Werden, 'The "No Economic Sense" Test for Exclusionary Conduct' (2006) 31 *Journal of Corporation Law*, 293, 302; E. Elhauge (*supra* n. 1) 826-827. In Europe a safe harbour for prices above AVC or AAC has only gained modest support, see, e.g., G. Goeteyn, S. Mavroghenis, M. Piergiovanni, E. Reed and D. Ridyard (*supra* n. 5) p. 81.

[114] See M. Motta, *Competition Policy: Theory and Practice* (Cambridge, 2004), p. 441.

[115] See Enforcement Communication (*supra* n. 8) para. 65.

[116] See H. Hovenkamp (*supra* n. 59) p. 166.

[117] See Enforcement Communication (*supra* n. 8) para. 65.

[118] *Ibid.* para. 66.

B. Anti-competitive foreclosure

1. Price/cost-considerations and recoupment of losses

a) General principle

Proof of sacrifice alone does not suffice to find a low price strategy abusive. The Commission only wants to intervene under Article 102 TFEU where, on the basis of cogent and convincing evidence, the allegedly abusive conduct is likely to lead to anti-competitive foreclosure.[119] As vigorous price competition is generally beneficial to consumers an intervention only seems in order if the pricing policy under investigation has already been or is capable of hampering competition from competitors which are 'as efficient as the dominant undertaking'.[120]

The 'as' or 'equally efficient competitor test', originally developed by *Posner*,[121] asks the question whether the dominant company itself would be able to survive the exclusionary conduct if it were the target. The Commission has applied this test in previous cases,[122] and the CFI (now: the General Court) has approved it under the condition that the assessment is based exclusively on the dominant firm's costs.[123] The Enforcement Communication reflects this important precondition for lawfulness. To see whether a hypothetical competitor could efficiently compete against the dominant firm, the Commission wants to rely on another price/cost-comparison and measure whether the dominant undertaking has priced its products or services below LRAIC.[124]

The as efficient competitor test laid down in the Enforcement Communication seems to cut back the second *AKZO*-rule. Under this rule, prices below ATC are abusive when predatory intent can be proven. ATC includes all fixed and variable cost. In the case of multi-product firms, a share of common costs to produce a given product or service are also included. In turn, the LRAIC-standard does take common costs into account. When assessing the conduct of a multi-product firm which has economies of scope, LRAIC are thus below ATC.

---

[119] *Ibid.* para. 20.

[120] *Ibid.* para. 23.

[121] See R. Posner (*supra* n. 23) pp. 195 *et seq.*

[122] See Commission Decision, *Deutsche Telekom*, Case No. COMP/C-1/37.451, 37.578, 37.579 [2003] OJ L 263/9 para. 102.

[123] See *Deutsche Telekom v. Commission*, Case No. T-271/03, n.y.r., para. 192.

[124] See Enforcement Communication (*supra* n. 8) para. 67.

This would make the finding of anti-competitive foreclosure slightly more difficult than under the second *AKZO*-rule.[125]

b) No strict recoupment test

Whereas a price/cost-comparison is judged useful in testing for anti-competitive foreclosure, the Commission rejects – in line with the *France Télécom* judgment of the ECJ[126] handed down after the adoption of the Enforcement Communication – the idea that a strict recoupment test should be conducted to prove that the price cutting strategy may hurt consumers. Although the Commission acknowledges that in general consumers will only to be harmed if the dominant undertaking can expect to 'benefit from the sacrifice'[127] by having a greater market power after the predatory conduct comes to an end, it is of the opinion that identifying consumer harm 'is not a mechanical calculation of profits and losses, and proof of overall profits is not required.'[128] To investigate whether anti-competitive foreclosure leads to likely consumer harm the Commission essentially opts for an assessment of structural factors and strategic considerations (which are dealt with in more detail below at 2.). A showing that the incumbent has a chance to charge supra-competitive prices in the post-predation phase is therefore not necessary. It suffices to show, for instance, that the predatory strategy would be likely to lead to 'a strong foreclosure effect'.[129]

2. Market structure and context

The inquiry as to whether the incumbent has priced its products or services below LRAIC is only the starting point when assessing anti-competitive foreclosure. The emphasis of the analysis lies on a thorough assessment of the structural factors and strategic considerations which indicate that a predatory pricing strategy is a rational business practice to exclude or discipline current rivals or to deter prospective ones.

---

[125] For exceptions resulting from the possibility of handling the as efficient competitor test flexibly in order to be able to take into account special features of markets susceptible to monopolisation see infra IV. B. 2.

[126] See *supra* II. C. 3. b).

[127] Cf. Enforcement Communication (*supra* n. 8) para. 70.

[128] *Ibid.*

[129] *Ibid.* para. 71.

a) Structural factors

As it is generally accepted that profitable predation strategies can only be executed in certain market settings, the Commission first wants to take a closer look at a variety of structural factors to show that the incumbent can success-fully dampen competition. The factors to be taken into account in this respect are well known from the Commission's prior decision practice and the case law. Thus anti-competitive foreclosure is likely, *inter alia*, if the predator has a strong market position and excess capacity and its competitors are much smaller, the market is characterised by high entry barriers, and the price cutting is of a long duration and targeted against specific competitors.[130] Moreover – and here the more economic approach comes into play – the Commission also wants to investigate and take into account possible evidence of actual foreclosure, such as changes in market-shares over time, notwithstanding that the European courts in abuse cases do not demand such a thorough effects based analysis.[131]

b) Strategic considerations

A further important enhancement of the analytical framework to test for predatory pricing laid down in the Enforcement Communication is the inclusion of insights generated by game-theoretic models. These models of predation discussed in modern industrial organisation literature have shown that the dominant undertaking can successfully use information asymmetries about entry cost or its capability to sustain a long price war to deter or delay entry or to encourage the exit of a newcomer. Essentially three main scenarios have been identified in modern industrial organisation literature, which are commonly labelled as reputation, signal jamming and financial predation.[132]

---

[130] *Ibid.* paras 71 and 72. Such factors were, e.g., considered in *Tetra Pak v. Commission*, Case No. T-83/91 [1994] ECR II-755 paras 186 and 202; Commission Decision, *Wanadoo Interactive*, Case No. COMP/38.233 paras 337-364.

[131] See *British Airways v. Commission*, Case No. C-95/04 P [2007] ECR I-2331 paras 107 and 123.

[132] For an overview of the recent theories of predation see J. Tirole, *The Theory of Industrial Organization* (Cambridge/Mass., 1988), pp. 372-380; R.T. Rapp, 'Predatory Pricing Analysis: A Practical Synthesis' (1991) 59 *Antitrust Law Journal*, 595-607; J.A. Ordover (*supra* n. 1) pp. 80-81; P. Bolton, J.F. Brodley and M.H. Riordan (*supra* n. 1) 2239-2330; M. Motta (*supra* n. 114) pp. 415-441; J. Haucap and J. Kruse (*supra* n. 1) pp. 50-53; R. O'Donoghue and A.J. Padilla (*supra* n. 35) pp. 243-244; D. Howarth (*supra* n. 23) pp. 281-283; W. Wurmnest, Markt-macht und Verdrängungsmissbrauch: Eine rechtsvergleichende Neubestimmung
cont.

The Enforcement Communication makes clear that credible theories of harm may be built upon these predation tests and models. For instance, anti-competitive foreclosure can be assumed if the dominant undertaking is better informed about cost, or can distort market signals about profitability so as to influence the expectations of potential entrants and thereby deter entry.[133] If the conduct and its likely effects are felt on multiple markets and/or in successive periods of possible entry, the same would hold true where the dominant undertaking is seeking a reputation for predatory conduct.[134] The *Tetra Pak II*-case reflects such a scenario as the incumbent used aggressive pricing strategies across a range of different – but closely connected – geographic and product markets.[135] The overall conditions of this strategy seemed consistent with the underlying principles of reputation effect predation. Finally, the Commission wants to take into account whether the predation campaign affects the targeted firms access to external financing, as substantial price decreases or other predatory conduct by the dominant undertaking could adversely affect the competitor's performance so that its access to further financing may be seriously undermined.[136] With regard to proving the anti-competitive foreclosure requirement, the Commission intends to rely on internal documents which contain direct evidence of an anti-competitive strategy to exclude competitors.[137]

C. Objective justifications

The showing of sacrifice and anti-competitive foreclosure alone is not sufficient to find low prices predatory. The Commission further wants to examine claims put forward by the dominant undertaking that purport to explain why its conduct is justified and therefore not abusive in the context of Article 102 TFEU.[138] The assessment of so-called objective justifications or efficiencies overlaps in part with the evaluation of the requirements of sacrifice and/or anti-competitive foreclosure. For instance, if the dominant undertaking claims that its low price strategy is not anti-competitive as it merely sold off some phased out products,

---

des Verhältnisses von Recht und Ökonomik in der Missbrauchsaufsicht über marktbeherrschende Unternehmen (Tübingen, 2010), pp. 394 *et seq.*
[133] See Enforcement Communication (*supra* n. 8) para. 68.
[134] *Ibid.*
[135] See *supra* II. C. 3. a).
[136] See Enforcement Communication (*supra* n. 8) para. 73.
[137] *Ibid.* para. 20.
[138] *Ibid.* para. 28.

one could argue that the incumbent did not sacrifice profits (if the stock could not be sold at higher prices due to new and better products on the market) and that the strategy could not lead to anti-competitive foreclosure likely to cause consumer harm (if the total amount of the stock sold at below-cost prices is of a *quantité négligable*). Such a strategy could also be objectively justified, as Article 102 TFEU – in the words of the ECJ – only prohibits 'recourse to methods different from those which condition normal competition in products or services' hindering the maintenance of the degree of competition still existing in the market.[139] The selling of old stock at below cost prices which otherwise could not be sold at all is a business practice often used in commerce and therefore usually normal competition on the merits.

Whereas the Discussion Paper addressed at length some defences discussed in modern industrial organisation literature, such as the meeting competition defence or below cost pricing to minimise losses in response to changed market conditions,[140] the Enforcement Communication explicitly mentions only the efficiency-defence.[141] The efficiency-defence is modelled after Article 101(3) TFEU and shall, as senior officials of the Commission have pointed out on several occasions, play a more important role in the assessment of future abuse cases.[142]

The recognition of a non-exclusionary explanation for prices below cost may be important in markets in which efficiencies can only be achieved over a long time. This might be the case in markets which require large, up-front investments and involve start-up losses in order to increase demand and thereby acquire the scale to reduce costs over time.[143] The Commission is however of the opinion that such efficiencies occur rather rarely when such low pricing

---

[139] Cf. *Hoffmann-La Roche v. Commission*, Case No. 85/76 [1979] ECR 461 para. 91; *AKZO v. Commission*, Case No. C-62/86 [1991] ECR I-3359 para. 70; see also *Tetra Pak Rausing SA v. Commission*, Case No. T-51/89 [1990] ECR II-309 para. 23.

[140] See Discussion Paper (*supra* n. 9) paras 130-133.

[141] See Enforcement Communication (*supra* n. 8) para. 74.

[142] See M. Albers, 'Der "more economic approach" bei Verdrängungsmissbräuchen: Zum Stand der Überlegungen der Europäischen Kommission', in *Marktmacht und Missbrauch*, B. Ahrens, P. Behrens and P. v. Dietze (eds) (Baden-Baden, 2007) p. 11, 24; E. Paulis, 'Roundtable Discussion, General Approaches to Defining Abusive/Monopolistic Practices', in *Fordham Competition Law Institute, International Antitrust Law & Policy 2006*, B.E. Hawk (ed.) (Huntington/NY, 2007), p. 541, 554.

[143] See R. O'Donoghue and A.J. Padilla (*supra* n. 35) p. 292; for further examples see J. Haucap and J. Kruse (*supra* n. 1) pp. 45 *et seq.*

strategies are pursued by dominant undertakings.[144] The Enforcement Communication acknowledges – despite the official parlance that it follows a consumer welfare approach – that rivalry between undertakings, i.e. the protection of the competitive process, is the essential driver of economic efficiency and the guarantor that efficiency gains are passed onto consumers.[145] Therefore, conduct which maintains, creates or strengthens a market position approaching that of a monopoly can normally not be justified on the grounds that it also creates efficiency gains.[146] As price cutting can only lead to anti-competitive foreclosure when the predator has a very strong position in the market, i.e. is in a position close to a monopoly, there is not much room for the efficiency defence.

Even if the room for objective justifications for price cutting strategies leading to anti-competitive foreclosure is limited, the Enforcement Communication makes clear that a dominant undertaking may also have legitimate reasons for temporarily pricing below cost. This has to be read as a correction of the ECJ's broad statement in *Tetra Pak II*, according to which prices below AVC are *always* abusive,[147] a correction which the ECJ seems to have embraced in its recent *France Télécom* judgment.[148]

IV. Assessment

A. Sacrifice

1. Establishing AAC as a baseline-test for sacrificed profits

From an economic perspective, the technical refinement of the first *AKZO*-rule by establishing AAC as a yardstick to test for sacrificed profits makes sense. Many economists agree today that the economic costs of a predation strategy are often well captured by comparing whether it would be more profitable for the dominant undertaking to exit the market than continuing to produce a given

---

[144] See Enforcement Communication (*supra* n. 8) para. 74.

[145] *Ibid.* para. 30.

[146] The Enforcement Communication does not define when a position close to a monopoly is reached. The Discussion Paper assumed such a position when the market share of the dominant undertaking exceeds 75% and there is essentially no competitive pressure left from other competitors in the market, cf. Discussion Paper (*supra* n. 9) para. 92.

[147] *Tetra Pak v. Commission*, Case No. C-333/94 P [1996] ECR I-5951 para. 41.

[148] Cf. *France Télécom v. Commission*, Case No. C-202/07 P [2009] ECR I-2369 para. 111.

output.[149] In comparison to the AVC-test, the AAC-standard has the advantage of not requiring a segregation of fixed and variable costs and the allocation of common costs, which is often a rather arbitrary undertaking: Splitting up common costs to single product lines of a multi-product firm can be done according to a variety of different standards with different outcomes[150] and whether costs are variable or fixed depends largely on the time frame on which the assessment is based: In the long run all costs are variable.[151] Further, AAC includes additional fixed costs entailed by the predatory pricing campaign which better reflects that in a mid-range time frame a dominant undertaking also has to recover investments in such fixed costs to stay in business.[152] Finally, the fact that the firm is losing more money by embarking on the alleged predatory pricing campaign than it would by exiting the product line is usually a good indication that profits have been deliberately sacrificed to monopolise the market. Against this background, the AAC-benchmark appears better able to represent the economically relevant costs of an exclusionary strategy in many markets.

The shift from AVC to AAC is also compatible with the general principle set forth by the ECJ in *AKZO* that only such price cuts that drive rivals from the market 'which are perhaps as efficient as the dominant undertaking'[153] shall be deemed predatory. As AAC may better reflect the economic background of the predation strategy it serves exactly the same purpose: to prevent the foreclosure of potentially as efficient rivals of the dominant undertaking.[154]

Making AAC the appropriate measure of cost to test for sacrifice does not however mean that the well known practical problems of cost calculation will be eased. Under the AAC-standard as well the outcome varies with the time frame on which the evaluation is based: In the short run, few costs are avoidable whereas in the long run, many costs can be avoided.[155] Moreover, applying the AAC-standard raises the intricate problem of measuring the cost of an event that

---

[149] See, e.g., W.J. Baumol (*supra* n. 97) 49, 56; R. O'Donoghue and A.J. Padilla (*supra* n. 35) p. 242.

[150] See D. Schwarz, 'Wettbewerbspolitische Problematik des Predatory Pricing' [1987] *Wirtschaft und Wettbewerb*, 93, 96.

[151] See H. Fleischer (*supra* n. 1) 80; L.A. Sullivan and W.S. Grimes, *The Law of Antitrust: An Integrated Handbook* 2nd ed (St. Paul/Minn., 2006), p. 167.

[152] See R. O'Donoghue and A.J. Padilla (*supra* n. 35) p. 241.

[153] Cf. *AKZO v. Commission*, Case No. C-62/86 [1991] ECR I-3359 para. 72.

[154] See F. Schuhmacher (*supra* n. 110) 352, 363.

[155] See R. O'Donoghue and A.J. Padilla (*supra* n. 35) p. 243. Measuring AVC and AAC often yield similar results as usually only variable costs are avoidable in the short run.

has not taken place: the market exit of the incumbent. The cost of such a hypothetical market exit cannot be quantified with accurate precision, as there are no objective criteria for assessing the cost of transferable assets or the dissolution of certain production facilities at market prices.[156] Finally, the AAC-standard might be inaccurate as it ignores common costs. For example, if an airline sells tickets for business and economy class seats, most of the cost of the transportation of a passenger are common, e.g. the fuel or the salaries of the personnel on board. So considering the AAC of only one class of tickets might yield a blurred outcome.[157] Against this background, the AAC-standard should only be viewed as a first screen which needs refinements to reflect the market setting in which the low pricing campaign takes place.

2. Sacrifice and above-cost predation

In light of the above, one can applaud the Commission for not declaring above-cost pricing legal *per se*. The Commission's wide perception of sacrifice as including prices above AAC or even ATC reflects the fact that economic theory does not establish any single cost measure as the definite competitive benchmark.[158] The marginal cost curve of a firm is a theoretical concept which differs from accounting cost concepts applied in practice, and marginal costs usually cannot be measured in real-life competition cases with accurate precision.[159] Looking at proxies for marginal costs (such as AVC, AAC or LRAIC) as well as the ATC-benchmark may thus lead to the result that they indicate predation where a true marginal cost test would not or vice versa.[160] Rigid price/cost comparisons are therefore very blunt instruments for testing for predatory pricing which need to be complemented by an analysis of the market realities and the strategic thinking behind the pricing policy. The *Compagnie maritime*

---

[156] See C. Ewald (*supra* n. 1) 1165, 1172; K.W. Lange and T. Pries (*supra* n. 1) 62.

[157] See W.J. Baumol (*supra* n. 97) 59-60; D. Howarth (*supra* n. 23) p. 255.

[158] See generally D. Howarth (*supra* n. 23) p. 259; C. Ewald (*supra* n. 1) 1171-1172; see further E.M. Iacobucci (*supra* n. 1) 320.

[159] See the critique voiced by O.E. Williamson (*supra* n. 23) 284-340; E.-J. Mestmäcker (*supra* n. 23) p. 195; M.A. Salinger (*supra* n. 22) p. 7; L.A. Sullivan and W.S. Grimes (*supra* n. 151) p. 168; D. Howarth (*supra* n. 23) p. 259.

[160] See the examples given by D. Howarth (*supra* n. 23) pp. 259-262.

belge case is a striking example that a pricing strategy combined with additional measures, such as the scheduling of services may unduly restrict competition.[161]

Against this background a safe harbour for above-cost pricing would only make sense when there is a strong risk that a non-tolerable number of false positives (type I-errors) will be committed, i.e. that pro-competitive low pricing strategies will be prohibited on a large scale. In the US, many speak in favour of such a safe harbour given that the enforcement of the law lies primarily in the hands of private parties, often competitors, who suffer directly from a low pricing campaign. As described above,[162] the missing dominance threshold coupled with a treble damages remedy and a plaintiff-friendly litigation system creates many incentives which can lead to the prohibition of beneficial conduct as clear-cut rules to distinguish between anti-competitive above cost price cuts and aggressive competition are difficult to design.[163]

In Europe, the enforcement arena is, however, quite different. Predatory pricing allegations are foremost investigated by the Commission or national competition authorities. Moreover, cases in which defendants were condemned for charging unduly low prices are few in number.[164] Even though the Com-

---

[161] Other examples are provided by S. Bishop and M. Walker, *The Economics of EC Competition Law: Concepts, Application and Measurement* 2nd ed (London, 2002), para. 6.79; see further A.S. Edlin (*supra* n. 1) 941-991; L.A. Sullivan and W.S. Grimes (*supra* n. 151) p. 168.

[162] See *supra* II. C. 2.

[163] See, e.g., *Barry Wright Corp. v. ITT Grinnell Corp.*, 724 F.2d 227, 235-236 (1st Cir. 1983), per (then) Judge Breyer: 'In sum, we believe that such above-cost price cuts are typically sustainable; that they are normally desirable (particularly in concentrated industries); that the "disciplinary cut" is difficult to distinguish in practice; that it, in any event, primarily injures only higher cost competitors; that its presence may well be "wrongly" asserted in a host of cases involving legitimate competition; and that to allow its assertion threatens to "chill" highly desirable procompetitive price cutting. For these reasons, we believe that a precedent allowing this type of attack on prices that exceed both incremental and average costs would more likely interfere with the procompetitive aims of the antitrust laws than further them. Hence, we conclude that the Sherman Act does not make unlawful prices that exceed both incremental and average costs.'; see further P. Areeda and H. Hovenkamp, *Antitrust Law: An Analysis of Antitrust Principles and their Execution* 3rd ed, vol. III A (New York, 2008), § 739c2; E. Elhauge (*supra* n. 1) 826-27; but see A.S. Edlin (*supra* n. 1) 941-991 (proposing a test to condemn anti-competitive above-cost pricing).

[164] From 1990 until 2009, the Commission took up two cases concerning selective above-cost price cuts (rebate-cases not counted), see Commission Decision,
cont.

mission is currently pursuing plans to strengthen private enforcement in Europe, the ideas discussed so far make it highly unlikely that in the near future a 'European private attorney general' will have a similar arsenal of weapons at his disposal as does his US counterpart.[165] Against this background, in Europe the risk of chilling price competition does not appear high enough to sustain a safe harbour above an appropriate measure of cost, for instance AAC or ATC.

B. *Anti-competitive foreclosure*

Given that cost measures are not as accurate for detecting anti-competitive conduct as once thought, the Commission's approach correctly states that sacrifice alone does not suffice to make a low pricing strategy predatory. If there is no danger that a firm is excluded or disciplined or entry or growth of competitors is delayed, then predation is not a rational strategy that will harm competition. A thorough assessment of likely effects and the strategic rationale behind the pricing policy is thus crucial to avoid false positives. Older decisions of the European courts sometimes only dealt cursorily with the effects of an abusive conduct on the market. Anti-competitive effects in abuse cases were sometimes inferred from the fact that the dominant undertaking held a high market share and acted with anti-competitive intent.[166] The Enforcement Communication seems to correct this shortcoming by tightening the standards of proof for showing that the conduct is capable of anti-competitive foreclosure.

CEWAL, Case No. IV/32.448 and IV/32.450 [1993] OJ L 34/20; Commission Decision, *Irish Sugar*, Case No. IV/34.621, 35.059/F-3 [1997] OJ L 258/1.

[165] For example, the White Paper on damages actions presented by the Commission in April 2008 does not mention the introduction of a double (let alone treble) damages-rule as policy option, see White Paper on damages actions for breach of the EC antitrust rules (2 April 2008), COM(2008) 165 final. The national tort or competition laws also do not provide treble damages for violations of European competition law. For the pros and cons of strengthening the enforcement of the European competition rules, see the contributions in J. Basedow (ed.), *Private Enforcement of EC Competition Law* (Alphen aan den Rijn, 2007).

[166] See Commission Decision, *Eurofix-Bauco/Hilti*, Case No. IV/30.787, 31.488 [1988] OJ L 65/19 para. 80, upheld in *Hilti v. Commission*, Case No. T-30/89 [1991] ECR II-1439, 1483 para. 100; *Hilti v. Commission*, Case No. C-53/92 P [1994] ECR I-667; Commission Decision, *Irish Sugar*, Case No. IV/34.621, 35.059/F-3 [1997] OJ L 258/1 para. 134, upheld in *Irish Sugar v. Commission*, Case No. T-228/97 [1999] ECR II-2969 para. 185 (both cases concerned selective price cuts coupled with other abusive practices).

1. Market structure and strategic theory

In this regard, the Commission not only wants to rely on a thorough assessment of structural factors facilitating the success of a predatory pricing campaign targeting a smaller competitor, the Enforcement Communication also integrates post-Chicago models and tests into the analysis for showing that the price cutting strategy is capable of dampening competition. Although modern industrial organisation theory provides many useful insights and their results are vital for understanding predation cases, one has to bear in mind that 'hard facts' which make a predation strategy rational, for instance by considering signal-jamming or reputation effects caused by information asymmetries in the markets, are often hard to prove in real life competition cases.[167] This diminishes their practical value. If, for example, the incumbent cuts prices to distort information about the cost of doing business in that market to prevent a newcomer from learning about market conditions and thereby discourage entry, such price cuts can also be a perfectly normal response to potential competition.[168] The construction of a plausible predation scenario based on signal-jamming or repudiation models must therefore be supported by clear and convincing evidence that the facts assumed by the models are present in the market realities of the case at hand to minimise decision errors.

Besides practical application problems, the theoretical underpinnings of game theoretic models have been questioned by proponents of Behavioural and Experimental Economics, two newer branches of economic theory within the post-Chicago family.[169] Game-theory is based on the classical rational choice

---

[167] See D. Howarth (*supra* n. 23) p. 294; K.W. Lange and T. Pries (*supra* n. 1) 63; see further F.M. Fisher, 'Games economists play: A noncooperative view' (1989) 20 *RAND Journal of Economics*, 113; K.G. Elzinga and D.E. Mills, 'Predatory Pricing and Strategic Theory' (2001) 89 *Georgetown Law Journal*, 2475, 2494.

[168] The example is based on the 'test market predation'-scenario described by P. Bolton, J.F. Brodley and M.H. Riordan (*supra* n. 1) 2311-2313.

[169] For an introduction to Experimental Economics see A.E. Roth, 'Introduction to Experimental Economics', in *Handbook of Experimental Economics*, J.H. Kagel and A.E. Roth (eds) (Princeton, 1995), pp. 1-109; C.F. Camerer, *Behavioral Game Theory* (Princeton, 2003), pp. 20-25. For an introduction to Behavioral Economics see C.F. Camerer, G. Loewenstein and M. Rabin (eds), *Advances in Behavioral Economics* (Princeton, 2004); M. Altman (ed.), *Handbook of Contemporary Behavioral Economics: Foundations and Developments* (New York, 2006); D. Fudenberg, 'Advancing Beyond Advances in Behavioral Economics' (2006) 44 *Journal of Economic Literature*, 694-711; W. Pesendorfer, 'Behavioral
cont.

model of neoclassical economics. However, empirical evidence which has been gathered gives much reason to doubt these assumptions and – as a consequence – the game-theoretic predictions of human behaviour. Due to limited cognitive resources market actors exhibit bounded rationality, bounded self-interest, and bounded willpower and seem to systematically deviate from the rational choice assumptions.[170] The proponents of a behaviourally informed approach therefore claim that various biases in judgments of risks, costs and benefits as well as heuristics (such as endowment or framing effects as well as the psychology of risk-taking) should be included in the analysis of competition law in general and the assessment of predation cases in particular.[171]

Given the empirical evidence, one can indeed hardly deny that decision-makers deviate more often from the rational choice model than traditionally assumed. These deviations seem to be of a systematic nature and therefore cannot be ignored in the economic analysis of competition cases. The detected deviation effects are however very situation specific and may contradict each other. Future (empirical) analysis will have to refine these effects to allow more generalised predictions of predatory conduct. The work undertaken thus far confirms however the validity of the general basic predation scenarios de-veloped by game theory, especially the reputation scenario,[172] and refines the understanding of such strategies for instance by showing that repudiation effects may be greater due to loss aversion strategies pursued by the prey.[173]

The Commission thus far has not taken recourse to insights discussed in the Experimental and Behavioural Economics literature. As these branches of eco-nomics are in their incipiency, the reluctance of the Commission is understand-able. With their further progress a cautious and gradual incorporation of insights generated by these newer branches of economic analysis seems advisable. It can

---

Economics Comes of Age: A Review Essay on Advances in Behavioral Eco-nomics' (2006) 44 *Journal of Economic Literature*, 712-721.

[170] For an overview of the analysed deviations from the rational choice model, see C. Jolls, C.R. Sunstein and R.H. Thaler, 'A Behavioral Approach to Law and Economics' (1998) 50 *Stanford Law Review*, 1471-1550.

[171] See H.S. Gerla, 'The Psychology of Predatory Pricing: Why Predatory Pricing Pays' (1985) 39 *Southwestern Law Journal*, 755-780; A. Tor, 'The Fable of Entry: Bounded Rationality, Market Discipline, and Legal Policy' (2002) 101 *Michigan Law Review*, 482-568.

[172] See Y.J. Jung, J.H. Kagel and D. Levin, 'On the existence of predatory pricing: An experimental study of reputation and entry deterrence in the chain-store game' (1994) 25 *RAND Journal of Economics*, 72-93.

[173] See A. Tor, 'Illustrating a Behaviorally Informed Approach to Antitrust Law: The Case of Predatory Pricing' (2003) 18 *Antitrust*, 52, 56.

however be predicted that also a behaviourally informed approach to predatory pricing will not alleviate the difficulty of measuring key assumptions of post-Chicago models in real life antitrust cases.

Against this background, it can be predicted that in the near future the Commission will ground its analysis of anti-competitive foreclosure primarily on a thorough assessment of structural market factors which facilitate the success of a predation strategy and use post-Chicago models as supportive evidence to round-up the analysis.

2. The as efficient competitor test

To minimise the risk of over-enforcement, the Commission further refines the general principle that European law condemns only price cuts capable of driving out competitors 'which may be as efficient as the dominant undertaking',[174] by subscribing to the view that usually only pricing below LRAIC is capable of achieving this result.[175] From an economic standpoint, this measure of cost is a good starting point for assessing foreclosure effects. This cost benchmark does not focus on short-run production decisions but tries to take into account profit maximising goals in the long run, by an estimation of the total cost of supplying a specific product or service, including all product specific costs incurred in the research, development and marketing of the product.[176]

Mechanically applied, the as efficient competitor test can however unduly restrict competition. Its focus is too narrow, as it concentrates on a price/cost-comparison without taking into account the market context in which the predation campaign is executed. Yet many markets prone to monopolisation exhibit significant economies of scale or scope, network effects or bottlenecks. In such cases, a dominant company with a high market share has significant cost advantages over any smaller actual or prospective rival. As the dominant firm always produces in greater quantity than its competitors, its average costs can be lower than those of its rivals.[177] If so, practices that would not exclude an equally efficient firm of the same size as the dominant market player may in fact exclude the only actual rivals the dominant is ever likely to face. In addition, the quantification of LRAIC raises difficult allocation problems (as would any other price/cost-test) and also depends on the willingness of the dominant undertaking

---

[174] Cf. *AKZO v. Commission*, Case No. C-62/86 [1991] ECR I-3359 para. 72.

[175] See Enforcement Communication (*supra* n. 8) para. 67.

[176] See R. O'Donoghue and A.J. Padilla (*supra* n. 35) p. 269.

[177] H. Hovenkamp (*supra* n. 59) p. 153.

to account for and supply all the relevant information on its cost structure. Consequently, the practical value of this test is limited.[178]

The Commission does not overlook these application problems. Consequently, the Enforcement Communication contains a variety of safety valves to minimise decision errors. In this regard, attention should be drawn to three important provisos contained in the Enforcement Communication, which indicate that the Commission wants to pursue a 'modified' as efficient competitor test.

First, in case that common costs are significant, the Commission intends to factor a fair share of these costs into the calculation of LRAIC when assessing that the pricing strategy is capable of hampering competition.[179] This variation of the as efficient competitor test is a continuation of the Commission's prior practice and comes into play when dealing with predation allegations lodged against multi-product firms with significant common costs.[180]

Second, the Commission will take a 'dynamic view' and accepts that a not yet as efficient rival may also stimulate competition, as in the absence of the abusive conduct such a competitor may benefit from demand-related advantages such as network and learning effects which will tend to enhance its efficiency.[181]

And third, the Commission is aware of the difficulties in obtaining reliable information on pricing conduct and costs of the dominant company. As the quality of cost data depends to a large extent on the willingness of the dominant firm to cooperate with the competition authority, the Commission is aware that there might be cases in which the submitted data will not suffice to infer from it that the pricing strategy is capable of excluding an as efficient competitor. In such a case, the Commission wants to use the 'cost data of competitors or other comparable data'.[182]

In sum, these refinements of the as efficient competitor test ensure that it can be adapted to the specific market circumstances governing the case at hand so as

---

[178] See the critique voiced by A.I. Gavil, 'Exclusionary Distribution Strategies by Dominant Firms: Striking a Better Balance' (2004) 72 *Antitrust Law Journal*, 3, 59; R.E. Bloch, H.-G. Kamann, J.S. Brown and J.P. Schmidt, 'A Comparative Analysis of Art. 82 of the EC Treaty and Sec. 2 of the Sherman Act' [2005] *Zeitschrift für Wettbewerbsrecht*, 325, 348; W. Wurmnest, 'The Reform of Article 82 EC in the Light of the Economic Approach', in *Abuse of Dominant Position: New Interpretation, New Enforcement Mechanisms?*, M.-O. Mackenrodt, B. Conde Gallego and S. Enchelmaier (eds) (Berlin, 2008), p. 1, 18-19.

[179] See Enforcement Communication (*supra* n. 8) para. 26 with note 2.

[180] See *supra* II. A. 2. a).

[181] See Enforcement Communication (*supra* n. 8) para. 24.

[182] *Ibid.* para. 25.

to make sure that Article 102 TFEU will not become a blunt sword in fighting predatory conduct.

3. Recoupment

The Commission was also right to disregard the view that without a strict recoupment test, the interpretation and application of Article 102 TFEU rests on an economically weak fundament.[183] The strict recoupment test is flawed for various reasons: Foreclosing a competitor from the market can make economic sense even if not all losses will be recouped. For instance, if the newcomer has a better technology than the monopolist, the latter might find an unprofitable predation strategy more preferable to a loss of market share, which is an even more disastrous outcome.[184] Thus, a non-recoupment is not in all cases a boon to consumers. Moreover, the strict recoupment test focuses on losses and gains in one given market. Financial gains stemming from reputation effects in other markets – which are usually not quantifiable – are left out of the analysis. This narrow focus ignores that modern industrial organisation literature has identified recoupment across several markets fostered by reputation effects as one decisive factor which makes predatory price cutting strategies by dominant undertakings an economically successful (and thus rational) business strategy.[185] Therefore, the strict recoupment test is potentially under-inclusive. Such a test might be necessary in the US to protect price competition but not in Europe where the risk of over-enforcement is much lower.[186] Furthermore, profits and losses can often not be calculated with the necessary accurateness as they have to be estimated against a hypothetical market price which depends on a multitude of factors.[187] These deficiencies counsel against the incorporation of the strict recoupment-test into EU predatory pricing law.

Against this background, it makes more sense – as the Enforcement Communication does and as the ECJ hinted in *France Télécom*[188] – to focus on a

---

[183] This view was taken by, e.g., R.J. Van den Bergh and P.D. Camesasca (*supra* n. 4) p. 299.

[184] C.S. Hemphill (*supra* n. 50) 1592; C. Ritter (*supra* n. 99) 645.

[185] See *supra* III. B. 2. b).

[186] This point of view is shared by H. Schweitzer, 'The History, Interpretation and Underlying Principles of Section 2 Sherman Act and Article 82 EC', in *European Competition Law Annual 2007*, C.-D. Ehlermann and M. Marquis (eds) (Oxford, 2008), p. 119, 154-55.

[187] See C.S. Hemphill (*supra* n. 50) 1596-1598.

[188] See *supra* II. C. 3. b).

'structural recoupment-test' to assess anti-competitive foreclosure. This test looks at the structure of the market to see whether the predator can successfully implement his predation strategy. Factors to be considered are, *inter alia*, changes of market shares, the duration of the low pricing campaign, capacity restraints or barriers to entry. Such a recoupment test is not superfluous because Article 102 TFEU applies only to firms with a high degree of market power. The market shares under which the ECJ presumes dominance are rather low. According to the case law, firms with a stable market share of 50% can be found dominant.[189] Whether such a market position suffices to successfully implement a predation strategy is more than debatable. Thus, a closer look at the chances of recoupment is indispensable. The same holds true in situations of multi-market predation as in these cases the dominant firm sells at below-cost prices only in markets other than the dominated one.[190]

C. Pricing below AAC is not always anti-competitive

Finally the Commission's move to correct the overbroad holding in *Tetra Pak II*, according to which prices below AVC must *always* be assumed as predatory, deserves approval. Most economists agree today that in special circumstances dominant firms may have legitimate business justifications for pricing their goods or services for a given period of time below AVC, AAC or LRAIC.[191] For example, special technology markets require large investments involving start-up losses in order to increase consumer uptake, acquire scale, or to gain the learning experience necessary for reducing costs over time.[192] Under such market conditions dominant firms will have to price below cost to stay in the market. Against this backdrop, the finding of the ECJ in *Tetra Pak II* does not make economic sense.

It has to be pointed out that the Commission never followed the strict approach voiced by the ECJ in its elder case law and always investigated

---

[189] *AKZO v. Commission*, Case No. C-62/86 [1991] ECR I-3359 para. 60; for a critical assessment of this broad statement see T. Eilmansberger (*supra* n. 42) Art. 82 EG para. 105.

[190] See R. O'Donoghue and A.J. Padilla (*supra* n. 35) p. 259.

[191] See, e.g., G. Goeteyn, S. Mavroghenis, M. Piergiovanni, E. Reed and D. Ridyard (*supra* n. 5) pp. 78-79; R. O'Donoghue and A.J. Padilla (*supra* n. 35) p. 283; M. Hellwig (*supra* n. 5) pp. 6-8; K.W. Lange and T. Pries (*supra* n. 1) 63.

[192] See R. O'Donoghue and A.J. Padilla (*supra* n. 35) pp. 292-294.

whether the selling at a loss served some form of legitimate conduct.[193] In its latest case law, also the ECJ seems to accept that it overshot the mark. Some passages in the recent *France Télécom* judgment indicate that the Court is willing to soften its tough stance against prices below AVC. For example, instead of reiterating that such prices are *always* abuse, the Court reasoned that prices below AVC are to 'be considered prima facie abusive inasmuch as, in applying such prices, an undertaking in a dominant position is presumed to pursue no other economic objective save that of eliminating its competitors'.[194]

This reasoning reads like an endorsement of the refined approach proposed by the Commission in the Enforcement Communication as it opens the door for the incumbent to rebut the abuse-presumption by showing a legitimate reason why its below cost pricing campaign is a rational business strategy.

V. Conclusion

The more economic approach to predatory pricing laid down in the Enforcement Communication brings the assessment of predation cases closer to contemporary economic thinking without causing a radical shift in enforcement policy. It carefully incorporates theories of harm developed by modern industrial organisation theory into the analysis thereby advancing the interpretation of Article 102 TFEU in the right direction. The strategic approaches for modelling a firm's pricing behaviour applied by the various strands of post-Chicago economics have demystified the categorical position once voiced by some economists and lawyers affiliated with the Chicago School that predatory pricing is always irrational and therefore not an issue competition law should deal with. Rather, under special circumstances low prices can be a threat to the competitiveness of markets which merits 'vigilance and vigorous countermeasures, but only if based on careful analysis'.[195] Post-Chicago economics further support the insight that rigid price/cost-rules are blunt instruments for distinguishing between aggressive competition and predatory price cuts. Therefore, a careful analysis of the market setting and the strategy pursued with the low price policy is crucial to avoid either false negatives or false positives. The three step approach (sacrifice, anti-competitive foreclosure, lack of an objective justification) proposed by the

---

[193] See., e.g., Commission Decision, *Wanadoo Interactive*, Case No. COMP/38.233 paras 305-331.
[194] Cf. *France Télécom v. Commission*, Case No. C-202/07 P [2009] ECR I-2369 para. 109.
[195] Cf. W.J. Baumol (*supra* n. 1) p. 37.

Commission is a workable analytical framework for solving the inevitable Scylla/Charybdis problem posed by predatory pricing. It provides a unifying analytical framework for assessing both below-cost pricing in the sense of *AKZO* and above-cost price cuts as dealt with in *Compagnie maritime belge*, and it corrects the overbroad holding in *Tetra Pak II*, that prices below AVC are always abusive in the sense of Article 102 TFEU.

Bringing the interpretation of Article 102 TFEU in line with modern economic insights does not mean that EU competition law will travel down the same path as US antitrust law. Even under the refined approach proposed by the Commission, the scope of intervention under Article 102 TFEU will be broader than under US antitrust law: The Enforcement Communication does not contain a safe harbour for prices above an appropriate measure of cost (whereas most US courts consider at least prices above ATC legal *per se*) and also rejects the strict recoupment-test which seems to be favoured by the US Supreme Court. To show that the predatory pricing strategy makes economic sense, the Commission seems to be committed to a more structural recoupment-test which looks at the market setting and strategic context of the incumbent's behaviour.

These strong transatlantic differences as to which prices should be deemed predatory are not necessarily the result of different economic theories followed by antitrust authorities and courts. The stricter standards for condemning low prices as anti-competitive prevailing under US are primarily the consequence of the court's efforts to correct perceived failures of the law and the enforcement system. Especially the introduction of a rather strict recoupment threshold must be seen as an effort to construe the scope of application of the predatory pricing law as narrow as possible to minimise the risk of false positives that result from frivolous predatory pricing allegations brought forward by private plaintiffs.

Given that in Europe a very different enforcement system prevails, the risk of over-enforcement is not overly strong. Against this backdrop, the more nuanced approach proposed by the Commission reflects the transatlantic differences with regard to the enforcement of the law and has a good chance of being endorsed by the European courts. In light of the recent *France Télécom* judgment, it can be assumed that the ECJ will not oppose a more refined approach to test for anti-competitive pricing abuses.

As the refinement of the operating principles is an on-going process, the Enforcement Communication will however not close the discussion on a sound economic framework for analysing predatory pricing allegations. The next challenge on the horizon will be the incorporation of insights developed by the behavioural approach to EU Competition law. This refinement will again require a combination of economic knowledge and a sound proportion of legal judgment to gradually develop an accurate analytical framework tailored to the needs of the legal institutions applying and enforcing Article 102 TFEU.

PREDATORY PRICING: A COMMENT

Philippe Choné[*]

I. Introduction

In his article on predatory pricing, *Wolfgang Wurmnest* offers an in-depth comment on the Commission's Enforcement Communication on exclusionary abuses covered by Article 82 EC (which has become Article 102 TFEU after the Treaty of Lisbon entered into force)[1], concluding that 'the more economic approach to predatory pricing laid down in the Communication brings the assessment of predation cases closer to contemporary economic thinking without causing a radical shift in enforcement policy.' Beyond the special case of predation, his view on the Communication is rather positive.

---

[*] This paper is based on my article 'A welcome advance in antitrust enforcement', [2009] (2) *Revue Concurrences*, 9-39.

[1] Communication from the Commission – Guidance on the Commission's enforcement priorities in applying Article 82 of the EC Treaty to abusive exclusionary conduct by dominant undertakings [2009] OJ C 45/7 (hereinafter 'Enforcement Communication').

The current paper shares this assessment. It first recalls the numerous difficulties the Commission had to overcome and argues that the Communication does a good job at promoting a modern and consistent approach to exclusionary conduct. Although the paper expresses nuances on minor points, the central message is that the Communication offers valuable guidance on the treatment of abuses of dominant positions under Article 102 TFEU. On a number of instances, *Wolfgang Wurmnest* highlights the practical difficulties that enforcers will face while implementing the methodology suggested by the Commission. This paper illustrates these difficulties with several recent French cases.

II. Providing guidance on Article 102 TFEU enforcement: a challenging task

The European case law often refers to 'the special responsibility of dominant firms' and to the idea of 'competition on the merits'. It is fair to say that the content of these phrases is vague. Obviously, going beyond these conventional expressions was an urgent need. But 'one abandons ambiguity only at one's peril' as was known by *Cardinal de Retz*. The Commission's task was therefore both necessary and risky.

As observed by *Wolfgang Wurmnest*, the Enforcement Communication is shorter than the 2005 Discussion Paper. The Commission has dropped a number of technicalities and has greatly improved the readability of the text. The Communication is policy-oriented, with a clear focus on enforcement, and can be adopted as a 'user's guide' for practitioners. Indeed, numerous documents in legal proceedings (complaints, replies to statement of objections, etc.) already refer to the Communication, suggesting that it is well accepted by the antitrust community.

While drafting the Communication, the Commission faced many constraints and aimed at many targets. Policy choices had to be consistent with both, the CFI (which is now the General Court) and ECJ case law as well as modern economic thinking. Above all, they had to be consistent with administrable legal rules. Moreover, the text was intended to enhance legal certainty and improve the predictability of decisions, while allowing for flexibility and a case-by-case approach. Finally, in spite of the complexity of the topic, the text had to be sufficiently short and simple to help businesses in their day-to-day life.

Some of the above constraints clearly pull in opposite directions. Consider the consistency with existing case law on the one-hand and with modern economic thinking on the other. It is not a secret that economists have heavily criticized several recent CFI judgments related to the enforcement of Article 82

EC/102 TFEU.[2] Especially criticized are statements such as: 'Exclusion is the only possible rationale for a given type of behaviour.'

Some economists have promoted an integrated, effects-based approach, whereby market power and harm to competition would be examined simultaneously. They have argued that such an approach need not reduce the predictability of competition policy.[3] On the other hand, some lawyers think of economic analysis as being intrinsically in flux and criticize the Commission for giving too much weight to economics in the Communication and for using this opportunity to go against settled case-law.

You can't please all of the people all of the time. The abovementioned goals and constraints may conflict, and trade-offs (or 'compromises' as *Wolfgang Wurmnest* puts it) are inevitable. For instance, the Commission decided to stick to the traditional, sequential approach: market definition, assessment of dominance, theory of harm, and, if needs be, 'efficiency defence'. Economists may regret this sequential process, but they should be happy that the possibility of efficiency gains is unambiguously acknowledged. Moreover, the Communication clearly sets forth the general rules that the dominant undertaking should follow to demonstrate the efficiencies its conduct generated and how they outweigh consumer harm.

III. General standards for exclusionary conduct

There is now a broad consensus on the idea that competition law should deter conduct that harm consumers. The Communication reaffirms this view, making it clear that the enforcement of Article 102 TFEU aims at protecting competition, not competitors. This premise leads the Commission to support the so-called 'as efficient competitor test' for the assessment of price-based exclusionary conduct. The underlying rationale is the following: in a competitive environment, the entry of efficient firms brings about lower prices and better quality, increases diversity. In short, it enhances consumer surplus. Therefore, the foreclosure of efficient competitors through artificial entry barriers deprives consumers of all these benefits.

---

[2] The CFI seems to integrate more economics when it reviews merger cases than when it reviews antitrust cases.

[3] J. Gual, M. Hellwig, A. Perrot, M. Polo, P. Rey, K. Schmidt and R. Stenbacka, 'An Economic Approach to Article 82' (2006) 2 *Competition Policy International*, 111 (so called 'EAGCP-Report').

The recent report on unilateral conduct by the US Department of Justice[4] lists no less than four possible standards for assessing unilateral conduct (each of which has a number of variants): effects-balancing test[5], equally efficient test, sacrifice test, disproportionality test.[6] The DOJ seems to favour the latter.

As mentioned earlier, the Communication primarily endorses the equally efficient competitor test. But it mentions other tests as well. According to the Communication, the Commission will make the ultimate assessment 'based on a weighing-up of any apparent anticompetitive effects against any advanced and substantiated efficiencies'.[7] This is reminiscent of the 'effects-balancing test'. Finally, the Communication mentions the sacrifice test in the section on predation.[8]

The debate on which test should be preferred is largely academic. The above typology is nothing but an intellectual construction designed to organize ideas. General standards are useful only to the extent that they express how the competition authority thinks. In this respect the sections on price based exclusionary conduct contained in the Enforcement Communication are conceptually simple and convey a clear message to markets.[9]

IV. The central role of time

Consumer welfare is 'multi-faceted' as the EAGCP report of 2005 puts it. A particular conduct may affect more than one market. Also, it may benefit consumers in the short run and harm them in the long run, creating a trade-off for competition authorities. The Communication puts great emphasis on time considerations and on the dynamics of competition. It rightly insists on time playing

---

[4] US Department of Justice, *Competition and Monopoly: Single Firm Conduct under Section 2 of the Sherman Act* (Washington, September 2008) <www.justice.gov/atr/public/reports/236681.htm>, 12 October 2010.

[5] This test asks 'whether a particular conduct reduces competition without creating a sufficient improvement in performance to fully offset these potential adverse effects on prices [...]. [It] entails quantifying and weighing procompetitive and anticompetitive effects of the challenged conduct.', *ibid*.

[6] 'Under the disproportionality test, conduct that potentially has both procompetitive and anticompetitive effects is anticompetitive under section 2 if its likely anticompetitive harms substantially outweigh its likely procompetitive benefits.', *ibid*.

[7] Cf. Enforcement Communication (*supra* n. 1) para. 31.

[8] Cf. *ibid.* para. 63.

[9] Cf. *ibid.* paras 23-27.

a critical role at each step of the analysis: the assessment of market power, the possible responses of competitors, the likelihood of foreclosure and consumer harm, and the assessment of efficiencies and of their passing-on to consumers.

Time is a central ingredient of competition policy in general and of particular importance in the area of exclusionary conduct. When a dominant firm feels that its position is becoming threatened by emerging competition, it may try to deter entry or to force competitors out of markets. But it may also try to *delay* the entry and the expansion of competitors.

Some economists, in line with the Chicago tradition, are concerned with the risk of over-enforcement: excessive intervention by competition agencies might induce dominant firms to refrain from cutting prices for fear of antitrust prosecutions. Accordingly, it would be more efficient to let markets correct themselves: dominant firms ultimately end up losing their market power to the benefit of efficient challengers. This approach, however, forgets that consumers suffer while waiting for the correction to occur.[10] Competition enforcers should not allow monopolists to buy extra monopoly time at the expense of consumers.

The Commission rightly notices that less efficient entrants can exert a competitive pressure on an incumbent, dominant firm. Such entrants may need some time to acquire a critical size, achieve the efficient production scale and benefit from network or learning effects. Accordingly, the Communication takes 'a dynamic view of the efficiency constraint', thereby introducing a caveat to the general 'as-efficient competitor' rule.[11] Admittedly, this caveat could introduce some degree of legal uncertainty.[12] But, as mentioned earlier, this sort of trade-off is inevitable. The equally efficient competitor test is not to be taken literally; it should allow for sufficient flexibility.

V. Cost tests as 'screening devices'

The Communication presents cost tests as 'screening devices': They serve to separate cases that deserve further investigation from cases that are prima facie of minor interest. Economists generally think that cost tests should not entail

---

[10] FTC Commissioners *Pamela Jones Harbour*, *Jon Leibowitz* and *J. Thomas Rosch* make this point very clearly in their statement, see P.J. Harbour, J. Leibowitz and J.T. Rosch, *Statement of Commissioners Harbour, Leibowitz and Rosch on the Issuance of the Section 2 Report by the Department of Justice* (8 September 2008) <www.ftc.gov/os/2008/09/080908section2stmt.pdf>, 13 October 2010.

[11] Cf. Enforcement Communication (*supra* n. 1) para. 24.

[12] For instance, the caveat may directly impact the result of a squeeze test.

definitive conclusions, drawn irrespectively of market circumstances, nor should they create safe harbours or per se prohibitions. The Communication is consistent with this general view.

Cost tests, however, could create rebuttable presumptions. Yet the Communication does not explicitly discuss the implications of cost tests on the allocation of the burden of proof.

For instance, one could envision the following legal rule to allocate the burden of proof on the basis of a two-tier cost test:

1) When the price does not cover the average variable cost ('AVC') or the average avoidable cost ('AAC'), a negative rebuttable presumption of anticompetitive effect would exist. The defendant could rebut the presumption by offering an alternative explanation to its conduct, based on verifiable evidence and grounded on facts;

2) When the price covers AAC but does not cover the average total cost ('ATC') or the long run average incremental cost ('LRAIC'), the competition agency would bear the burden of proving that the pricing policy is part of an exclusionary strategy aiming at foreclosing or disciplining competitors. The authority should articulate a fact-based theory of harm and gather a convincing body of evidence to support it. Direct evidence of exclusionary conduct would be particularly welcome in this configuration.

Such a rule would have the advantage of being administrable. However, it is not alluded to in the Communication. The Commission does not go as far as formally linking cost tests to the administration of proof. Admittedly, it is for the courts to establish and validate the legal rule in force; furthermore, this issue was out of the scope of the exercise, which has been limited to the presentation of the Commission's enforcement priorities.

VI. Predation

The Communication rightly indicates that the proof of actual recoupment is not required to establish predation. Nor is it required to show that competitors have exited the market. This is because predation should be assessed from an *ex ante* perspective. Predatory strategies may fail for various reasons[13], making retrospective assessments potentially misleading. As *Wolfgang Wurmnest* puts it, 'the Commission was also right to disregard the view that without a strict recoup-

---

[13] For instance, an intervention of a competition authority during the predation phase may prevent the predator from recouping its initial losses.

ment test', the interpretation and application of Article 102 TFEU 'rests on an economically weak fundament.' This approach is in line with the ECJ judgment of 2 April 2009, in the *France Télécom* case.

The distinction between AVC and AAC is especially relevant when the dominant firm increased its capacities during the predation phase. The estimation of the AAC requires determining a proper counterfactual to serve as a benchmark. The Enforcement Communication states that 'the Commission may also investigate whether the allegedly predatory conduct led in the short term to net revenues lower than could have been expected from a reasonable alternative conduct.'[14] Should competition authorities examine each and every possible alternative conduct? What forms may be assumed by 'reasonable alternative conduct'? In *Eurostar*[15], the Conseil de la concurrence (hereafter, 'the Conseil') concluded that it does not have the burden of examining alternative capacity strategies and of verifying that dominant firms use their capacity so as to maximize their short-term profits. The Conseil argued that perfect profit maximization only exists in textbooks and determined that, to establish predation, competition authorities should observe changes in pricing policy that reduce short-run profits. In other word, the Conseil considered the status quo as the most natural counterfactual to compute avoidable costs and establish sacrifice.

The distinction between ATC and LRAIC is particularly relevant for multi-product firms. Following the *Deutsche Post* decision[16], the Conseil used the LRAIC measure in a case where a public operator, in charge of a service of general interest, was also active on a competitive market. This cost threshold has the advantage of allowing dominant firms to pass on the benefits of scope economies to consumers. However, the Conseil's experience confirms *Wolfgang Wurmnest's* point that the estimation of LRAIC may be difficult. First, fixed costs incurred prior to the practices must be taken into account; second, the identification of incremental costs (as opposed to purely common ones) must rely on assumptions about a hypothetical scenario. In *Vedettes vendéennes*[17], the Conseil de la concurrence had to imagine what would have happened had the public operator never entered the competitive market. In a judgment of 17 June 2008, the Cour de cassation established a high standard of

---

[14] Cf. Enforcement Communication (*supra* n. 1) para. 65.

[15] Conseil de la concurrence, *Eurostar*, Decision 07-D-39 (23 November 2007).

[16] Commission Decision, *Deutsche Post*, Case No. COMP/35.141 [2001] OJ L 125/27.

[17] Conseil de la concurrence, *Vedettes vendéennes*, Decision 04-D-79 (23 December 2004).

proof for determining the parameters (e.g. the incumbent's capacities) that would prevail in such a counterfactual world.

The assessment of predation in a multi-product context is complicated also when it concerns private firms. The *GSK France* case involved two distinct relevant markets (markets 'A' and 'B' hereafter), both concerning anti-infective drugs sold to hospitals.[18] The patent of GSK's product expired three years earlier in market B than in market A. In the intermediate period, GSK was dominant on market A (as patent protection still applied) and had engaged in below variable cost pricing on market B. The defendant argued that the latter market did not exhibit any entry barrier after patent expiration and, consequently, that recoupment of losses on that market was not possible. The Conseil replied that recoupment could be achieved on market A, where GSK was still a monopolist at the time of the practice. The Conseil explained that GSK's below cost pricing on market B could serve to build a reputation of aggressiveness, thereby delaying entry on market A after patent expiration. Such a strategy is alluded to in the Enforcement Communication: 'If the conduct and its likely effects are felt on multiple markets and/or in successive periods of possible entry, the dominant undertaking may be shown to be seeking a reputation for predatory conduct'.[19] The Cour d'appel de Paris and the Cour de cassation concluded, however, that the Conseil failed to properly prove that such a mechanism was at work in *GSK France*.[20] The judges noticed that the majority of potential entrants on market A were not active on market B and that there was no cogent evidence that a potential entrant had given up entering market A after observing GSK's conduct on market B. In short, the Cour d'appel and the Cour de cassation judged that the Conseil failed to demonstrate the existence of a causal link between below cost pricing on market B and a potential foreclosure effect in market A, such a link, however, being required by the case law to establish unlawful conduct.[21] In particular, the proximity of markets (same type of drugs and same buyers) is not enough to establish causality. A reputation mechanism can help establish a causal link only if it is substantiated by concrete evidence; according to the judges, such evidence was missing. Modern economic theory has shown how firms can use sophisticated strategies to harm

---

[18] Conseil de la concurrence, *GSK France*, Decision 07-D-09 (14 March 2007).

[19] Cf. Enforcement Communication (*supra* n. 1) para. 68.

[20] Judgment of 8 April 2008 of the Cour d'appel de Paris; judgment of 17 March 2009 of the Cour de cassation.

[21] *AKZO v. Commission*, Case No. C-62/86 [1991] ECR I-3359 Recitals 35-45; *Tetra Pak International v. Commission*, Case No. C-333/94 P [1996] ECR I-5951 Recitals 21-33.

competition in multi-product environments. These insights, however, are hard to apply in practice. The *GSK France* case illustrates how difficult it is to legally prove anticompetitive conduct absent hard evidence of an eviction plan.[22]

VII. Squeeze and refusal to deal

The Communication rightly points out that *ex ante* incentives to invest are an important driving force behind competition, and it recognizes that over-enforcement may chill competition and innovation. However, it also underlines specific circumstances in which these concerns are not likely to arise. The specific cases mentioned in the Enforcement Communication are of particular interest: (i) the upstream market is regulated and the design of regulation has taken the balancing of incentives into account; (ii) the upstream market position of the dominant undertaking has been developed under the protection of special or exclusive rights or has been financed by State resources.[23] Most recent squeeze cases -in France as well as in other European countries- satisfy at least one of these conditions.

This approach contrasts with the position of the US Supreme Court in its recent *Linkline* judgment.[24] It is worth noticing that both the economic context (the state of the liberalization process in network industries) and the institutional arrangements (the respective role of courts and regulatory agencies) are very different on both sides of the Atlantic Ocean. These differences could in part explain the gap between the squeeze doctrines that prevail in Europe and in the United States.

VIII. Rebates

The methodology presented in the 2005 Discussion Paper is still present in the Commission's Enforcement Communication, but many technical aspects have

---

[22] *Wolfgang Wurmnest* makes the very same point in his paper: 'Although modern industrial organization theory provides many useful insights and their results are vital for understanding predation cases, one has to bear in mind that 'hard facts' which make a predation strategy rational, for instance by considering signal-jamming or reputation effects caused by information asymmetries in the markets, are often hard to prove in real life competition cases'.

[23] Cf. Enforcement Communication (*supra* n. 1) para. 82.

[24] *Pacific Bell Telephone Co. v. Linkline Communications Inc.*, 139 S. Ct. 1109 (2009).

been removed, making the text more readable. The Commission announces that it 'will estimate what price a competitor would have to offer in order to compensate the customer for the loss of the conditional rebate if the latter would switch part of its demand ("the relevant range") away from the dominant undertaking.'[25] The 'effective price' is then compared to the two cost thresholds mentioned earlier (AAC and LRAIC).

In the recent *NMPP* case[26], the Conseil experienced the difficulty of carrying out this methodology. The concerned market was the market for press distribution services, a duopoly with an incumbent, super-dominant firm and one challenger. Buyers were press editors. The dominant firm granted a rebate to editors on the condition that they purchase distribution services exclusively from it. The rebate was 'retroactive', according to the Commission's terminology, as it applied to all of the editor's publications. The rebate consequently created incentives for editors to use the dominant firm as their sole distributor, and it tended to turn competition for each and every publication into competition for editors (that is to say, competition for the set of all the publications of each editor). It remained to assess the strength of this effect.

To this aim, it was necessary to compute the effective price, which, in turn, required identifying 'contestable shares'. Indeed, according to the Communication, for 'retroactive rebates, it will generally be relevant to assess in the specific market context how much of a customer's purchase requirements can realistically be switched to a competitor (the "contestable share" or "contestable portion").'

The contestable share of each editor's demand turned out to be difficult to compute. The dominant firm claimed that the total demand expressed by the editors was contestable. It was, however, prepared to work under the milder assumption that weekly newspapers were not (or not particularly) contestable[27] and argued that most of the other (allegedly contestable) publications belonged to editors for which weekly newspapers accounted for less than 10% of their publications. It followed that, according to the defendant, the competing distributor could easily match its prices for a vast majority of publications. Conversely, the competing distributor argued that it could only contest market segments comprising publications of categories (e.g. TV journals, news magazines)

---

[25] Cf. Enforcement Communication (*supra* n. 1) para. 41.
[26] Conseil de la concurrence, *NMPP v. MLP*, Decision 09-D-04 (27 January 2009).
[27] Daily newspapers were outside the scope of this case.

for which it already had some experience.[28] Editors' testimonies supported this view. Additional evidence in the case file (very asymmetric market shares, capacity constraints, high fixed costs) suggested that the dominant firm seriously overestimated the share of the demand the challenger could realistically contest in the short run. It was not possible, however, to obtain sufficiently precise estimates of the contestable shares to compute the effective price for each editor.

More generally, the methodology set out in the Communication may be computationally demanding or not feasible because of data requirements. As the Commission recognizes, the quantification of the foreclosure effect is often difficult, if not virtually impossible. Accordingly, competition authorities often have to rely on qualitative evidence to demonstrate the potential foreclosure effect.

IX. Bundling

Concerning mixed bundling, the Communication suggests comparing incremental prices and incremental costs. For a bundle of two goods A and B, the incremental price of good A is defined as the price of the bundle minus the price of the stand-alone product B. However, according to the Enforcement Communication, 'if the evidence suggests that competitors of the dominant undertaking are selling identical bundles, or could do so in a timely way without being deterred by possible additional costs', then the Commission will regard this as competition 'bundle against bundle'.[29]

The abovementioned DOJ report doubts the administrability of the 'as efficient competitor test' in multi-product settings. The DOJ stresses that there is difficulty in comparing the efficiency of two firms doing different things: 'A diversified firm may enjoy superior efficiencies in joint production and marketing, as compared to a firm that is arguably as efficient with respect to the one target product. Thus, it may be difficult to conclude that a firm would be equally efficient based on the analysis of only the one targeted product. Moreover, it is difficult to measure and compare efficiencies in multi-product cases where there are joint costs.' Admittedly, these remarks make sense in the context of mixed bundling, as the following case illustrates.

---

[28] The reason was that the distribution of a publication requires determining the number of copies that are to be delivered to each press retailer, which in turn requires a good knowledge of the demand for the particular type of publication.

[29] Cf. Enforcement Communication (*supra* n. 1) para. 61.

In *Canal Plus v. TPS*[30], the Conseil examined discounts granted by the dominant French pay-TV operator for the joint subscription to the premium channel Canal+ and to the satellite bouquet CanalSat. In this case, the challenger was also running a premium channel, but of less notoriety than Canal+. The incremental price of the bouquet CanalSat in the bundle did not cover its incremental cost, yet the Conseil dismissed the case, arguing that only the total bundle price mattered and its decomposition into a stand-alone price and an incremental price was irrelevant. Whether or not competition was 'bundle against bundle' was hard to decide. The decisive argument, however, concerned efficiency gains in accordance with the DOJ observations mentioned above. The bundle rebate reflected the cost economies achieved by the dominant firm that were subsequently passed on to consumers.[31] On top of the rebate, consumers benefited from reduced transaction costs (one invoice and one decoder instead of two).

X. Conclusion

The Conseil de la concurrence (now the Autorité de la concurrence) has long advocated a more effects-based approach for the assessment of unilateral conduct. The Communication published by the Commission clearly supports this view. It will help to develop a balanced and administrable approach towards exclusionary practices. It might even influence future judgments by European courts. The pedagogical value of the Communication is unquestionable. The methodology presented by the Commission is fairly simple and can be understood by non-specialists.

Although the Communication is not binding for national competition authorities, it may hopefully help to improve the consistency of antitrust enforcement throughout the European Union.

---

[30] Conseil de la concurrence, *Canal Plus v. TPS*, Decision 05-D-13 (18 March 2005), upheld by the Cour d'appel de Paris (judgment of 15 November 2005).
[31] Invoicing and decoder management costs were reduced.

DISCUSSION

At the outset of the discussion *Jürgen Basedow* raised the question how the as efficient competitor test and the assessment whether a dominant firm has sacrificed profits can be translated into proper legal standards. A true as efficient competitor test would necessitate an evaluation and comparison of the cost structures of the targeted rivals and of the dominant undertaking. Such an approach might be proper from an economic point of view but not from a legal one: A dominant undertaking usually does not know the cost structures of its competitor and the targeted competitors are usually not willing to disclose such information to the dominant undertaking. Consequently a dominant undertaking cannot assess whether its pricing policy violates Article 82 EC/102 TFEU. This result violates the principle of legal certainty. Also the sacrifice test has some flaws as it is difficult to evaluate whether a business decision was taken 'but for' the exclusion of an as efficient competitor. Against this background *Jürgen Basedow* wondered whether the Commission's approach would yield satisfactory outcomes.

Wolfgang Wurmnest agreed that in practice it might be very difficult for the Commission to gather the relevant economic cost data in order to apply the as efficient competitor test but pointed out that the Commission does not seek to focus on the cost structures of *actual* competitors so that competitors do not have to disclose their cost structures. The test proposed in the Communication wants to assess whether a *hypothetical* as efficient competitor could withstand the competitive pressure waged against him by the dominant undertaking. To assess whether such a hypothetical competitor would be excluded from the market, the Commission will rely on cost-data from the dominant undertaking itself and will check whether the dominant firm has priced its goods or services below a given measure of cost. Only when the necessary cost-data is not available may the Commission rely on cost data of other firms in the market, provided that this data can be taken as a proxy for the costs of the dominant undertaking. In sum the as efficient competitor test is more a hypothetical market analysis than a hard-and-fast-rule. In addition he pointed out that price/cost-comparisons, irrespective of the cost benchmark (AAC, AVC, LRAIC or ATC) applied, are very blunt tools for assessing anticompetitive foreclosure and that the assessment therefore needs to be complemented by a thorough analysis of the market setting and the predatory strategy behind the pricing policy. *Christian Ewald* added that in this regard the requirement of sacrifice may serve as a tool for showing that a rational market actor would not have pursued such a pricing policy, which is often a good indication that the pricing conduct serves no legitimate business goal other than the exclusion of rivals.

Martin Hellwig shared the view that price/cost-comparisons often yield arbitrary results, which make the as efficient competitor test a doubtful criterion in the assessment of pricing abuses. *Christian Ewald* drew attention to the fact that the Commission's Communication leaves the door open for a case-specific handling of the as efficient competitor analysis to minimise decision errors (so-called modified as efficient competitor test). As a general rule pricing above LRAIC is not a violation of Article 82 EC/102 TFEU. This allows dominant undertakings to avoid abusive conduct by simply monitoring their costs. Pricing above LRAIC is, however, only a 'soft safe-harbour', as in certain market settings a dominant undertaking can exclude newcomers also by pricing above LRAIC, for example on markets with strong network effects and economies of scale on which the dominant undertaking holds a very strong position. In such a setting, the Commission will intervene to avoid false negatives, as a strict as efficient competitor test would allow a dominant undertaking to exclude the only competitors the monopolist is ever likely to see. Against the background of these difficulties *Jürgen Basedow* remarked that one should be cautious in declaring one specific economic test as the general yardstick for testing for abusive pricing strategies. Once a specific approach is endorsed by the courts, it becomes a legal concept which will be applied by lawyers for many years and will be difficult to change.

The remaining discussion focused on the recent French predation cases high-lighted by *Phillippe Choné*. *Thomas Lübbig* asked whether it would make sense to appoint some economists as judges at the ECJ as has apparently been done in France. Additionally, *Wolfgang Wurmnest* wanted to know whether French courts had put the threshold of proving predatory pricing claims too high such that the French competition authority is having difficulties stopping anticom-petitive conduct. *Phillippe Choné* confirmed that the French Cour de Cassation has appointed an economist as a judge and agreed that such appointments are useful given the importance of the economic background in competition cases. He further pointed out that the economic assessment of predation cases is very complex. The facts on which modern predation models rely, for instance signalling-strategies, are very difficult to prove in practice. Moreover, the details of price-cost comparisons give rise to quite an amount of debate as there are often various possibilities for allocating certain costs. Infusing more economics into the analysis certainly can, in certain instances, make it more difficult for a competition authority to prove predatory pricing. But, as a general rule, economic analysis enhances the effectiveness of antitrust enforcement and helps reduce the risk of type I and type II errors (false negatives and false positives). Against this background, one cannot say that the standards of proof have been set too high so that competition authorities are not able any more to stop anticompetitive pricing strategies.

Dominik Massing

PART III: STUDIES ON STATE AID

EUROPEAN STATE AID CONTROL – THE STATE AID ACTION PLAN

Ulrich Schwalbe

I. Introduction

In many areas of European competition policy such as merger control as well as the application of Article 102 TFEU to exclusionary abuses, methods of modern industrial organisation have increasingly been used in recent years. Guidelines on horizontal and non-horizontal mergers have been adopted, and a guidance notice on abusive practices by dominant firms has been published that all rely on approaches based on modern industrial organisation theory. Further, many recent decisions made by the Directorate-General for Competition and the Court of Justice employ arguments from modern industrial organisation. These are examples of the so called 'more economic approach' in competition policy. However, one area that has been an integral part of European competition policy since the Treaty of Rome has been exempt from this development for quite a long time. This is the area of European State aid control. A more economic approach has only recently been introduced into that area. There are a number of reasons for this delay in the adoption of a refined economic analysis in State aid control. First, in contrast to other areas of competition policy, State aid control does not merely rely on efficiency considerations. Instead, normative and social objectives, as e.g. equity, are of major importance. Secondly, tax-financed State aid amounts to a redistribution scheme, and thirdly, the economic relationships between Member States are directly concerned. That is, State aid control relates to several areas of economics, including besides industrial organisation also the theory of public finance as well as international trade theory, which are all of major importance with respect to the economic foundations of State aid control. Another reason for the fact that a more economic approach has been introduced into the analysis of State aid control only quite recently is due to the complexity of the subject. Only specialists have an overview of the extensive case law the knowledge of which is indispensable for the assessment of new cases. For these reasons, State aid control has formally taken into account economic concepts only in recent years. One important step in this development is the State-Aid Action Plan ('SAAP') adopted by the European Commission in the course of the Lisbon strategy in 2005.

This essay discusses the economic foundations as well as the most important points of the SAAP. It is organised as follows: The second part characterises State aid control as a part of European competition policy and outlines the legal foundations of State aid control as well as its practice (II.). The third part deals with the economic justification of controlling State aid, and gives a summary account of the way it has hitherto been practiced (III). The fourth part presents the SAAP and describes the 'balancing test' that enables competition policy to arrive at an economics based assessment of the positive and negative impacts of

State aid (IV.) and in the fifth part conceptually related problems are mentioned (V.). This essay concludes with a brief summary of the results.

II. State aid control as an integral part of competition policy

A. Legal foundations of State aid control

European State aid control has been forming an integral part of European competition policy ever since its beginnings. The introduction of State aid control was aimed at preventing individual Member States from gaining an advantage over other Member States through supporting their domestic industries. This highlights a major difference between State aid control and other areas of competition policy. In contrast to e.g. merger control or control of abusive practices, State aid control is not aimed at firms but at the Member States themselves. The firms are merely the beneficiaries of State aid. One could say that the Member States compete by means of the firms by subsidising them.

Since the coming into force of the Treaty of Lisbon, the legal foundations of State aid control are laid down in Article 107 TFEU.[1] According to Article 107(1) TFEU, State aid is prohibited (as far as it is incompatible with the internal market), provided that the Treaties (TFEU/TEU) do not determine anything else. However, an explicit definition of the term 'State aid' is not provided for in the TFEU. Indeed, the European Commission and legal practice have developed a number of criteria that distinguish State aid from other payments. Thus, a payment is considered to be State aid incompatible with the common (now: internal) market if the following 4 conditions are satisfied: First, State aid is a transfer of public funds. Secondly, the aid favours the beneficiary. The third condition is of particular importance from an economic point of view: The aid granted is capable to distort competition, or at least there is a threat that competition be distorted. The fourth condition applies to trade between the Member States of the EU. An aid granted is incompatible with the internal market if, in addition to the criteria just mentioned, the aid affects the trading conditions between Member States. However, State aid is not absolutely prohibited – there are two types of exceptions from the negative presumption. There are several types of State aid that are compatible with the internal market without further qualification. They are specified in Article 107(2) TFEU and include socially motivated aid to individual consumers as well as aid to repair damages caused

---

[1] Under the EC Treaty, the State aid control regime was laid down in Articles 87-89 EC.

by natural disasters. Finally, Article 107(2) TFEU contains a third type of exemption: aid for i.e. regions disadvantaged by the division of Germany, e.g. regions close to the former inner-German border (the so called 'German clause'). This type of aid is also admissible without further preconditions. The second exemption from the negative presumption is contained in Article 107(3) TFEU. It refers to types of State aid where the European Commission has a certain margin of discretion when deciding about the admissibility of the aid. These types of State aid are of particular interest from an economic point of view as the question of compatibility with the internal market usually requires an economic analysis. These include aid for the development of areas characterised by abnormally low standards of living or high unemployment (Article 107(3) TFEU), aid that promotes important projects of common European interest or remedy a serious disruption in the economy of a Member State (Article 107(3) TFEU). The latter section has become particularly relevant in the course of the current economic and financial crisis as many measures taken by governments have been declared as compatible with the internal market by the European Commission since they are considered necessary in order to remedy a serious disruption of the economy of the Member States. Further, payments that are compatible with the internal market comprise aid for the development of certain economic activities or areas, provided that the trading conditions are not adversely affected (Article 107(3)(c) TFEU). These aid measures have an unequivocal economic-policy objective and are thus of particular interest for an economic analysis. Further, Article 107(3)(d) TFEU states, that aid to the promotion of culture and heritage conservation is compatible with the internal market provided that it does not adversely affect the conditions of competition and trade. Finally, the European Commission may propose aid that will then be specified by decision of the Council with qualified majority (Article 107(3)(e) TFEU. Apart from these rules, the TFEU allows for exemptions such as agriculture (Article 42 TFEU) or transport (Article 93 TFEU) that restrict the rules stated in Article 107 TFEU. In what follows, these exemptions will be excluded from consideration since they are not mentioned in the SAAP.

B. *Economic foundations of State aid control*

From an economic point of view, there are several arguments in favour of State aid control. These considerations stem from the theory of strategic trade policy on the one hand, and an argument known as the 'soft budget constraint' on the other. Strategic trade policy has shown that supporting domestic industries or firms affects the competitive position of the industry or the firm, in comparison with the respective industries or firms in other Member States. For instance, a tax-financed aid secures the receiving firm an advantage over other firms that do not benefit from State aid. This may affect the welfare within the country that offers State aid. For this reason, each State has an interest in supporting its domestic industries. But the welfare in the country will increase only if the other states refrain from granting State aid themselves. In contrast, if other States also grant State aid, welfare in each country is diminished because of negative spill-over effects between the countries. This situation corresponds to a prisoner's dilemma situation where there is a danger that non-coordinated behaviour of the Member States gives rise to excessive aid payments.[2] In such a situation, it makes sense to prohibit State aid in order to prevent a Pareto inferior situation from arising.

The argument of the 'soft budget constraint' was first presented by *Janos Kornai*.[3] The problem is that if a government is unable to commit to a fixed budget, it will always be able to grant firms additional means – the budget constraint is not binding. This adversely affects the firms' incentives to produce efficiently. In case of corporate distress, a firm may rest assured that the respective Member State will support the firm by granting State aid in order to prevent problems such as mass layoffs. But if this is the case, the firms' incentives to produce efficiently are reduced, which in turn gives rise to welfare losses. State aid control may serve as an instrument to avoid the problem of the soft budget constraint since it creates a commitment mechanism that each individual Member State would be unable to achieve. State aid control ensures that the governments of the Member States do not grant any required aid to needy firms. Since the firms anticipate this practice, they face a strong incentive to produce efficiently from the outset.

C. *Previous practice*

The previous practice is characterised by an implicit balancing of the positive (e.g. reaching an objective of common interest) and negative effects (e.g.

---

[2]   See e.g. J.A. Brander and B.J. Spencer, 'Strategic Commitment with R&D: The Symmetric Case' (1983) 14 *Bell Journal of Economics*, 225-238; A.J. Brander and B.J. Spencer, 'Export Subsidies and International Market Share Rivalry' (1985) 18 *Journal of International Economics*, 83-102.

[3]   J. Kornai, 'The Soft Budget Constraint' (1980) 39 *Kyklos*, 3-30; J. Kornai, E. Maskin and G. Roland, 'Understanding the Soft Budget Constraint' (2003) 41 *Journal of Economic Literature*, 1095-1236.

creating market power or distorting competition) of the aid in question. This implicit weighing of the effects is based on the concept of 'eligible costs' that are paid to a certain extent by the State, provided that the corresponding conditions are satisfied, e.g. 50% of the expenses for measures for environmental protection. This should provide an upper bound on State aid in order to limit possible distortions of competition while the subsidised measure is an objective of common European interest.[4] In practice however, according to *Hans W. Friederiszick et al.*, these rules were applied in a strict and often rather formalistic way. As a consequence, even State aid that was likely to induce positive welfare effects was not granted when it failed to satisfy the specified criteria. The effects of State aid on market performance were not analysed explicitly. In recent years however, the European Commission has issued a number of regulations aimed at following a refined economic approach, using criteria such as a firm's market share in the context of regional aid for large investments, or the type of research (basic vs. applied research), as well as the incentive effects of State aid for research and development with respect to the extent of research in the EU.[5] In spite of these economic criteria, State aid control was stuck to the formal criteria rather than judging them by the expected effects on market performance. *Hans W. Friederiszick et al.* summarize the previous practice as follows: 'In sum, the current legal context of European state aid control is based on relatively simple to administer indicators, primarily the transfer of State resources, the existence of an economic advantage and the criterion of selectivity. The competition analysis and the assessment of the negative effects on trade are rudimentary. Economic analysis is limited mainly to the assessment of the "economic advantage" of an aid measure.'[6] However, this practice involves the risk of granting aid that, while satisfying the formal criteria, fails to induce any positive economic effects (type I-error), or that aid is prohibited even though it would entail significant welfare gains just because it violates the formal criteria (type II-error).

---

[4] See H.W. Friederiszick, L.-H. Röller and V. Verouden, 'European State Aid Control: An Economic Framework', in *Advances in the Economics of Competition Law*, P. Buccirossi (ed.) (Cambridge, 2008), p. 630.

[5] Community Framework for State Aid for Research and Development and Innovation [2006] OJ C 323/1.

[6] H.W. Friederiszick, L.-H. Röller and V. Verouden (*supra* n. 4) p. 631.

III. The SAAP

The SAAP was adopted by the European Commission in 2005.[7] It is a consultation document that spells out the objectives of State aid reform and contains
a roadmap that indicates the steps taken during the years 2005 to 2009.

A. Objectives of the SAAP

In the context of the Lisbon-strategy, the main objective of the SAAP is the
realisation of less and better targeted State aid by concentrating on innovation,
research and development, investment in human capital and the start-up of new
enterprises. To reduce the level of State aid, all measures that do not serve an
objective of common interest should be minimized. To ensure better targeted
State aid, only measures with no or limited distortions of competition and trade
should be granted, i.e. aid measures should mainly be used to correct market
failures. In addition, State aid should not be granted as sectoral aid that benefits
only some commercial sector but rather as horizontal aid, comprising several
sectors of the economy. Aid measures to rescue and restructure enterprises are
especially problematic from an economic point of view and should be avoided.
This would contribute to a reduction of distortions of competition and trade
between the Member States. However, the European Commission cannot influence the level of State aid directly, as this is determined by the fiscal policies
of the Member States, but a policy of better targeted State aid is an important
contribution to reduce the level of State aid in the EU.

1. More effective procedures, better enforcement, higher predictability and
    enhanced transparency

To assess State aid measures, the reform of State aid control has suggested a
threefold procedure where the basis is provided by a reformed *de minimis*
Regulation.[8] In addition, a General block exemption Regulation ('GBER') has

---

[7]   State Aid Action Plan: Less and better targeted state aid: a roadmap for state aid
      reform 2005-2009 (7 June 2005), COM(2005) 107 final.
[8]   Commission Regulation (EC) No. 1998/2006 (15 December 2006) on the appli-
      cation of Articles 87 and 88 of the Treaty to *de minimis* aid [2006] OJ L 379/5;
      see also section V.A.

been adopted, covering a large number of different State aid measures.[9] An additional block exemption Regulation adopted covers regional aid.[10] These Regulations increase the effectiveness of the procedures, enhance the transparency and also contribute to a higher degree of legal certainty. As the enhanced effectiveness of the procedures reduces the workload of the European Commission, it can concentrate on the more problematic cases, i.e. State aid measures of large amounts not covered by block exemption Regulations. This contributes to a better assessment of those cases. With respect to a more effective enforcement of State aid control, a monitoring of the implementation of the European Commission's decisions by the Member States is necessary, especially with respect to the execution of recovery decisions of illegal or incompatible State aid. The European Commission intends to increase the awareness and the understanding of State aid control on all levels and will more actively pursue non-compliance.

In addition to the block exemption rules, the European Commission has issued several guidelines concerning regional aid,[11] risk capital investments in small and medium-sized enterprises,[12] and environmental protection.[13] The Community framework for State aid for research and development and innovation[14] also deserves mentioning as it exemplifies how the 'more economic approach' is implemented in the course of the reform of State aid control.

2.   Shared responsibility between European Commission and Member States

As the regulations have to be implemented by the Member States, an improved execution of State aid policy, an increased efficiency and enhanced transparency on the Member State level is necessary. An increased quality of the notifications by the Member States would reduce the time the European Commission needs to

---

[9]   Commission Regulation (EC) No. 800/2008 (6 August 2008) declaring certain categories of aid compatible with the common market in application of Article 87 and 88 of the Treaty (General block exemption Regulation) [2008] OJ L 214/3; see also section V.B.

[10]   Commission Regulation (EC) No. 1628/2006 (24 October 2006) on the application of Articles 87 and 88 of the Treaty to national regional investment aid [2006] OJ L 302/29.

[11]   Guidelines on National Regional Aid for 2007-2013 [2006] OJ C 54/13.

[12]   Community Guidelines on State Aid to Promote Risk Capital Investments in Small and Medium-sized Enterprises [2006] OJ C 194/2.

[13]   Community Guidelines on State Aid for Environmental Protection [2008] OJ C 082/1.

[14]   Community Framework for State Aid (*supra* n. 5).

verify whether the State aid is compatible with the internal market. In this context, the European Commission considers to issue 'best practice guidelines'. In addition, independent authorities in the Member States could support the European Commission in the screening of State aid measures, in the monitoring of the implementations of decisions and in the execution of recovery decisions. Such independent authorities conducted the screening of State aid measures in the new Member States in the context of the enlargement of the EU.

3. A refined economic approach

In particular, State aid policy is required to follow an approach that is based to a larger extent on economic criteria. According to the SAAP, State aid should primarily serve to correct possible market failures. It is argued that, if markets fail to produce efficient outcomes, State aid might contribute to correcting the failure. When firms make incorrect decisions from a welfare point of view, State aid may provide incentives for the firms to make better decisions,

The SAAP lists a number of types of market failure that may be corrected by granting State aid. In the presence of either positive or negative externalities, State aid may ensure that the efficient quantity of the good is provided. The new economic geography points out another reason for market failure.[15] It shows that the geographical distribution of economic activities has an impact on both efficiency and social objectives such as an equal standard of living within a country. E.g., a firm's choice of location directly affects the regional job market. That is, the firm's location choice induces externalities, but the firm does not take these externalities into account in its decision making process. Such externalities may give rise to inefficient location choices. State aid, if chosen properly, may reduce or even eliminate such inefficiencies. Further, if employees invest inefficiently into human capital, e.g. due to hold-up problems, State aid may induce them to opt for a higher and more efficient level of education. Similarly, market failures arise in the case of public goods such as environmental protection or public broadcasting. Further, the existence of asymmetric information might induce market failures, e.g. in the presence of moral hazard or adverse selection.[16] For instance, asymmetrically informed banks may refuse to

---

[15] M. Fujita, P.R. Krugman and A.J. Venables, *The Spatial Economy: Cities, Regions, and International Trade* (Cambridge, 2001).

[16] Cf. e.g. G.A. Akerlof, 'The Market for "Lemons": Qualitative Uncertainty and the Market Mechanism' (1970) 84 *Quarterly Journal of Economics*, 488-500.

give credit to small firms on the capital market.[17] Credits or debt guarantees provided by the State for small and medium sized firms could alleviate this problem. Another cause for market failure is that of coordination problems that arise e.g. in the context of infrastructure, the setting of standards, and innovation. Another obstacle to efficient market outcomes is the existence of market power that leads to an inefficient allocation. In these cases, State aid could improve market performance e.g. by facilitating market entry or by removing barriers to entry.

4. Form-based vs. effects-based approach

However, State aid usually induces also effects that severely impede competition, and significantly reduce welfare. These effects may even eradicate the possible positive effects of State aid.

An assessment of the actual or imminent impediments to competition induced by State aid and its adverse effect on cross-border trade requires an estimation of the economic effects of aid measures. In this context, it has to be taken into account that different types of State aid, depending on the particular situation, may lead to similar or identical outcomes. Conversely, identical aid measures may induce different economic outcomes if there is a significant difference in the basic conditions under which the aid is being granted. Put differently, identical forms of aid may induce different outcomes in different situations, while different forms of aid may induce the same outcome. This is why an analytical approach that takes into account only the form of an aid measure usually does not achieve appropriate results. As in other areas of European competition policy a purely form-based approach should be replaced by an effects-based approach that takes into account the impact of every individual aid measure on competition, trade, and the performance of markets. The SAAP as well as the measures taken so far have paved the way for the transition from the form-based approach to an effects-based one. The desired effects-based approach in State aid control has been implemented by using a three-stage test, the so-called balancing test described in the following section.[18]

---

[17] J. Stiglitz and A. Weiss, 'Credit Rationing in Markets with Imperfect Information' (1981) 71 *American Economic Review*, 393-410.

[18] The balancing test applies only to aid measures that are not covered by the *de minimis* Regulation or some other block exemption Regulations, i.e. only to aid measures that exceed a certain threshold.

B. The balancing test

In order to examine whether an aid measure is compatible with the internal market, a three-stage balancing test is applied.[19] This test serves to balance the positive and negative effects of an aid measure and substantiates the conditions for the discretionary decision that is characterised by huge leeway of the European Commission due to the framing of the reasons for justification of Article 107(3) TFEU.

1. Positive effects of State aid (stages 1 and 2 of the test)

At the first stage of the test it is examined if the aid serves to achieve an objective of common European interest, i.e. to correct a market failure or to achieve an objective motivated by social, equity or regional reasons. In the case of a market failure, competition does not induce an efficient market outcome. But even if the resulting allocation is economically efficient, the market outcome may turn out to be undesirable for social or political reasons.

If the necessary condition holds that there is an objective of common interest, i.e. the elimination of a market failure or an equity objective, the second stage of the balancing test consists in analysing whether or not State aid is the most adequate measure to reach the given objective. The question is whether the aid will eliminate the existing market failure specifically and effectively. The reason is that, even if a market failure exists, it is not automatically guaranteed that the situation will be improved by State aid. On the contrary, it may be the case that the aid fails to achieve the desired effect, and adversely affects the situation, if the government has misinterpreted the situation. Therefore, it should also be analysed if there are possibly other market failures. In this case, the competitive situation might deteriorate if only one failure is mended by the State aid.[20] It could also be the case that there are other policy instruments available that are better fitted to the problem. For instance, if distribution is concerned, the objective may be reached through changes in the tax policy that is better able to achieve the desired goal, such that State aid may be dispensed with. Further, it has to be analysed if State aid induces an incentive effect, i.e. if it affects the behaviour of the beneficiaries either directly or indirectly. If the aid does not induce a change in the behaviour of the beneficiaries, no additional economic benefit will occur. Instead, it is a waste of taxes paid by consumers. The analysis

---

[19] See H.W. Friederiszick, L.-H. Röller and V. Verouden (*supra* n. 4) pp. 625-669.
[20] These problems are known as 'second best problems'. See section IV.B.

always has to take into account the welfare of all parties concerned either directly or indirectly by the aid. These include not only the recipients of the aid and their actual or potential competitors, but also firms located upstream or downstream in the value chain. Finally, the consumers have to be taken into consideration. Since the aid affects the restrictions as well as the incentives faced by a firm, it is to be expected that the firm will change its behaviour e.g. with regard to the quantity supplied, market entry or exit, or its research, development, and innovation activities. This in turn induces changes in the competitors' behaviour, or that of other parties concerned and thus the market outcome. In this context, cross-border effects are of particular interest, especially the effects on employment and on input markets. Further, it has to be examined what the firm would do if it did not receive any State aid. Finally, it has to be analysed if the aid is proportional, i.e. if it is impossible to achieve the given objective with lesser means, e.g. a smaller amount of State aid.

Examining whether the conditions of stages one and two of the balancing test are satisfied, turns out to be difficult for several reasons. The effects of a market failure are usually hard to quantify, i.e. estimating the welfare loss induced by the failure. This will be the case especially if several types of market failure coexist (e.g. information and coordination problems). However, if this problem cannot be solved, it will also not be possible to tell whether or not the aid is proportional. Only if the extent of the market failure is known, authorities will be able to calculate the amount of aid needed to eliminate the failure. In order to answer the question if the aid is the most adequate instrument to correct the market failure, it is necessary to examine a variety of alternative policy measures, and compare them with the State aid, which incurs considerable time and effort.

2. Adverse effects of State aid and balancing (stage 3 of the test)

If the intended aid has passed the first two stages of the test, the third stage of the test consists in identifying the possible effects that may distort competition and impede trade. Also, the actual balancing of the positive and negative effects is carried out at this stage. The State aid should be granted only if the positive effects outweigh the negative ones. As a first step, balancing the effects requires a definition of the relevant welfare standard, and the relevant market has to be delineated. Finally, the possible impediments to competition have to be determined. In this context, these effects may be measured by identifying the parties that benefit from the aid, the restrictions imposed with the aid, the characteristics of the market, and, finally, the extent of the aid and the type of aid measure under consideration. These aspects will be dealt with below.

Evaluating the effects of State aid requires a distinction between the economic objectives, i.e. the elimination or correction of a market failure on the one hand, and the normative or equity objectives on the other, such as the adjustment of regional differences in the standards of living. With respect to the economic objectives, the efficiency criterion is used to weigh the welfare increasing effects against the welfare reducing ones. With regard to the normative aims, in contrast, it is only possible to say whether the aid is the appropriate measure to reach the normative objective, i.e. if the aid is efficient and if it minimises the induced adverse effects on competition, or if there are other, more efficient instruments available. The normative objective as such defies economic analysis. The adverse effects on competition that may result have to be put up with. Economic theory can only determine whether an aid is the best and most suitable instrument to achieve the desired objectives, or if these objectives could not be achieved through other, more efficient instruments. The cases considered below involve aid measures that are aimed at reaching an economic objective, i.e. aid that is designed to increase efficiency or welfare in a market or in an economy by correcting a market failure.

3. The relevant welfare standard

The assessment of State aid from an economic point of view requires the definition of a welfare standard as a criterion. In this context, the focus is on the efficiency aims. Up to now, the praxis of granting State aid has been relying on the so-called effect-on-rival standard that measures the effects of the aid on the rivals of the firm that receives the aid. This concept is closely related to the idea of equal conditions of competition, i.e. a level playing field. According to this criterion, an aid measure reduces competition if it changes the relative positions of the firms in the market. However, this is a common effect of State aid. As a consequence, this criterion would imply that virtually any aid measure limits competition and is therefore unacceptable.[21] Using this criterion would imply that there is no way to correct a market failure and thereby increase welfare through State aid. Further, this concept does not correspond to the effects-based approach since its focus is not on the effects of an aid measure on markets, i.e. competition and consumers, but first of all on producer surplus of the rivals of the beneficiaries. From an economic point of view, however, this restriction to the effects on rivals as a decisive criterion is questionable. Usually, the competition reducing effects of an aid measure do not only affect the firm's rivals,

---

[21] See H.W. Friederiszick, L.-H. Röller and V. Verouden (*supra* n. 4) p. 646.

but they affect primarily the consumers. The criterion of producer surplus is too narrow since the efficiency of the allocation is determined by the economic surplus, i.e. the sum of producer and consumer surplus. One could argue that, in the long run, the adverse effect of an aid on the firm's competitors will also adversely affect consumers. From an economic point of view, however, considering the effect on consumer surplus directly is preferable.

In other areas of European competition policy, the consumer welfare standard has been established as the relevant criterion. Applying this criterion to State aid control would restrict attention to the effects on the final consumer. For this purpose, a short-run price development that results from the aid on the relevant product markets could serve as a criterion. From an economic point of view, however, this is just as problematic as the focus on the firm's rivals. If attention is restricted to the effects of an aid measure on consumers in the relevant product market, the effects on the firms, i.e. the one that receives the aid as well as its competitors, will be excluded from consideration. In this case, an aid might reduce the receiving firm's marginal cost and thus induce lower prices in the short run, which in turn increases consumer surplus.[22] In the medium to long run, however, State aid may induce restrictions to competition, e.g. more effective barriers to entry. Firms that profit from the aid will extend their market shares at the expense of their competitors even if the latter are more efficient. These adverse effects may be captured if the change in producer surplus is taken into consideration. In addition, aid measures may affect the incentives faced by upstream and downstream firms. This should also be taken into account in the economic analysis of State aid. It reduces the cost pressure on the receiving firms, which may result in a kind of mentality that induces production inefficiencies. A firm that can count on State aid in time of dire circumstances will not have an incentive to produce efficiently, to carry out investments, or to invest in research and development. This may induce production efficiencies since the firm does not produce at minimum cost. On the other hand, considerable dynamic inefficiencies are bound to arise. If State aid is granted not only once but repeatedly, this may induce a lasting distortion of the relative prices, as well as allocation inefficiencies.[23] Restricting attention to consumer surplus, as practised in other areas of competition policy, seems to raise prob-

---

[22] German Monopolies Commission, *The 'More Economic Approach' in European State Aid Control – Translated Version of Chapter VI of the Biennial Report 2006/2007* (Bonn, 2008) para. 201. The translated version of the German Monopolies Commission's chapter on State aid can be found in the Annex to this book.

[23] *Ibid.* para. 202.

lems in the context of State aid control.[24] For these reasons, a more general criterion should be used to assess the effects of State aid. In this context, the total welfare standard could be considered, where consumer and producer surplus on the relevant market as well as on upstream and downstream markets are taken into consideration. This standard captures all direct effects of an aid measure on the parties concerned, i.e. consumers and producers. From an economic point of view, however, the total welfare standard seems still too restrictive. State aid constitutes a transfer of money, i.e. it is a measure of re-distribution. Thus, even the total welfare standard is unable to take into account the financing side of the aid. Since the tax induces consumers to change their behaviour in order to evade the tax, allocative distortions will result. These have to be taken into account in the assessment of the aid measure. Otherwise, the benefits of State aid would be systematically overrated. As a consequence, the Eurpean Commission should follow the suggestion made by the former chief economist of the Dircetorate-General for Competition who stated that the tax payers' interests should be taken into consideration in the evaluation of the effects of State aid.[25]

The SAAP does not contain any statements on the relevant welfare standard. However, there are hints at the opportunity cost of taxation.[26] The Community Framework on State aid for Research, Development, and Innovation points out that the total welfare standard has to be applied in cases of State aid since it takes into account both consumer and producer surplus.[27] Likewise, a study commissioned by the European Commission on the economic assessment of State aid recommends a 'social welfare standard'.[28]

At this stage, it is necessary to define the relevant product and geographical market. Without such a definition of the relevant market an economic assess-ment of the effects of State aid on competition would be impossible. Basically, the same conceptual framework may be used as in merger control, i.e. the

---

[24] In the very long run however, the negative impact of State aid on competition could also be covered by the consumer welfare standard, as any distortions of competition would result in higher prices or lower quality.

[25] See H.W. Friederiszick, L.-H. Röller and V. Verouden (*supra* n. 4) p. 647.

[26] State Aid Action Plan (*supra* n. 7) para. 8.

[27] Community Framework for State Aid (*supra* n. 5) fig. 1.1, para. 3, fn. 3.

[28] R. Nitsche and P. Heidhue, 'Study on Methods to Analyse the Impact of State Aid on Competition', Final Report ECFIN/E/2004/004, CRA International (2005), p. 5.

hypothetical monopoly test, or SSNIP-Test.[29] However, in the context of State aid control some modifications have to be made. The need for modifications results from the fact that the effects of State aid may extend across various markets and economies. In order to determine these effects, it is inevitable to track these effects on firms and markets. This is the main difference between market delineation in the case of State aid and e.g. in merger control.[30] It is suggested that the concept of demand substitution be used to define the relevant market. Supply substitution is taken into consideration only after the market has been defined. The reason is that, in the case of State aid control, the distribution of gains and losses induced by the aid have to be taken into account. Therefore, it seems expedient to capture the effects on consumers and producers separately.[31] Here, all markets have to be considered where the beneficiary of the aid is active, or where it could become active in the short run. The cross-border effects of State aid make it necessary to put a higher weight on the delineation of the relevant geographical market in market definition. Similarly, the role of potential competitors should be taken into account already at the market definition stage and not, as in other areas of competition policy, in the assessment of the competitive situation on the market. It could be the case that the aid measure brings about potential competition in the first place. This in turn may be important in the context of the creation of a internal market.[32]

The adverse effects of State aid on competition may be classified into three categories, regarding productive, allocative, and dynamic efficiency.[33] In a market, productive efficiency might be impaired when an inefficient firm, or an inefficient branch of industry, is able to survive only if it receives State aid. In such a case, granting the aid will imply that the output is not produced at minimum cost, or that the output does not correspond to that desired by the consumers. In either case, a considerable welfare loss may result, in particular with respect to consumer surplus.

---

[29] The hypothetical monopoly test is explained in U. Schwalbe and D. Zimmer, *The Law and Economics in European Merger Control* (Oxford, 2009), pp. 63-78.

[30] 'With antitrust policy, the market is delineated to see whether the market mechanism will ensure competition. With state aid control, the definition of the market is required to trace the effects of aid across markets.', J. Fingleton, F. Ruane and V. Ryan, 'Market Definition and State Aid Control' (1999) 3 *European Economy*, 83.

[31] J. Fingleton, F. Ruane and V. Ryan (*supra* n. 30).

[32] *Ibid.*

[33] With respect to these efficiency concepts, see U. Schwalbe and D. Zimmer (*supra* n. 29) pp. 3-10.

Adverse effects of State aid on allocative efficiency may arise when market power, or a dominant position, is created or strengthened. Thus, an aid measure might enable a firm, or a group of firms, to gain such an advantage over its competitors that its market share or market power, increases to an extent that enables the firm to significantly raise its price, and thus its profits. These additional profits may be used to strengthen the position of the firm in other markets. Moreover, the firm could secure its position by creating barriers to entry, or drive competitors out of the market through abusive practices such as predatory pricing.

State aid may also have an impact on the firms' location decisions, and thus on the geographical allocation of economic activity. This in turn affects cross-border trade, since the streams of goods between the Member States are changed.[34]

Finally, the effects of State aid on dynamic efficiency have to be mentioned. In particular, dynamic efficiency may be reduced by changing the dynamic incentives with respect to e.g. investment decisions. In the case of aid for research, development, and innovation, it is possible that an aid measure induces the firms to invest too much in R&D.[35] The effects on dynamic efficiency are especially important from the economic point of view, since they have a great impact on the economic development of the EU as a whole.

In order to estimate the adverse effects of State aid on competition, characteristics of the relevant market[36] may be used, as well as the type and the extent of the aid, and, finally, the procedure of granting the aid.[37] After the relevant product and geographical market has been defined, the market shares of the beneficiaries may be determined, as well as the market shares of their competitors. If a firm holds a large market share already, this might indicate existing market power. The same is true in the case of significant asymmetries between the market shares. If the asymmetries are increased by the aid, i.e. if the market share of the firm that profits from the aid is enhanced in comparison with its rivals, competition will probably be distorted by the aid. In the case of differentiated products, however, market shares are less meaningful, since sub-

---

[34] These effects could also increase the welfare if firms would choose an inefficient location without State aid.

[35] A State aid measure could start a patent race where each firm invests more than the social efficient amount.

[36] A detailed survey on the relevant market criteria is provided by R. Nitsche and P. Heidhue (*supra* n. 28).

[37] The criteria to assess the competition distorting effects of State aid, see H.W. Friederiszick, L.-H. Röller and V. Verouden (*supra* n. 4) pp. 654 *et seq.*

stitutability between products plays a major role. Further, the degree of concentration is a major criterion. If the market is highly concentrated, problems with respect to competition will be more likely to occur. The existence of barriers to entry is also evidence of competitive distortions. If the market is characterised by significant excess capacities, low investment, and a non-transitory decrease in demand, probability is high that State aid will merely stabilise existing inefficient structures. Further, the effects on upstream and downstream markets are of importance. For instance, if the aid results in an increase in the price of an indispensable input, this may adversely affect other Member States. Other important characteristics refer to the kind of product and its diffusion. If the receiver of the aid is a firm that is operating in several Member States, it will probably be the case that the aid will affect the trade between the Member States, or the location decisions made by the firms.

The type and the amount of State aid also allow for conclusions with respect to the effects on competition. However, it is not possible to derive a general relationship between the amount of an aid measure and the extent of the impediment to competition. The impact of an aid measure also depends on the size of the market. While a minor aid may cause huge distortions in a small market, it is possible that even a substantial aid will not have any considerable impact if the market is sufficiently large. For a given market size, however, it is certainly true that higher aid is more likely to distort competition than a smaller one. But not only the amount of the aid is important, but also its intensity. In general, a higher aid intensity will induce more drastic distortions. It is also important to note if the aid is paid only once or repeatedly. Especially in the case of repeated payments, there is a danger that the firms learn to rely on the aid, which adversely affects productive efficiency. The type of State aid also makes a difference. Thus, aid that promotes the normal operating schedule of a firm has other effects than an investment aid. If the aid acts as a subsidy for the variable costs of production, this usually causes a direct effect on the prices, and thus on competitors and consumers. In contrast, an investment aid does not induce any immediate effects. However, long-term effects such as market entry or exit may ensue, or the location decisions of the firms may be affected. Finally, it matters if the aid is paid directly to the firm or if it is indirect aid such as a tax reduction or a guarantee. In general, the former will have a stronger impact on competition.

With respect to the procedure, State aid is granted, the degree of selectivity and the transparency of the procedure are of importance. Further, one has to differentiate between ad hoc aid and State aid schemes. The smaller the degree of selectivity, the lesser will be the ensuing distortions of competition. If the aid is given e.g. to all firms in a certain region, or all firms that exceed a certain size, this will not affect competition as strongly as a more selective aid, where just one or a few firms receive aid. A non-discriminating, open, and transparent procedure is unlikely to cause problems since it may not be used to enforce industrial policy goals such as the creation of national champions. State aid schemes are less likely to cause distortions than State aid given ad hoc. However, State aid schemes may also induce adverse effects, namely if only a small group of firms in a specific industry is eligible as a recipient of aid, if the intensity of State aid is high, and if the receiving firms may possess market power. In such a case, even an aid scheme may help to create or strengthen market power, of it may affect the geographical allocation of economic activity.

An efficiency defence, as used e.g. in merger control, is not possible in the context of State aid control. The reason is that the originator of distortions of competition is not just another firm but the State. However, the criterion of market failure, the major economic justification for granting State aid,[38] may be considered as a kind of efficiency defence. This is because a market failure always occurs when such friction prevents the market from inducing an efficient outcome. Since the Member States bear the burden of proof of the existence of a market failure, and such a proof is not easy to demonstrate, it is likely that the more economic approach in State aid control will tend to induce a more critical view of State aid, and a more restrictive control.[39]

IV. Conceptual problems of the refined economic approach

The fact that economic theory has hitherto little to say to questions of State aid control is partly due to the complexity of the matter, compared with other areas of competition policy. A well-founded economic analysis of State aid control has to be based on three areas of economic theory: Industrial organisation that analyses the effects of aid measures on competition, public finance that deals with tax financed transfers, and international trade that analyses competition between countries. Further, knowledge of economic geography and regional economics are helpful. On the other hand, difficulties arise since State aid is intended to affect the condition of both efficiency and distribution, i.e. equity. That is, positive and normative aspects have to be assessed at the same time. In addition, there are to important conceptual problems related to State aid that are discussed in the following two sections: The financing side of State aid should

---

[38] See section III.A.
[39] See German Monopolies Commission (*supra* n. 22) para. 213.

be taken into account and the correction of market failures may give rise to so called 'second-best problems'.

A.   Financing of State aid

As explained above, from an economic point of view it makes sense to grant aid if the measure enhances social welfare, or at least consumer welfare. In this respect the objective of a better economic foundation is the same as in merger control that attempts to prevent the creation or strengthening of market dominance in order to avoid losses in efficiency induced by significant market power. However, State aid control differs fundamentally from other areas of competition policy in one important respect: State aid is a transfer that extracts income from one group of individuals, the tax payers, and transfers this income to another group, the recipients of the payment. If an aid measure is tax financed, the tax will usually affect the consumers' decisions since they adapt their behaviour to the tax. The literature refers to the resulting inefficiencies and welfare losses as the 'shadow costs of taxation'. Recent studies have shown that these shadow costs may be quite substantial.[40] While the effect of the tax on the individual tax payer is negligible, the total effect may induce changes in the factor supply that encompass welfare losses that significantly exceed existing estimations.

   This is why the welfare analysis of State aid has to take into account both sides, the revenue side as well as the expenditure side. This is widely accepted in the economic literature on State aid control. 'Last but not least, it must be born in mind the government's expenditure in implementing the policy has to be financed and this is likely to lead to some loss of efficiency in other parts of the economy.'[41] Therefore, the effects of tax financed aid should be taken into account in the assessment: 'As a result we propose that the opportunity costs of funding, that is, both the direct cost of the subsidy and the deadweight loss due to distorting taxes, need to be included in the standard of State aid.'[42] The fol-

---

[40]   Cf. e.g. W.H. Parry and W.E. Oates, 'Policy Analysis in a Second Best World', Discussion Paper 98-48 (Washington/DC., 1998) <ageconsearch.umn.edu/bit stream/10687/1/dp980048.pdf>, 15 October 2010; E.K. Browning, 'A Neglected Welfare Cost of Monopoly – And Most Other Product Market Distortions' (1997) 66 *Journal of Public Economics*, 127-144.

[41]   R. Meiklejohn, 'Introduction and Synopsis' (1999) 3 *European Economy*, State Aid and the Single Market, 9.

[42]   H.W. Friederiszick, L.-H. Röller and V. Verouden (*supra* n. 4) p. 632.

lowing proposal is being made: 'Governments should undertake efforts to measure the shadow costs of using funds for State aid and require a level of benefits of State aid that is above the identified costs.'[43] The SAAP also mentions the revenue side: 'Tax payers in the end have to finance state aid and there are opportunity costs to it. Giving aid to undertakings means taking funding away from other policy areas.'[44]

However, in most cases the authors confine themselves to merely mentioning the problem. While a few empirical studies of State aid are mentioned, these are ignored in the welfare analysis.[45] The problem is exacerbated by the fact that the empirical studies of the shadow costs of taxation cannot be directly applied to the problem of State aid in the EU. The reason is that the data were derived in a framework that is not qualified to analyse the total effects of State aid.[46] Moreover, the data stem from other countries (e.g. the US, New Zealand, Australia) that are characterised by different basic conditions.[47]

The vast majority of the literature restricts attention to the expenditure side of State aid: A payment should be granted if it serves to achieve an objective of common European interest, i.e. correct a market failure or achieve a social or equity goal. If this is the case, the literature states that the payment should be made, provided that granting the aid does not itself induce substantial distortions of competition and trade. This would be the case if e.g. the aid measure ensures the survival of an inefficient firm that would otherwise have had to exit from the market.

---

[43] R. Nitsche and P. Heidhue (*supra* n. 28) p. 13.

[44] State Aid Action Plan (*supra* n. 7) para. 8.

[45] The essays by *Collie* that take into account the shadow costs explicitly are an exception. R. Collie, 'State Aid in the European Union: The Prohibition of Subsidies in an Integrated Market' (2000) 18 *International Journal of Industrial Organization*, 867-884; R. Collie, 'Prohibiting State Aid in an Integrated Market: Cournot and Bertrand Oligopolies with Differentiated Products' (2002) 2 *Journal of Industry, Competition and Trade*, 215-231; R. Collie, 'Trade liberalization and State Aid in the European Union', in *Trade Liberalization, Competition and the WTO*, C. Milner and R. Read (eds) (Cheltenham, 2002), pp. 190-206; R. Collie, 'State Aid to Investment and R&D' (2005) *European Economy*, European Commission DG EcFin, Economic Papers.

[46] The estimations mentioned above stem from models of partial equilibrium analysis, i.e. models that are restricted to the analysis of an isolated market. The analysis of State aid control, however, requires an approach that takes all markets into consideration.

[47] E.g. E.K. Browning, 'On the Marginal Welfare Cost of Taxation' (1987) 77 *American Economic Review*, 111-123.

However, systematically underrating or even ignoring the welfare losses resulting from the financing side of State aid, and focussing on the expenditure side instead, involves the danger of overrating the positive effects of State aid on welfare, and thus granting payments too generously.

In order to arrive at an economically sound estimation of the welfare effects induced by State aid, the revenue side should receive the same weight as the expenditure side. Unfortunately, this is not the case. Thus, a study on economic criteria to assess the impact of State aid commissioned by the Directorate-General for Economic and Financial Affairs states that 'While theoretically and empirically very relevant, there is little explicit use of the shadow costs in theoretical models and practical appraisal in the context of State aid control.'[48]

After all, it is exceedingly difficult to take into account the revenue side of State aid in an adequate manner. It is conceivable to use models that are employed in public finance in order to assess the effects of certain taxes. These are the so called computable general equilibrium ('CGE') models.[49] Within the framework of such empirical models, the welfare effects of e.g. a tax may be analysed, where the tax is used to finance a policy measure or a certain project. In these models, both the revenue and the expense side are taken into account in the calculation of the total effect. Further, all feedback effects of tax financed State aid can be taken into consideration. But this is exactly the issue to be estimated in the calculation of welfare effects of State aid. Of course, developing a specific model for each individual aid measure would be of little use, since the ensuing expense would be prohibitive. *Friederiszick et al.* point out a similar problem: 'As indicated above, an economic approach does not mean a full economic assessment in all cases. The obvious solution – like in all other areas of competition policy, such as mergers and antitrust – has to be a sensible combination of safe harbour thresholds and prohibition thresholds and a more complete economic assessment for those cases (limited in number) which fall in between these two thresholds.'[50] CGE-models may contribute to determining a threshold above which State aid is prohibited since they allow for a better assessment of the welfare costs of financing State aid, compared with a simple project-based cost-benefit analysis that tends to underrate the costs of financing the measure. Because of the welfare losses induced by distortions through taxes, it is to be expected that the threshold is lower than hitherto believed.

---

[48] R. Nitsche and P. Heidhues (*supra* n. 28) p. 70.

[49] An introduction to CGE-models is provided by J.B. Shoven and J. Whaley, *Applying General Equilibrium* (Cambridge, 1992).

[50] H.W. Friederiszick, L.-H. Röller and V. Verouden (*supra* n. 4) p. 658.

B. Second-best problems

Apart from the problem of the welfare effects of tax-financed State aid, the economic analysis of State aid faces another basic problem that has at best been mentioned in a footnote in existing economic studies, even though it makes the concept of State aid seem dubious as such. This is the class of problems usually referred to as 'second-best problems' in the economic literature. These problems go back to an analysis of general equilibrium models by *Richard Lipsey* and *Kelvin Lancaster* where at least one condition for Pareto optimality is violated due to institutional or other restrictions.[51] *Kelvin Lancaster* and *Richard Lipsey* show that, in this case, it is generally welfare decreasing to try to meet all other conditions for a Pareto optimum. Instead, a higher degree of welfare could be achieved by violating one or more of the other conditions as well. Put differently: In the presence of several allocative distortions, eliminating merely one of them does usually not lead to a Pareto improvement. If the optimality conditions for a welfare optimum are not satisfied e.g. because of an externality and, at the same time, the allocation is distorted e.g. due to asymmetric information, the correction of the externality might induce a reduction in welfare. The reason is that the externality acts as a counterbalance to the inefficiency with respect to the allocation induced by asymmetric information. Eliminating the externality would diminish this counterbalance, and thus reduce welfare. That is, the correction of a market failure by means of State aid does not necessarily imply an increase in welfare. The well-meaning attempt to induce a better, more efficient allocation through State aid may have the opposite effect.

This is a well-known fact in economic theory that is mentioned sometimes the economic literature on State aid control. E.g. *Gual* states that '... government intervention to achieve the social optimum is subject to the usual caveats of second-best analysis. If other distortions are present in the economy, there is no guarantee that social welfare is increased ...'[52] However, the discussion of the second-best problem does not go beyond mentioning the existence of the problem. The reason is that, in order to provide a well-based analysis of the problem, it does not suffice to restrict attention to the market where the failure occurs. Instead, a simultaneous analysis of all markets is required. However, the

---

[51] K. Lancaster and R.G. Lipsey, 'The General Theory of Second Best' (1956) 24 *Review of Economic Studies*, 11-32.

[52] J. Gual, 'Reducing State Aid in the European Union', in *The Political Economy of Industrial Policy in Europe and the Member States*, D.J. Neven and L.-H. Röller (eds) (Berlin, 2000), p. 11, 15.

complexity of the problem, the restricted availability of data as well as measurement problems render such a task impossible.

Only if the market failure corrected by the aid measure is of comparatively small size, one would expect the ensuing second-best problems to be negligible. In this case, their counterbalancing power would be insignificant. But this implies that State aid does not induce any considerable welfare effects either, since the correction of a small market imperfection implies only small welfare effects. To summarize: If a State aid measure corrects or diminishes a significant market failure, considerable second-best problems are likely to arise. On the other hand, if the market failure addressed by State aid is only small, the measure will usually not induce any noticeable effects. It is not clear how this problem should be dealt with in practice. More likely than not, one will have to assume that second-best problems do not exist, or that they are of minor importance.

V. The implementation of the SAAP – some examples

In the course of implementing the SAAP, the European Commission has devised a number of guidelines, communications, and block exemption regulations in recent years. Some examples are considered in the following sections.

A. The de minimis Regulation

The new *de minimis* Regulation has doubled the existing upper bound on aid measures of 100.000 Euros within three years.[53] That is, 200.000 Euros within a time horizon of three years are now subject to the *de minimis* Regulation. Credit guarantees are admissible up to 1.5 million Euros. However, the regulation applies only to 'transparent' aid, i.e. aid whose gross grant equivalent can be calculated exactly, and where no risk assessment has to be carried out. The gross grant equivalent is defined by the cash value of the economic benefit, excluding possible taxes on the aid. While this condition is satisfied e.g. by grants, interest grants, or limited tax concessions, capital injections from the public sector does not fulfil the condition. This implies that e.g. municipal projects that are carried out by a public-private partnership are not subject to the *de minimis* Regulation. According to Article 108(3) TFEU, such projects have to be notified, which incurs considerable transaction costs. However, restricting the *de minimis*

---

[53] Regulation 1998/2006 (*supra* n. 8).

regulation to transparent aid induces a higher degree of legal certainty, since the rules of the regulation are unequivocal and easy to apply. Further, the regulation induces significant cost savings for the European Commission, since a large number of cases may be handled without major administrative effort.

From an economic point of view, it makes sense to exempt aids of minor extent. However, there is still room for improvement. It is doubtful whether a fixed amount of for all branches and industries will induce efficient outcomes. This kind of regulation ignores the size of the market, the position of the receiving firm, as well as the competitive situation on the market. If State aid is primarily aimed at eliminating market failures, the amounts stated in the *de minimis* Regulation may suffice in some markets. In other markets, however, higher amounts than 200.000 Euro would be necessary. The amounts stated in the *de minimis* Regulation would have no effect. In smaller markets, in contrast, even a small aid might distort competition.

Thus, from an economic point of view, it makes sense to make the payments dependent on the size of the market (e.g. the total turnover), the market position of the recipient of the aid (i.e. its market share), and the intensity of the aid (the share of the aid in relation to the total expenditure on the project). This might be achieved by using graduated lump sum payments.[54] A firm that holds a large share of a small market is assigned a lower amount of aid by the regulation than a firm with a smaller market share and/or in a larger market. In the case of aid that exceeds a certain threshold (e.g. 1 million Euros), the European Commission could be granted a certain margin of discretion to decide whether to deploy a procedure. Below the threshold, the (refutable) conjecture holds that the aid does not cause any conceivable distortion of competition, where the conjecture should hold in cases of aid of minor intensity tied to certain activities (e.g. less than 30%) that were approved in a transparent procedure.[55] On the one hand, the specific competitive situation should be taken into account regularly when the *de minimis* Regulation is applied. On the other hand, however, this would incur prohibitive costs, time and effort for the authorities, as well as legal uncertainty. Further, the transparency criterion could be applied less stringently in order to be able to grant aid to public-private partnerships as well.

---

[54] Cf. German Monopolies Commission (*supra* n. 22) para. 175.
[55] *Ibid.* para. 176.

B.   The GBER

The General block exemption Regulation ('GBER') issued in 2008 summarises the hitherto existing five block exemption regulations for State aid to small and medium sized firms ('SMF'), research and development aid for SMF, employment aid, education aid, and regional aid.[56] Further, the GEBR comprises additional aid groups such as environmental protection, venture capital, and research and development aid for large firms. In total, the rather complex block exemption Regulation lists nine different aid groups with 26 different categories of aid that do not require any specific examination. For instance, in certain conditions, aid for disadvantaged or disabled employees, female entrepreneurs, or aid for the loan of highly qualified personnel are exempt from a detailed inspection. The GBER applies only to transparent aid, just like the *de minimis* Regulation.

Categories of State aid that are exempt from specific examinations are first of all those that are generally suited for correcting a market failure, e.g. aid for environmental protection (externalities), risk capital and other types of aid for SMF (information problems), or training aid (hold-up problem). Other groups include social or normative objectives (female entrepreneurs, regional aid, aid for disadvantages and disabled employees).

The regulation assigns thresholds of the gross subsidy equivalent to the various blocks of exemption to deal with a number of individual aid measures that lie between 2 million Euros (e.g. for SMF firms in order to participate in trade fairs or to avail of consultants) and 20 million Euros (e.g. for basic research). In accordance with the balancing test, the aid must have an incentive effect, i.e. it has to have the potential to change the behaviour of the beneficiary. For instance, incentive effects are absent if the firm would have realised the project even without any State aid. In the case of small and medium sized firms, it is assumed that such an incentive effect exists whenever the aid is applied for before starting the project. In contrast, large firms face more stringent conditions. Thus, the Member State has to examine (Article 8(3) GBER) whether the firm has *ex ante* analysed the practicability of the project by using quantitative as well as qualitative indicators for both cases, with and without State aid. An incentive effect will be likely to exist if the aid significantly increases the extent or the scope of the project, if the total amount of the investment is significantly increased, or if the termination of the project is significantly sped up.

---

[56]   Regulation 800/2008 (*supra* n. 9).

The GBER regulates the maximum admissible intensities of the aid as well as the eligible costs. The amount of the admissible intensity, i.e. the share of the total (acknowledged) cost of the project that may be paid by the Member State, is considered as evidence for the degree of risk of a distortion of competition of a certain kind of aid on the one hand, and for its social benefit estimated by the European Commission on the other. Here, a smaller admissible intensity is taken as an indicator of more significant distortions of competition. Fixing the intensity of State aid indirectly provides a measure for the positive and negative effects of an aid, albeit a rather coarse one. For instance, the admissible intensity for research and development projects for basic research is 100%, but only 50% for industrial research. This difference shows that basic research is less likely to be provided in efficient quantity by the market. The main reason is that basic research does not directly generate monetary returns. An intensity of 65% is admissible in the case of general education measures that provide transferable qualifications. In contrast, the intensity is limited to 35% for specific education measures that primarily inure to the benefit of the educating firm. If an aid measure fulfils the conditions named in the regulation, and does not exceed the respective block specific intensity, it shall be assumed that it is compatible with the internal market.

From an economic point of view, it is positive that the hitherto existing block exemption Regulations have been subsumed into a single Regulation as transparency as well as legal certainty are increased. Block exemption regulations may provide an important contribution to the simplification of the procedure. However, they will serve this purpose only if the exemption rules are stated clearly, and their realisation is straightforward. In contrast, the regulation stipulates a positive proof of the incentive effect of State aid to large firms, which renders the procedure costly and time-consuming.

Indeed, large firms regularly present a business plan that contains a detailed (counterfactual) analysis prior to filing for an aid. However, a closer inspection of the analysis by the authorities of the Member States induces a considerable amount of red tape, which is hardly efficient since the control is given over to the authority that will grant the aid. Therefore, it is at least doubtful whether the simplification of the procedure effected by the GBER is not counteracted by the additional red tape induced by checking the incentive effect of aid to large firms. Moreover, it is not clear if the additional benefit from verifying the incentive effect, and thus avoiding aid that does not induce incentive effects, outweighs the additional cost incurred by the inspection, especially since the firms possess an information advantage over the authorities.

C. The CFRDI

The Community Framework for Research and Development and Innovation ('CFRDI')[57] defines various aid categories, e.g. aid for R&D projects, where a differentiation is made between different categories such as basic research, industrial research, and experimental research; aid for studies of technological feasibility, aid to young innovative firms, or to innovation clusters. The admissible aid intensities are stated for each type of aid. The intensity may be the higher the less likely the subsidised activity is to be provided by the market. Thus, the intensity is equal to 100% in the case of basic research, 50% in that of industrial research, and 25% for experimental research. These differences are motivated by the reflection that competition will be more likely to be distorted if the planned investment is aimed at developing new or modified products or technologies.

Depending on the kind of aid and on its amount, the CFRDI stipulates two different inspection practices, one of which is simplified and quick and relies on legal conjectures, while the other is based on the three-stage balancing test. The simplified method is applied when the aid does not exceed certain upper bounds that differ according to the type of aid and the subsidised activity. If the upper bound is exceeded, however, a detailed analysis will take place, where the CFRDI provides specifications with respect to the inspection of the incentive effect induced by the aid. In the case of certain aid measures such as project aid for large firms, project aid for SMF above 7.5 million Euros, aid for the inno-vation of processes and organisation in the service sector, and aid for innovation clusters, the incentive effect has to be proved by the Member States that apply for the aid. In relevant cases, the Member States have to provide an *ex ante* assessment of the increased R&D&I activities, no matter if the aid exceeds the upper bound or not. The assessment is based on a comparison of the situation with and without the aid measure. Possible indicators of the incentive effect are the increase of the extent of the project, its scope, the acceleration of the process, and the increase in the total expenditure on R&D&I.

As far as the aid under consideration fulfils the criteria stated in chapter 5 of the CFRDI, and does not exceed the threshold assigned to the subsidised activity as stated in chapter 7 CFRDI, and if the incentive effect is verified according to the procedure described in chapter 6 CFRDI, there will not be any further examination. Instead, it is assumed that the three-stage balancing test yields a positive outcome. Since the European Commission gears to thresholds rather

---

[57] Community Framework for State Aid (*supra* n. 5).

than market shares, this conjecture applies independent of the size of the market and of the market position of the receiving party. If the aid exceeds the threshold assigned to the corresponding activity, the balancing test will apply. At the first stage, the Member State has to prove that the aid is used to reach an objective of common interest. The only possible justification is that of the intended correction of a market failure. This may be e.g. knowledge spillovers, incomplete or asymmetric information, or a coordination failure. Social or distributive objectives are excluded from the R&D&I framework. The Member State in question has to verify the market failure in each case.

If this condition is satisfied, stage 2 of the balancing test consists in examining whether the aid is suitable and proportional in order to correct the market failure, and if it provides an incentive effect. A measure will be considered appropriate if the Member State has already considered alternative measures in the framework of an impact assessment, but has come to the conclusion that granting a selective aid is advantageous. In this context, the European Commission allows its Member States a certain scope with respect to the assessment of the aid. Examining the proportionality aspect requires that the Member State discloses the details of the selection procedure, and proves that the aid does not exceed the upper bound assigned to the corresponding activity. Further, the Member State has to provide positive proof of the incentive effect. This in turn requires a complex and time consuming analysis. The determination of the incentive effect forms the most important component of an R&D&I aid.[58]

If the aid has passed the first two stages of the test, the third stage conducts the actual balancing of the positive effects due to the elimination or reduction of a market failure with the possible distortions of competition or trade. A sound standing economic analysis of possible adverse effects on competition of R&D&I aid requires a correct definition of the relevant product and geographical market. However, this is problematic especially in dynamic industries, since, due to technological developments, the outlines of the market are not clearly defined.[59]

In general, R&D&I aid measures may induce several types of competition distorting effects, that are divided into static and dynamic effects. Thus, an

---

[58] *Ibid.* p. 21.
[59] With respect to market definition in the case of dynamic industries, see e.g. D.S. Evans and R. Schmalensee, 'Some Economic Aspects of Antitrust Analysis in Dynamically Competitive Industries', NBER Working Paper No. W8268 (Washington/DC., 2001); D.J. Teece and M. Coleman, 'The Meaning of Monopoly: Antitrust Analysis in High Technology Industries' (1998) 52 *Antitrust Bulletin*, 801-857.

R&D&I aid may create or enhance the market power of one or several firms. Indicators of increased market power are the effectiveness of the barriers to entry to the market, possible buyer power, as well as the selection process. It is agreed upon that market shares below 25% and a Herfindahl-Hirschman-Index ('HHI') below 2000 do not cause any problems with respect to market power. Another adverse effect of an R&D&I aid may consist in maintaining inefficient market structures. Such a case may occur if the market is characterised by considerable excess capacities, if the market is shrinking, or if the sector in question is particularly sensitive.

The most important adverse effect of an R&D&I aid is the reduction of dynamic innovation incentives faced by competitors due to an increased presence of the receiving firm on product markets, i.e. a crowding-out effect might occur. However, this effect is counteracted by possible knowledge spill-overs from the beneficiary to its rivals. These effects may in turn promote the dynamic development of the market. Indicators of these effects are e.g. the amount of the aid, the type of aid, its proximity to the market, and the method the aid is granted. Economic indicators comprise possible barriers to exit, competition incentives for a future market, the degree of product differentiation, and the intensity of competition.

The classification of possible adverse effects on competition provided by the CFRDI and the transparent disclosure of the assessment criteria are beneficial, from an economic point of view, since they enhance transparency and increase the economic foundations of aid decisions in the R&D&I sector, compared with the former practice. The pivotal role of the incentive effect and the possible dynamic distortion of competition is justifiable from an economic point of view since the dynamic development of the economy is primarily influenced by R&D&I investments, where the dynamic incentive effects are of particular importance. In many cases, positive externalities due to knowledge spillovers exist in the area of R&D, such that, without State aid, innovative activity would fall short of its optimal level. In contrast, if the aid does not induce a change in behaviour with respect to the subsidised project, this means that the receiving firm would not take other quantity or pricing decisions with or without the aid. The level of R&D would then remain on an inefficient level. For this reason, the central role of the incentive effect in the context of R&D&I aids seems legitimate. If there is no incentive effect, i.e. if the behaviour of the firm remains unaffected by the aid, the market failure will persist. Further, the firm will be able to use the aid payment in order to gain a competitive advantage in adjacent markets.

To summarise, in recent years the European Commission has made extensive efforts to tackle and to enforce the reforms scheduled in the SAAP. The new block exemption Regulations, the communications and the Community Frameworks are suitable devices to simplify the procedure of granting State aid, and to render it more transparent. Further, the predictability of State aid decisions is enhanced.

VI. Conclusion

To summarise, the SAAP has contributed considerably to the realisation of a more economic approach in European State aid control. The process of granting State aid has been simplified considerably through a series of block exemption Regulations. Community Frameworks, guidelines and communications with respect to different classes of State aid have increased the transparency of the process as well as its predictability. From an economic point of view, the balancing test for State aid measures is a useful approach in order to decide whether or not an aid should be granted. As a caveat, the revenue side of financing State aid should play a more prominent role in the assessment of aid measures. While this aspect has been mentioned, it has not as yet been adequately taken into account. Including this problem into consideration would probably render State aid control more restrictive. This would certainly promote the aim of less and better targeted State aid, as required in the SAAP.

THE GENERAL BLOCK EXEMPTION
FOR STATE AID

Piet Jan Slot

I. Introduction

In June 2005 the European Commission ('the Commission') published a consultation document: 'State Aid Action Plan: Less and better targeted aid: road map for state aid reform 2005-2009.'[1] The aim of the State Aid Action Plan ('SAAP') is to provide support for the renewed Lisbon strategy and to create better governance and transparency. The SAAP has the following objectives:

– Less and better targeted aid;
– A refined economic approach;
– More efficient procedures, better enforcement, higher predictability and enhanced transparency;
– Shared responsibility between the Commission and the Member States.

---

[1] (7 June 2005), COM(2005) 107 final.

So far, 12 new instruments have been adopted pursuant to the plan.[2] The centerpiece of these instruments is the new General Block Exemption Regulation ('GBER').[3] As a result of the new block exemptions, some 65% of the State aid measures is now block-exempted. This figure will even be higher after the raising of the threshold for exemptible aid under the revised *de minimis* rule in December 2008 from 200.000 to 500.000 Euros.[4] It should, of course, be observed that this figure of 65% is somewhat optimistic in the sense that the remaining 35% are the really difficult cases with often a high political profile such as the State aid measures for banks. State aid in the EU is a very hot topic

---

[2] Community Framework for State Aid for Research and Development and Innovation [2006] OJ C 323/1; Commission Decision (28 November 2008) on the application of Article 86(2) to State aid in the form of public service compensation granted to certain undertakings entrusted with the operation of services of general economic interest [2005] OJ L 312/67; Community framework for State aid in the form of public service compensation [2005] OJ C 297/4; Commission Directive 2005/81/EC (28 November 2005) amending Directive 80/723/EEC on the transparency of financial relations between Member States and public undertakings as well as on financial transparency within certain undertakings [2005] OJ L 312/47; Communication of the Commission to Member States amending the communication pursuant to Article 93(1) of the EC Treaty applying Articles 92 and 93 of the Treaty to short-term export credit insurance [2005] OJ C 325/22; Guidelines on National Regional Aid for 2007-2013 [2006] OJ C 54/13; Community Guidelines on State Aid to Promote Risk Capital Investments in Small and Medium-sized Enterprises [2006] OJ C 194/2; Commission Regulation (EC) No. 1628/2006 (24 October 2006) on the application of Articles 87 and 88 of the Treaty to national investment aid [2006] OJ L 302/29; Commission Regulation (EC) No. 1998/2006 (15 December 2006) on the application of Articles 87 and 88 of the Treaty to *de minimis* aid [2006] OJ L 379/5; Community Guidelines on Staid Aid for Environmental Protection [2008] OJ C 82/1; Communication from the Commission on the revision of the method for setting the reference and discount rates [2008] OJ C 14/6; Commission Notice on the application of Articles 87 and 88 of the EC Treaty to State aid in the form of guarantees [2008] OJ C 155/10; Commission Regulation (EC) No. 800/2008 (6 August 2008) declaring certain categories of aid compatible with the common market in application of Articles 87and 88 of the Treaty (General block exemption Regulation) ('GBER') [2008] OJ L 214/3.

[3] See *supra* n. 2.

[4] Communication from the Commission – Temporary Community framework for State aid measures to support access to finance in the current financial and economic crisis [2009] OJ C 83/1.

these days. There is plenty of action in Brussels, the Member States and in the literature.[5]

II. The State Aid Action Plan[6]

As in antitrust law, there is a trend to apply economic reasoning to State aid rules. *Damien Neven* and *Vincent Verouden* explain the Commission's economic approach.[7] The economic rationale for State aid control is based on the following five arguments:

–   Member States aim to foster their own economic development by attracting investment;
–   Member States may also affect the competitive position of domestic firms in international markets;
–   Member States do not consider spill-over effects on other Member States. This may shift employment, rents and reduce investment abroad;
–   Uncoordinated actions may degenerate into excessive support;
–   But State aid can still contribute to sound public policy objectives and should not be banned *per se.*

The approach consists of striking a balance between the benefits of State aid and its costs. According to *Damien Neven* and *Vincent Verouden* this balancing test asks:

---

5   Recent books are: W. Mederer, N. Pesaresi and M. van Hoof (eds), *EU Competition Law*, vol. IV, book 1 and 2 (Leuven, 2008) (a 1596 page compendium written by 40 officials of the European Commission); see also P. Vesterdorf and M. Uhd Nielsen, *State Aid of the European Union* (London, 2008); J. Flett, *EC State Aid Law/Le droit des aides d'Etat dans la CE: Liber Amicorum Francisco Santaolalla Gadea* (Alphen aan den Rijn, 2008); a useful guide to the case law of the Community courts broken down by subject matter, R. Barents, *Directory of EC Case Law on State Aids* (Alphen aan den Rijn, 2008), the book covers the case law until March 2008 to the extent that judgments have been translated into English.

6   See T. Kleiner, 'The State Aid Action Plan (SAAP)', in *EU Competition Law*, vol. IV, book 1, W. Mederer, N. Pesaresi and M. van Hoof (eds) (Leuven, 2008), pp. 65-98.

7   See D. Neven and V. Verouden, 'Towards a more refined economic approach in State aid control', in *EU Competition Law*, vol. IV, book 1, W. Mederer, N. Pesaresi and M. van Hoof (eds) (Leuven, 2008), pp. 99-121.

'(i) Whether the state aid addresses a market failure or another objective of common interest;

(ii) Whether there is an incentive effect (i.e. whether the aid affects the behaviour of the recipient in a way which meets the objective);

(iii) Whether the aid leads to distortions of competition and trade;

(iv) Whether given the magnitude of the positive and negative effects, the overall balance is positive.'[8]

The benefits to be taken into account for the balancing test are efficiency rationales and equity rationales. The former consist of a correction of market failures. The latter consist of redistribution and cohesion objectives. The question is, are the distortions of competition and the effects on trade limited, so that the overall balance is positive? Therefore the aid should be aimed at well-defined objectives of common interests. It should also be well designed to deliver the objective of common interest. The market failures lead firms to make incorrect decisions from a public policy perspective. They do not take account of positive externalities. Imperfect and asymmetric information also lead to market failure. As far as cohesion objectives are concerned, it is important that positive effects are felt in less developed regions and that socially disadvantaged groups benefit.

Damien Neven and *Vincent Verouden* explained that these principles have been incorporated in the Guidelines for Risk Capital, R&D&I, Regional Aid and in the GBER and the Guidelines on Environmental Protection.[9]

III. The General Block Exemption Regulation

A. Introduction

The General Block Exemption Regulation constitutes the centerpiece of the new system. Its enactment crowns a decade-long development of block exemption regulations beginning with the enabling Council Regulation 994/98.[10] The Regulation is designed to consolidate and simplify the hitherto existing block

---

[8]   D. Neven and V. Verouden (*supra* n. 7) p. 100.

[9]   *Ibid.* p. 104.

[10] Council Regulation (EC) No. 994/98 (7 May 1998) on the application of Articles 92 and 93 of the Treaty establishing the European Community to certain categories of horizontal State aid [1998] OJ L 142/1.

exemption regulations into one single instrument.[11] A look at the GBER shows that this first objective has certainly been met. It is doubtful however, to say the least, whether the second objective, to simplify, has been achieved. The new GBER is a very complex piece of legislation and certainly not an easy read. Not only are the rules complex, there are also many exceptions. One also wonders whether this Regulation will be helpful for national courts applying the State aid rules. The Commission may well end up having to issue guidelines to facilitate its application, as it has done in the area of antitrust, e.g. for the block exemption for vertical agreements.

The GBER comprises three chapters. Chapter I contains common provisions, chapter II sets forth specific provisions for the different categories of aid and chapter III lays down final provisions.

B. Chapter I: Common provisions

The scope rules of Article 1 GBER look more like a legal labyrinth than the acclaimed simplified system of application. On a horizontal level it may be noted that the GBER is applicable to all sectors of the economy even though this simple starting point is then considerably weakened with exceptions, followed by exceptions to those exceptions. Such is the case for the following sectors: agriculture,[12] fishery and aquaculture,[13] coal,[14] regional aid in the steel sector, shipbuilding and synthetic fibres,[15] road and air freight transport.[16] Furthermore, the GBER shall not apply to regional aid schemes targeted at specific sectors of the economy.[17]

On a vertical level the GBER does not apply to *ad hoc* aid granted to large enterprises[18] or to undertakings in difficulty.[19]

---

[11] See A. Fort and H. Nyssens, 'General Framework and Block Exemption Regulations', in *EU Competition Law*, vol. IV, book 2, W. Mederer, N. Pesaresi and M. van Hoof (eds) (Leuven, 2008), pp. 762-797.

[12] Article 1(3)(b) GBER.

[13] Article 1(3)(a) GBER.

[14] Article 1(3)(d) GBER; this exception does not apply to training aid, R&D&I aid and environmental aid.

[15] Article 1(3)(e), (f) and (g) GBER, respectively.

[16] See Paragraph 35 of the preamble of the GBER.

[17] Article 1(4) GBER; schemes aimed at tourism activities are not considered targeted at specific sectors.

[18] Article 1(5) GBER with again an exception as provided for in Article 13(1) GBER.

According to Article 3 GBER, aid schemes and individual aid fulfilling all the conditions of the Regulation shall be compatible with the common market, or as we have to say after the Treaty of Lisbon has entered into force – with the internal market. There are quite a number of conditions in order for the GBER to apply. In other words the exemption comes with strings attached. It is therefore important to identify aid that is below the *de minimis* threshold because such aids come with no, or few, strings attached.[20] Furthermore, as has been outlined above in section II, it is important to identify financial compensation measures that under the *Altmark* rules are not State aid.[21]

Article 4 GBER provides rules for calculating the aid intensity and the eligible costs.

---

[19] Article 1(6)(c) GBER.

[20] Regulation 1998/2006 (*supra* n. 2). The *de minimis* block exemption excludes export aid, agriculture and fisheries as well as the transport sector. It also excludes aid that cannot be calculated precisely in advance, Article 2(4) and Paragraph 7 of the preamble of the Regulation.

[21] *Altmark Trans GmbH und Regierungspräsidium Magdeburg v. Nahverkehrsgesellschaft Altmark GmbH*, Case No. C-280/00 [2003] ECR I-7747. The gist of the judgment is that: 'Public subsidies intended to enable the operation of urban, suburban or regional scheduled transport services are not caught by that provision [Article 87(1) EC – now Article 107(1) TFEU] where such subsidies are to be regarded as compensation for the services provided by the recipient undertakings in order to discharge public service obligations. For the purpose of applying that criterion, it is for the national court to ascertain that the *following conditions* are satisfied:
– first, the recipient undertaking is actually required to discharge public service obligations and those obligations have been clearly defined;
– second, the parameters on the basis of which the compensation is calculated have been established beforehand in an objective and transparent manner;
– third, the compensation does not exceed what is necessary to cover all or part of the costs incurred in discharging the public service obligations, taking into account the relevant receipts and a reasonable profit for discharging those obligations;
– fourth, where the undertaking which is to discharge public service obligations is not chosen in a public procurement procedure, the level of compensation needed has been determined on the basis of an analysis of the costs which a typical undertaking, well run and adequately provided with means of transport so as to be able to meet the necessary public service requirements, would have incurred in discharging those obligations, taking into account the relevant receipts and a reasonable profit for discharging the obligations'.

According to Article 5 GBER, the Regulation only applies to aid that is transparent.[22] The second sentence of Article 5(1) GBER states that: 'In particular, the following categories of aid shall be considered to be transparent.' This would appear to allow aid to be considered transparent even though it is not listed in the Regulation. Aid is transparent if it is possible *ex ante* to calculate, precisely, the gross grant equivalent. The transparency condition is fulfilled when the methodology for calculating it has been approved by the Commission following notification. This system is applicable to aid below the maximum amount of aid exempted under the GBER. Larger amounts of aid should be notified individually. The maximum amounts should be expressed in terms of aid intensities in relation to eligible costs. For aid to large undertakings that are within the scope of the GBER, Member States have to ensure that the beneficiary has analysed, in an internal document, the viability of the project for which aid is foreseen. Article 9 GBER requires Member States to forward to the Commission a summary of the exempted aid measure. The summaries shall be published in the Official Journal. According to Article 10(1) GBER the Commission shall regularly monitor the aid measures it has been informed of. Article 10(2) GBER requires that Member States maintain detailed records of exempted aid for a period of 10 years. Article 10(3) GBER provides that the Commission may request information for the monitoring of the Regulation. The Article provides for sanctions when the Member State concerned does not provide the information. It further allows the Commission to require the Member State that has failed its duties under Article 10(2) and (3) GBER to notify all future aid to which the GBER applies. In other words it may withdraw the benefit of the block exemption for the Member State concerned. It should be noted that this is a different type of withdrawal than the withdrawal which is common for antitrust block-exemptions where the withdrawal has effect *erga omnes*.

Anne Fort and *Harold Nyssens* write that the Commission may open the procedure of Article 108(2) TFEU if a Member State fails its duties.[23] It is doubtful whether this is correct. The Commission can only withdraw the benefit of the GBER when this is clearly stipulated in the Regulation. Now that it has adopted the Regulation, the Commission is no longer free to follow the procedure of Article 108(2) TFEU whenever it feels like it. The Commission cannot have its cake and eat it. This seems to be contrary to the principle of

---

[22] A similar transparency requirement was laid down in the previous block exemption regulations.

[23] A. Fort and H. Nyssens (*supra* n. 11) p. 785.

legitimate expectations. It should also be noted that this provision does not address the situation where the Commission does receive the necessary information, but considers the measure to be incompatible. If the Commission considers that such aid measure does not satisfy the conditions of the GBER, it may avail itself of the Article 108(2) TFEU procedure because the Regulation does not apply. On the other hand, the Commission cannot use that procedure in the situation that the conditions of the GBER are satisfied. However, such situations will be rare.

Article 6 GBER lays down the maximum amount of aid that is block exempted. There are 14 different maximum amounts varying from 2 million Euro for training aid, to 20 million Euro for aid for fundamental research.

The GBER specifies when aids may be cumulated thus addressing the situation that arose in the Dutch petrol stations case.[24] Genuine individual investments below the threshold comes within the scope of the GBER while a series of investments by one and the same undertaking will not. The main rule is found in Article 7(2) GBER, which states that aid may be cumulated with any other type of exempted aid under the GBER as long as those aid measures concern different identifiable eligible costs. According to Article 7(3) GBER, aid exempted by the GBER shall not be cumulated with any other aid exempted by it or by the *de minimis* Regulation in relation to the same eligible costs when such cumulation would result in exceeding the highest aid intensity. According to paragraph 27 of the preamble, it may be necessary to have a look at the relevant guidelines in case of cumulation of aid that is not covered by the GBER.

According to Article 8 GBER, only aid that has an incentive effect shall be exempt. Aid shall only be considered to have an incentive effect if the beneficiary has submitted an application before actually starting work on the project. For large enterprises there are several additional requirements. These rules are an incorporation of the compensatory justification principle of the *Philip Morris* judgment.[25] This principle was formulated by the European Court of Justice ('ECJ') following its general case law according to which exceptions to a basic prohibition have to be necessary. It also follows from the wording of Article 107(3) TFEU that aid 'may be considered to be compatible with the internal market.' In the context of the State aid exemptions, this means that the aid will not be considered necessary if the undertaking itself would have made the

---

[24] *Netherlands v. Commission*, Case No. C-382/99 [2002] ECR I-5163. Article 7 GBER.
[25] Paragraph 28 of the preamble of the GBER.

investment. The requirement of the incentive is also a reflection of the economic approach. Without such an incentive effect there will be market distortions.[26]

The GBER also incorporates the principle laid down by the ECJ in the *Deggendorf* judgment that no fresh aid may be granted before previously granted aid that is subject to a recovery order is repaid.[27]

The GBER includes an anti-circumvention rule in that it specifies that aid may not be artificially divided into subprojects so as to escape the notification threshold.[28] This rule was established in the ECJ judgment on the Dutch petrol stations near the German border.[29]

C. Chapter II: Specific provisions for the different categories of aid

The GBER consolidates previous block exemption regulations and provides for new block exemptions for environmental aid, aid for SME's by women or in assisted regions, innovation aid and aid the form of risk capital.

Articles 13 and 14 GBER lay down rules for the exemption of regional aid. Article 13 GBER replaces the Block Exemption Regulation for Regional Investment Aid.[30] The GBER refers to regional investment and employment aid. The exemption applies to aid schemes. Article 13(1) second paragraph also provides a block exemption for *ad hoc* aid that does not exceed 50% of the total aid. The most important difference between the GBER and the previous regulation is found in the transparency requirements. Article 14 GBER provides for an exemption for a new type of aid: aid for newly created small enterprises. Article 15 GBER provides an exemption for SME investment and employment aid. The rules are very similar to the SME Block Exemption Regulation.[31]

---

[26]   A. Fort and H. Nyssens (*supra* n. 11) p. 779.

[27]   Article 1(6)(a) GBER; *TWD Deggendorf v. Commission*, Case No. C-355/95P [1997] ECR I-2549.

[28]   Paragraph 41 of the preamble GBER. Similar rules apply in the public procurement regulations.

[29]   *Netherlands v. Commission*, Case No. C- 382/99 [2002] ECR I-5163; see P.J. Slot and B. van Bockel, 'A case of Borderline Schizophrenia? An interesting case of interaction between the rules of State aid and the competition rules in the Dutch downstream oil market', in *Das neue Energierecht in der Bewährung: Bestandsaufnahme und Perspektive, Festschrift zum 65. Geburtstag von Prof. Dr. Jürgen F. Baur*, U. Büdenbender and G. Kühne (eds) (Baden-Baden, 2002).

[30]   Regulation 1628/2006 (*supra* n. 2).

[31]   Commission Regulation (EC) No. 70/2001 (12 January 2001) on the application of Articles 87 and 88 of the EC Treaty to State aid to small and medium-sized

cont.

Article 16 GBER, providing an exemption for aid to small enterprises newly created by female entrepreneurs, is new. The provision is designed to tackle the specific market failures women encounter with respect to access to finance. Women also face particular difficulties linked to bearing care costs for family members.[32]

Articles 17-25 GBER deal with exemptions for environmental aid. This section is new. It has to be read together with the revised 2008 environmental guidelines.[33] The calculation method for eligible costs has been substantially simplified when compared to the method embodied in the guidelines. The basic principle is that the aid may only be designed to meet the extra costs an undertaking incurs which are necessary to meet an environmental objective. The extra benefits an undertaking enjoys because of such extra investment, may be disregarded. The provisions include exemptions for investment in energy saving, high-efficiency cogeneration and renewables. The provisions on environmental aid in the form of tax reductions include only a part of the guidelines.

Article 29 GBER provides for an exemption for aid in the form of risk capital. This is a new form of aid block exempted under the Regulation. The rules are similar to those laid down in the Risk Capital Guidelines.[34] Only public equity participations in investment funds are block exempted.

Articles 30-37 GBER provide rules for the exemption of aid for research, development and innovation. They incorporate the rules of the 2004 Block Exemption Regulation.[35] The GBER also covers R&D project aid and aid for technical feasibility studies for large enterprises. This was not the case under the 2004 rules which restricted the exemption to SME's.

Article 38 and 39 GBER block exempt training aid. The rules largely correspond to the rules of the 2001 Block Exemption Regulation.[36] The notification ceiling has been raised from 1 to 2 million Euro. *Ad hoc* training aid for

---

enterprises [2001] OJ L 10/33, amended by Commission Regulation (EC) No. 364/2004 (25 February 2004) amending Regulation (EC) No. 70/2001 as regards the extension of its scope to include aid for research and development [2004] OJ L 63/22.

[32] Paragraph 44 of the preamble of the GBER.

[33] Community Guidelines on Staid Aid for Environmental Protection (*supra* n. 2).

[34] Community Guidelines on State Aid to Promote Risk Capital Investments in Small and Medium-sized Enterprises (*supra* n. 2) section 4.

[35] Regulation 364/2004 (*supra* n. 31).

[36] Commission Regulation (EC) No. 68/2001 (12 January 2001) on the application of Articles 87 and 88 of the EC Treaty to training aid [2001] OJ L 10/20.

large undertakings is not covered whilst under the previous rules it was. On the other hand, the eligible costs basis for providing the aid has been extended.

Articles 40-42 GBER provide a block exemption for disadvantaged and disabled persons. There are some minor differences between the Regulation and the corresponding rules in the 2002 Employment Regulation.[37] The definition of disadvantaged worker has been simplified and a new category of severely disadvantaged worker has been introduced. The provision on aid for the recruitment of disabled and disadvantaged persons has been clarified.

D. *Chapter III: Transitional provisions*

Article 44(1) GBER provides that the Regulation shall apply to individual aid granted before its entry into force if it fulfills all the conditions of this Regulation. Exemptions under the previous block exemption regulations continue to apply. The enactment of the GBER does not create an obligation for Member States to amend existing aid schemes not covered by the previous block exemption regulations.[38]

IV. Comment

The GBER is a rather complex piece of legislation. The rules are differentiated according to different criteria and there are several exceptions to the main rule and, furthermore, there are exceptions to the exceptions. This will not make it easy for national courts to apply. Furthermore, it should be noted that, at the same time, the Commission has continued to adopt guidelines, communications and notices. As a result a substantial body of substantive rules has been developed.

It may therefore be useful to sketch the way in which Member State measures under the new State aid rules will be analysed. First, it should be

---

[37] Commission Regulation (EC) No. 2204/2002 (12 December 2002) on the application of Articles 87 and 88 of the EC Treaty to State aid for employment [2002] OJ L 337/3, corrected by Corrigendum to Commission Regulation (EC) No. 2204/2002 (12 December 2002) on the application of Articles 87 and 88 of the EC Treaty to State aid for employment [2002] OJ L 349/126.

[38] A. Fort and H. Nyssens (*supra* n. 11) p. 796. They refer to the judgment *Belgium v. Commission*, Case No. C-110/03 [2005] ECR I-2801.

verified whether or not the aid is exempted by the *de minimis* rules.[39] If it is not, it should be ascertained what type of aid is involved. Next it should be checked whether the measure is exempted under the GBER. If not, it should be assessed whether the measure is exempted by any other block exemption. If not, then it should be analysed under the relevant guideline or communication. Finally, if there are no guidelines or communications or relevant individual Commission decisions, an individual assessment should be made. When making such an individual assessment the principles laid down in the regulations and the guidelines and communications will be applied in the context of such cases.

It remains to be seen whether the Commission's objective of simplifying the application of the rules will be achieved.

---

[39]   It should be remembered that Regulation 1998/2006 (*supra* n. 2) was temporarily amended in December 2008 so that the minimum was raised to 500,000 Euro.

DISCUSSION

At the outset of the discussion *Jürgen Basedow* stressed the political dimension of State aid, which often forms a popular instrument for attracting votes. Therefore, there is a certain tension between politicians, who, in a rather short-time perspective, dislike State aid control, and the long-term perspective of the respective departments of government which have to deal with the resulting problems created by State aid in later years. He further pointed out that the European State aid policy can only be understood if one has its origins in mind. After World War II competition was not so much viewed as a rivalry between single undertakings, but rather between national economies. The task of the European competition rules was therefore to keep national markets open to competition. Although in the course of the last fifty years the understanding of competition has changed as the internal market has developed, the single market goal is still important. State aid control is still a key to ensure that national borders are not resurrected to the detriment of competition. Afterwards he highlighted the significant differences between the enforcement mechanisms of Articles 81 EC/101 TFEU and 82 EC/TFEU on the one hand and Article 87 EC/107 TFEU on the other. In cases of an infringement of Articles 81 EC/101 TFEU and 82 EC/102 TFEU there exists a possibility of private enforcement, not necessarily in the sense of damages actions, but in the sense of questioning the validity of an agreement under Article 81(2) EC/101(2) TFEU. In turn, in State aid cases such remedies exist only to a very limited extent. It is exclusively Article 88(3) EC/108(3) TFEU that is potentially enforced by private action. But all decisions relating to the substance of State aid control are taken by the Commission. Thus, there is no other decision-making body in respect of these matters. The powers of the European Court of Justice are equally limited; it may only be asked to review the respective decisions of the Commission to the extent the law has been applied.

Ulrich Schwalbe agreed that often political considerations which are unsound from an economic point of view are used to pay out State aid. As a striking example mentioned the *Holzmann*-case, where the political motivation behind the aid granted turned out to be very costly for the tax-payer. In that case, the German Chancellor *Gerhard Schröder* decided to grant a considerable amount of money to a failing construction company which went bankrupt a few years later.

Martin Hellwig added that the very beginning of the common market was characterised by the abolition of tariff barriers. There was a concern that this abolition of trade barriers, mandated by the EEC Treaty, might be compensated by Member State governments through State aid. One of the forms of State aid contemplated at the time had been subsidies afforded to a particular national industry. In his view those concerns have very little to do with competition but are primarily related to industrial policy. This leads to the question why the provisions on State aid control were placed in the competition section of the EEC Treaty. But it also raises the question whether we are nowadays justified in thinking about it mainly in terms of the individual player-orientated approach of competition policy. Thus, he wondered whether it is appropriate to address the wide array of political economy issues that form part of the analysis of State aid in the general framework of competition analysis.

In the further discussion it was agreed that State aid control must at least to ask the question whether or not an aid has a specific bearing on competition in a given market. *Justus Haucap* stressed that in this context one has to decide what type of competition should be regulated by the State aid rules: the competition between Member States or the one between firms in the market. In the former case one has to bear in mind that the overall economic effects are rather unclear. There appears to be agreement that increases in subsidies are harmful because they are likely to damage the national budget. But it is still open if they are harmful from a welfare perspective as they may benefit consumers and producers. Thus, a balancing test might lead to a positive overall welfare effect. He also pointed out that in large investment cases a competition analysis is included in the review of regional aid. The question is whether the size of the investment or the market share of the respective firm in the relevant market is the optimal trigger for an investigation. In all other areas of competition policy the market share or an equivalent threshold forms the relevant trigger. Thus, regional aid is the only area in competition policy in which the size of the investment forms the relevant threshold. *Justus Haucap* questioned whether the size of an investment could really be the optimal trigger, since it is not linked to the size of the relevant market. In small markets a small investment may seriously affect the market structure whereas the same investment in a bigger market may not have any effect on competition at all. Thus, market share considerations may be more appropriate even in State aid cases.

Against this background *Lukas Repa* first clarified that in the field of State aid the threshold is actually often a combination of market shares and the size of investment. It would certainly be interesting to discuss whether the investment size rather than market shares is an 'ideal' threshold. Indeed, while in other areas of EU competition policy the Commission uses market shares for determining whether an investigation should be started, while in the field of State aid, absolute figures such as the size of the investment are more important. One factual problem the Commission services face with establishing market shares in the field of State aid is that the Commission does not dispose of the same powerful investigative tools to obtain relevant data directly from companies as it does, for instance, dispose of in antitrust or in merger investigations. As a consequence, the application of thresholds which are exclusively or predominantly linked to a market share may be difficult in the State aid practice. Member States also need legal security when deciding on whether or not to notify an aid. This, too, speaks in favour of (also) using absolute figures rather than (only) market shares.

Dominik Massing

PART IV: ROUND TABLE ON STATE AID

THE NEED FOR A MORE ECONOMIC APPROACH

Jürgen Kühling

I. Introduction

Before evaluating the consequences of the application of the more economic approach in the field of State aid law, one has to clarify what exactly is meant when referring to a more economic approach. In this paper a more economic approach refers to a more reflected approach when applying the law – an approach which considers the economic effects of the application of law more precisely and an approach which applies the law in a way as to achieve a better economic outcome. Thus, it does not imply a specific economic concept and, particularly, not necessarily a more effects based approach or an industrial economics approach.

Furthermore, what kind of concept is to be applied is the result of a more economic approach and not an underpinning assumption. Hence the concept may vary within the various fields of competition law.

The basic aims of the application of the more economic approach to State aid law as outlined by the European Commission ('the Commission') in the State Aid Action Plan[1] are convincing: less and more targeted State aid, stricter cost-benefit-analysis, a stricter test whether there is a market failure or a cohesion justification for a State aid, more transparency, more legal certainty. Only the consequences of a better reflection on the principle of subsidiarity in the area of State aid law remain unclear. Maybe the Commission is being too modest here.[2] Even if the main subject of State aid law is to avoid negative cross-border effects, one may argue from a point of view of federal economics that avoiding self-commitment problems is a sufficient rationale as well. This is, in fact, the case as national authorities tend to damage national economies by giving too many State aids and central authorities such as the Commission might be in a better position to solve such problems.

If we have a look at the implementation of the more economic approach one has to differentiate between the application of a more economic approach at the first stage of State aid control – the so called jurisdictional stage – guided by the question 'Is there a State aid in the sense of Article 107(1) TFEU?', and the second step of the assessment, the compatibility test, guided by the question 'Facing the aims pursued by the State aid and the disadvantages for the competition and trade within the EU, can we accept the State aid according to Article 107(2) and (3) TFEU?'. Moreover, particularly with a view to the second step of the assessment one has to differentiate between general rules on the application of law and individual impact analyses.

II. The notion of State aid

With respect to the first step, the notion of State aid, the European Court of Justice ('ECJ') usually refers to four conditions which a measure must satisfy under Article 107(1) TFEU to be regarded as State aid:

---

[1] State Aid Action Plan: Less and better targeted state aid: A roadmap for state aid reform 2005-2009 (7 June 2005), COM(2005) 107 final; cf. also *Ulrich Schwalbe* pp. 161 *et seq.* in this book.

[2] Cf. H.W. Friederiszick, L.-H. Röller and V. Verouden, 'European State Aid Control: An economic framework', in *Advances in the Economics of Competition Law*, P. Buccirossi (ed.) (Cambridge/Mass., forthcoming), section IV.

- first, advantage on a specific[3] recipient,
- second, there must be an intervention by the State or through State resources,
- third, it must distort or threaten to distort competition and
- fourth, the intervention must be liable to affect trade between Member States[4]

So far, the more economic approach has hardly played any role at the level of Article 107(1) TFEU. One reason for this is of course that it is the ECJ which ultimately decides on the application of Article 107(1) TFEU and not the Commission. Thus, it is not within the power of the Commission to attach more influence to a more economic approach at that level. The Commission may try, but it all depends on the ECJ. This does not mean, of course, that there is no economic reflection at that level. For instance, the market economy investor test[5] is certainly influenced by an economic reflection.

In some recent decisions the ECJ has underlined its full review and factually reduced any leeway of the Commission at the first level. As far as the review by the Court is concerned, the ECJ has ruled in a number of cases that the legal concept of State aid must be interpreted on the basis of objective factors. Therefore, the European courts carry out a comprehensive review as to whether or not a measure falls within the scope of Article 107(1) TFEU. Thus, the courts do thoroughly review the Commission's appraisal of the facts and the applicable rules.[6]

---

[3] More precisely, specificity is a further criterion, cf. C. Koenig, J. Kühling and N. Ritter, *EG-Beihilfenrecht* 2nd ed (Frankfurt am Main, 2005), pp. 124 *et seq.*
[4] *Confédération nationale du Crédit mutuel v. Commisson*, Case No. T-93/02 [2005] ECR II-143 para. 77.
[5] Cf. L. Hancher, 'Public Sector Aid', in *EC State Aids* 3rd ed, L. Hancher, T.R. Ottervanger and P.J. Slot (London, 2006), para. 8-016 *et seq.*
[6] See *France v. Ladbroke Racing and Commission*, Case No. C-83/98 P [2000] ECR I-3271 para. 25; *Linde v. Commission*, Case No. T-98/00 [2002] ECR II-3961 para. 40; J.-D. Braun and J. Kühling, 'Article 87 EC and the Community courts: From revolution to evolution' (2008) 45 *Common Market Law Review*, 465, 468 *et seq.*

A. Case review by the Court and proof that there is an advantage – the necessity for a more economic approach at the level of the notion of State aid

Nevertheless, there is one important exception to this principle. In cases in which a complex economic assessment is involved case review by the courts can be restricted.[7] This case law has been refined by the ECJ in the *Valmont*[8] case with a view to the criterion of an advantage for sales of land and buildings by public authorities. Initially, the ECJ only states that there is a full review by the Courts on the question if there were reports devoid of any evidential value referred to by the Commission in order to conclude that there was an element of State aid in the sale of land. This is persuasive as such a question does not involve any complex economic appraisal.[9] But the following review of the Court goes far beyond such a rather self-evident statement. The Court analysed in depth whether the Commission had found sufficient proof to assume that there was State aid. This comprised a strict analysis of all the evidence provided by the Commission. At the end of the day this strict control by the ECJ implies that the Commission has to provide 'proof' of a difference in price between the actual sale and the market prices at that specific time. Even if the Commission may refer to consultants in order to find such proof, this does not exempt the Commission from assessing their work as it is its central and exclusive responsibility to ensure that 107 TFEU (ex-Article 87 EC) is observed and Article 108 TFEU (ex-Article 88 EC) is implemented.[10] This responsibility is subject to full judicial review. As the Commission's conclusion in *Valmont* was not sufficiently supported by the expert's report to which the Commission referred, it had misapplied EU State aid law.[11]

Apart from what follows from the *Valmont* case, the task of the Commission is additionally burdened by the fact that the ECJ has recently applied a strict standard in assessing the quality of the reasons given by the Commission in order to identify measures treated as State aid. In the case *Crédit mutuel*[12] the

---

[7] See *Belgium v. Commission*, Case No. C-56/93 [1996] ECR I-723 para. 11; *Italy and SIM 2 Multimedia v. Commission*, joined Cases No. C-328/99 and C-399/00 [2003] ECR I-4035 para. 39.

[8] *Valmont Nederland BV v. Commission*, Case No. T-274/01 [2004] ECR II-3145.

[9] *Ibid.* para. 43.

[10] *Ibid.* para. 72.

[11] *Ibid.* paras 88-90.

[12] *Confédération nationale du Crédit mutuel v. Commission*, Case No. T-93/02 [2005] ECR II-3145 paras 120-127.

Court referred to its *BASF* judgment[13] and stated that with regard to the principle of collegiate responsibility the operative part and the statement of reasons of a Commission decision constitute an indivisible whole. This is the case for all decisions which must be reasoned under Article 296 TFEU (ex-Article 253 EC). Commission decisions on State aid clearly belong to that category. Thus, the reasoning of a decision cannot be changed by the Commission's agents before the Court but only by the College of Commissioners. By consequence, the reasoning put forward in front of the Court must at least be implied by the Commission's original decision and cannot be considered by the Court if it is contradicted by passages of the decision in question. Otherwise the decision does not state sufficient reasons and is in breach of Article 296 TFEU (ex-Article 253 EC).

Thus, the Commission will in the future need to deploy *more economic* reasoning in order to prove that there is a State aid. This will open the door for a more economic approach also at the level of the notion of State aid.

B. A more economic reflection on the application of the criterion 'State resources'

With respect to the interpretation of the criterion of State resources there is definitely the need for a better economic reflection. However, it is not the Commission but rather the ECJ which must be blamed for creating unnecessary confusion. In the *PreussenElektra* judgment the Court said that there must be a burden on State resources in order to fulfil that specific criterion.[14] As a result, the State measure at issue, a purchase obligation of energy at prices fixed by law, was not considered to be State aid. In contrast, the Court considered in the more recent *Bayrischer Rundfunk* judgment public broadcasting fees as State aid.[15] Even if this decision refers to the public procurement framework, two notions of State financing should not exist – one with view to State aid law and one with view to public procurement law. Thus, it seems contradictory that the

---

[13] *Commission v. BASF and Others*, Case No. C-137/92 P [1994] ECR I-2555 paras 66-68.

[14] *PreussenElektra v. Schleswag*, Case No. C-379/98 [2001] ECR I-2099.

[15] *Bayerischer Rundfunk a.o. v. GEWA*, Case No. C-337/06 [2007] ECR I-11173 para. 41 *et seq.*; cf. also *SIC v. Commission*, Case No. T-442/03 [2008] ECR II-1161 para. 45, in which the requirement concerning the involvement of State resources was not in dispute and it was not contested that it was fulfilled. But the case concerned tax exemptions which are a clear case of advantages emanating from State resources.

European courts exclude the purchase obligation in the *PreussenElektra* situation as not emanating from State resources whereas the German public broadcasting fees do. The Court emphasises three aspects in its line of argument in the *Bayrischer Rundfunk* case: (1) the fees have been introduced by legislation, (2) they are guaranteed by the State and (3) recovered with State support. Points 1 and 2 do not differ in the *PreussenElektra* situation. Hence, one has to wonder whether it should really be relevant if a certain claim is collected by State authorities or if one ultimately has to go to court to litigate one's claim against a consumer. From an economic point of view that cannot make any difference. Thus, it is true what the Court emphasises: It cannot make a difference whether a private party is the direct beneficiary of monetary aid (either by fees collected from third parties and later distributed by the State or by immediate payments required of third parties to the advantaged private party) or whether a private party benefits from a purchase obligation requiring third parties to buy a particular good or service. In other words, the ECJ was wrong in *Preussen-Elektra*.[16] The distribution of all resources directed by the State should be considered as State resources in the sense of Article 107 (1) TFEU. A more economic approach may help to decide on those questions in any case.

C. A stricter and more economic approach to the criteria of 'distortion of competition' and 'trade between Member States'?

Some economists have asked the Commission to apply the more economic approach with respect to the criterion of distortion of competition and trade between Member States[17], even if it may mean that the reach of State aid control is reduced to some extent. Again, this mostly depends on the case-law of the ECJ. Some recent developments indicate that the Commission may now be subject to stricter scrutiny in respect to its duty of showing that there is a distortion of competition and that trade between Member States is affected.

---

[16] C. Koenig, J. Kühling and N. Ritter (*supra* n. 3) pp. 162 *et seq.*; W. Möschel, 'Der „more economic approach" in der Beihilfenkontrolle – Überlegungen aus juristischer Perspektive', in *Der „More economic approach" in der Beihilfenkontrolle*, P. Oberender (ed.) (Berlin, 2008), pp. 39, 43 *et seq.*

[17] Very prominently, the German Monopolies Commission, *The 'More Economic Approach' in European State Aid Control – Translated Version of Chapter VI of the Biennial Report 2006/2007* (Bonn, 2008) para. 122 *et seq.* The translated version of the German Monopolies Commission's chapter on State aid can be found in the Annex to this book.

So far it is established case-law that the scheme of the decision of the Commission must set out sufficiently the facts and legal considerations of essential importance, 'allowing the applicants and the Court to ascertain the reasons for the Commission's view that the transaction at issue led to a distortion of competition and affected trade within the Union'.[18] As it is also settled case-law that any State measure which can relieve an undertaking of the expenses which it usually has to bear in principle distorts competition[19], it has thus far not been very difficult to establish that this condition was satisfied. Yet in its *Ter Lembeek* judgment, the Court of First Instance ('CFI'), which has recently become the General Court, added with reference to its *Vlaamse Gewest* judgment[20] that a distortion of competition or a risk of such a distortion usually occurs in a sector characterised by intense competition. If this turned into a necessary precondition, the Commission would then be forced to dwell on the question how intense the competition is in the sector at issue. But the CFI does not really seem to imply such a strict test as it refers in its *Ter Lembeek* judgment merely to the fact that the sector is 'entirely open to competition' which is a much more lenient test. As it is sufficient to establish that the State measure 'threatens to distort competition' according to the wording of Article 107(1) TFEU, it is submitted that such a more lenient test is also the more convincing one. Even if competition is distorted to a lesser extent it will still be distorted, and thus this condition of Article 107(1) TFEU is satisfied; State aid may only be justified more easily as a result.

With respect to the affection of trade between Member States things might be different as distortions of competition do not necessarily have to have negative cross-border effects; it is the central rationale for EU State aid control to avoid such cross-border externalities.[21] By consequence, in absence of such effects the legitimacy of European State aid control might be questioned.[22] Thus it would not be surprising if the Commission and the Court took this criterion more seriously in future and ask for a more developed reasoning on this point. So far it has always been sufficient to show that there is trade between the

---

[18] Cf. most recently *Ter Lembeek International NV v. Commission*, Case No. T-217/02 [2006] ECR II-4483 para. 246.

[19] Cf. *ibid.* para. 177.

[20] *Vlaamse Gewest v. Commission*, Case No. T-214/95 [1998] ECR II-717 para. 46.

[21] Cf. H.W. Friederiszick, L.-H. Röller and V. Verouden (*supra* n. 2) section IV.

[22] Although one may argue that avoiding commitment problems is a sufficient rationale as well since national authorities tend to damage national economies by giving too many State aids and central authorities such as the Commission might be in a better position to solve such problems, cf. for this discussion, *ibid.*

Member State in question and other States and/or that the undertaking at issue is exporting its products[23] or – at least – that future influences cannot be excluded.[24] A harbinger of such a development is the famous *Dorsten* decision[25] in which the Commission referred to this criterion and decided that a public swimming pool as the one *in casu* did not attract costumers living more than 50 kilometres away from it and since the Dutch-German frontier was in such a distance that trade between Member States could not have been affected.[26]

With respect to both the conditions, 'distortion of competition' and 'affecting trade between Member States', the *Le Levant* case of the CFI (now: the General Court) seems to be quite remarkable as it is one of the few[27] cases in which the Court has declared the Commission's reasoning on the condition 'distortion of competition' as insufficient.[28] The case dealt with a decision in which the Commission considered a French State aid as being incompatible with the internal Market and ordered its recovery. The measure in question consisted of ensuring under a French law the financing and operation of the cruise vessel Le Levant by investors. Those investors were natural persons who founded one-person limited liability undertakings, constituted solely for that purpose and brought together in a co-ownership. The vessel was then leased to another undertaking (La Com-

---

[23] Cf. recently *Ter Lembeek International NV v. Commission*, Case No. T-217/02 [2006] ECR II-4483 para. 177.

[24] *Philip Morris Holland BV v. Commission*, Case No. 730/79 [1980] ECR 2671 para. 11; for further references, cf. C. Koenig, J. Kühling and N. Ritter (*supra* n. 3) para. 181 *et seq.*

[25] Commission Decision, *Freizeitbad Dorsten*, N 258/00 (12 January 2001) para. 3.

[26] Although one has to keep in mind that the *Dorsten* constellation was a very special one. However, a similar approach has been adopted by the Commission in a number of subsequent cases, see, e.g., Commission Decision, *Espacio Editorial Andaluza Holding*, N 458/04 (14 December 2004) para. 8 *et seq.* (concerning State aid for local newspapers); Commission Decision, *Ayudas a la producción teatral, musical y coreográfica*, N 448/2005 (25 January 2006) para. 16 (concerning State aid for small and medium-sized cultural enterprises in Madrid); Commission Decision (26 November 2003) on the aid scheme which Italy (Region of Piedmont) is planning to implement for the reduction of airborne pollution in its territory [2006] OJ L 32/82 para. 59 (concerning State aid directed at the extension of the network of service stations in Piedmont for the distribution of natural gas (methane) used as motor fuel).

[27] For an older example, see *Italian Republic and Sardegna Lines – Servizi Marittimi della Sardegna SpA v. Commission*, joined Cases No. C-15/98 and C-105/99 [2000] ECR I-8855 para. 66 *et seq.*

[28] *EURL Le Levant 001 a.o. v. Commission*, Case No. T-34/02 [2006] ECR II-267 para. 109 *et seq.*

pagnie des Iles du Levant – CIL). According to the French law, the investors were able to deduct from their taxable income the costs of their investments and any losses incurred in operating the vessel.

The (then) CFI first underlined that the region directly affected by the State measure was one of the 'overseas countries and territories' ('OCTs') of France which are not part of the territory of the Union. Thus, the CFI asked for some extra reasoning why the trade between Member States could be affected. As the Commission's decision did not refer to that point at all, the statement of reasons was flawed.[29] Although, of course, OCTs are a very special case, the point that the CFI asked for further reasoning should not be underestimated and could lead to a relevant strengthening of this criterion in further cases.[30]

The same holds true with a view to the element of distortion of competition. Here the CFI first of all asked for a clear explanation how in triangular situations, in which a private person obtains an advantage (such as the fiscal advantage for the investors *in casu*) and in which the relevant distortion of competition takes place with regard to a third party (such as the operator of the vessel – CIL), the advantage is transferred to the third party.[31] But what seems even more striking is the fact that the CFI has asked the Commission to define exactly the markets which might be affected by the distortion of competition and why this might be the case.[32] This will definitely force the Commission to offer some additional reasoning. Nevertheless, at the end of the day it will only support the Commission in its approach to have a more elaborated economic reasoning it its decisions anyway.[33]

In this context, there might be some more economic reflection on setting the *de minimis* threshold as well. It might also be analysed if it is not more convincing to have a bundle of criteria including the specific market situation and

---

[29] *Ibid.* paras 115-117.

[30] A similar view seems to be taken by A.W.H. Meij, 'Balancing Substance and Procedure in State Aid Practice – An update on recent developments in EC Case Law', in *Proceedings of the 5th Annual Experts' Forum on new developments in European State aid Law: 2 years into the SAAP*, A. Bartosch (ed.) (forthcoming), section II.2.

[31] *EURL Le Levant 001 a.o. v. Commission*, Case No. T-34/02 [2006] ECR II-267 paras 118-120.

[32] *Ibid.* paras 123-125.

[33] It is noteworthy that *A.W.H. Meij*, Judge at the Court of First Instance, who did not decide on the *Le Levant* case, understands the CFI as asking 'for a full-fledged economic analysis of the alleged distortion', cf. A.W.H. Meij (*supra* n. 30) section II.2. with note 30.

the position of the undertaking in the market, i.e. its market shares, as the Commission tried to introduce with its LET-approach.[34]

III. Exceptions from the prohibition of State aids

So far the more economic approach has been much more important with respect to the exception from the prohibition of State aids and particularly with a view to Article 107(3) TFEU.

At this juncture, the way the more economic approach is implemented in the Commission's first decisional practice in State aid matters is basically reasonable. The application of Article 107(3) TFEU has always been open to arbitrariness to some extent. In contrast to the Courts' strict control of the Commission's activities under Article 107(1) TFEU, there is a significant discretion the Commission enjoys in granting a derogation from Article 107(1) TFEU, particularly on the basis of Article 107(3) TFEU. Here, the Commission has only to adhere to its own rules laid down in the legal or soft law instruments on the application of Article 107(3) TFEU, if applicable. As a consequence, judgments annulling decisions of the Commission for having breached Article 107(3) TFEU (or Article 107(2) TFEU) are very rare.[35] Thus, the application of the more economic approach of the Commission in the field of State aid law is to be welcomed in principle as it will bring about the opportunity to have a stricter rationale in the application of the Article 107(3) TFEU exemption.

The more economic approach will not only raise the Commission's level of rationality in the justification of State aids, but will also increase its predictability and thus enhance legal certainty rather than lessen it. This may be different from other fields of competition law. One important difference is of course the fact that State aid control is a form of *ex ante* control. And also, from a constitutional point of view there is quite a difference if an undertaking asks for State aid from government or if a State prohibits certain private activities.

The Commission's new catalogue of questions on Article 107(3)(c) TFEU is convincing.[36] There should be a strict test whether a State aid measure aims at a well-defined objective of common interest and is well designed to deliver this objective, i.e. it should address a market failure or another clear objective of

---

[34] LET = Lesser effect on trade.
[35] Cf. J.-D. Braun and J. Kühling (*supra* n. 6) 465, 486 *et seq*.
[36] Cf. the decisions quoted in the following footnotes and also H.W. Friederiszick and L.-H. Röller, 'Weniger und effektiver – Ökonomische Prüfverfahren könnten die EU-Beihilfenkontrolle stärken' (2006) 111 *WZB-Mitteilungen*, 27, 29.

common interest. There should be a strict proportionality test (including an incentive-test). Finally the Commission should inquire whether the distortions of competition and the effect on trade are limited, so that the overall balance is positive. These questions have not been a clear standard of EU State aid control yet. One can assume that State aid control will become stricter once the more economic approach is fully applied. Within this proportionality test, it is in fact important to identify to which extent the State measure may improve the situation – even if this approach is contested by legal experts on State aid law who claim that the Commission can only identify the positive and negative outcome for competition law[37]. That is not convincing at all and has not been the practice within the proportionality test. One may additionally wonder to what extent the loss of State funds as such are reflected in the balancing test. This is particularly relevant with a view to regional aid.

Furthermore, the first decisions which explicitly reflect the more economic approach in State aid matters and which applied the catalogue mentioned did in general profit from this approach. As the quality of the Commission's line of argument improves, this will also be fruitful with a view to the recent case-law of the European courts which burden the tasks of the Commission with also stating sufficient reasons for its decisions in the field of State aid law.

To take just four examples: In the Commission decision of 19 July 2006 on the measure No C 35/2005 which the Netherlands are planning to implement concerning a broadband infrastructure in Appingedam,[38] there was indeed neither a market failure nor a cohesion objective. And in the Commission decision of 24 January 2007 on State aid C 52/2005 implemented by the Italian Republic for the subsidised purchase of digital decoders[39] there were indeed unnecessary distortions of competition. As a consequence, a justification of the measures on the basis of Article 107(3)(c) TFEU (then Article 87(3)(c) EC) was duly rejected in both cases. In the Commission decision of 24 January 2007 on the measure N 270/2006 implemented by the Italian Republic for subsidies to

---

[37] A. Bartosch, 'Der „More Economic Approach" in der Entscheidungspraxis der Europäischen Kommission in Beihilfesachen' [2007] *Recht der Internationalen Wirtschaft*, 681, 688.

[38] Commission Decision (19 July 2006) on the measure No. C 35/2005 (ex N 59/2005), which the Netherlands are planning to implement concerning a broadband infrastructure in Appingedam [2007] OJ L 86/1.

[39] Commission Decision (24 January 2007) on State aid C 52/2005 (ex NN 88/2005, ex CP 101/2004) implemented by the Italian Republic for the subsidised purchase of digital decoders [2007] OJ L 147/1.

digital decoders with open API,[40] there was an objective of common interest as there was a market failure (externalities) and the remedies were proportionate and without unnecessary distortions of competition. As there was an overall balance in respect of the measure as well, the conclusion of the Commission that the measure constituted an aid compatible under 107(3)(c) TFEU (then Article 87(3)(c) EC) is convincing.[41] Finally, in the Commission decision of 24 April 2007 on State aid E 3/2005[42] for public broadcasters in Germany on the basis of fees which were used for the online expansion, the Commission developed a convincing three-step test. This test shall particularly guarantee that there really is a market failure, i.e. some lack of public value in the existing content provided for by private entities.

IV. Outlook

To sum up, one can say that there is a need for a more economic approach not only at the level of Article 107(3) TFEU but also with respect to the (very) notion of State aid (itself).

But even if the decisions at the level Article 107(3) TFEU have been quite convincing so far, the costs of producing them should be of more relevance. One has to exercise caution in order to avoid making the test so complicated that ultimately only big enterprises with their own State aid justification department will be able to obtain State aids. This would be contrary to the important aim of supporting SME. In any case, one can hardly see in what respect the costs of State aid control are reflected in the more economic approach.

Moreover, information asymmetries might become a problem in the long run. Some questions might well be answered by Commission officials handling the cases. This will be the case for market failure analysis – even though there will always be a vigorous discussion if the Commission is right in its analyses. On some other questions one could be rather sceptical. This seems to be particularly the case as far as the incentive effect according to the new R&D&I

---

[40] Cf. Commission Decision, *Contributi ai decoder digitali con API aperta*, N 270/2006 [2007] OJ C 80/3.

[41] Cf. also Commission Decision, *Aide du Sicoval pour un réseau de très haut débit*, N 890/2006 [2007] OJ C 218/1.

[42] Cf. Commission Decision, *Die Finanzierung der öffentlich-rechtlichen Rundfunkanstalten in Deutschland*, E 3/2005 [2007] OJ C 185/1.

framework[43] is concerned. In order to correctly analyse all those incentive effects[44] at the project level on an *ex ante* basis, one may need an economic *Hercules*. Even if, for example, the 'Net present Value' approach[45] is widely accepted and robust in theory, one may wonder how the Commission could really control and apply it because it all depends so much on the data given by the Member State and the undertaking seeking the State aid. A more refined economic approach at that level might just lead to a more refined lobbying approach – and the biggest incentive effect will be to assemble information and know-how within undertakings and Member States to show such incentive effects.[46]

In addition to that, one may wonder if the Commission is setting the right priorities. In order to apply such a more refined economic approach one needs to build up organisational capacities both at the Commission and at the Member States level.[47] To my mind, priorities should be different. The main task is still to guarantee that there is control on the obligation to notify and not necessarily to refine the control of measures having been notified to the Commission by Member States. Thus, measures are necessary in order to enforce the willingness of Member States to notify (possible) State aids. But also the application of the more economic approach in certain areas of notified State aids is doubtful, e.g., it does not seem very fruitful to apply the more economic approach in the area of regional aid if the basic assumption is that below average State economies should have more leeway to spend money in a manner which might not other- wise be reasonable from an economic point of view.[48] Before refining regional

---

43 Community Framework for State Aid for Research and Development and Inno- vation [2006] OJ C 323/1; cf. also T. Kleiner, 'The new Framework for Re- search, Development and Innovation, 2007-2013' [2007] *European State Aid Law*, 231 *et seq.*

44 On the incentive effect in general cf. also P. Nicolaides, 'Incentive Effect: Is State Aid Necessary when Investment is Unnecessary?' [2003] *European State Aid Law*, 230 *et seq.*

45 H.W. Friederiszick and L.-H. Röller, 'Using Economic Analysis to Assess R&D&I State Aid Measures' [2007] *European State Aid Law*, 592, 602.

46 Cf. also T. Jaeger, 'Systemfragen des More Economic Approach im Beihilfe- recht' [2008] *Wirtschaft und Wettbewerb*, 1064, 1068 *et seq.*

47 H.W. Friederiszick and L.-H. Röller (*supra* n. 45) 592, 604.

48 See for such a convincing critique J. Haucap, 'Regionalbeihilfen bei Unterneh- mensansiedlungen im Lichte eines stärker ökonomisch fundierten Ansatzes', in *Der „More economic approach" in der Beihilfenkontrolle*, P. Oberender (ed.) (Berlin, 2008), p. 107, 126 *et seq.*

aid on a very elaborated level, it might be more important to develop that point first.

Thus, the Commission should pursue the further aims of its State Aid Action Plan. Particularly, better control and enforcement at the national level is of key importance. Here, we face two options: Either one introduces at the national level independent authorities controlling the compliance by Member States with EU State aid law as is the case with general EU competition rules as laid down in Articles 101 and 102 TFEU and sector specific regulation, e.g. in the telecom markets; or, alternatively, one could seek inspiration from other branches of competition law and particularly public procurement law. Here we have an enforcement directive[49] which is supposed to guarantee the full application of the substantive rules. Something comparable could help to reinforce the federal forces for implementation of State aid law.[50]

Finally one has to emphasise that a more economic approach should be applied to more sectors of competition law such as sector-specific competition law or, more precisely, sector-specific regulation in the telecommunications and energy sectors as well. There is not enough consistency in the Commission's overall approach yet. Thus, we need more of the more economic approach.

---

[49] Directive 2007/66/EC of the European Parliament and of the Council (11 December 2007) amending Council Directives 89/665/EEC and 92/13/EEC with regard to improving the effectiveness of review procedures concerning the award of public contracts [2007] OJ L 335/31.

[50] See for problems with respect to the implementation of State aid law at the level of Member States the various contributions to P.F. Nemitz (ed.), *The Effective Application of EU State Aid Procedures: The Role of National Law and Practice* (Alphen aan den Rijn, 2007).

SOME REMARKS FROM A JUDICIAL POINT OF VIEW

Josef Azizi[*]

I. Introduction

Let me thank you for the invitation to add to the interesting contributions of this morning and for the opportunity to make some remarks, which will have to be very short given the limited time available.

Unfortunately, I have to apologize for not being in a position to comment in detail on the contents of the various speeches. Indeed, as a judge of the Court of First Instance of the European Communities ('CFI') – which after the Treaty of Lisbon became effective has been renamed General Court ('GC') –, I may easily have to examine, in the frame of future cases brought to our forum, many of the questions dealt with this morning. I, thus, have to refrain from giving an opinion which might be misunderstood as prejudging in an inappropriate way the

---

[*]   All views expressed are strictly personal.

Court's future proceedings. I therefore shall limit myself to making some general remarks in the light of the recent development of our case law.

II. GC's scope of control

A. General remarks

First, let me recall, as a general point of departure, the scope of the GC's control of administrative decisions issued by the Union's institutions:[1] The GC has to exercise full control regarding questions of law as well as – in principle – regarding the facts. However, it flows from consistent case law that the GC limits its judicial review as to Commission findings involving the assessment of complex economic facts: Indeed, according to jurisprudence, the Commission enjoys a large margin of appreciation as to the appraisal of complex economic facts, and the scope of the judicial control to which the Commission is subjected in that regard is limited to one of *manifest error*. Thus, the GC confines its review of the Commission's assessment of complex economic facts to ascertaining whether the Commission committed a manifest error. In that context, the GC has to determine whether the evidence adduced by the applicants is sufficient to render the underlying assessment implausible in terms of probability and, thus, to shift the burden of proof. But, except for that review of plausibility, it is not the GC's role to substitute its assessment of the relevant complex economic facts for that made by the institution which adopted the decision.

In such a context, review by the GC consists of ascertaining that the Commission complied with the rules of procedure and the rules relating to the duty to give reasons and also that the facts relied on were accurate and that there has been no error of law, no manifest error of assessment or misuse of powers.

---

[1] For a more thorough analysis, see J. Azizi, 'The tension between Member States' autonomy and Commission control in State aid matters: selected aspects', in *EU Competition Law in Context: Essays in Honour of Virpi Tiili*, H. Kanninen, N. Korjus and A. Rosas (eds) (Oxford, 2009), pp. 307-320.

B. Scope of judicial control in State aid matters

1. Variations according to the specific legal basis applied

In State aid matters, according to the case law as it stands, the above considerations imply the following consequences:

In State aid matters, the case law has refrained from recognizing a wide margin of appreciation for the Commission as far as concerns the interpretation and application of Article 107(1) TFEU (ex-Article 87 EC) for ascertaining the presence of State aid, which is considered as involving essentially *questions of law.*

Therefore, in principle, there is *full judicial review* as to the Commission's findings and appraisal under (now) Article 107(1) TFEU[2] concerning the existence of State aid falling under the criteria mentioned in that provision, namely

– Transfer of State resources
– Economic advantage
– Selectivity
– Effect on competition and trade

Nonetheless, the case law has acknowledged that the application of the private investor test implies an analysis of complex economic facts. Therefore, the GC limits its control in this respect only to the above-mentioned restricted grounds for annulment (manifest error, breach of rules of procedure or breach of duty to state reasons).

In contrast with the full in-depth control exercised in principle by the GC as to the application of Article 107(1) TFEU, Union case law has recognized a large margin of appreciation of the Commission as to the application of Article 107(2) and (3) TFEU.[3]

With regard to Article 107(2) and – above all – (3) TFEU, the GC's control is thus limited to one of manifest error, given the Commission's discretionary power in defining the way in which it wishes to shape its economic policy under the relevant exceptions to the general prohibition rule contained in Article 107(1) TFEU.

When it comes to identifying the existence of a Service of General Economic Interest ('SGEI') within the meaning of Article 106 TFEU,[4] it follows from the case law that this matter falls under the exclusive competence of the Member

---

[2]   *Ibid.* p. 314.
[3]   *Ibid.* pp. 317 *et seq.*
[4]   *Ibid.* p. 317.

States. Indeed, the Member States have the prerogative and a wide discretion in defining what they regard as SGEI's. In this respect, the definition of such services by a Member State can be questioned by the Commission itself only in the event of manifest error. The GC's review of the Commission's assessment in turn must observe the same limit. Accordingly, its review – though careful – must be confined to ascertaining whether the Commission properly found or rejected the existence of a manifest error by the Member State.[5]

2. Examples from recent case law

Now, let me give you a few illustrations from the GC's case law as to economic aspects:

One example amongst others for the in-depth control as to the fulfilment of the criteria under Article 107(1) TFEU is the judgment of 22 February 2006 in Case T-34/02, *EURL Le Levant 001 v. Commission*, paragraphs 114 et seq.

See also, in this sense, the earlier judgment of 28 February 2002, in Case T-155/98, *Société Internationale v. Commission*, as to the definition of the export market for French language books.

Another example concerning the detailed judicial control under Article 107(1) TFEU would be the examination of new versus existing aid in the judgment of 28 November 2008 in Case T-254/00, *Hôtel Cipriani v. Commission*. In addition to this point, that judgment also concerns judicial review under Article 107(3) TFEU as well as a brief statement on the calculation methods for interest levied on the amounts to be recovered, and it touches upon many other economic aspects.

As to the necessity, under certain circumstances, to carry out a private investor test, see for instance the judgment of 17 December 2008, Case T-196/04, *Ryanair ltd. v. Commission*.

Let me also stress a new accent in the recent case law as to the importance of the link between a failure to state sufficient reasons on the one hand and the failure to comply with the obligation of diligence, i.e. the duty of care in the conduct of administrative proceedings, on the other. I am talking about the judgment of 22 October 2008 *in Cases T-309/04 and others, TV2/Danmark A/S and others v. Commission*, paragraphs 233 and 234. In this judgment, not only is this important link between reasoning and diligent conduct underpinned, but it also underlines the increased importance of the Commission's providing detailed reasoning by giving a precise and detailed assessment of the relevant

---

[5] *Ibid.* p. 318.

actual legal and economic conditions, this being seen as a counterweight to the Commission's wide discretion as to questions involving complex economic issues.

As it seems, – step by step in its evolution over time – some of the more recent case law could to a certain extent be perceived as also assuming some control on rather economic matters.

In this regard, one can find some elements of economic reasoning or control amongst others in the following judgments:

The judgment of 29 March 2007, Case T-366/00, *Scott SA v. Commission*: Here, one of the questions at stake was the method of calculation for determining the value of an aid consisting in the allegedly too low price paid for an estate property. In this respect, I would like to mention the detailed and critical analysis of this judgment in the article by *Thomas Jaeger* on 'Recovering illegal State aid in Real Estate contracts'.[6]

In a similar respect see also the more recent judgment of 18 December 2008 in Case T-455/05, *Componenta OY v. Commission*, as to the economic evaluation of the acquisition price for real estate property.

III. Possible future consequences of the 'new approach' for the judicial practice

Nonetheless and in spite of my introductory remark, allow me the following additional observation: it is obvious that, in the future, the new secondary State aid rules discussed today will be the legal basis of the Commission's State aid decisions in the years to come.

In that respect, these rules shall also be part of the yardstick against which the GC will appraise the legality of such future Commission decisions.

In this sense, generally speaking, I would like to welcome these new rules in as much as they contribute to the rule of law. Because of their precision they add to the clarity of EU law, thus contributing to the foreseeability of the Commission's State aid proceedings and easing the tasks of its judicial control.

Indeed in several respects, it seems to me that these new rules shall increase the foreseeability of the application of State aid rules.

Let me mention two aspects in that regard which are in the interest of the involved enterprises as well as of the Member States in particular:

On the one hand, the laying down of specific and more precise rules for a more economic approach will increase transparency and legal certainty, as it

---

[6] [2007] *European State Aid Law Quarterly*, 578-585.

seems to me, specifically in the field of economic assessment which hitherto, as I already mentioned, was largely left to the sole discretion of the Commission. The result will be improved predictability.

It is, no doubt, in the interest of EU law that these rules are rendered more precise in the future. This might also facilitate the task of the Union judge and further increase his willingness to resist the temptation of substituting himself for the Commission in the field of economic assessment.

On the other hand, the second aspect I would like to mention is that I have noted with pleasure that the new rules, in the large sense of the word, somewhat broaden the possibilities for interested third parties to contribute efficiently to the Commission proceedings. As to the possible outcome of this new factor for the GC's burden of work, I am slightly more optimistic than as stated by *Piet Jan Slot* in his oral assessment. Indeed, as a matter of fact, in terms of the GC's current workload things could hardly become worse. On the contrary: The new forms developed for gathering the opinion of interested third parties to be contacted on the Commission's initiative may well lead to clarifying essential points of the case already during the administrative proceedings; this hopefully shall help avoid certain questions of substance being raised for the first time before the Union judge. It may thus even help us to avoid some future litigation.

Let me finally mention a positive side effect of the new General Block Exemption Regulation: It will perhaps also help, through its new efficiency, to slow down a bit the steady increase of State aid cases brought before the GC.

TOWARDS A MORE ECONOMIC CONTROL OF STATE AID IN EUROPE

Lukas Repa[*]

I. Introduction

The conference on 'Structure and Effects in EU Competition Law' at the Max Planck Institute has provided an excellent overview of the Commission's new economic approach in applying EU competition law. Instruments as different as the fiercely discussed Commission guidelines on the former Article 82 EC which after the Treaty of Lisbon entered into force became Article 102 TFEU in the antitrust area and the Commission's 2008 General Block Exemption Regulation ('GBER') for controlling State aid have served as illustrations for discussing the impact of industrial economics on the Commission's policy. My contribution shall add to this discussion by explaining from a practitioner's

---

[*] The author thanks *Harold Nyssens*, *Wouter Pieké*, *Oliver Stehmann*, *Andras Tari*, *Vincent Verouden* for their useful comments and help. The views presented in this article are, however, only those of the author and do not constitute an official position of the European Commission.

viewpoint why a less formalistic and more economic assessment of State aid may make sense. It, however, also tries to point to some practical challenges this 'refined' economic approach poses in practice.

II. SAAP and the 'aid balancing test'

When in 2005 the European Commission adopted its 'State Aid Action Plan' ('SAAP'), it built on a number of conclusions reached by the European Council since the launch of the so-called Lisbon agenda for growth and jobs in 2000. The SAAP set out a roadmap for reforming State aid control in the period of 2005 to 2009. Both in designing State aid rules and in assessing individual cases, the Commission intended to henceforth pay more attention to when State aid is useful in improving the market outcome and when the effect of an aid is rather to distort competition and/or trade between Member States.[1] This new/refined economic approach initially stems from merger control and from antitrust. It is based on the general policy perception that an intervention by the Commission should only occur if the effects of an undertakings' actions or a State's intervention are ultimately detrimental for consumers.

The SAAP recognises two legitimate aims of using State aid: First, it can alleviate market failures, that is, State intervention may improve the functioning of a market where competitive forces alone cannot provide an efficient outcome (efficiency objective), and second, it can bring about a socially more acceptable outcome of the competitive process (equity objective). Both legitimate aims are to be tested in a so-called 'balancing test'.

This balancing test is a conceptual framework which assesses (i) whether the State aid addresses a market failure or other objective of common interest; (ii) whether there is an incentive effect (i.e. whether the aid affects the behaviour of the recipient in a way which meets the objective); (iii) whether the aid leads to distortions of competition and trade and (iv) whether, given the magnitude of the positive and negative effects, the overall balance is positive.

The incentive effect is arguably the centre piece of the balancing test. Its aim is commonsensical: no undertaking should receive aid if it would already perform the desirable economic activity without being subsidised. Granting aid for such projects is a squandering of taxpayer's money which harms private initiatives by distorting competition.

---

[1] See also H. Friederszick, L.-H. Röller and V. Verouden, 'European State aid control: An Economic Framework', in *Handbook of Antitrust Economics*, P. Buccirossi (ed.) (Cambridge/Mass., 2007).

Between 2005 and 2009 the Commission subsequently introduced this balancing test in its State aid instruments, starting with the Restructuring Aid Guidelines and the R&D&I Framework of 2006.[2]

III. The R&D&I Framework 2006

The new R&D&I Framework[3] increases the range of projects which may benefit from such aid but also introduces thresholds that trigger an in-depth assessment of an R&D&I project under the SAAP balancing test. The *NeoVal* case was the first R&D&I project to be assessed under the balancing test.[4] Another instrument, where *some* of the principles of the SAAP have been implemented, is the regional aid guidelines. *NeoVal* is not only interesting from an economic perspective, it also put the spotlight on the core legal difference between the refined economic approach and the 'old' approach of controlling the proportionality of State aid. In analysing the counterfactual situation[5] to test the incentive effect (step 2 of the balancing test), the case team was faced with the argument of the aid beneficiary that – despite a positive net present value ('NPV') of the project – due to *internal* profit targets imposed on STS by Siemens, STS could not finance the project on its own. Thus, the aid was necessary for the project to proceed. Internal profit targets are, however, normally set by the company's management and it becomes an evidentiary matter whether these profit targets indeed existed before the company applied for State

---

2   Community Framework for State Aid for Research and Development and Innovation [2006] OJ C 323/1.

3   *Ibid*. Point 6 of the Framework sets out that if the aided R&D&I project has not started before the application, the Commission considers that the incentive effect is automatically met for a number of aid measures such as project aid and feasibility studies where the aid beneficiary is an SME and where the aid amount is below 7,5 million Euro for a project per SME, aid for industrial property rights costs for SMEs, or aid for young innovative enterprises. *E contrario*, for other aid projects Member States must demonstrate an incentive effect.

4   Commission Decision, *Soutien de l'Agence de l'innovation industrielle en faveur du projet NeoVal*, N 674/2006 (21 February 2007).

5   Economists refer to a 'counterfactual' in assessing the hypothetical situation 'in the absence of' some predicate fact. A counterfactual test is common in other areas of EU competition law, such as in antitrust where the objective necessity of a competitive constraint between two undertakings is regularly analysed by benchmarking the situation in the presence and absence of the restraint. In EC merger control, too, case teams assess the hypothetical situation under the hypothetical presence of the merger, again a 'counterfactual'.

aid. Hence, the assessment becomes one of adducing evidence (e.g. minutes of board meetings, shareholder reports or annual statements) rather than evaluating static parameters such as the intensity of aid or the cash grant equivalent of an aid.

IV. The refined economic approach in regional aid

The 2006 Regional Aid Guidelines[6] have indeed been influenced by the refined economic approach in at least a two-fold manner. First, the regional aid ceilings for large investment projects (in short 'LIPs') above 50 million Euro must be progressively scaled down. Second, the framework foresees individual notifications and the SAAP balancing test for LIPs above 100 million Euro. A formal investigation rather than a block exemption is required if the market share of the beneficiary lies above 25% and if the aid leads to a capacity increase of more than 5% in underperforming markets. The rationale for applying the SAAP balancing test to LIPs is that LIPs are typically less affected by region-specific problems. Larger companies also have easier access to capital and credit and skilled labour. They are more capital intensive and can typically be less expected to create jobs than, for instance, Small and Medium Sized Enterprise ('SME's').

Already before these Guidelines on regional aid were adopted in 2006, the Commission's policy on regional aid had increasingly become more 'economic' and, hence, evidence based.

The *IBIDEN Hungary* case of April 2008[7] was still based on the 2002 Multisectoral Framework on regional aid for large investment projects ('MSF'), i.e. a legal instrument predating the 2005 SAAP. Yet, in that case, the case team entered into a sophisticated definition of the relevant market. The assessment was reminiscent of a merger or antitrust case: it entailed a substitution analysis whether substrates for diesel oxidation catalysts and diesel particulate filters belong to the same product market.

The *IBIDEN Hungary* case is of broader interest because it also demonstrates the advantages of the SAAP balancing test. Under the MSF, market shares played a role because regional aid to large investment projects was deemed disproportionate if the market share of the beneficiary exceeded a certain thresh-

---

6 [2006] OJ C 54/13.
7 Commission Decision (30 April 2008) on State aid C 21/07 (ex N578/06) which Hungary is planning to implement in favour of IBIDEN Hungary Gyártó Kft. [2008] OJ L 295/34.

old. Thus, the delineation of the relevant market was crucial for concluding whether or not the aid was compatible with the TFEU. Under the 2006 Regional Aid Guidelines, in contrast, market shares merely trigger the in-depth investigation and the balancing test. So, under the new approach, regional aid for large investment projects can, in theory, be allowed even if the beneficiary has a large market share. It depends on the incentive effect and the balancing of pro- and anticompetitive effects. This difference between the two regional aid instruments is also highlighted in a Commission paper which sets out the refined economic approach in regional aid.[8]

In the author's view, market shares should never *per se* determine the compatibility of State aid with the TFEU, because large companies may be large precisely because they are efficient. Excluding such companies from State aid *ab initio* can lead to an outcome that is socially and economically undesirable. However, special vigilance is warranted when States grant aid to large companies. This is why the incentive effect must be assessed with particular care.

V. The General Block Exemption Regulation

One of the aims of the SAAP was to create one consolidated and coherent set of legislative rules applying to those types of aid which can be considered as passing the compatibility test as outlined in Article 107(3) TFEU. Following the risk capital guidelines (2006) and the environmental guidelines (2008), the Commission announced that it would simplify its existing block exemption regulations ('BERs') and consolidate them into one instrument, the General Block Exemption Regulation ('GBER')[9].

As *Piet Jan Slot* pointed out,[10] the GBER is a somewhat complex instrument. Obviously, it is. The Commission sought to strike the right balance between two objectives: the necessity of simplifying the assessment of straightforward cases and the need to ensure that effects on competition are reduced to the minimum

---

[8]   Point 6 and 7 of the Commission Communication on criteria for an in-depth assessment of regional aid to large investment projects, see <ec.europa.eu/com petition/state_aid/regional_aid/guidance_regional_large_investment_en.pdf>, 20 September 2009.

[9]   Commission Regulation (EC) No. 800/2008 (6 August 2008) declaring certain categories of aid compatible with the common market in application of Articles 87 and 88 of the Treaty (General block exemption Regulation) [2008] OJ L 214/3.

[10]   Cf. pp. 193 *et seq.* in this book.

necessary.[11] The provisions of the GBER are largely based on the different BERs, guidelines and frameworks which existed before. As a block exemption is an instrument with direct effect, it must be clear and straightforward. And that implies a casuistic way of regulating matters which differs from the less detailed and prescriptive approach chosen for other forms of horizontal instruments such as guidelines and frameworks. General Court Judge *Josef Azizi* rightly pointed out that there is an evident trade-off between legal security and flexibility.[12] The more casuistic rules are, the less scope for interpretation and hence uncertainty. While introducing a more refined economic analysis, the Commission also attributed much importance to legal security.

The refined economic approach has clearly left its imprint on the GBER. The GBER imposes a new affirmative requirement to demonstrate the incentive effect of an aid, i.e. the second step of the SAAP balancing step.[13] This, however, is only required for aid to large enterprises. If an aid does not change the behaviour of the beneficiary, then the aid should not be granted. The recitals of the GBER set out that the Commission services will usually assess the incentive effect on the basis of 'business documentation prepared by the beneficiary and verified by the Member States'.[14] Under Article 8(3) GBER, large enterprises will typically have to produce a business plan indicating how they fulfil the conditions of the balancing test.

This raises the question whether companies could not be tempted to 'write' the incentive effect 'into' their business plans if they intend to apply for an aid in the next business period. The GBER tries to address that difficulty by obliging beneficiaries and Member States to 'maintain detailed records' regarding any individual aid or aid scheme exempted under this Regulation and, in particular, 'including ... information on the incentive effect of the aid'.[15]

VI. SAAP and the balancing test under Article 106(2) TFEU

It is an open question to which extent the 'balancing test' in the SAAP is justified in controlling the proportionality of State aid which finances services of general economic interest ('SGEI').

---

[11] See H. Nyssens, 'The GBER: bigger, simpler and more economic' [2008] (3) *Competition Policy Newsletter*, 12.
[12] Cf. pp. 225 *et seq.* in this book.
[13] Article 8 GBER.
[14] Recital 28 GBER.
[15] Article 10(2) GBER.

The criteria developed in the 2005 SGEI Framework, which are in turn based on the ECJ's *Altmark* judgment, do not foresee any test which would be remotely comparable to the balancing test of the SAAP. In particular, the first step of the SAAP balancing test is sometimes interpreted as implying a test whether the Member State concerned could achieve the economically and socially desirable aim by means other than granting State aid, for instance, through statutory regulation. Applying this principle and the incentive effect requirement to SGEI appears politically explosive. Notably German Scholars attending the conference organised by the Max Planck Institute have questioned such understanding of Article 106(2) and 107 TFEU. They have argued that the duties of the Commission are limited to control distortive effects of EU State aid and that it would be beyond the Commission's task to 'tell' Member States which policy instrument they should choose in pursuing social aims.

It would appear that the Commission has so far been prudent in not expanding the SAAP balancing test to services of general economic interest. One example is the public broadcasting sector. Here, the balancing test introduced in the 2009 Broadcasting Communication does not contain either of the first two elements of the 'standard' balancing test as set out in the SAAP.[16] Similarly, the necessity of State aid as an appropriate instrument is not at issue and the incentive effect is not being tested. This deviation from the general pattern is arguably due to the specific legal basis for the Commission's State aid control as set out in the so-called Amsterdam Protocol, which was also annexed to the Treaty of Lisbon.[17] The author of this article anticipates that similar prudence will be observed when it comes to the application of the SGEI

---

[16] Communication from the Commission on the application of State aid rules to public service broadcasting [2009] OJ C 257/1. According to para. 88 of the Broadcasting Communication, Member States must consider, by means of a prior evaluation procedure based on an open public consultation, whether the launch of significant new publicly financed audiovisual services actually serve the democratic, social and cultural needs of the society without leading to undue distortions of competition. In the case of predominantly negative effects on the market, State funding for audiovisual services is proportionate only if it is justified by the added value in terms of serving the social, democratic and cultural needs of society.

[17] The Protocol clarifies in an interpretative way that the provisions of the Treaty of Lisbon (or before this Treaty entered into force, the provisions of the Treaty establishing the EC) shall be without prejudice to the competence of Member States to provide for the funding of public service broadcasting, see Protocol (No 29) on the System of Public Broadcasting in the Member States [2010] OJ C 83/312.

Framework and Article 106(2) TFEU. In general, the SAAP balancing test is a useful tool for analysing large State aid projects under Article 107(3) TFEU, but the Commission does not follow a 'one size fits all' approach in adopting a more economic analysis overall.

VII. Outlook from a practitioner's perspective

My presentation at the Max Planck Institute has put an emphasis on factual difficulties Commission case handlers may face in applying the refined economic approach in practice. These difficulties stem from the fact that, contrary to merger control and antitrust control, the Commission has no powers to obtain high quality data directly from companies. In antitrust or merger, when proving a counterfactual scenario, case handlers can issue requests for information to companies.[18] Under the threat of fines, companies must disclose highly sensitive data; even banks cannot invoke a bank secret. The situation is entirely different in a State aid case.

In State aid proceedings, the Commission depends on the goodwill of a Member State to exert pressure on the beneficiary companies or on third parties to provide data. Case handlers will obviously try to rely on any external industry study which happens to be publicly available. Also, after opening proceedings, companies other than the beneficiary sometimes make themselves known to the Commission services and provide data which either corroborates or rebuts arguments of the beneficiary company on the incentive effect and on the counterfactual situation absent an aid. However, as already pointed out by the case team in *IBIDEN Hungary*, 'the opening of the formal investigation procedure may not always help in gathering relevant information from interested parties as some of them might have no incentive to reply or might not be aware of such a procedure being initiated'.[19] It therefore appears that the collection of evidence is the '*Achilles heel*' of the SAAP balancing test.

Modern industrial economics depends on data and more data will allow for a more reliable econometric analysis. The balancing test of the SAAP may therefore in the long run lead to consideration of a procedural reform which

---

[18] See, for instance, Article 18 of Council Regulation EC No. 1/2003 (16 December 2002) on the implementation of the rules on competition laid down in Articles 81 and 82 of the Treaty [2003] OJ L 1/1.

[19] E. Tumasonyte, Z. Didziokaite and A. Tari, 'State aid to IBIDEN Hungary: Assessing the relevant market in the context of a large investment project' [2008] (2) *Competition Policy Newsletter*, 76.

would provide the Commission and/or Member States with investigative instruments comparable to those in antitrust and merger proceedings. That would obviously be a political matter with wider implications. To mention but one: Considering that complainants can legally challenge decisions approving new aid, the question also arises the extent to which third parties should be able to gain access to evidence on the incentive effects. Without seeing such evidence, third parties can hardly challenge the Commission's conclusions in favour of a beneficiary. As long as the assessment of the Commission mainly relies on market studies and evidence collected by a Member State, third party access will not pose a central problem in State aid proceedings. However, were State aid control assimilated to the procedure applied in mergers and antitrust, it can be expected that the European courts will extend their jurisprudence on access to the file and third party rights to this field of EU competition policy as well.

VIII. Conclusion

The Commission has kept its promise to implement the refined economic approach in the field of European State aid control. The balancing test has been introduced in most areas of State aid control, and more economic thinking has influenced the increased block exemption of unproblematic aid. Together with the Commission's ongoing procedural reforms, this should enable the Commission services to gradually concentrate their forces on large and potentially more problematic State aid cases.

There are however constraints on the Commission's capabilities to engage in a full-fledged economic analysis, but a first step is completed. In the long run, the Commission may not wish to implement the new economic approach to the same extent as it has done in antitrust. There are procedural constraints (lack of investigative tools), legal constraints (Article 106(2) TFEU and Amsterdam Protocol) and there is a pronounced need for legal security and certainty for companies and Member States as to the orientation the Commission is taking in State aid cases. The more in-depth analysis of large State aid cases and the less formalistic approach have certainly advanced the Commission's State aid policy.

EU STATE AID POLICY, ECONOMIC APPROACH, BAILOUTS, AND MERGER POLICY: TWO COMMENTS

Wolfgang Kerber

I. Introduction

The EU State aid policy is both a successful and a deeply troubled policy. Since the 1980s, it has succeeded in implementing step-by-step a regime for monitoring direct and indirect subsidies of the Member States, leading to an overall reduction of State aid within the EU. The Member States lost much of their previous discretion for arbitrarily granting State aid to all kinds of firms and industries. In that respect, EU State aid policy has proved an effective restriction for the Member States. However, in the recent financial crisis the authority of the EU State aid policy was seriously challenged by the Member States, and – at least for some time – the EU Commission seemed to have lost control over the national State aid for troubled banks and other firms. Despite having achieved some limitations and modifications of national measures for helping firms during the financial crisis, there are many doubts whether the Commission has been really able to control State aid effectively in regard to its distorting effects on competition.

However, EU State aid policy is also a deeply troubled policy in other respects. In the last thirty years, it has evolved extensively in many different directions, leading to a situation in which the rules of EU State aid policy must

241

be taken into account in nearly all kinds of economic and social policies, both on the level of the Member States and on the level of regions and even communalities. The manifold rules and extensive practice show the breadth, complexity, and intransparency of EU State aid policy. The ensuing uneasiness about the existence of a clear, consistent, and transparent approach for EU State aid control suggested that the 'more economic approach' might also help to develop a more consistent analytical framework for EU State aid policy: It can help to develop a common theoretical framework for deriving general principles and criteria for all these very different kinds of State aid (for example, by using a market failure test). An economic analysis is also necessary because the compatibility of State aid with the internal markets should be determined through the analysis of the economic effects of State aid. Therefore it can be expected that the use of more economic analysis can lead to a larger effectiveness of EU State aid policy.

In this comment I want to focus on two specific topics: In section II., I contend that we need a careful analysis about the goals of EU State aid policy. I will argue that the current economic approach to EU State aid policy tends to be more a general control of the effectiveness of all subsidies in the Member States, which goes far beyond the initial intention of the EU competition rules of Articles 107 to 109 TFEU that wanted to control subsidies in regard to their distorting effects on competition through spillover effects between Member States. I will discuss from an economic perspective whether the EU Commission should have the authority for an overall control of all subsidies in the EU Member States, or whether this authority should be limited to their effects on distortion of competition. In section III., I will suggest seriously considering the possibility of also using EU merger policy to prevent firms from becoming 'too big to fail', and therefore reducing the danger of bailouts which can lead to significant distortions of competition. I will briefly discuss the possibility of a bailout test in merger policy and show that such an approach might be implemented within the scope of the SIEC (significant impediment to effective competition) test in the current Merger Regulation.[1] Although such an approach for solving the bailout problem has to be developed very carefully and needs much more research, it might complement the traditional instruments of EU State aid policy.

---

[1]   Council Regulation (EC) No. 139/2004 (20 January 2004) on the control of concentrations between undertakings (the EC Merger Regulation) [2004] OJ L 24/1.

II. What do we want EU State aid policy do for us?

During the last decade and reinforced by the State Aid Action Plan of 2005 ('SAAP') and the current efforts for a 'more refined economic approach', the objectives and scope of EU State aid policy have changed considerably. The basic concern in EU competition policy in regard to (direct and indirect) subsidies and the main rationale for Article 107 TFEU was that subsidies given by Member States to firms can distort competition between firms from different EU countries (and also competition between Member States). Therefore inefficient firms might survive in the internal market, and subsidy races between the Member States can emerge, which both waste resources and delay necessary restructuring processes. Therefore the justification of EU State aid policy was based upon the externalities (spillover effects) of the national subsidies in regard to other Member States in an integrated European market. This is reflected in the criterion 'in so far as it affects trade between Member States'. But in regard to the exemptions of the general prohibition of State aid that (threatens to) distort competition, a number of other policy objectives must be taken into account. This has led to the wide range of specific EU State aid rules and practices in regard to many different policies of Member States, in which subsidies are used as a policy instrument. Here a balancing is necessary between the justification of subsidies for achieving these policy objectives and their negative impact on competition through their distorting effects.

The new approach to State aid control takes a very different perspective on the tasks of EU State aid policy. This can best be demonstrated by a brief analysis of the three-stage balancing test of the European Commission, which is the basic element of the more refined economic approach:[2] (1) Is the planned aid aimed at a well-defined objective of common interest? (2) Is the planned aid a well-designed policy instruments, i.e. is it appropriate, has it incentive effects, and is it proportionate? (3) Are the negative effects of aid (primarily through distortive effects) outbalanced through their positive effects, i.e. is the overall balance positive?

I will not discuss the merits and problems of this three-stage balancing test here in detail,[3] but focus only on one specific point. The test can be interpreted

---

[2] See European Commission, *Vademecum – Community law on State aid* (30 September 2008) <ec.europa.eu/competition/state_aid/studies_reports/studies_re ports. html), 13 October 2010.

[3] See in much more detail German Monopolies Commission, *The "More Economic Approach" in European State Aid Control – Translated Version of Chapter VI of the Biennial Report 2006/2007* (Bonn, 2008). The English translation of the
cont.

as a sequence of filters for allowing State aid of Member States. Through the first two filters, the Commission attempts to ensure that within the EU only those State aid measures are allowed which can be justified through market failures (efficiency) or other common (regional, distributional) objectives – both in respect to their objective but also in respect to their specific suitability. From an economic policy perspective, such an approach seems to make much sense, and in that respect economics can contribute a great deal in regard to its specific implementation. This approach can now be used for scrutinizing all kinds of subsidies that Member States grant to firms and industries, whether they can be defended from the perspective of economic efficiency or other clearly defined policy objectives.

This new approach of EU State aid policy aims at a comprehensive control of all direct and indirect subsidies given by the Member States. If a subsidy cannot be defended as a necessary and proportionate policy measure for solving a clearly defined market failure problem or for achieving another objective of common interest, then it is deemed as not compatible with the internal market. This is an extension of the task of EU State aid policy, which goes far beyond the traditional objective of preventing distortion of competition and trade through State aid. Since neither the assessment in Article 107(1) TFEU nor the first steps of this balancing test require any real test whether there are spillover effects between Member States or whether such an aid does lead to any kind of distortion of competition, the new approach to State aid of the Commission is no longer directed at distortions of competition, but claims to assess the effectiveness of all subsidies of the Member States, irrespective of the question whether they have distortive effects on competition through cross-border spillover effects. This gives the EU Commission the possibility to influence deeply a wide variety of economic, social, and environmental policies of the Member States, which are not in the competence of the EU. A brief look in the new General Block Exemption Regulation as well as the Vademecum about the EU law on State aid already shows to what extent the EU State aid control claims the right to monitor and influence policies of the Member States as far as they use State aid as a policy instrument.[4] Especially, the test for the necessity and proportionality of State aid gives the EU Commission a broad authority for monitoring

---

German Monopolies Commission's chapter on State aid can be found in the Annex to this book.

[4] See Commission Regulation (EC) No. 800/2008 (6 August 2008) declaring certain categories of aid compatible with the common market in application of Articles 87 and 88 of the Treaty (General block exemption Regulation) ('GBER') [2008] OJ L 214/3; European Commission (*supra* n. 2).

policies because, ultimately, these tests require a comparative analysis of different policy options in order to determine whether another kind of policy could have achieved this policy objective with less State aid.

This interpretation of the new approach to State aid policy as a general control of subsidies is also suggested clearly by the objectives stated by the Commission in its Vademecum. Besides ensuring a level playing field for European companies (through avoiding subsidy races), EU State aid control should have the task to 'redirect aid to Lisbon-related objectives' in order to strengthen the competitiveness of the EU's economy, and to 'require the stakeholders to verify whether State aid is an appropriate policy instrument'[5] (contributing to the avoidance of wasteful use of public resources and protecting the taxpayers' money). It should be emphasised that also subsidies can be a legitimate and suitable policy instrument for solving different kinds of market failures under certain circumstances (and might also be defended for achieving a number of other legitimate policy objectives). However, usually far too many and often ineffective subsidies are granted, primarily due to rent seeking activities of interest groups. Therefore from an economic perspective, establishing an institutional solution (as, for example, an agency) for controlling the granting of subsidies in regard to their effectiveness can be very important for reducing the wasting of public resources through rent-seeking activities and for enhancing the effectiveness of public policies in Europe. A market failure framework as well might be very helpful for such an assessment. However, it should also be noted that such a task does not seem far removed from the tasks of State audit agencies (such as the *Bundesrechnungshof* in Germany or the European Court of Auditors in the EU), because a modern interpretation of their role would also include an assessment of the effectiveness of policies as far as the spending of taxpayers' money is involved.

The questions I want to raise here are (1) whether such a huge task of controlling all subsidies in regard to their effectiveness in the EU should be carried out on the EU level, and (2) whether the DG Competition would really be the most appropriate agency for such a task. The application of the more economic approach to State aid policy should also extend to these institutional questions. The economic theory of federalism as well as institutional economics offer a broad set of well-established economic criteria which can be used for analysing the question of the optimal design of an effective system of State aid supervision in Europe (both in regard to the optimal vertical allocation of com-

---

[5]   European Commission (*supra* n. 2) p. 5.

petences/subsidiarity and in regard to the institutional design of such agencies). Here I can only hint at some arguments for such a discussion.

The most important argument from an economic perspective for controlling State aid on the EU level are externalities (spillover effects) between Member States, and this is exactly the traditional rationale for EU State aid control (avoidance of subsidy races and distortion of competition). Another argument is that the Member States might have problems in committing themselves to not granting State aid for political reasons, and therefore an independent agency on a higher jurisdictional level might help to resist rent seeking efforts of interest groups. This is an interesting argument which, however, does not lead at all to the conclusion that this should be a task of DG Competition because the latter is definitely not an independent agency. The most important counterargument from an economic perspective for a comprehensive control of all subsidies at the EU level is in my view that such a task requires a large amount of specific infor-mation, expertise, and staff (well-trained and experienced in many different policy fields) for fulfilling this task appropriately. A brief glance at the Block Exemption Regulation or the Commission's Vademecum already shows the wide range of very different policies that EU State aid policy is dealing with. Whether a State aid is a necessary and proportionate policy instrument in a certain case requires an intimate knowledge both of the specific situation and of this field of policy in general. Such an agency would need to develop rather clear notions about what the best policies are for achieving the respective policy objectives (for assessing whether these objectives can also be achieved with less or no State aid).

First, I strongly doubt that any central agency at the EU level is capable of carrying out such a task for all State aid in the 27 Member States of the EU (especially if we keep in mind the very broad definition of State aid). However, in any case, the DG Competition with its small amount of resources devoted to State aid control cannot fulfil such a task. Secondly, and in my view no less important, is the problem that with such a competence, the Commission is capable of influencing significantly all kinds of policies which are in the competence of the Member States. This leads to a de facto shifting of com-petences to the EU level through using the possibilities of formulating policies about the compatibility of State aid. Such an implicit shifting of competences, which is not the result of an explicit decision about the appropriate vertical allocation of powers, can already be observed in many policy fields.[6] This

---

[6] See for this danger of an implicit shifting of competences to the EU level being effected through EU State aid policy W. Kerber, 'Die EU-Beihilfenkontrolle als

cont.

problem can be considerably aggravated by an explicit recognition of a general competence of the EU Commission for controlling all direct and indirect subsidies in the Member States in regard to their effectiveness. Therefore, in my view a thorough analysis about the appropriate task of EU State aid policy should also take into account its indirect (and perhaps unintended) effects for the vertical allocation of powers within the EU, which requires a much more comprehensive analysis of advantages and disadvantages of centralisation and decentralisation of competences.

What preliminary conclusions can be drawn from this brief (and very incomplete) discussion? I expect that a comprehensive economic analysis would lead to the result that EU State aid policy would not have the objective of a comprehensive control of the effectiveness of all direct and indirect subsidies in the EU. An economic approach as well does not lead to such a conclusion because economics of federalism and institutional economics can provide good arguments why this might not be the optimal institutional solution. Instead, it can be presumed that an overall economic analysis would point in the direction of a sophisticated two-level system of State aid supervision in which (1) the EU State aid control focuses primarily on State aid with spillover effects on other Member States and (2) national agencies for controlling subsidies focus on subsidies with their primary effects within the Member States. This would without doubt limit the scope of EU State aid policy but would also allow it to concentrate its limited resources to the still too many serious cases of State aid. For solving the problem of self-commitment due to political economy pressures, it might be necessary to establish all these agencies for subsidy control as independent agencies. This can also be recommended for the EU State aid control itself, which might also enable it to also control the effectiveness of the subsidies granted by the EU itself. Through the establishment of a well-designed two-level system of these agencies, the independence of the particular agencies in regard to their respective governments (Member States and the EU Commission) might be strengthened. It is certainly true that such a two-level system of State aid control might deprive the EU Commission of some power in regard to making policy decisions about general principles for granting State aid in certain policy fields, but this depends (1) on the specific design of such a system, and (2) might also be more appropriate in regard to the subsidiarity principle. However, within such a two-level system of State aid control, a more

---

Wettbewerbsordnung: Probleme aus der Perspektive des Wettbewerbs zwischen Jurisdiktionen', in *Europäische Integration als ordnungspolitische Gestaltungsaufgabe, Probleme der Vertiefung und Erweiterung der Europäischen Union*, D. Cassel (ed.) (Berlin, 1998), pp. 37-74.

economic approach for the assessment of the compatibility of State aid with the internal market and for safeguarding the effectiveness of the use of State aid in economic and social policies might be very helpful.

Such a solution would be close to the proposals of the German Monopol-kommission in their Biennial Report 2006/2007 on the application of the more economic approach to European State aid control.[7] The Monopolkommission clearly welcomes a more economic approach to State aid policy. However, based upon their economic and legal analysis they clearly insist that 'the European ban on aid only takes effect and justifies intervention by the European Commission as the controlling body if a risk of distortion of competition on the internal market has been established'. Therefore the 'objective likelihood of an aid noticeably distorting competition should be examined under Article 107(1) TFEU. This should be combined with a restriction of the area of application of aid control by the European Commission, and should be flanked by the intro-duction of complementary aid control on national level and by private right to appeal'.[8] Therefore also the Monopolkommission is in favour of a kind of two-level system of State aid control agencies, with the EU State aid policy focussing on 'ensuring less distortion to competition through aid and on better targeting aid to keep cross-border distortion of competition in the EU internal market as low as possible'.[9]

My main point in this section is that we need a very careful and explicit discussion about the proper task of EU State aid policy.[10] Both the practice and the general argumentative framework of EU State aid policy has evolved very dynamically in the last decade, partly also through applying the more economic approach to this part of EU competition policy. The EU State aid policy has evolved from a policy that controlled subsidies in regard to their distortive effects on competition to a policy which increasingly and, in the meantime, also explicitly claims the authority to monitor all (direct and indirect) subsidies in the EU in regard to their effectiveness as a policy instrument. The central role of testing for the necessity and proportionality of State aid for achieving certain

---

[7] See German Monopolies Commission (*supra* n. 3).

[8] *Ibid.* p. 69.

[9] *Ibid.* p. 50.

[10] See also J.L. Buendia Serra and B. Smulders, 'The Limited Role of the "Refined Economic Approach" in Achieving the Objectives of State Aid Control: Time for Some Realism', in *EC State Aid Law, Liber Amicorum Francisco Santaolalla Gadea* (Alphen aan den Rijn, 2008), pp. 1-26. M. Blauberger, 'Of "Good" and "Bad" Subsidies: European State Aid Control through Soft and Hard Law', in: West European Politics 32 (4), 2000, pp. 719-737.

policy objectives in comparison to the question of assessing distortive effects on competition and cross-border spillover effects demonstrates this development clearly. Two important questions have emerged: (1) Should such a huge task be fulfilled by the EU Commission (and carried out by the DG Competition)? The discussion above suggests that we should be very sceptical about such an institutional solution. In any case, it would require an extensive discussion and analysis, which so far does not seem to exist. (2) Does the EU Commission have the legal competence for fulfilling such a *general effectiveness control of subsidies* on the basis of Articles 107 et seq. TFEU? This is a question that must be clarified by lawyers, but I strongly doubt that this is the case.[11]

III. State aid, bailout problem, and merger policy

The State aid of the Member States in the financial crisis seriously threatened the authority of EU State aid policy. Although it was evident that the huge sums expended by the Member States for bailing out banks (and also other firms that came into difficult financial problems as a consequence of the financial markets) would distort competition in the internal market, the EU Commission struggled heavily to defend its authority for controlling these State aid. It can be left open here how well the EU Commission succeeded in really preventing or limiting distortions of competition through its attempts to enforce some limits and conditions as to these kinds of State aid. In fact, the financial crisis, in which each Member State rushed to save its domestic banks and firms without considering spillover effects on other countries, demonstrated very clearly the necessity of a strong EU State aid control. However, this example also showed the political difficulties for the EU Commission in enforcing State aid rules in serious cases of bailouts. Therefore it might make sense to think about complementary policies which help to prevent the emergence of significant bailout situations. The problem of 'too big to fail' has already been discussed extensively in regard to the banking sector. The regulatory framework of banks and financial markets can be used for addressing this problem – either by limiting the size of financial institutions or by taking care that insolvencies would not jeopardize the stability of the financial system. In this brief chapter I want to consider the admittedly far-reaching idea that also merger policy might be an instrument for preventing the danger of bailout problems.

Can EU merger policy be used for reducing the danger of bailouts? According to the EU Merger Regulation, a merger must be prohibited if it would

---

[11] See, e.g., German Monopolies Commission (*supra* n. 3), p. 50.

lead to a 'significant impediment to effective competition' (Article 3(2) Merger Regulation). If a firm is so large or in other way important that a Member State seems not to be able to let this firm go bankrupt (due to a huge loss of jobs and so forth), the ensuing bailout problem distorts competition in the market. If bailed out inefficient firms can survive in the market, other more efficient firms are harmed and incorrect incentives are set for competition and the efficient allocation of resources. The State aid rules about aid for rescue and restructuring of firms in difficulty attempt to limit the extent of exactly this kind of distortion of competition. However, it should be seen clearly that the bailout problem does not only distort competition *ex post*, i.e. when a firm in difficulty is actually getting aid from the State. On most markets, competition between firms is already being distorted by the expectation that some firms are more prone to being bailed out than other firms, i.e. if their bailout probability is different. If, for example, in Germany a very large private bank on account of its size or a German *Sparkasse* for political reasons has a larger probability for being bailed out than, for example, a smaller private bank, then competition between these firms is distorted because customers, suppliers and creditors need to care less about their insolvency. In this respect, also large manufacturing firms might have similar artificial competitive advantages in comparison to their small- and medium-sized competitors. In addition to the negative effects on the taxpayer, positive bailout probabilities can have two negative economic effects: (1) Any positive bailout probability of a firm leads to a lower level of diligence and scrutiny of the risk of doing business with these firms (especially creditors) and therefore leads to economic inefficiency. (2) The existence of different bailout probabilities for firms that compete on the same market leads to a direct distortion of competition.

If a merger leads to an increasing probability that the new entity will be bailed out in case of an imminent bankruptcy, the ensuing distortions of competition could be used as an argument that the merger should be prohibited, because it leads to a 'significant impediment to effective competition' according to the Merger Regulation. The reform of the Merger Regulation in 2004 led to the new assessment criterion 'significant impediment to effective competition' ('SIEC test'), which opened the merger policy to a broader set of arguments how a merger might significantly impede effective competition. The main reason for this reform was the potential existence of non-coordinated effects of mergers, which were assumed of not being grasped appropriately by the traditional market dominance test. From an economic perspective, it is no problem to add an additional bailout test to the list of reasons why a merger can significantly impede effective competition.

The basic idea of such a bailout test might be put as follows: Before the merger the firms might not be big and/or important enough to trigger the State to save one of these firms if they get into difficulties. Therefore the bailout probability before the merger might be zero (or low), leading to no (significant) distortions of competition through the bailout danger. However, after the merger the new entity might have a high bailout probability due to its much increased size and importance. Therefore the merger has caused this high bailout probability, leading to significant distortions of competition on (some or all of) the markets, on which this firm is doing business. If the merger leads to a situation in which one of the firms in the market is de facto protected against insolvency by the State, this can be interpreted as a significant impediment to effective competition according to the Merger Regulation. In that respect, the prohibition of a merger is only another alternative (structural) instrument for avoiding distortions of competition through the possibility of State aid. On first sight, it seems that we would not need this kind of instrument if we have a well-functioning system of State aid control. However, experience shows again and again the limits of the credible enforcement of State aid control. Beyond that, also the EU State aid rules on aid for the rescue and restructuring of firms in difficulty do not eliminate distortive State aid to failing firms, but only limit the extent of these distorting effects. Both consequences are not so surprising because State aid policy does not address the cause of the problem, which are the huge economic and social effects in the case of the failing of such a big firm. Using merger policy for preventing the emergence of firms 'too big to fail', which significantly impede effective competition through a high bailout probability, would be in line with the traditional role of merger control as a preventive instrument for protecting competition in a market economy.

Of course, the next important question is: How could such a bailout test be implemented? What kind of criteria can be used for assessing the bailout probability before and after a merger? Should the increase of the bailout probability be decisive or would it be better to have a critical threshold that should not be surpassed? Should there be exemptions for allowing mergers that would lead to 'too big to fail' firms in exceptional cases? I think that so far we lack ready-made answers for these difficult questions.

But I think it might not be so difficult to explore more deeply how such an assessment might be carried out. Most important is that we have to know more about the determinants of the bailout probability of firms. This might be dependent on the extent of a variety of negative effects of a failing firm. It can be presumed that not always the absolute size of a firm (and therefore the absolute size of possible job losses) might be most important, but also whether these job losses are concentrated in a specific region. In that respect, empirical research

251

about the determinants of past cases of aid for rescue and restructuring of firms in difficulty might be very helpful. Another important determinant might be the specific political institutions in a Member State, which can be more or less prone to rent seeking activities. Here the political-economic and rent seeking literature might be helpful. If, for example, a Member State can credibly demonstrate (such as through the establishment of an independent national agency for the control of State aid) that it would not succumb to bailout claims, then a lower post-merger bailout probability might be expected, leading to the clearance of mergers which otherwise would be prohibited.

These considerations can only give some preliminary ideas about how possible arguments, assessment criteria and even remedies might look like. Although this is an approach that still has to be worked out in detail, the difficulties might not really be so much larger than in many other difficult merger cases, where, for example, we try to assess the extent of non-coordinated effects or the increase of the probability of coordinated effects.

These are only very preliminary ideas about such a new bailout test within EU merger control. At this stage of research, I would not claim that such a bailout test should be introduced in EU merger policy. However, due to both the huge bailout problems that all Member States – as well as the EU Commission itself – are facing and the limited capability of EU State aid policy to solve this problem, we should seriously think about possibilities for addressing the root of the problem, which is that there might be too many firms that are so big or so important that they can force States into bailing them out. In order to limit the danger of bailout problems, merger policy might be a good candidate for an appropriate policy instrument which helps to prevent serious bailout problems.

Of course, it should not replace other instruments from, for example, establishing effective institutional safeguards for preventing the State from giving in to bailout claims due to political reasons, as, for example, EU State aid policy or independent national agencies for controlling State aid. However, merger policy might complement these efforts by reducing the danger that firms emerge with high bailout probabilities. Since, from an economic perspective, such a bailout test might be carried out within the overall assessment criterion of 'significant impediment to effective competition', it might even be feasible within the scope of the current Merger Regulation. However, such a task requires much more research. My contention here is that the bailout problem is big and serious enough that we should think earnestly about this possibility. Such a discussion might also help to see the great dangers of an alternative (and in the financial crisis often favoured) solution for bailout problems, namely merging these failing firms with other large firms. This is exactly the wrong solution, and one which only aggravates future bailout problems.

ANNEX

MONOPOLKOMMISSION

The "More Economic Approach" in European State Aid Control

Translated Version of Chapter VI of the Biennial Report 2006/2007

Bonn, November 2008

Contents

The "More Economic Approach" in European State Aid Control[†*]

1. Introduction

1.1 The Issue

1. The idea of a "more economic approach" is widely discussed in the general public[†] and in research on European competition policy. The Directorate-General for Competition of the European Commission has for some years been pursuing the aim of gradually redirecting competition law towards a more economic approach. The aims and substance of the new approach are the subject of much controversy amongst economists and legal experts. So far European antitrust law has been the main focus of the general interest.[1] (Arts. 81, 82 EC Treaty and the EC Merger Regulation), together with the reforms in this field proposed by the European Commission.[2] However, the regulations in EU antitrust law, which are intended for companies operating on the European internal market, are not the subject of this chapter. The concern here is the possible application of a more economic approach in the field of EU state aid control (Arts. 87ss. EC Treaty). These articles form the second part of the European rules on competition, and they deal with restraints of competition caused by sovereign states through state aid. The European Commission intends to reform this area fundamentally by applying a more economic approach.[3] The present European Commissioner for Competition, Neelie Kroes, attaches considerable importance to reform of the legislation on state aid, indeed she calls it the "flagship project" of her term in office.[4]

2. The new approach in state aid law is not the same as the methods and concepts which the European Commission applies as a more economic approach in EU antitrust law. Certainly, just like EU antitrust law, the legislation on state aid is designed to protect competition in the

---

[†] The German *Monopolkommission* (Monopolies Commission), www.monopolkommission. de, is an independent advisory body to the German Government in the areas of Antitrust and Regulated Industries (a.o. Telecommunications, Energy, Mail and Railways). In its Biennial Reports (this document is a translated version of Chapter VI of the Biennial Report 2006/2007, published 2008) and in its Special Reports, the Monopolkommission scrutinizes systematically for systemic and economic soundness the decisional practice of the *Bundeskartellamt* (German Competition Agency) and of the *Bundesnetzagentur* (German Regulatory Agency for Network Industries) as well as the underlying legal framework, to a lesser but growing extent also the EU Commission's enforcement policy. While without decisional powers, the Monopolkom-mission's recommendations in the past were regularly followed both by Agencies and the Legislator.

[*] The Monopolkommission would like to thank Mrs. Eileen Martin for translating the original German text into English.

[1] The term "antitrust law" is used very broadly in this chapter, covering all the competition regulations that concern companies, including merger control.

[2] Currently in particular aspects of abuse control, Art. 82 EC Treaty.

[3] In discussing the desired reform of state aid control the European Commission uses the expression "refined" economic approach as well as a "more economic" approach.

[4] Neelie Kroes, "European Competition Policy in a changing world and globalised economy: fundamentals, new objectives and challenges ahead", SPEECH/ 07/364, GCLC/College of Europe Conference on "50 Years of EC Competition Law", Brussels, 5 June 2007.

common market.[5] Nevertheless, there are decisive differences. In the legislation on state aid the instigators of possible restraints of competition are not companies and market participants but sovereign states. Moreover, other aims beside economic objectives – social and distribution policy and cultural interests – are important in the law on state aid. European state aid control is also characterised by a transfer mechanism. The grants are paid out of tax revenue, which in turn causes loss of welfare, or revenue is absorbed that could be used for other purposes (opportunity costs).

1.2 State Aid as a Particular Form of Subsidisation

1.2.1 The Concept of State Aid

3. The concept of state aid is used in European law for subsidies to which the European ban on state aid in Art. 87, Para. 1 EC Treaty applies.[6] State aid is defined as follows: "Save as otherwise provided in this Treaty, any aid granted by a Member State or through State resources in any form whatsoever which distorts or threatens to distort competition by favouring certain undertakings or the production of certain goods shall, in so far as it affects trade between Member States, be incompatible with the common market."

So five conditions must be met for a measure to be classified as state aid and be subject to European state aid control:

- It must "favour" certain companies or production processes, that is, it must create an economic advantage for the recipient.
- It must be granted to "certain undertakings or the production of certain goods", so it must have a selective effect.
- It must be granted "by a member state or through state resources". So only a transfer of a member state's resources, not aid granted by the EU itself, is state aid.
- It must also "distort or threaten to distort competition" .
- It additionally must "affect trade between member states".

4. Measures that qualify as state aid are on principle incompatible with the common market under Art. 87, Para. 1 EC Treaty. Under Art. 88, Para. 3, Sentence 1 EC Treaty member states must inform the European Commission of any aid which they intend to introduce or alter

---

[5] This is already evident in the subdivisions in the law. The chapter "Rules on Competition" in Title VI of the EC Treaty is divided into "Section 1 – Rules applying to undertakings" and "Section 2 – Aids granted by States". While Section 1 contains Arts. 81 to 86 of the Treaty with the antitrust regulations, Section 2 contains the European regulations on state aid (Arts. 87 to 89 EC Treaty).

[6] In practice the term "state aid" is used in a very different ways. In the national accounts drawn up by the German Federal Statistical Office, and consequently in fiscal policy economics, a narrow concept is used, meaning only positive financial grants (monetary transfers) to companies. Cf. Federal Statistical Office, Statistisches Jahrbuch 2007, p. 439; Brümmerhoff, D., Finanzwissenschaft, Munich 2007, pp. 17ss. But the Kiel Institut für Weltwirtschaft, for example, holds the view that all the advantages that are distorted by the allocation of macroeconomic resources should be designated state aid. Cf. Boss, A., Rosenschon, A., Beihilfen in Deutschland: Eine Bestandaufnahme, Kieler Arbeits-papiere, No. 1267, Kiel 2006, pp. 4ss.

– 3 –

early enough for the European Commission to respond (obligatory notification).[7] The European Commission will examine whether a particular aid may by way of exception be permitted, for the ban in Art. 87, Para. 1 EC Treaty is not absolute. The Treaty lists a number of conditions that will allow an exemption to be made (Art. 87, Paras. 2 and 3, Art. 86, Para. 2), and these are in general terms which allow the European Commission wide scope for judgement in exercising its control. State aid for economic purposes can be approved, for example, if the measure is "to facilitate the development of certain economic activities or of certain economic areas" (Art. 87, Para. 3 c)). Secondly, the EC Treaty also allows aids with a social or distribution policy background – especially aids to promote disadvantaged regions[8] or aid for cultural objectives[9] – to be exempt.

5. It will already be clear that European supervision of state aid – unlike the application of the antitrust regulations (Arts. 81 and 82 EC Treaty, merger control regulations) – is a political part of European competition law. Beside aspects of competition policy social and distribution policy aspects also play an important part. In judging an aid the European Commission must weigh these aspects against each other as well as considering the effects on competition.

1.2.2 The Macroeconomic Importance

6. The aids given by member states that fall under European control of state aid are of great macroeconomic importance. The level of all the aids granted in the EU has fallen, from an average of EUR 104 billion in the years 1993 to 1995, but according to information from the European Commission it was still EUR 67 billion in 2006.[10] That is a ratio of about 0.6% of the EU gross domestic product (GDP).

7. The level of aid granted varies between member states, in some cases considerably. In

---

[7] The obligatory notification only applies to "new aids", cf. Art. 1, c) of Procedural Regulation No. 659/1999. For "existing aid" (cf. definition in Art. 1, b) of the Procedural Regulation), the procedure laid down in Art. 88, Paras. 1 and 2 EC Treaty applies.

[8] 8 Art. 87, Para. 3 a) and c), EC Treaty.

[9] Art. 87, Para. 3 d) EC Treaty.

[10] CF. Commission Report, State Aid Scoreboard, Autumn 2007, COM(2007) 791 final, p. 3, fn.1 The figure quoted includes aids for the manufacturing industry, the services sector, coal mining, agriculture, fisheries and parts of the transport sector. But it does not include aids for rail transport or compensation payments for services of general economic interest (for more detail see 5.4.3), as according to the Commission comparable data was not available. The nominal level of EU aid shown is relatively low compared with the volume of subsidies, namely EUR 45.8 billion, shown in the 21st Subsidisation Report of the Federal Government, just for Germany in the same period, 2006. The figure consists of the financial aids and tax concessions granted by the Federal Government, the Länder and the municipalities without the expenditure by the EU on market regulation and without the ERP financial aids. Cf. Bericht der Bundesregierung über die Entwicklung der Finanzhilfen des Bundes und der Steuervergünstigungen für die Jahre 2005-2008 (21st Subsidisation Report), p. 22. http://www.bundesfinanzministerium.de/nn_53848/DE/BMF_Startseite/Service/Broschueren_Besteller-service/Finanz_und_Wirtschaftspolitik/40200,property=publicationFine/pdf. However, it must be remembered in this context that the EU statistics, unlike the Federal Government's Subsidisation Report, only include pure grants, that is, in exchange contracts only the subsidisation equivalent is calculated and shown compared with the assumed behaviour of a private investor.

absolute figures Germany was in the lead in 2006, with EUR 20 billion, or 30% of the entire volume of aid given in the EU. It was followed by France with EUR 10 billion, Italy with EUR 5.5 billion and Spain with EUR 5 billion. Measured by GDP other member states are relatively higher on the list. But Germany gave 0.87% of its GDP in financial aids and so was above the EU average of 0.58.[11]

8. EU statistics on the distribution of state aid by economic sector in percent of total state aid show that the greater part, 66%, of the state aid granted in Germany flows into manufacturing (EU average 58%), with 20% going to agriculture (EU average 24%) and 11% to hard coal mining (EU average 5%). Of the aid granted for horizontal effect, that is, not intended right from the start for specific sectors but to serve objectives in every sector, the aid given for environmental protection measures and energy saving in Germany tops the list.[12] The above-av-erage aid granted for environmental protection and hard coal mining in Germany is the main reason for the high level of state aid in this country compared with the other EU member states.[13]

1.3 Effects on Competition

9. Granting state aid involves various costs and has various repercussions. On the cost side, first the financing or opportunity costs must be taken into account, as must the welfare losses incurred by the need to raise taxes in other areas (the "shadow cost" of taxation). In addition, state aid can lead to inefficient use of public funds through free riding and erroneous prognoses.

10. In addition to the economic costs there is the danger of disadvantageous effects on competition. The considerable distortion to competition that state aid can cause on the product and services markets affected can be of immense importance for competition policy. Restraints of competition thus induced create misguided incentives in allocative, productive and dynamic respects.

11. In regard to allocation it should be borne in mind that existing resources can be drawn into less productive use through state aid. If competition is workable the market will send clear signals to suppliers on which products and services consumers want. If a state aid induces the companies favoured to lower their prices, these signals may be distorted, and so more resources are used for the subsidised activity. If an entire sector is favoured this can have disadvantageous effects on other sectors. Moreover, finance is withdrawn from market participants in other branches in their function as taxpayers. Such allocative misguidance is evident, for example, in coal mining.

---

[11] Malta was in the lead with 2.29% of GDP, followed by Latvia with 1.8%, Finland with 1.53%, and Sweden with 1.15%. Great Britain (0.22%), Greece (0.26%) and Luxemburg (0.32%) all had particularly low levels.

[12] This is probably due particularly to the selective exceptions created for German energy-intensive firms, for measures that affect all companies equally are not aid: the criterion of selectivity required under Art. 87, Para. 1 EC Treaty is not met. If all the companies producing in Germany were to be equally affected the measure would be a general economic policy measure and it would not appear in the statistics on state aid.

[13] Cf. 21st Subsidisation Report of the Federal Government, loc. cit., p. 43.

12. State aid can also mean that less efficient companies are artificially maintained, thus making it more difficult for new and efficient companies to enter the market. The productive efficiency of companies can also be impaired if they use their resources for rent-seeking activities, whereas if the market forces were free to operate they could use them productively. And companies have less incentive to produce efficiently and invest if they can assume that the state will come to their aid (to save jobs) if they are in financial difficulties (reducing cost pressure).

13. If state aid changes the profitability of an investment companies may be induced to change the level, nature and timing of their investment. In this way distorting investment decisions may be made and dynamic efficiency impaired.

14. State aid that helps to increase the market power of a single company is particularly problematic. Granting state aid to established companies can result in a barrier to market entry for newcomers, help to seal off the domestic market and facilitate displacement practices. If the company can also transfer market power thus acquired to adjoining markets through crosssubsidisation the competition problem is further intensified.

2. Possible Purposes in Granting State Aid

2.1 Types of State Aid

15. State aid can be found in many forms; the differences are:

- the form in which it is granted[14],
- if it is tied to specific projects[15],
- the absolute amount and size relative to the costs of the activity subsidised,
- the method of giving the aid[16],
- the duration[17],
- the breadth of the effect[18], and
- the purpose for which the aid is given.

16. The purposes for which state aid is given will now be examined in more detail, in order to assess the suitability of aid as an economic policy instrument. These purposes play a big part in the legality of state aid. State aid can serve to cure market failure. Removing market failure is the classical economic justification for granting state aid and other forms of subsidisation. The classical features of market failure are discussed in 2.2. But there are also aims outside economics which state aid is intended to achieve. These non-economic aims are the subject of 2.3.

---

[14] For instance, a loan or tax concession.
[15] The aid can be tied to a specific activity or given as operational aid which the company is free to use as it will.
[16] For instance using a transparent tender.
[17] The aid can be given as a single payment or in instalments.
[18] State aid can be individual in nature and only benefit a specific company; but some state aid measures benefit all the companies in a certain sector; finally there is aid with a horizontal objective that is not limited right from the start to a specific economic sector.

– 6 –

2.2 Compensating for Market Failure as a Reason for Granting State Aid

17. On principle state aid can help to reduce market or competition failure. The causes of market or competition failure given in the economic literature are serious external effects, public goods, natural monopolies, asymmetrical information and adjustment shortfalls. It must always be remembered that intervention by the state often itself leads to inefficiencies that in turn can lead to state or policy failure. The main factors that lead to state or policy failure when state aid is granted can be lack of information, erroneous analyses and prognoses, delay in decision-making and in the effects of the use of the funds and mis-incentives within politics and the public administration. In view of this, before aid is granted an examination should be made using a comparative institutional economic approach, in which the possible market failure is weighed against the threat of state failure. Finally, market failure does not in itself justify state aid, the aid is only justified when it is particularly suited to correct this market fail-ure.[19]

2.2.1 External Effects

18. Positive and negative external effects will occur if the activity of one economic subject (e.g. production or consumption) has effects on the benefit to other economic subjects (increasing or decreasing it), without these effects being taken into account in the market pricing system or without any other compensation.[20] External effects are the direct result of property rights that are inadequately defined or definable, or that cannot be adequately implemented.

19. Negative external effects are familiar from environmental policy. If those affected by environmental pollution have no enforceable property rights in the commodity environment, they will typically not succeed in preventing the pollution or in charging the (external) costs to the polluter. The failure to include these external costs in the market pricing mechanism (lack of internalisation) results in excessive environmental pollution. For instance, CO_2 emission, such as occurs through electricity generation (especially from coal-fired power stations), has negative external effects, unless these costs can be internalised through appropriate political means (e.g. taxes or emission trading certificates).

20. The occurrence of positive external effects is for instance assumed in basic research. Basic research is characterised by the fact that third parties can hardly be excluded from benefiting from the knowledge gained, as the lack of possibilities for patenting mean that there are no enforceable property rights. As they cannot be excluded, third parties also profit from basic research without having to pay for this.

21. As property rights cannot be assigned, the price mechanism alone cannot ensure efficient market results in the case of either negative or positive external effects. In a pure market

---

[19] Cf. Coase, R.H., The Problem of Social Cost, Journal of Law and Economics 3, 1960, pp. 1-44 and Demsetz, H., Information and Efficiency, Another Viewpoint, Journal of Law and Economics 12, 1969, pp. 122.

[20] These effects are called external effects because they occur outside the voluntary market relations.

solution more than the economically efficient quantity of CO2 would be emitted and less would be spent on basic research than economically efficient. In the case of serious external effects state intervention must aim to ensure that the divergence between costs and yields that are individually taken into account and actually incurred for society as a whole is eliminated by measures to internalise the external effects.

22. On principle state aid, e.g. in the form of an investment bonus for reducing pollution, can help to internalise negative external effects. State aid can have a similar effect on basic research. However, one must heed that the external effect must first be identified as serious and quantified in the form of external costs.[21] Furthermore must be kept in mind that the assessment of the external effect is influenced by the decision-maker's subjective sensation and the level of his information. In addition, the period for observing the extent of the external effect or the level of the external costs is also relevant. Finally, state aid as an economic policy instrument must be examined for its particular suitability to internalise the external effects. As with taxes, the socially optimal quantity of a good can only be achieved approximately or in a lengthy process of trial and error. Moreover, in view of this granting state aid to the originator of a negative external effect seems dubious, because he is being rewarded for reducing or avoiding the external effect whereas in fact, the originator of the external effect should be obliged to bear the external costs thus incurred.

2.2.2 Public Goods

23. A good that creates no rivalry in consumption and thus can be used by many without marginal costs, and from the use of which no one can be excluded at justifiable expenditure and with justifiable means, is a pure public good.

24. In some economic literature the lack of rivalry in consumption is itself regarded as sufficient to identify a public good, the private provision of which without state intervention would lead to market failure.[22] The lack of rivalry for an existing commodity means that additional demand for the same commodity does not require additional costs to provide it, that is, the marginal costs of an additional user are zero. In the ideal case, therefore, no-one should be excluded from use of the good. However, at a zero price such good would never be produced in the private sector without subsidisation.[23]

25. However, the lack of rivalry is not in itself sufficient to identify market failure. For if it is possible to exclude potential demand from use of the good a supplier can take the one-off

---

[21] Strictly speaking, it is hard to imagine an economic activity that does not give rise to any positive or negative externalities (external effects are ubiquitous). If the state attempted to internalise all externalities this would be tantamount to comprehensive interventionism, which would paralyse much private economic activity.

[22] Typical goods that are characterised by lack of rivalry in consumption are virtual goods like software and the contents of television and radio programmes and the Internet.

[23] This applies particularly in view of the fact that a supplier generally has fixed costs for providing a commodity. The provision of software, for example, which is also characterised by lack of rivalry in consumption, requires one-off research and development costs, while the costs of reproducing it are negligible.

provision costs into account in his pricing (e.g. with multi-part tariffs). In a comparative perspective this need not necessarily be inefficient supply.[24]

26. Hence economists usually only speak of a public good and of market failure induced by it if potential users who are not willing to pay cannot be excluded with justifiable means, as property rights are not adequately defined or definable. Examples of a pure public good are the internal and external security of a country, or ensuring competition on markets. No consumer can be excluded from the advantages of competition with justifiable means, and no citizen can be excluded from his country's internal and external security.

27. Non-exclusivity leads to free riding. As no-one can be excluded from a public good noone has a strong incentive to participate in financing it (unless forced to do so). As a result a pure public good can generally not be provided efficiently without state intervention.

28. Nonetheless, a public good need not necessarily be provided by the public authorities. It can be provided by private companies, if they can cover their costs with a public grant.[25] Such a grant can constitute state aid in the meaning of Art. 87, Para. 1 EC Treaty. However, if a proper tender has been held for the private provision of the public commodity, and the company that puts in the best bid in price and performance is awarded the contract, the public grant given in this context is not regarded as state aid by the European courts.[26]

2.2.3 Size Advantages in Relevant Demand

29. Size advantages on the supply or demand side of the relevant market can give rise to a natural monopoly. In this case a single supplier will provide the quantity in demand on the market at the most favourable cost. Supply-side size advantages are to be found on electricity grids, for example, where they are caused mainly by installing dense electricity distribution networks.

30. Demand-side size advantages are created when major positive network effects occur. A positive network effect is the phenomenon that new demand for the same good increases the benefit to current users. A new user for an application software, for example, will increase the benefit to other users because he is an additional potential exchange partner (e.g. for text processing documents or information). The resultant desire to join as big a network as possible can in the extreme case lead to monopolisation of the entire market by one supplier.[27]

---

[24] This is evident on various markets for virtual goods, the provision of which is not characterised by general market failure. Moreover, the skimming pricing system is often used by innovators in early marketing phases, in order to ensure rapid amortisation of their research and development costs. It is a frequent strategy on the market for PC processor chips, for example, where it can be observed that the supplier who has developed the next generation of chips initially charges high prices, which come down markedly as soon as competitors put a chip of the same performance on to the market.

[25] In Germany, for instance, some prisons have been part-privatised.

[26] For more detail see 5.3.4.

[27] This will occur if one of a number of incompatible proprietary technologies has achieved a critical mass of demand. Owing to the positive back-coupling effect that then starts this technology, after achieving the critical mass, will attract the entire market demand (winner takes all / winner takes most). This form of de-mand-side induced competition for the dominant market position is particularly evident on markets for virtual network goods, as there are no supply-side restrictions here.

cont.

A well known example of a demand-side induced (quasi-) monopoly is the application software Microsoft Office.

31. Often the marginal costs of a natural monopoly are below the average costs, so that a marginal cost price would cause a deficit for the operator of the monopoly. Deviating from the marginal cost price, on the other hand, leads to a loss of allocative efficiency, in contrast to the theoretical ideal case. In theory, state aid could be justified economically. In practice, however, natural monopolies do not generally require state aid. The loss of allocative efficiency is more of a theoretical nature and without practical relevance. In many cases natural monopolies actually require state price supervision, in order to protect users from exploitation by too high prices. These cases occur when the monopoly supplier is protected from potential competitors by high barriers to market entry and so can keep his price above competitors' levels.

2.2.4 Asymmetrical Information

32. There is asymmetrical information if one side of the market participants concerned is better informed than the other. The undesirable effects this causes can be moral hazard[28] and ad-verse selection.

33. There is asymmetrical information on credit markets, for example. The suppliers of loans are not fully informed of the exact risk of default posed by each borrower. Consequently they will set the interest rate for their loan (the price for the loan) by the estimated average default risk. Would-be borrowers with low individual risk of default (good risk customers) will regard this price as too high and may possibly decide against taking up the loan. Would-be borrowers that are an above-average risk, on the other hand (bad risk customers) benefit from the price, which is relatively favourable for them. The systematic displacement of the good risks by the bad (adverse selection) can in extreme cases lead to market failure, as beneficial transactions are not undertaken.[29]

34. Particularly in regard to raising capital for small and midsize companies it is suspected that there are major information asymmetries that could cause market failure. It is assumed for both venture capital markets and for lending by banks in the private sector that the suppliers of capital systematically overestimate the risk of default on loans to this group of companies and so set the price too high.[30] As a result raising capital is made more difficult for

---

A supplier of software, for example, can adapt his supply to changes in demand at almost any speed (instant scalability).

[28] There is moral hazard when one market side has the possibility of changing key items that are relevant to the transaction secretly and at the expense of the other side (owing to the asymmetrical information) after the contract is signed (ex post).

[29] The classical example of negative selection caused by information asymmetries at the expense of the demand side is the market for used cars. Cf. Akerlof, G., The Market for 'Lemons': Quality Uncertainty and the Market Mechanism, Quarterly Journal of Economics 84, 1970, pp. 488-500.

[30] One reason for this is that potential investors are faced with relatively greater problems in obtaining reliable information on the business prospects for small and midsize companies than for large firms. Cf. European Commission, Community Guidelines on state aid to promote capital investments in small and mediumsized enterprises, OJ EU C 194 of 18 August 2006, p. 2.

smaller and midsize companies than for larger firms, so that they can suffer considerable competitive disadvantages.

35. Public authorities often grant small and midsize companies loans at favourable conditions with the aim of compensating for these competitive disadvantages. As the award is selective these loans take on the character of state aid. Hence before state interventions, as by granting a soft loan, it should always be examined whether protective mechanisms are not forming on the market itself that could prevent market failure. Possible protective mechanisms are effective screening or signalling, which reduce the danger of moral hazard and adverse selection. An exact examination is also indicated in view of the fact that information asymmetries on capital markets do not necessarily lead to less lending, as inefficiently high lending can also be shown to be the result of underestimating risks. In this case state lending would lead to further loss of efficiency.

2.2.5 Shortcomings in Adjustment

36. Adjustment shortcomings are, firstly, a situation in which a market equilibrium does not exist, owing to unfavourable supply and demand constellations, or a new equilibrium does not evolve, or not at the desired speed, especially owing to lack of flexibility by market actors. One example of lack of flexibility is the ruinous competition that is caused by the "wrong" order in which suppliers leave a market (e.g. in inland waterways and agriculture).

37. State aid is often used as an instrument of sectoral structural policy in the EU and by member states. The aim here is to cushion the problems caused by structural change from the agricultural (primary) and manufacturing (secondary) sectors to the services sector (tertiary sector) and make them socially bearable. The need for a sectoral structural policy is seen in the lack of flexibility outlined above.

38. Economically, adjustment aids (or restructuring aids in EU law) can at most be justified as an economic policy instrument for sectoral structural policy under certain conditions. Adjustment aids are given to companies with the aim of simplifying the process of adjustment to the given economic conditions. After German reunification, for example, adjustment aids were given particularly to agricultural production cooperatives in the new Federal Länder. The grants, which were given e.g. for purchases of modern agricultural equipment, were to enable the farmers to move to market economy conditions more quickly.

39. On principle adjustment aid is intended to be help to self-help. It should only be paid until the necessary adjustment to changing structural conditions has been made. However, it has frequently been evident in the past that under political pressure a grant that was originally intended to be a short-term measure became a permanent subsidy to a particular sector or certain enterprises. This maintained the old structures and counteracted the original intention to accelerate the adjustment process. Permanent subsidisation is not an appropriate way to remove market failure caused by shortcomings in adjustment. On the contrary, permanent aid that assumes the character of maintenance grants serves other economic policy aims.

2.3 The Non-Economic Aims of State Aid

2.3.1 Regional, Distributional, Employment and Industrial Policy Aims

40. Maintenance subsidies, also called rescue aid in European law, are used as a structural policy instrument to maintain economic, cultural and regional cultural structures. They are given in the form of a compensation grant, for example, in agriculture and mining. Maintenance aids are intended to keep the incomes of those employed in the sector affected by structural change (e.g. hard coal mining) on a certain, socially desirable level (distribution policy aim), and avoid excessive unemployment in the regions concerned (employment policy aim).[31] Purchases to support prices have also been a well known form of maintenance subsidy in the EU.[32]

41. In general a critical attitude should be taken to the use of state aid as a structural policy instrument, in the form of both an adjustment aid and as a maintenance aid, because it is not precise enough and can have negative side effects. Maintenance aids in particular set the wrong price signals on product markets, and so cause considerable distortion to competition to the benefit of the subsidised industry. Moreover, the resulting wrong income signals cause workers to remain in jobs that have no future prospects. This hinders the necessary structural adjustment process, which causes more loss of economic efficiency. Other instruments, like individual financial support for the workers, are better suited to achieve employment and distribution policy aims. Targeted promotion of the workers in old industries, e.g. in the form of further training and retraining courses, will achieve these aims more efficiently and more permanently without the negative side effects.

42. The focus of regional policy is on the distribution of the production potential and the development of the infrastructure in areas within an economy. The aim of regional policy measures is to create equal living standards in a region. Against this background, i.a. financial incentives are offered to companies in branches with good future prospects to induce them to move into structurally weak areas that have high unemployment, and so increase the demand for labour. The political decision-makers also hope that the arrival of these companies will have other positive effects as well, like agglomeration advantages.[33] But state aid motivated by regional policy bears a considerable prognosis risk and so can fail to have the intended effect.

---

[31] Besides employment policy and distribution policy aims, the argument put forward for subsidies in hard coal mining and agriculture, which have assumed outstanding importance in Germany in the past, was particularly the need to secure supplies nationally. This national argument loses significance in the European context.

[32] This practice has been particularly frequent on the agricultural market, where a minimum price was set to guarantee a specific income level in the sector. The minimum price was set above the market equilibrium price, and the surplus production that resulted, and which the farmers could not sell on the market at the fixed minimum price, was bought up by the state decision-makers at the previously fixed intervention price and − as far as possible − stored. This led to the well know butter and meat mountains. Alternatively, price support can also be achieved by paying a grant tied to capacity limitation (e.g. closure premiums).

[33] State aid given as part of regional policy can lead to competition between different jurisdictions "to attract private investment", which in regard to dynamic can lead to gains in efficiency. It is
cont.

43. On national level targeted promotion of large companies, i.a. through selective tax concessions, has been evident in recent years. The intention of the state decision-makers was partly to strengthen their international competitiveness by promoting these national champions. According to the theory of strategic foreign trade policy, if considerable advantages of scale and scope exist, an active industrial policy can result in the domestic company achieving gains abroad in the medium to long term, which then benefit the domestic economy.[34]

44. The Monopolkommission has explained in the past that for several reasons it takes a very critical view of the promotion of national champions, as is currently being practised in Germany in the railway and postal services sectors, for example.[35] It doubts that subsidising domestic industry benefits the state that is giving the aid; it also doubts that the benefit from the gains that may (possibly) be achieved abroad through the promotion exceed the costs of disabling the markets at home.[36] Even those who support the theory of strategic foreign trade policy assume that in constellations where all the states are granting aid they will all in the final result be worse off (the prisoners' dilemma),[37] and an inefficient aid race (a rat race) will en-sue.[38]

2.3.2 Merit Goods and Basic Security

45. In many cases aid is also granted to ensure the provision of a socially desirable quantity of goods. For goods that on principle are provided through the market mechanism, but are not regarded as provided in sufficient quantity, the term "merit goods" has been coined in the literature on fiscal policy.[39] Those who advocate this concept see the reason for the inadequate provision of merit goods as errors in estimating the benefit to themselves of these goods by private users, which in turn were caused by distorted preferences, lack of information or false information, and irrational decisions by members of the general public. This causes inadequate willingness to pay and consequently insufficient demand for merit goods. To avoid the economic inefficiencies that this undesirable development involves the political decisionmakers must promote the provision of merit goods, e.g. with state grants (aid), to such an extent that the price people have to pay for the socially desirable quantity of consumption corresponds to their "inadequate willingness to pay". The advocates of this theory name education, culture, health care and provision for old age as typical merit goods.

---

conceivable that of several incentive packages on offer the most efficient will become established – and with it the region that attaches the greatest value to attracting companies. This is discussed separately in Section 3.

[34] Cf. Brander, J., Spencer. B., Export Subsidies and International Market Share Rivalry, Journal of International Economics 18, 1985, pp. 83-100.

[35] Cf. Monopolkommission, Wettbewerbspolitik im Schatten "Nationaler Champions", Hauptgutachten 2002/2003, Baden-Baden 2005, Items 1ss.

[36] Loc. cit., Item 16.

[37] The prisoners' dilemma is a situation where individually rational behaviour by single members of the group leads to a bad result for the group as a whole.

[38] Rat races are competition processes where growing expenditure is not matched by expectation of higher earnings overall; consequently a rat race is a waste of resources.

[39] Cf. Musgrave, R.A., A Multiple Theory of Budget Determination, Finanzarchiv N.F. 17, 1956/1957, pp. 333-343.

46. As an economic concept the principle of merit goods plays hardly any role in economic theory today, as it is problematic even in its basic approach. Firstly, there is the problem of which good should be classified as deserving promotion (identification problem). This generally results in state intervention in individual people's preferences, when state decision-mak-ers also have to fix the degree of intervention (the quantity to be consumed) as a norm. This contains considerable potential for error and conflict, as the decision by a collective – or the decision-makers authorised by a collective – is set above that of the individual.[40] Moreover the state elite do not have sufficient knowledge of how demand will react to a change in price. It is also unclear where the state decision-makers are to obtain information on the optimal quantity of a merit good, if the people themselves do not know their preferences. Where this greater insight is to come from remains in the dark. So the politically desirable quantity of the merit good can only be achieved, even in the best case, through an elaborate process of trial and error. In view of this it seems more than questionable to justify huge areas of state policy, like health care and pension provision, with the merit argument. Ultimately, this is always a value judgement, which is unavoidable in weighing between individual preferences and preferences set collectively.

47. In some cases alternative reasons could be found for state aid given on the questionable grounds of merit. Assuming that the modern social state will support an individual even when he is in a desperate situation he has caused himself, certain insurance obligations can also be seen as means of preventing free riding.[41] Workers might make no provision for their old age if they could assume that after leaving working life they will receive state transfer payments. In this case the possible free riding could be prevented by making provision for old age obligatory. Similar arguments can be put forward for health and care insurance. Some state funding of culture and education can also be justified on the grounds of positive external effects.

48. The concept of services of general interest that is used in administrative law (Daseinsvorsorge) is also used to justify state aid in connection with some goods that are provided or subsidised by the state (like local transport, health care and broadcasting).[42] Under the term "services of general interest" are subsumed all state measures intended to secure the 'essential supply' ("Grundversorgung") of the population. Unlike merit goods, such supply is not justified with the argument that owing to erroneous estimates of individual needs the provision of these goods has become insufficient : it is rather argued that the market does not provide such services of general interest to the politically desired extent. The politically desired extent need not be the same as the economically efficient quantity. The loss of economic efficiency which this entails is generally accepted for the sake of other political aims. The Monopolkommission regards the pursuit of these other aims as an entirely legitimate procedure in a democracy. However, in providing the politically desired amount of funding to cover people's basic needs care should be taken to ensure that this is done at the least possible economic cost, to avoid unnecessary distortion to competition and the resultant inefficiencies.

---

[40] The argument is only uncontested in a few exceptional cases, where the decision-making competence of an individual cannot be regarded as given (e.g. children up to a certain age).

[41] There will be free riding if persons in need are not to be excluded from the state transfer system. This would be tantamount to a negative external effect.

[42] On existential support see 5.3.4 below as well.

49. An efficient provision of goods to cover people's basic needs can be achieved through competitive tender procedures. The tenders must be held so that the company that can provide the good in the desired quality and quantity at the lowest cost is awarded the contract. The part of the costs that is not covered by the market process can be compensated by state grants. As outlined above in regard to the private provision of public goods these grants do not qualify as state aid in EU law in the meaning of Art. 87, Para. 1 EC Treaty, if they are given as part of a proper temporary tender procedure. The provision of the politically desired quantity of services of general interest in conformity with competition can thus actually help to increase the public and political acceptance of reforms to the general order.

2.3.3 Politico-Economic Grounds

50. The above remarks make it clear that state aid is intervention in the market mechanism, and so can result in considerable distortions to competition. In this context state aid can cause considerable economic costs. As it is paid out of tax revenue, it first constitutes diminution of income, which is then disbursed in selective form to privileged branches of industry or enterprises. Granting state aid also involves bureaucracy costs and transaction costs for the enterprises (e.g. for consultancy on the aid, to make the application and for the obligatory reporting). Particularly protecting a stagnating branch with maintenance aid withdraws further funds from an economy. In addition, state aid has undesirable side effects, e.g. in the form of price distortions, which can result in further state maintenance payments.

51. Despite these well known disadvantages of state aid, it is evident in political practice that the aids are given even when other instruments would be better suited to achieve certain competitive or non-competitive purposes. One-off direct subject-related transfer payments (e.g. single payments to persons employed in mining), for example, have a better economic costbenefit ratio. Inefficient granting of state aid is also due to the fact that it is given as part of the political process, and those responsible for political decisions are also pursuing their own interests. The danger of self-centred behaviour by political decision-makers, who are concerned with their own re-election chances, or those of their party, is particularly high. Shortterm populist measures can give the (wrong) impression that the state aid will permanently secure jobs or create jobs in a region. State aid given in large and very noticeable amounts to a small group (like one company) has a very marked effect. The big group of taxpayers are financing it, on the other hand, with relatively small amounts that are individually hardly noticeable. While the fact that the taxpayers hardly notice the amount means that they do not take any action, the entrepreneurs and workers affected generally act in a way that the general public does notice, and so their response can help to secure an election victory for a politician or a party.

3. Possible Alternative Concepts to European Control of State Aid

3.1 Full Harmonisation of the Economic Policy Conditions?

52. Distortion to competition within the Community can be caused not only by state aid with selective effect but also by general economic policy measures by member states. There are proposals to remove these distortions to competition within the EU through full harmonisation of the economic policy rules, namely the national regulations (in labour market policy, environmental and product standards, company law), company taxation and public expenditure.[43] Banning state aid on European level is not enough, the need is to go further and aim for a level playing field throughout the EU. This can help to remove artificial distortions to competition caused by national states, enable companies to make the best use of the cost advantages of production and maximise welfare on the European internal market.

53. Harmonisation of legal requirements can be a meaningful instrument in some areas, for instance if it considerably reduces the transaction costs where cross-frontier movements are involved. But full harmonisation throughout the EU is not to be recommended, in the view of the Monopolkommission, as it would exclude all systems competition between member states and regions in the EU. Moreover, it would ignore the fact that member states have different customs and preferences in regard to their economic policy conditions.[44] In systems competition institutions are competing for efficient and mobile factors that will be strong in value creation, like companies, financial capital and mobile workers.[45] The economic policy parameters that are available to states and regions to attract mobile factors or prevent their departure consist on the one side of public assets like infrastructure, the wages level, the level of training and technology and product regulation, and the taxes and charges raised to finance these on the other. Systems competition can help to reveal the true preferences of potential users, that is, the decision-makers on mobile factors, in regard to the state offer of taxation and performance.

54. In addition, systems competition – independently of the mobility of the factors – also opens up the possibility of trying out and comparing various concepts to solve socio-political problems through a competition for ideas. The political actors in systems competition have the incentive to develop attractive institutional regulations, and reduce superfluous regulations and bureaucratic obstacles, leading to a discovery procedure. In view of this the Monopolkommission speaks out against full harmonisation of the economic policy framework conditions within the EU. It would eliminate systems competition.

3.2 Location Competition by Granting (Relocation) State Aid?

55. In view of the positive effects of systems competition some writers argue that the supervision of state aid assigned to the European Commission should be abolished – at least for businesses relocating to an area – while member states and regions within the EU should be allowed to use (relocation) state aid as a competition parameter.[46] An appropriate offer of

---

[43] For more detail see Ehlermann, C.-D., Ökonomische Aspekte des Subsidiaritätsprinzips: Harmonisierung vs. Wettbewerb der Systeme, Integration 19, 1995, pp. 11-21.

[44] Systems competition, which is also referred to as institutional, inter-jurisdictional or location competition, means that not only companies but economic systems or locations as well are competing with each other.

[45] Cf. Monopolkommission, Systemwettbewerb, Sondergutachten 27, Baden-Baden 1998, Item 9.

[46] For more detail see Gröteke, F., Europäische Beihilfenkontrolle und Standortwettbewerb – eine ökonomische Analyse, Stuttgart 2007, pp. 182ss. Opponents of this extreme approach to systems competition, by contrast, see granting state aid as a potential cause of inefficient allocation of enterprises between the various locations; they regard European supervision of state aid as a necessary institutional framework condition. For example cf. Koenig, C., Kühling, J., Reform des EG Beihilfenrechts aus der Perspektive des mitgliedstaatlichen Systemwettbewerbs – Zeit für eine Neuausrichtung?, Europäische Zeitschrift für Wirtschaftsrecht 10, 1999, pp. 517-523.

state aid can help to ensure that companies or investors make efficient location decisions, they say. In politico-economic regard it can be assumed that political decision-makers are extremely keen to attract companies into their area of jurisdiction, to create jobs and increase their tax basis. On the other side mobile companies want the best possible conditions in a location to allow them to produce and meet demand at the lowest possible cost. State aid can be an effective instrument to incorporate and internalise the positive effects that attracting companies into a particular region will have, especially in the form of agglomeration advantages to the authority granting the aid. As the positive effect could vary in intensity, depending on the characteristics of the company willing to relocate and of the region, it is efficient for sovereign authorities to create price differentiation with state aid in the form of discounts on tax payments. In location competition that region will win through that offers the greatest advantages to companies willing to locate there.

56. It is also argued that many companies would necessarily have to make long-term investment specific to that location if they settled there. That would be the case for suppliers of infrastructure facilities like energy, transport or telecommunications. In these cases there is a risk that the sovereign authority could subsequently change the framework conditions to the company's disadvantage, for instance through subsequent tax increases or other regulations.[47] Location aid can be a means to secure specific investment against later deterioration and exploitation by the authority (the hold-up problem). Moreover, granting state aid in location competition between authorities is one possible competition parameter among many. So the question arises why specifically that parameter must be regulated. EU supervision of state aid merely shifts location competition on to other parameters, like improving the physical infrastructure, free or subsidised training for workers, building regulations, etc.

57. In the view of the Monopolkommission the proposal to abolish supervision of state aid for newly locating companies to encourage competition between locations is an interesting concept in theory. However, this extreme form of systems competition, in which (location) aid would be a permissible competition parameter for local authorities and not subject to prior control would in practice only be fully functional if the principle of fiscal equivalence were realised.[48] Fiscal equivalence means that the aid would be financed entirely by the region granting it and be subject to strict budget restrictions, so that a region in financial difficulties could not expect assistance from another sovereign authority. Otherwise there would be a risk that the costs involved in a corporate location would be shifted to other authorities. This externalisation of costs could mean that a region would offer excessively high aid and consequently inefficient location decisions would be made. However, the principle of fiscal equivalence can scarcely be realised. Indeed, it is unclear on which level it should be realised – in the individual municipality, in parts of a Federal Land, throughout one Federal Land, in several Länder (e.g. North Germany) or throughout Germany. The problem would not be solved if one Federal Land were the reference unit. That would imply that cross-subsidisation was accepted within one Federal Land while subsidisation across the borders between the Länder had to be stopped. Each Federal Land would then have to fix its tax rates and decide

---

[47] Cf. Haucap, J., Hartwich, T., Fördert oder behindert die Beihilfenkontrolle der Europäischen Union den (System-)Wettbewerb, in: Schäfer, W. (ed.), Wirtschaftspolitik im Systemwettbewerb, Schriften des Vereins für Sozialpolitik, N.F., Vol. 309, Berlin 2006, pp. 93ss.

[48] This view is shared by those who support this approach. For more detail see Gröteke, F., loc. cit., pp. 206ss.

on grants to investors in location competition. This premise of free competition in aid between the Länder would be clearly contrary to the fiscal constitution in the Basic Law. In so far as tax revenue is joint revenue and also accrues to the Länder under Art. 106 of the Basic Law – and this applies to the greater part of the revenue from income, corporation and turnover tax – the Federal Government still has (competing) legislative powers, and the consequence is uniform taxation that does not depend on the domicile of the taxpayer. The obligatory financial equalization for the Länder under Art. 107, Para. 2 Basic Law also prevents the realisation of fiscal equivalence. Furthermore, there is a political obligation to redistribution between regions within the EU as well. Under Arts. 158ss. of the EC Treaty the most disadvantaged regions are to be promoted in the interests of economic and social cohesion within the Union. This results in payment flows of considerable size, motivated by distribution policy (and frequently in the form of EU subsidies).

58. There is also the risk that a state granting aid may err in its estimates, with the result that the hoped-for positive effects for the region concerned do not materialise in the long term. This prognosis risk can theoretically be reduced if the aid is repaid if the expected positive effects for the region do not materialise. However, it is only possible to concretise and implement a repayment obligation of this nature if it has involved guarantees for which the recipient of the aid is responsible, like the commitment to create a certain number of jobs. It cannot include the actual external effects which the new location could create in the region as a whole, as these are difficult to measure and cannot be exactly forecast. Moreover, the aid can prove to be inefficient if the political decision-makers are acting in self-interest in granting it (mindful of a coming election) and thus take short-term popular measures or are promoting particular interests. The danger of a hold-up described in Item 941 can also occur for the converse reasons. Conceivably, a company that has received aid could build up a potential to exert pressure that will grow with the increasing size of the company, and threaten to move elsewhere, with the loss of jobs for the region this would entail. However, to what extent companies or authorities have such potential power does depend on the specific nature of the investment made and in how far it is reversible. A company that has invested considerable amounts in facilities specific to a location (e.g. in the infrastructure) cannot issue very credible threats to leave.

59. A further consideration to support supranational aid control is that aid granted by one member state can cause negative effects in another member state in the form of distortion to competition on product and services markets. That applies particularly in cases where large companies domiciled in that member state, or the companies in a specific branch, are built up and promoted to strengthen their international competitiveness. European supervision of state aid can help to reduce cross-frontier distortion to competition on the EU single market.

60. The Monopolkommission is not in favour of abolishing European control of state aid. This is because the principle of fiscal equivalence cannot be sufficiently realised, moreover granting state aid involves prognosis problems and can cause cross-frontier distortion of competition on product and services markets. It must also be borne in mind that the ban on state aid in Art. 87, Para. 1 EC Treaty is normed and does not apply absolutely, indeed numerous exceptions are envisaged. Member states are not prevented right from the start from granting location aid under the present system, but the European Commission should take greater account than hitherto of the positive effects that competition between locations to attract companies can have.

– 18 –

4. The Tasks for the European Commission in State Aid Supervision under Arts. 87ss. EC Treaty

4.1 Possible Economic Grounds for Shifting State Aid Control to a Supranational Body

61. In the economic view there are two possible reasons for transferring supervision of the award of state aid to a supranational body like the EU. Such powers can be created with the aim of avoiding the negative effects which state aid can cause in other states through distortion of competition. Another possible reason may be to have the efficient use of public resources appraised externally and avoid commitment problem with this form of budget con-trol.[49] Owing to political pressure sovereign powers sometimes find it difficult to refuse to give aid. They are not willing to tie themselves in advance to a long-term ban on aid and a fixed budget. If giving state aid is likely to increase support in the short term, and win more votes in a coming election, politicians may be inclined to grant it even if the aid is not economically efficient and ultimately constitutes a waste of public resources. Delegating control of state aid to a higher authority that is politically independent can help to avoid such commitment problems.

4.2 Protection of Competition in the EU Internal Market as Sole Objective – No Budget Policy Powers

62. Both the systematic position of Arts. 87ss. EC Treaty in the legislation and the wording of Art. 87, Para.1 EC Treaty suggest that aid control is exclusively intended to protect competition on the internal market. The regulations on state aid (Arts. 87ss. EC Treaty) are contained in Chapter 1 of Title VI to the EC Treaty, that is headed "Rules on Competition". So just like the antitrust regulations in Arts. 81, 82 EC Treaty, which are in the same chapter, they relate to the aim named in Art. 3, Para. 1 g) EC Treaty, namely to set up a system that will protect competition within the internal market from distortion. Art. 87, Para. 1 EC Treaty expressly names distortion of competition and restriction of trade between states as the main criteria. Preventing negative spill-over effects in the form of distortion to competition in the EU internal market is consequently the protective purpose of European state aid control. It was introduced with the aim of promoting the establishment of a single internal market and preventing member states from using state aid to counteract the lowering of trade barriers and the realisation of the basic freedoms named in the EC Treaty. State aid to national companies can have an effect similar to protective customs barriers in sealing off a market.[50] In recent years attempts by member states have been evident to compensate for the loss of state control through the former state monopolies or network industries by making greater use of state aid and by permitting major national mergers, and to this extent to hamper the EU internal market. The Monopolkommission rejects this protectionist industry policy, which is directed to promoting domestic industries and sealing off national markets.

---

[49] Cf. Friederiszick, H.W., Röller, L.-H., Verouden, V., European State Aid Control: an Economic Framework, in Buccirossi, P. (ed.), Handbook of Antitrust Economics, Cambridge, Mass. 2008, pp. 625-669.

[50] Cf. Mestmäcker, E.-H., Schweitzer, H., Europäisches Wettbewerbsrecht, 2nd edition, Munich 2004, § 42, No. 20.

63. However, the Community has no powers to control member states' budgets. The EU has so far only been granted power of budget control to supervise adherence to the Maastricht criteria (Art. 121 EC Treaty). It is not one of the European Commission's tasks in state aid control under Arts. 87ss. EC Treaty to supervise the right use of member states' resources as such.[51] As long as there are no such powers the member states are responsible for setting up effective control mechanisms and a stringent system within their borders to prevent an economically harmful waste of state funds through the inefficient award of state aid. In accordance with the aim formulated in Art. 3, Para. 1 g) EC Treaty the sole protective purpose of the European regulations on state aid is to avoid distortion to competition on the product and services markets on the European internal market.

64. This aim has been taken out of the final version of the Lisbon Treaty, the future EU reform treaty.[52] Owing to the negative signal effects it will have for European competition policy the Monopolkommission regards this with concern. In legal terms, however, no direct changes will result for the implementation of the competition regulations in EU antitrust law and state aid law.[53] Under Art. 3, Para. 3 of the Lisbon Treaty the realisation of the internal market is one of the primary aims of the Community, and a protocol annexed to it states that the internal market also includes a system that will protect competition from distortion.[54] Protocols that are added to the primary law Community treaties have binding legal force and the same primary law ranking.

4.3 Improving the National Means of Control

65. It is essential for the public authority granting state aid to know the foreseeable effects of this on the general welfare (macro welfare oriented cost-benefit comparison). However, as explained above, in its control of state aid the European Commission is only obliged to assess those costs that can be incurred through state aid in the form of restraints of competition in the internal market, and weigh them against the desired benefit.

66. On national level, on the other hand, the other economic costs induced by granting state aid must be taken into account beside the expected distortion to competition. Member states must calculate the cost of financing the state aid, and the opportunity costs and loss of net welfare (the shadow costs of taxation), and ensure that the aid is given efficiently, avoiding any waste of public funds.

67. Germany has a large number of promotional programmes with some overlapping objectives, initiated by various public authorities and sovereign bodies (the EU, the Federal Government, the Länder and the municipalities). Owing to the resultant intransparency it is difficult for companies (especially small and midsize companies) to gain an overview of whether and to what level they could obtain promotional funds. In some cases they have to

---

[51] Cf. Bartosch, A., Der More Economic Approach in Beihilfesachen, Recht der Internationalen Wirtschaft 53, 2007, pp. 681-690.

[52] Treaty of Lisbon amending the Treaty on European Union and the Treaty establishing the European Community, signed at Lisbon, 13 December 2007, OJ EU C 306, 17 December 2007, p. 1.

[53] Arts. 81, 82 and 87ss. of the EC Treaty were retained with only a few modifications, cf. Art. 2, Fig. 75ss. of the Lisbon Treaty.

[54] Protocol on the internal market and competition, OJ EU C 306, 17 December 2007, p. 156.

spend considerable resources on clarifying the question. Owing to the lack of coordination there is also a risk that aid in pursuit of specific objectives will be given in inefficiently high amounts or that contrary aims will be pursued. The coordination could be improved if state aid and state aid programmes had to be published by all the donors in advance on a central website on the Internet, with a description of their objective, their volume and the qualities expected of their actual or potential recipients. For practical reasons this obligation should only apply to state aid that exceeds a certain volume still to be determined. A central website of this nature could help to lower the transaction costs for the acquisition of information by potential applicants for state aid. Another possible way of lowering transaction costs – especially for smaller and midsize companies – could be to allow companies to apply for state aid on their tax declaration forms, with the factors that qualify them for the aid clearly formulated. The aid should then be given in the form of tax reductions.

68. The Monopolkommission recommends subjecting the national state aid programmes to regular success control, in which an independent body would examine whether the objectives, that should be clearly formulated in advance, had been achieved, and which disadvantageous effects had occurred as a result of the state aid. To avoid the creation of a subsidisation mentality and ensure efficient appraisal a time limit should be set for state aid right from the start (sunset regulation). Degressive state aid for longer term promotion is also to be recommended.

69. Beside ex post success control there is also the possibility of prescribing ex ante control for particularly serious cases, where the aid programme, or the intended individual grant, is for a volume still to be determined. In the ex ante control the entire economic effects of an aid, including the consequences for competition, should be forecast. The examining body would not be empowered to make a political decision instead of the public authority granting the aid, but it should check whether the donor has taken all the foreseeable economic costs into account in its decision. It should also consider whether the aid is on principle a suitable and necessary means of achieving the desired effect, and whether the expected costs are not out of proportion to the expected benefit. The powers to undertake this form of macro national aid control and assessment could be given to the national audit courts, for example, as they already have the task of checking the budgets and economic management of the public administration. Alternatively, an independent national body of experts (a subsidisation control council) could be considered.[55] The competent body could be given powers to hold hearings, make statements and report as part of its ex ante control, and it could make recommendations. But it could also be given right of objection, similar to the powers the European Commission has in European state aid control.

70. In addition, state aid should on principle be given in an open and transparent procedure, as is prescribed for the award of public contracts (§§ 97ss. Act Against Restraints of Competition – GWB). For a general, abstract aid programme the funds should be available to all companies that meet certain criteria. In the case of individual aids there should be competition in a transparent tender. This would avoid inefficiently high and discriminatory aid and unnecessary additional distortion to competition.

---

[55] Cf. Monopolkommission, Wettbewerbspolitik in Zeiten des Umbruchs, Hauptgutachten 1994/1995, Baden-Baden 1996, Item 154.

71. Finally, subjective rights and an efficient system of legal protection should be created for potential recipients of the aid, competitors affected and their associations. Permitting private lawsuits would, in the view of the Monopolkommission, increase the efficiency of macroeconomic national state aid control. The regulations on checking the award of public contracts (§ 104ss. GWB) could serve as a model. Under these regulations companies that have failed to obtain a public contract can obtain legal protection under §§ 107ss. GWB before independent awarding chambers in a formal ex post appraisal procedure, if certain thresholds have been reached or exceeded. Immediate objection to the decision by the awarding chamber is permitted. An award senate of the Intermediate Court of Appeal in whose jurisdiction the awarding chamber is located (§ 116 GWB) decides on the appeal. This procedure also raises the question of the protection of confidential business data. To prevent the beneficiary's operating and business secrets having to be revealed to the competitor who has brought the case the awarding chambers and senates are to be allowed to refuse the right to access files containing the relevant data.[56] In addition, regulations could be introduced to accelerate the procedure, analogous to the legislation on the award of contracts, to avoid delays and legal uncer-tainties.[57]

72. State aid that is designed right from the start for individual companies and so for which no tender is held, and state aid for the benefit of specific, already established branches, should on principle be forbidden on national level and at most permitted in exceptional cases. Aid of this kind regularly proves particularly problematic in the macroeconomic regard. This applies, for instance, to rescue aid designed to maintain a specific company. As well as the risk that the aid will fail to have the desired effect (securing jobs), may be given to an excessive level or be the result of self-interest on the part of politicians, this kind of state aid can cause considerable distortion of competition because inefficient companies are promoted, and access to the market is made more difficult for efficient newcomers.

73. In regard to the politico-economic context explained in 2.2.3 above, the introduction of effective control of state aid on national level is not very likely. The political interest in maintaining the financial scope to serve the politicians' own clientele is too strong, and it is presumably for these reasons that the European authorities have extended their area of application of state aid control fairly widely, with a broad interpretation of Art. 87, Para. 1 EC Treaty.[58] This fills a gap, so to speak, in the institutional structure of member states. Because they do not effectively control their own subsidisation practice, but on the other hand acknowledge the budget policy need to limit this, member states generally do not protest much if the European Commission also examines the award of state aid where noticeable restraint of competition and restriction of trade between states is not seriously evident, so ultimately where the issue is budget policy discipline. The Monopolkommission sees its proposals to reduce European state aid control onto aid relevant to competition, and to create a national aid control system, as a package of complementary measures that can only be realised as a whole.[59]

---

[56] Cf. § 111 GWB. § 120, Para. 2 GWB states that this is applicable to the immediate appeal to the awarding senates.

[57] § 113 GWB provides for acceleration of the ex post appraisal procedure before the awarding chambers.

[58] For more detail see 5.2.4 and 5.3.5 below.

[59] See 5.2 and 7.1 below.

– 22 –

5.   The Legal Framework Conditions and their Traditional Interpretation by the European Institutions

5.1 Subsidies given by the EU and Third Countries: Art. 87 EC Treaty does not apply

74. The EU itself grants subsidies to a considerable extent. The figure given in the 2007 budget plan was EUR 126.5 billion.[60] The 25 EU member states, by contrast, gave state aid totalling "only" EUR 66.5 billion in 2006.[61] EU distribution and agricultural policy measures have so far predominated. The regional structural measures that are intended to improve cohesion between the various regions and member states accounted for 35.9% of the EU budget in 2007. EUR 45.5 billion was earmarked for these in the budget plan, with EUR 35.3 billion intended for the economically weakest regions in the EU. The share of aid for agriculture and rural development in the EU budget was set at 44.4% (EUR 56.3 billion) in the same period.[62]

75. Despite its importance aid from the EU does not come under the ban in Art. 87, Para. 1 EC Treaty. The definition "aid granted by a Member State or through State resources" only covers measures by member states and aid given by them. Aid given by the Community, a considerable share of which is not in pursuit of horizontal aims but flows to specific sectors (agriculture) and should be classified as particularly problematic in regard to competition policy, is therefore not subject to the strict control of state aid by the EU under Arts. 87ss. EC Treaty. EU aid is only subject to the regulations in WTO legislation. These are in both the General Agreement on Tariffs and Trade of 1994 (GATT 1994) and the Agreement on Subsidies and Countervailing Measures (SCM Agreement).[63] As well as the member states the EC itself is party to these international agreements under Art. 133 EC Treaty, making them binding for the institutions of the Community as well as for its member states (Art. 300, Para. 7 EC Treaty). The European legislation on state aid is a much more differentiated set of regulations than the WTO legislation, and its application is comprehensively designed to realise the Common Market and remove distortion to competition.[64]

---

[60]   European Commission: Survey of the 2007 EU Budget, http://ec.europa.cu/budget/publications/ budget_in_fig_de.htm.

[61]   Cf. Commission Report, State Aid Scoreboard, Autumn 2007, loc. cit., p. 10.

[62]   The direct payments to farmers and measures to sustain an orderly market account for EUR 45.8 billion of this.

[63]   Cf. OJ EU L 336 of 23 December 1994, p. 3, here pp. 156-183 (Annex 1A, Agreements and Countervailing Measures).

[64]   The SCM Agreement distinguishes between three categories of state aid (traffic lights approach): RED: banned aid (Part II SCM Agreement). This is aid tied to the export of goods or the use of domestic goods, which is banned per se. If the "special group" of the Dispute Settlement Body (DSB, a WTO organ) is involved and concludes that the measure is a banned form of aid it will "recommend" the state concerned to withdraw the aid without delay; if that is not done the state is restricted and may not take any countervailing measures. YELLOW (disputable) aid (Part III SCM Agreement): Aid can be disputed if it will have disadvantageous effects on the interests of other members (Art. 5, SCM Agreement). In this case the WTO member granting the aid can withdraw it or remove the disadvantageous effects; if it does not do so countermeasures (countervailing duties) may be imposed as protection against subsidised imports (Arts. 10ss. SCM Agreement). GREEN (non-
cont.

76. The present system of EU aid is characterised by the coexistence of a number of funds, whose tasks are not always clearly delimited. Institutionally, Community aid is given by the European Guidance and Guarantee Fund for Agriculture (Art. 34, Para. 3 EC Treaty), the European Social Fund (Art. 146 EC Treaty), the Structural Fund to Achieve Cohesion and Convergence (Arts. 158ss. EC Treaty), the European Investment Bank (Arts. 266f. EC Treaty), as well as in research and development (Arts. 163ss. EC Treaty).[65] In many cases the level of financing for the individual funds provided by member states is the result of political compromise.

77. As potential beneficiaries find the criteria for EU aid complex and difficult to understand current EU promotion runs the risk of excessive bureaucracy costs and lack of efficiency. The supervision of EU aid also has shortcomings, entailing the risk of free riding and fraud.[66] Due to the lack of transparency in the system and the amount of funds being awarded EU aid can, in the view of the Monopolkommission, give rise to considerable distortion of competition in the European internal market. The present WTO regulations, which are not very differentiated and mainly of significance in relations with third countries outside the EU, offer only rudimentary protection.

78. There are proposals to extend the control regime laid down in Arts. 87ss. EC Treaty to EU aid.[67] In the view of the Monopolkommission this would involve difficulties, not least because the EU would be controlling itself, through the same institution. For the European Commission has not only been entrusted with carrying out aid control, it is also responsible for the administration of European promotional finance and the European funds. A transfer of the control function to the European courts would be conceivable. However, traditionally they leave the European Commission wide scope for judgement in decisions of a political nature. So it appears questionable whether efficient control of EU aid could be achieved in this way.

---

disputable) aid (Part IV SCM Agreement). Certain research grants, aid for disadvantaged regions and environmental aid come into this category.

[65] The European Commission is also aiming to reform EU aid. For 2008, for example, a debate is planned on the principles of reorienting the EU Common Agricultural Policy, which will be implemented in 2013 at the earliest. In 1992 the EU began on the first of now three reforms to withdraw gradually from market and price support. In the last agricultural reform, in 2003, the member states decided to uncouple aid from production and replace it with a system of direct income support. The level of the lump sum payments, which farmers are now receiving, is oriented to the level of the operational aids granted in former years. The European Commission suggests limiting the aid to large agricultural enterprises and cutting back the direct EU payments to farmers in favour of a policy to promote rural regions. For more detail see Maas, S., Schmidt, P., Gemeinsame Agrarpolitik der EU, Wirtschaftsdienst 87, 2007, pp. 94-100 and Anon, EU-Kommission stellt Basis für Agrarhilfen in Frage, Frankfurter Allgemeine Zeitung, 31 October 2007, p. 15.

[66] In its annual report on the implementation of the budget plan for the financial year 2006 (OJ C 273 of 15 November 2007, pp. 1, 132, Col. 1, Item 6.39) the European Community Audit Court reaches the conclusion that in 2006, in structural policy for instance, at least 12% of the promotional funds should never have been granted. The reasons for the high error ratio are firstly carelessness and insufficient knowledge on the part of the offices disbursing the funds, and secondly specific attempts at fraud, facilitated by the lack of quality and the number of controls. In Germany fraud with promotional funds can be prosecuted under § 264 of the Criminal Code.

[67] For example Schwintowski, H.-P., Staatlich veranlasste Wettbewerbsbeschränkungen auf europäischen und internationalen Märkten, Rabels Zeitschrift für ausländisches und internationales Privatrecht 58, 1994, pp. 232-291, 245.

It would be preferable to transfer control to a new independent European supervisory authority, that could act free of political influence. Beside EU-related measures greater engagement on international level for the introduction of a better control regime within the WTO framework should also be considered.

79. European aid control fulfils an important and essential function in protecting cross-frontier competition on the EU internal market. Corresponding protective mechanisms are lacking in many states outside Europe, so that granting aid by the political decision-makers is not subject to strict control, as it is in the EU. Consequently, when there is international competition for major projects third countries may be able to hold out a prospect of higher grants (subsidies) to companies than EU member states can, as they are bound by Arts. 87ss. EC Treaty. In the view of the Monopolkommission the regulations on EU aid should not be reduced or relaxed even in such circumstances. The aim should rather be to establish better standards of protection on the international level and work for the introduction of more stringent rules on subsidisation (especially in the WTO), in relations with third countries as well.

5.2 The Factual Level (Art. 87, Para. 1 EC Treaty)

5.2.1 Granting Aid

80. Although Art. 87, Para. 1 EC Treaty contains a definition of aid, the criteria are given in indeterminate legal terms that are open to differing interpretations and need to be concretised. To make clear under which conditions a measure has so far been classified as aid and subject to European control the individual criteria named in Art. 87, Para. 1 EC Treaty and their traditional interpretation by the EU institutions will now be discussed.

81. A measure is only aid if it involves "favouring" in the meaning of Art. 87, Para. 1 EC Treaty. This can result from positive state payments. Hence a broad spectrum of forms of assistance are subsumed as aid. In contrast to the report on aid by the Federal Government, therefore, this also includes state guarantees. Measures are also classified as aid if they reduce the burden a company normally has to bear. Thus loans at preferential conditions and easier terms of payment for taxes and social insurance contributions also fall under European state aid control.

82. The ban on aid in Art. 87, Para. 1 EC Treaty covers not only one-way state measures, it also covers advantages which the state grants a company as part of an exchange. Member states can certainly take part in economic activity as investors aiming to make a profit (Art. 295 EC Treaty), but to prevent evasion of the regulations favourable treatment in the meaning of Art. 87, Para. 1 EC Treaty is assumed if the state payments are not matched by appropriate reciprocity (partial gratuitous transfer, e.g. the sale of land below market price). To what extent an injection of capital, compensation for loss or renunciation of profit constitutes aid or can be regarded as market behaviour is examined more closely by the European Commission in individual cases. According to long-standing jurisprudence, the "private investor test" is to be used to distinguish between favourable treatment and market action by the state.[68]

---

[68] In this context the European Court of Justice has stated that member states are interested less in short term than in longer term profitability for their investments. Their behaviour as public investors must

cont.

83. This is the only condition in Art. 87, Para. 1 EC Treaty that has been subject to extensive economic analysis over an extensive period. It is usual in practice for economic reports to be compiled and used in establishing whether there is favourable treatment, at least in difficult cases and especially as part of the private investor test. This contrasts with the approach to the other aid criteria.

5.2.2 Favouring "Certain Undertakings or the Production of Certain Goods"

5.2.2.1 Possible Beneficiaries

84. For a measure to constitute aid a company or branch of production must benefit from it. The concept of an "undertaking" in Art. 87, Para. 1 EC Treaty corresponds with that in the other EU competition rules. Just as in Art. 81, Para. 1 EC Treaty, for example, an undertaking is a unit that performs any economic activity independently of its legal form and the way it is financed (the function concept of an undertaking).[69] Grants that primarily benefit private households are not covered by the term. Under Arts. 87ss. EC Treaty aid supervision must cover not only aid to private enterprises but also aid to public enterprises (Art. 86, Para. 1 EC Treaty). Public enterprises are economically active units of any legal form, on whose business planning or activity public sovereign authorities can exercise a determinant influence, directly or indirectly (through ownership, shareholdings, voting rights or in any other way). Deutsche Bahn (the German Railway company) is one example.[70] If the beneficiary exclusively performs social tasks assigned to him by law, it is not an undertaking in the meaning of Art. 87, Para. 1 EC Treaty, according to jurisprudence by the European Court of Justice, as long as it performs its legal tasks independently of the level of contributions and entirely in accordance with the idea of solidarity (e.g. the statutory health insurance institutes).[71] The ban on aid applies not only to financial benefits to companies, it also applies to whole branches of production. This concept is interpreted broadly, as meaning branch or sector, and it also covers the services sector.

5.2.2.2 Selective Advantage

85. The measure must benefit specific companies or specific branches of production. So only state measures of a selective nature constitute aid. The selectivity makes the difference between the competence of member states to regulate general economic policy measures and the competence of the Community to protect competition from individual acts of intervention. State payments that benefit all the companies in the member state, without distinction (e.g.

---

therefore be compared with that of holding companies or groups of private companies, whose profitability thinking is more long term.

[69] ECJ, Judgement of 17 February 1993, Conn. Cases 159/91 and 160/91, Poucet/AGF and Camulrac and Pis-tre/Cancava, Rec. 1993, 1-637, No. 17.

[70] Cf. Art. 2 b) of Commission Directive 2006/111/EC of 16 November 2006 on the transparency of financial relations between Member States and public undertakings as well as on financial transparency within certain undertakings (the Transparency Directive), OJ EU L 318 of 17 November 2006, p. 17.

[71] ECJ, Judgement of 16 March 2004, Conn. Cases C-264/01, C-354/01, C-355/01, AOK-Bundes-verband et al., Rec. 2004, 1-2493, No. 48ss.

general labour market policy measures, general tax rules or infrastructure measures that will benefit all the corporate sector) are not aid in the meaning of Art. 87, Para. EC Treaty.

86. Differences in the initial conditions, and distortions to competition that result from member states making use of their powers to instigate appropriate general economic policy measures, can only be removed through legal harmonisation (Arts. 94ss. EC Treaty). If a measure introduces different treatment between companies, according to jurisprudence the decisive fact is whether this difference is due to the nature of the current system or its structure. If the difference is due to other than the objectives of the general system it is on principle assumed that the measure in question is to be classified as selective in the meaning of Art. 87, Para. 1 EC Treaty.

87. In general the fact of selectivity ("favouring certain undertakings or the production of certain goods") is interpreted very widely by the EU organs.[72] Accordingly, not only those advantages that a member state grants a certain company individually, or a certain branch, are subject to aid control. Rather, a measure is already regarded as selective if it covers
- only companies of a certain size, independent of their branch, e.g. only large firms or small and midsize firms
- only companies producing physical goods or
- only new companies making investment of a certain level and creating a certain number of jobs.

Measures to benefit companies of neighbouring branches are also included. Moreover, measures that will benefit all the companies and branches in a certain region are generally classified as selective.[73] So if, for example, a German Federal Land allowed all the companies that settled or were established in its territory a low rate of tax, this measure would be covered

---

[72] Cf. ECJ, Judgement of 13 September 2006, Case T-210/02, British Aggregates Association/Commission, Rec. 2006, II-2789, Nos.. 104ss.

[73] In its Azores judgement of 6 September 2006, Case C-88/03, Portugal/Commission the ECJ considered the question of the range covered by the concept of regional selectivity in aid law in more depth. It drew a distinction between the following groups of cases: Lack of devolution (that is, no transfer of sovereign powers to regional bodies): The central government sets a rate of tax for a certain region (to be paid by all the economically active) that is lower than the rate charged on national level. In the view of the Court such a measure is always selective, as it only applies to part of the geographical area for which the tax legislature is responsible. Symmetrical devolution: The model of divided taxation powers, in which all the territorial authorities of a certain level are free, within the limits of the competences assigned to them, to choose the rate of tax for their area of responsibility. In the view of the Court the criterion of selectivity is not fulfilled in such a constellation. The determinant frame of reference is the unit that is regionally responsible, not the member state as a whole. Asymmetrical devolution: In the exercise of its powers a regional or local body sets a rate of tax that is lower than the national rate and which applies only to the companies in its territory. In the view of the Court a tax measure in such a constellation is not selective in the meaning of Art. 87, Para. 1 EC Treaty only when the body is sufficiently autonomous in institutional, procedural and economic regard. Accordingly, the lower tax rate may not be cross-subsidised and the economic consequences of lowering this rate of tax must be borne by the region itself. In detail on the judgement see Arhold, C., Steuerhoheit auf regionaler oder lokaler Ebene und der europäische Beihilfenbegriff – wie weit reicht das Konzept von der regionalen Selektivität, Europäische Zeitschrift für Wirtschaftsrecht 17, 2006, pp. 717-721.

by the ban on aid, and it would be subject to control by the European Commission, even if the degree of selective effect were relatively slight.[74]

5.2.3 State Grants or Grants using State Funds

88. The ban in Art. 87, Para. 1 EC Treaty only covers "aid granted by a Member State or through State resources". Aid is state aid if the donor is a sovereign authority. So the ban applies not only to the member states as such but also to all their sovereign authorities (the Länder, municipalities, other bodies and institutes incorporated under public law). According to jurisprudence by the European Court of Justice, only those advantages that involve a transfer of state funds, or are paid out of the state budget are covered by the ban (the PreussenElektra jurisprudence).[75] So the criterion is not met if the state action only achieves a desired beneficial effect, while the cost is borne entirely by the private sector. Consequently the promotion under the German Renewable Energies Law, which includes an obligation to pay non-com-petitive prices, does not come under the European aid regime.[76]

89. In the economic view financial advantages to the private sector accruing from state regulation, the costs of which are to be borne by other members of the private sector, will have distorting effects on competition similar to the benefits that accrue directly or indirectly from state budgets. Consequently there is a risk that member states can evade the European regime on aid with skilful steering of the flows of funds. In the view of the Monopol-kommission the concept should nevertheless not apply to all the measures that arrange for transfer payments between different market participants. Such an interpretation would mean that many regulations in member states' legislation that cover the relation between different members of the private sector (e.g. obligatory liability or regulations in labour law) would be subject to European aid supervision. This would make all the legislation that places obligations on the private sector subject to aid supervision, which is unsuited for these purposes. In the view of the Monopolkommission, in cases where the legislature is obliged (under constitutional law) to en-sure that certain facilities can function and are financed, ordering a transfer of resources between these enterprises and their private users can, by contrast, be seen as saving expenditure which the state would otherwise have to make, and so

---

[74] Measures of this nature by the German Federal Länder would not be exempt from the ban on aid, according to the jurisprudence by the European Court of Justice on regional selectivity (the Azores judgement) outlined in the previous footnote, because the Länder are not sufficiently autonomous, especially as a result of the Länder financial compensation arrangements. This also applies to cases where the tax in question is not charged uniformly throughout Germany.Cf. also Arhold, C., loc. cit.

[75] In its judgement on the PreussenElektra case of 13 March 2001, Case C-379/98, Rec. 2001, I-2099, No. 59, the ECJ decided that a law that obliges electricity supply companies to buy the electricity produced in their distribution area from renewable energies (obligatory purchasing) and to pay a minimum rate for this electricity that is higher than its actual commercial value (the minimum remuneration regulation) is not state aid because there is no charge on the state budget.

[76] Act to Give Priority to Renewable Energies of 1 July 2004, BGBl. I, p. 1918; for more detail on the Renewable Energies Law see Monopolkommission, Strom und Gas 2007: Wettbewerbsdefizite und zögerliche Regulierung, Sondergutachten 49, Baden-Baden 2008, Items 79ss.

these measures can be classified as aid in the meaning of Art. 87, Para. 1 EC Treaty (e.g. financing the public radio corporations).[77]

90. The alternative "or through State resources" is intended to prevent evasion and also extend aid control to the indirect assignment of public funds through facilities that are not sovereign powers (e.g. a public enterprise like a state-owned bank). The criterion is met if the economic advantage ultimately comes from state funds and the aid is also assignable to the state.[78]

5.2.4 Restriction of Trade between Member States

91. Under Art. 87, Para. 1 EC Treaty measures are only subject to aid control if they "affect trade between Member States". This criterion is intended to exclude effects on purely national trade from the area of application of Art. 87, Para. 1 EC Treaty, and it serves to delimit the areas of competence of the Community and member states in the control of state aid. In many cases the European Court of Justice examines the criteria of "distortion of competition relevant to the Community" and "restriction of trade between Member States" as a single issue.

92. According to long-standing jurisprudence the European Commission is not obliged to prove the actual effects of state aid on trade within the Community,[79] it regards as sufficient a tendency to restrict trade. In so far the requirements are very slight. According to the jurisprudence, neither a relatively small amount of aid nor a relatively small company as beneficiary exclude the possibility of restriction of trade between member states.[80] So in contrast to the antitrust regulations in Arts. 81 and 82 EC Treaty noticeable restriction of trade has not so far been required as an unwritten rule. In the view of the Monopolkommission that is not appropriate. In aid control as well, it should be an unwritten rule that noticeable restriction of trade between states is an essential condition, to prevent matters of purely local significance coming under the European aid regime.

93. In aid supervision, unlike under EU antitrust legislation, the European Commission does not have the power to decide whether it should deploy a procedure. It is obliged to intervene in any measure that could be unlawful state aid. The De minimis regulation provides for some relief.[81] It states that certain cases of state aid that do not exceed a specific amount do not give rise to any restriction in the meaning of Art. 87, Para. 1 EC Treaty and consequently do not have to be

---

[77] Cf. Monopolkommission, Mehr Wettbewerb auch im Dienstleistungssektor! Hauptgutachten 2004/2005, Baden-Baden 2006, Item 788.

[78] If the advantage is granted by a public enterprise the mere fact that the state can exercise a dominant influence is not enough, according to jurisprudence by the ECJ. For financial support given by this enterprise to a third party to be classified as state aid the European Court deems it necessary for state offices to be involved in some way in issuing the specific measure. ECJ, Judgement of 16 May 2002, Case C-482/99, Stardust Marine, Rec. 2002, L-4397, No. 52.

[79] ECJ, Judgement of 15 June 1999, Case T-288/97, Friuli Venezia Giuali/Commission, Rec. 1999, II-1871, No. 47f; Judgement of 15 June 2000, Case T-298/97, Alzetta Mauro/Commission, Rec. 2000, II-2319, Nos. 76ss.

[80] ECJ, Judgement of 3 March 2005, Case C-172/03, Heiser/Innsbruck Tax Office, Rec. 2005, 1-1627, No. 25.

[81] Commission Regulation (EC) 1998/2006 of 15 December 2006 on the application of Arts. 87 and 88 EC Treaty to "De minimis" aid", OJ EU L 379 of 28 December 2006, p. 5.

notified to the European Commission under Art. 88, Para. 3 EC Treaty.[82] In addition, certain forms of aid are exempt from obligatory notification under block exemption regulations.

5.2.5 Distortion of Competition

94. Art. 87, Para. 1 EC Treaty prohibits aid granted by member states only if it "distorts or threatens to distort competition". According to the jurisprudence by the European Court of Justice the criterion of distortion to competition in Art. 87, Para. EC Treaty is met if aid strengthens the position of the beneficiary over (current or potential) competitors.[83] Initially the European Commission held the view that it did not need to detail the circumstances which, in its view, constituted (the threat of) distortion to competition in a specific case. Aid would always distort competition.[84] In 1985 the European Court of Justice decided that the Commission must at least name these circumstances in the justification of its decision, although in certain cases it could be clear from the circumstances in which aid was granted that it would distort or threaten to distort trade between member states.[85] However, the Court does not require a very detailed account. A summary of the circumstances relevant to competition and plausible explanation of the actual or threatened distortion to competition are regarded as sufficient "proof" that there is at least a risk of distortion to competition.[86] The European Commission only has to show which sectors are potentially affected by the aid, that there is competition in these sectors, that competitors are affected in different ways by the aid in question and that the favourable treatment is likely to affect competition.[87] A quantitative analysis of the possible effects of the aid on competition and an exact delimitation of the market are not required by the Court.[88]

95. The jurisprudence in connection with Art. 87, Para. 1 EC Treaty thus traditionally allows the European Commission a wide margin of appreciation. In contrast to Arts. 81 and 82 EC Treaty the European Court of Justice does not require a specific intensity or evidence of distortion to competition as an unwritten rule.[89] As a result cross-frontier distortion to competition is generally assumed as soon as it is clear that there is a selective benefit to

---

[82] The upper threshold has now been raised. Formerly financial aid that did not exceed a total amount of EUR 100,000 within three years was not state aid. In the new De minimis regulation that amount has been raised to EUR 200,000. Loan securities are permitted up to EUR 1.5 million.

[83] ECJ, Judgement of 13 June 2000, Case T-204/97, EPAC/Commission, Rec. 2000, II-2267, Nos. 87ss.

[84] Commission of the European Communities, Eleventh Competition Report 1981, Brussels, Luxemburg 1982, No. 176.

[85] ECJ, Judgement of 13 March 1985, Verb. Cases 296 and 318/82, Netherlands and Leeuwarder Papierwarenfabriek, Rec. 1985, No. 24.

[86] ECJ, Judgement of 15 June 1999, Case T-288/97, Friuli Venezia Giulia/Commission, Rec. 1999, II-1871, No. 48/50; judgement of 15 June 2000, Case T-298/97, Alzetta Mauro/Commission, Rec. 2000, II-2319, No. 95; judgement of 13 June 2000, Case T-204/97, EPAC/Commission, Rec. 2000, II-2267, Nos. 35/47s.; judgement of 29 September 2000, Case T-55/99, CETM/Commission, Rec. 2000, II-3207, Nos. 102ss.

[87] ECJ, Judgement of 13 June 2000, Case T-204/97, EPAC/Commission, Rec. 2000, II-2267, Nos. 87ss.

[88] ECJ,Judgement of 17 September 1980, Case 730/79, Philip Morris/Commission, Rec. 1980, 2671, Nos. 9 and 11s.

[89] ECJ, Judgement of 19 September 2000, Case C-156/98, Germany/Commission, Rec. 2000, I-6857, No. 32/29.

certain companies or production branches in the meaning of the above jurisprudence. Nor is this assumption prescribed in the wording of the norm. The use of the phrase "threaten to distort" in Art. 87, Para. 1 EC Treaty does show that simply the possibility of distortion to competition is sufficient, it need not actually materialise for the ban to be applied. But it cannot be deduced from this that a concrete account of the competition situation and the facts that give rise to the danger of adverse effects on competition could be dispensed with.

96. The formulation of the competition criterion in Art. 87, Para. 1 EC Treaty differs from that in the antitrust norm in Art. 81, Para. 1 EC Treaty, where the phrase "which distorts or threatens to distort competition" is not used; instead the reference is to certain practices "which have as their object or effect the prevention, restriction or distortion of competition within the common market". Nevertheless, in Art. 81, Para. EC Treaty the various practices that restrict competition are interpreted as inadmissible in order to protect competition.[90] Moreover, both Art. 87, Para. 1 EC Treaty and Art. 81, Para. 1 EC Treaty refer to the objective named in Art. 3, Para. 1 C) EC Treaty, namely to protect competition on the internal market from distortion. Therefore, it does not necessarily follow from the different formulations of the criterion of competition in Art. 81, Para. 1 EC Treaty on the one side and Art. 87, Para. 1 EC Treaty on the other that competition is to be interpreted differently in the legislation on state aid from the antitrust legislation.

97. The Monopolkommission regards the fact that the legislation on state aid does not require a detailed examination of the competition situation as dubious for several reasons. Firstly, because the criterion of trade between member states is interpreted very widely and extended to cover cases that are largely local, and secondly, because to meet the criterion of selective advantage ("favouring certain undertakings or the production of certain goods") a very low degree of selectivity is regarded as sufficient and is held to be evident even with measures that benefit all the companies in a region or all those of a certain size, and thirdly, because the level of state aid granted can be very low.[91]

5.2.6 Conclusion

98. In the past the criterion of distortion to competition has not been the subject of detailed economic study by the European Commission. The economic proof required by the European courts to establish distortion of competition has so far been minimal – unlike the requirements in the field of merger control and the antitrust regulations in Arts. 81 and 82 EC Treaty. Accordingly, the European Commission has usually limited its consideration of the criterion of distortion of competition to a general sector-specific examination. If, in its view, there is selectivity and favouring, distortion of competition and restriction of trade are generally assumed, although owing to the broad interpretation of selectivity, a large number of measures

---

[90] An examination of the actual effects of Art. 81, Para. 1 EC Treaty is not necessary, according to the jurisprudence of the European courts, if the agreement in question is objectively likely to cause distortion of competition. For the purpose in question, therefore, it is sufficient for disadvantageous effects on competition typically to occur, without proof being required that this was actually intended by the parties involved. For more detail see Bechtold, R., et al., EG Kartellrecht, Kommentar, Munich 2005, Art. 81 EC Treaty, Nos. 70ss.

[91] Under the revised De minimis Regulation only state aid of a promotional level up to EUR 200,000 is exempt.

with horizontal objectives and very broad effect come into the area of application of Art. 87, Para. 1 EC Treaty. In the case of restriction of trade between member states and distortion to competition it is not an unwritten rule that the threat of restriction should at least be "noticeable" – unlike under the antitrust regulations in Arts. 81 and 82 EC Treaty. Consequently, Art. 87, Para. 1 EC Treaty also applies to cases that are largely local. The Monopolkommission, by contrast, believes that – as with Art. 81, Para. 1 EC Treaty – the objective likelihood that an aid measure will noticeably distort competition and cause noticeable restriction of trade between member states should be examined in the state aid control procedure.

99. The broad interpretation of the concept of state aid and the low level of proof required mean that the European Commission must also follow up cases that are hardly relevant. Under Art. 10, Para. 1 of Procedural Regulation 659/1999[92] it must examine without delay all information of whatever origin on state aid that may be unlawful. Generally the European Commission is informed when competitors of the favoured company lodge a complaint of unlawful state aid that has not been notified. The European Commission's obligation under Art. 10, Para. 1 of the Procedural Regulation to examine such cases is very far-reaching. As soon as its examination of the information confirms that there may possibly be unlawful state aid the European Commission must continue the procedure, as for notified aid, and reach a decision.[93]

5.3   Justification – Examination of Compatibility (Art. 87, Paras. 2 and 3 EC Treaty, Art. 86, Para. 2 EC Treaty)

100. Measures to which the ban on state aid in Art. 87, Para. 1 EC Treaty applies can be granted exemption. The grounds for exemption are given in the EC Treaty, in particular in Art. 87, Paras. 2 and 3 and Art. 86, Para. 2.[94] The European Commission will decide whether a measure may be permitted by way of exemption either in an individual procedure or generally under a block exemption regulation. In the compatibility examination which it has been authorised to conduct the European Commission must weigh the intended and expected positive effects of the aid measure against the risk of negative consequences to competition.

5.3.1 Legal Exemptions in Art. 87, Para. 2 EC Treaty

101. Art. 87, Para. 2 EC Treaty contains the following grounds for exemption:
- exempts aid of a social character, if it is granted to individual consumers without discrimination related to the origin of the products.[95]
- exempts aid granted to remedy damage caused by natural catastrophes or other extraordinary events (e.g. the economic consequences of the Gulf War).

---

[92] Council (EC) Regulation 659/1999 of 22 March 1999 on laying down detailed rules for the application of Article 93 of the EC Treaty.
[93] See Art. 13, Para. 1 together with Art. 4 Procedural Regulation.
[94] There are also special rules on state aid for agriculture (Art. 36 EC Treaty) and transport (Arts. 73, 76 EC Treaty).
[95] This is firstly on condition that the measure is aid as defined in Art. 87, Para. 1 EC Treaty. This can only be assumed for advantages granted to consumers if certain companies or branches of production benefit indirectly. One example is tax exemptions granted by a member state to owners of private cars with catalytic converters, independent of the make of the car.

• finally, states that aid given to compensate for the economic disadvantages caused by the division of Germany is compatible with the Common Market.[96]

102. 987. If, after examining the results, the European Commission concludes that one of these three criteria for exemption is present it must declare the aid in question compatible with the Common Market. It has no scope for discretion in applying Art. 87, Para. 2 EC Treaty. However, the legal exemptions in Art. 87, Para. 2 EC Treaty are of little practical im-portance.[97]

5.3.2 Grounds for Exemption in Art. 87, Para. 3 EC Treaty

103. Unlike under Art. 87, Para. 2 EC Treaty the European Commission does have wide powers of discretion in applying Art. 87, Para. 3 EC Treaty. This disposition, frequently applied in practice, contains five, very generally formulated grounds for exemption, letters a) to e):

a) covers regional aid to promote the economic development of areas where the standard of living is extraordinarily low, or where there is serious underemployment. Under this condition only areas that are particularly weak economically, measured by the EU average, are eligible. Disadvantagement compared with the national average of the member state in question is not sufficient. This condition is to enable regional cohesion between member states to develop.

b) covers aid to promote important projects of common European interest or to remedy a serious disturbance in the economy of a member state. Projects of common European interest (the first alternative) can be aid for research and development projects, if the projects are important qualitatively and quantitatively, if the Community has a direct interest in them and if a number of member states are involved. A serious disturbance in the economy of a member state (the second alternative) is only assumed by the European Commission extremely rarely and only under very strict conditions.[98]

c) covers aid to promote the development of certain economic branches or economic areas. The first alternative (branches) covers a large number of different measures. As well as rescue packages and restructuring aid, measures with horizontal objectives (aid for research and development, environmental protection and exports) can be justified, as can sectoral aid (e.g. for the transport sector or the automotive industry). The second alternative, economic areas, again covers regional aid. Unlike the conditions in a) it is not necessary here for the region benefiting to be particularly disadvantaged by the EU average, regions with general development problems (compared with other regions within the member state concerned) can also benefit. In contrast to the areas regarded as particularly in need of promotion under a), promotion is only possible here if it "does not adversely affect trading conditions to an extent contrary to the common interest".

---

[96] The European courts interpret this exception, which was included in the Treaty long before German reunification, very narrowly. Only aid granted to compensate for disadvantages directly resulting from the physical construction and maintenance of the inner-German border is included. The exemption covers disadvantages caused by the break in the transport routes, for example.

[97] Cf. Jestaedt, T., Schweda, E. in Heidenhain, M. (ed.), Handbuch des Europäischen Beihilfenrechts, Munich 2003, § 14, No. 2.

[98] Since the start of the 1980s the European Commission has only applied this in the case of Greece; the consequences of German reunification were not regarded as sufficient economic disturbance.

d) refers to aid to promote culture and for heritage conservation. e) permits the Council to agree to other kinds of aid at the proposal of the European Commission if they are compatible with the Common Market.[99]

104. The criteria in Art. 87, Para. 3 EC Treaty which allow exemptions from the ban on aid not only for economic policy reasons but more particularly for non-economic considerations (regional policy, social, cultural reasons) are indeterminate legal concepts that allow the European Commission a wide margin of discretion. Consequently, despite supranational aid control the danger of intransparent decision-making and (industrial) policy influence is not excluded. This applies particularly in view of the fact that the European Commission is not designed as an independent competition authority, but as a political body with far-reaching legislative and executive powers, and consisting of a large number ofDirectorates-General . They are naturally pursuing contradictory aims in some cases (e.g. the DG Environment and the DG Trade and Industry). The member states also frequently pursue national interests on European level and attempt to exert influence to that effect. In practice most of the exemptions which the European Commission grants individually or under block exemption regulations are granted on the basis of Art. 87, Para. 3 a) or c) EC Treaty.

5.3.3 Publications to Date Concretising the European Commission's Approvals Practice

105. The European Commission has issued a large number of guidelines and Community frameworks in the past[100] to concretise the approvals conditions and typify the assessment procedure. The aim is ensure transparency and legal certainty in the application of Art. 87, Para. 3, EC Treaty and the justification given there, especially in a) and c). Hence a complex system of regulations has been created, most of which refer to the objective of the aid and differentiate between the categories below (see Table VI.1).

106. It is characteristic of these past publications (Community frameworks, communications, guidelines)[101] that several conditions are set that are relatively easy to establish and can be fulfilled cumulatively; moreover they automatically involve certain legal consequences (like the compatibility of aid with Art. 87, Para. 3 EC Treaty). Accordingly, the legal consequences do not depend on the economic effects of the measure, the right categorisation (for instance as

---

[99] The Council has used these powers to regulate aid to the shipbuilding industry and hard coal mining. Beside the option named in Art. 87, Para. 3 e) EC Treaty to extend the general list of aid that can be approved, the member states also have the possibility of taking a (political) decision in individual cases under Art. 88, Para. 2, Sentence 3 EC Treaty. If aid has not been approved by the European Commission under Art. 87, Para. 1 EC Treaty, under this regulation the Council, upon application by a member state, can decide unanimously and in deviation from the grounds for exemption in the EC Treaty, that a measure granted or planned by this state is compatible with the Common Market, if "exceptional circumstances" justify the decision. This political caveat has parallels with the ministerial approvals procedure provided for mergers in German antitrust law (§ 42, Act Against Restraints of Competition).

[100] In some cases with the participation of the European Council.

[101] Only the Community frameworks are general acts of legislation, not the guidelines and communications from the European Commission. These instruments, by which the European Commission undertakes a selfbinding obligation, are comparable to the "administration regulations" familiar in German law.

horizontal environmental protection aid or regional aid) plays a decisive part. That is why the approach used so far is known as the "form-based approach".[102]

Table VI.1:

Categories of State Aid

Guidelines and Community Framework Documents interpreting Art. 87, Para. 3 EC Treaty refer to:		
1) Horizontal Aid	**2) Regional Aid**	**3) Other Aid**
= aid with horizontal objective not limited right from the start to individual companies or branches for • research and development • small and midsize firms • risk capital • employment • and training environmental protection Aid with horizontal objectives is generally regarded by the European Commission as relatively less distortive of competition[1]	(aid to support regional development and cohesion, Art. 87, Para. 3 a) und b) EC Treaty Regional aid plays a big part in member states' promotional activities. There are also a number of Community regional promotion instruments (structural funds), with which member states' promotion policy is increasingly to be coordinated.	*a) Sectoral aid* Branch-specific Community framework under Art. 87, Para 3 EC Treaty for the following areas: • Iron and steel • Artificial fibres • Motor vehicles • Shipbuilding • Agriculture (Art. 36 EC Treaty) • Fishing (Art. 36 EC Treaty) • Air and sea transport • Electricity There are also special rules for rail, road and inland waterways transport (Arts. 73, 76 and 78 EC Treaty) *b) Special rescue and restructuring aid* (for companies and branches in difficulties) The European Commission regards this type of aid as particularly problematic.

1 Report by the European Commission, State Aid Scoreboard, Autumn edition 2006, COM(2006) 761, final, p. 18.
Source: Monopolkommission

107. Beside these measures (the justification level), which involve the examination of compatibility under Art. 87, Para. 3 EC Treaty, the European Commission has published communications and regulations on the following areas:[103]

---

[102] Cf. Lowe, P., Some Reflections on the European Commission's State Aid Policy, Competition Policy International 2, 2006, pp. 77ss.

[103] In some cases with the participation of the EU Council.

- The interpretation of the ban in Art. 87, Para. 1 EC Treaty (example: De Minimis Regulation)[104]
- Obligatory notification under Art. 88, Para. 3 EC Treaty (especially block exemption regulations)[105]
- Certain forms of aid (e.g. obligatory liabilities and guarantees)
- Financial transfers to public enterprises and companies providing services of general economic interest and
- The procedure to be carried out (preliminary examination and formal investigation procedure by the European Commission, injunction to recover unwarranted aid by member states)[106]

108. The above acts of secondary legislation and measures are mutually complementary and some of the objectives overlap. Regional aid for structurally weak areas with horizontal objectives, for example, is privileged. There are also several regulations that contain privileges for small and midsize companies (SMEs).[107] In the State Aid Action Plan (SAAP), in which the European Commission presents its new reform concept, it states aptly itself that over time the documents have grown in number and become increasingly complex, so that streamlining is now necessary[108].

5.3.4 The Special Area of Services of General Interest (Art. 86, Para. 2 EC Treaty)

109. The justification given in Art. 86, Para. EC Treaty is relevant in the field of what is known as "services of general interest ", a term which is used for state measures to ensure the basic welfare of the population.[109] Which areas are actually covered by such "essential supply" has not been finally clarified, and the range can be defined in various ways.[110] The term used in Art. 86, Para. 2 EC Treaty is not essential supply but "services of general economic interest". While services to provide basic welfare include both market related and nonmarket related activities, services of general economic interest are solely market related.[111] These services differ from

---

[104] This states that certain aid that does not exceed a fixed amount does not cause distortion in the meaning of Art. 87, Para. 1 EC Treaty and so does not need to be reported to the European Commission under Art. 88, Para. 3, Sentence 1 EC Treaty.

[105] In Regulation 994/98, OJ EC L142 of 14 May 1998, which is based on Art. 89 EC Treaty, the European Council has empowered the European Commission to issue block exemption regulations for certain groups of horizontal aid. Accordingly in certain horizontal areas of promotion the Commission may determine which aid projects are per se compatible with the Common Market.

[106] Cf. Procedural Regulation 659/1999.

[107] E.g. the Guidelines on State Aid to Promote Risk Capital Investment in Small and Midsize Enterprises (OJ EU C 194, of 18 August 2006, p. 2), the Guidelines for State Aid with Regional Objectives 2007-2013 (OJ EU C 54 of 4 March 2006, p. 13), which i.a. provide for business aid for small companies in promotional areas to assist their development in the start-up and early phases.

[108] SAAP, Item 17.

[109] Cf. Haucap, J., Daseinsvorsorge zwischen Beihilfenkontrolle und globalem Wettbewerb, Wirtschafts-dienst87, 2007, pp. 712-716.

[110] See 2.3.2 above.

[111] Cf. European Commission, Report for the European Council in Laeken, Brussels, 17 October 2001, COM (2001), 598, final version p. 24; Kallmayer, A., Jung. C., in: Callies, C., Ruffert, M. (eds.), EUV/EGV, 3rd ed., Munich 2007, Art. 16 EGV No. 2.

– 36 –

normal services in that in the view of the state they must also be provided if the market does not offer incentives for their provision to the politically desirable extent.[112] According to the jurisprudence of the European courts member states have a wide margin of appreciation over which type of services they regard as being of general economic interest. Labour placement, postal operations, telecommunications, transport, energy supply and public broadcasting are all recognised as services of general economic interest. In the view of the Monopolkommission, as an exception Art. 86, Para. 2 EC Treaty should be interpreted narrowly. Otherwise there is a risk that the efforts to liberalise the network industries could be counteracted with greater use of state aid and national markets could be sealed off.[113]

110. In November 2005 the European Commission published its decision that certain types of aid for essential supply are exempt from obligatory notification.[114] So this decision fulfils the same function as a block exemption regulation. It exempts compensation payments to enterprises whose annual turnover on all activities before tax did not exceed EUR 100 million in the two accounting years preceding the assumption of a service of general economic interest, and that receive a compensation payment of less than EUR 30 million per year for the service provided. The maximum limit of EUR 30 million for the aid is clearly above the general upper limit of EUR 200,000 in the De Minimis Regulation. Certain areas (social housing construction, hospitals, airports and seaports) are further privileged under this decision, because these upper limits for turnover and aid received do not apply to them.

111. Under Art. 86, Para. 2 EC Treaty the ban on state aid in Art. 87, Para. 1 EC Treaty only applies to (public or private) enterprises that are entrusted with the provision of services of general economic interest as long as "the application of such rules does not obstruct the performance, in law or in fact, of the particular tasks assigned to them". However, the justification in Art. 86, Para. 2 EC Treaty will only apply if the measure in question can in fact be classified as aid in the meaning of Art. 87, Para. 1 EC Treaty, and is not simply a compensation payment for services required by the public authorities.[115]

112. The relation between the ban in Art. 87, Para. 1 EC Treaty – to be more exact, the criterion of "favouring certain undertakings or the production of certain goods" (selectivity) – and the justification in Art. 86, Para. 2 EC Treaty is controversial. The following basic positions are taken. In the 'aid interpretation' state funds granted to an enterprise for the provision of services of general benefit are always state aid in the meaning of Art. 87, Para. EC Treaty, although it can be justified under Art. 86, Para. 2 EC Treaty.[116] In the 'compensation approach' state funding of services of general economic interest is only aid in the meaning of Art. 87, Para. 1 EC Treaty if and in so far as the economic advantage granted goes beyond adequate compensation for the

---

[112] Cf. also Art. 16 EC Treaty, which was introduced in the Amsterdam Treaty and is intended to underline the special importance of Community services.

[113] In the field of antitrust legislation there could be state distortion of competition in the form of allowing major national mergers or preventing cross-frontier mergers.

[114] Decision by the European Commission of 28 November 2005 on the application of Article 86, Para. 2 EC Treaty to state aid granted to certain enterprises that are entrusted with providing services of general economic interest, OJ EU L312, of 29 November 2005, p. 67.

[115] The European Court of Justice has given the conditions for this in more detail in the judgement on Altmark Trans; Judgement of 24 July 2003, Case C-280/00, Rec. 2003, I-7747.

[116] Cf. Koenig, C., Kühling, J., in: Streinz, R. (ed.), EUV/EGV, Munich 2003, Art. 87 EGV, No. 35.

provision of these services, or beyond the additional costs which this provision entails.[117] The difference is that in the compensation approach state financing of this kind is not subject to the notification requirement in Art. 88, Para. 3, Sentence 1 EC Treaty. Independent of the legal classification, however, there is agreement that overcompensation of the costs to enterprises of providing such services is generally impermissible, that is, the condition in Art. 87, Para. 1 EC Treaty is met and the aid is not justified under Art. 86, Para. 2 EC Treaty, either. However, the Monopolkommission believes it will be difficult in practice to calculate the additional costs of providing essential supply services.

113. In its more recent decision-making practice the European Commission has been pragmatic and used both the aid approach and the compensation approach. It has applied the same criterion, appropriate compensation, on both the factual level and the justification level. If the compensation can be identified as appropriate without difficulty, this in itself shows that the circumstances described in Art. 87, Para. 1 EC Treaty do not exist. If it cannot, the European Commission undertakes a detailed examination of the matter on the justification level (Art. 86, Para. 2 EC Treaty). The principles established by the European Court of Justice in the Altmark Trans judgement serve as the standard.[118] According to these, in the field of public welfare state aid in the meaning of Art. 87, Para. EC Treaty is not being given if the finance is clearly, transparently and directly a consideration for clearly defined obligations in the public interest and the beneficiary is not fixed right from the start. If these conditions are met in an individual case the European Commission assumes that the compensation paid for the provision of services of general economic interest is not favourable treatment in the

---

[117] European Court of Justice, Judgement of 22 January 2001, Case C-53/00, Ferring, Rec. 2001, I-907, Nos. 32s.

[118] ECJ, Judgement of 24 July 2003, Case C-280/00, Altmark Trans, Rec. 2003, I-7747, Nos. 89-93. The European Court names the following conditions under which financial compensation for services of general benefit is not to be classified as state aid:

First, the recipient enterprise must actually be required to discharge public service obligations, and those obligations have to be clearly defined. So the court had to examine whether the services of public interest which Altmark Trans was obliged to perform were clear from the national legal requirements and/or the approvals in dispute in the initial proceeding.

Secondly, the parameters on the basis of which the compensation is calculated must have been established beforehand, clearly and objectively. This is to prevent the compensation creating an economic advantage that would favour the enterprise to which it is granted over its competitors. So if a member state compensates the losses suffered by an enterprise before the parameters are established, because it subsequently becomes clear that these public obligations could not have been performed commercially, this constitutes financial intervention and is regarded as state aid in the meaning of Art. 92, Para. EC Treaty.

Thirdly, the compensation must not exceed the amount necessary to cover all or part of the costs of performing these public obligations, taking into account the relevant receipts and a reasonable profit for discharging these obligations. Only if this condition is met can it be ensured that the enterprise is not being given an advantage that will strengthen its competitive position and so distort or restrict competition.

Fourthly, if in a specific case the enterprise that is to perform public obligations has not been selected in a procedure for the award of public contracts which would enable that applicant to be chosen who can perform these services at the lowest cost for the general public, the level of compensation required must be determined on the basis of an analysis of the costs of performing these services to an average enterprise that is well managed, has the appropriate means of transport and can meet the public requirements. The income thereby earned and an appropriate profit are to be taken into account.

meaning of Art. 87, Para. EC Treaty. If aid that requires to be notified is being given this may be justified under Art. 86, Para. 2 EC Treaty, and here the decisive factor is whether the financing in question is necessary as compensation for the performance of public tasks and is appropriate to this purpose.

114. In the Community Framework of November 2005 the principles for the application of Art. 86, Para. 2 EC Treaty are concretised.[119] Accordingl to this framework, the level of compensation may not go beyond what is necessary to cover the costs incurred in fulfilling the public obligation, taking into account the income thereby earned and an appropriate return on the performance of these obligations.[120] Moreover, the compensation may only be used to en-sure that the service of general economic interest functions. Financial compensation used to operate on other markets is not justified and is classified as state aid that is incompatible with the Common Market. Under European competition law cross-subsidisation of this kind can come under both the legislation on state aid and the antitrust legislation. Under Art. 82 EC Treaty the European Commission or the national competition authorities can proceed against cross-subsidisation if the enterprise concerned has a dominant market position and attempts to extend this market power to a neighbouring competitive market by transferring profits. If the funds used are state grants the European Commission can intervene with reference to the legislation on state aid. The problem of cross-subsidisation through state payments for basic security arises particularly in the liberalised economic sectors like postal services, telecommunications and the energy sector.[121] In practice it is frequently extremely difficult to prove crosssubsidisation.

---

[119] Community framework for state aid given as compensation for the provision of public services, OJ EU C 297 of 29 November 2005, p, 4.

[120] According to No. 16 of Community framework 2005 the costs comprise:
- The variable costs incurred for the provision of services of general economic interest
- An appropriate contribution to the fixed costs, both those related to the public service provided and those incurred elsewhere.
- An appropriate return on the enterprise's equity capital that can be assigned to the services of general economic interest.

The appropriate return is to be calculated by a comparison of profits in accordance with the principles in No. 18 of the framework:
- An appropriate return is an appropriate yield on capital, taking into account the risk, if any, entered into by the enterprise from the state intervention. This applies particularly if the state grants exclusive or special rights.
- The appropriate return should correspond to the profitability shown for that sector and as a rule it may not exceed the average return obtained in that sector in the immediately preceding years.
- In sectors where there are no enterprises that can serve as standard of comparison for the enterprise entrusted with the provision of services of general economic interest enterprises in other member states, or if necessary in other sectors, may be used for comparison, on condition that the special characteristics of the sector in question are taken into account.

On the problem of Cost Standards cf. Monopolkommission, Preiskontrollen in Energiewirtschaft und Handel? Zur Novellierung des GWB, Sondergutachten 47, Baden-Baden 2007, No. 20.

[121] Cf. Mestmäcker, E.-J., Schweitzer, H., loc. cit., § 43, Nos. 35s.

5.4 The Procedural Aspects

5.4.1 Proceedings before the European Commission

5.4.1.1 Aid Duly Notified

115. Unless an exception is stipulated under a block exemption regulation member states are obliged to notify the European Commission of any new aid they intend to give (Art. 88, Para. 3, Sentence 1 EC Treaty).[122] As long as the aid has not been notified to and approved by the European Commission, the member state may not grant it (Art. 88, Para. 3, Sentence 3 EC Treaty). Infringements of this ban on execution can be brought directly before the national courts by competitors of the benefiting enterprise.[123]

116. The European Commission's procedure in state aid control, like its merger control, is divided into two phases, the preliminary examination and the formal investigation procedure, which follows if necessary. In the preliminary examination the European Commission examines whether the project notified gives cause for concern. After a full notification has been received the European Commission must decide within two months whether it will approve the aid or whether it wishes to make a detailed examination and initiate the formal investigation procedure. If it fails to give a decision by that deadline fictive approval can be assumed.[124] In this first phase of the supervisory procedure only the European Commission and the member state are involved, while the enterprise receiving the aid and its competitors are not admitted. Nor can the latter learn of the notification and the deployment of a preliminary examination, as these facts are not published. By far the greater majority of cases are concluded in this preliminary examination stage.[125]

117. If the European Commission was not able to clarify the question of the legality of the aid in the preliminary procedure it initiates the formal investigation procedure. The decision to do so is published in the Official Journal (Art. 26, Para. 2 together with Art. 4, Para. 4, Procedural Regulation). In the formal investigation procedure beside the member state concerned in accordance with Art. 20, Para. 1 Procedural Regulation, other "interested parties" may give a written statement. "Interested parties" here means "any Member State and

---

[122] While Art. 88, Para. 3 EC Treaty applies to new aid, Art. 88, Paras. 1 and 2 EC Treaty cover current aid, which, unlike new aid, does not have to be reported to the European Commission. The European Commission constantly appraises the current rules on state aid (Art. 88, Paras. 1 and 2 EC Treaty). Essentially, aid being given before the EC Treaty came into force on 1 January 1958 or before a member state joined the EU is classified as current aid, as is aid previously approved by the European Commission or the Council in some way.

[123] Cf. 5.4.3 for more detail.

[124] The aid is regarded as approved if the European Commission has not issued a decision within two months of receipt of a full notification. The member state may carry out the measure if it informs the European Commission of such intention and the European Commission has still not given a decision within a further 15 working days (Art. 4, Para. 6 Procedural Regulation).

[125] Between 2000 and 2006 the European Commission did not initiate a formal investigation procedure at all in around 95% of the cases duly notified, but gave a final decision in the preliminary procedure. Cf. Commission Report, State Aid Scoreboard, Spring 2007, COM(2007) 347, final, p. 15.

any person, undertaking or association of undertakings whose interests might be affected by the granting of aid, in particular the beneficiary of the aid, competing undertakings and trade associations" (Art. 1 lit. h) Procedural Reg.). This possibility for participation is intended not only to take account of the interests of parties that may be affected but also to open up a source of information for the European Commission. Under Art. 7, Para. 6, Sentence 2 Procedural Regulation the formal investigation procedure should if possible be concluded within 18 months. However, failure to keep to this deadline – which may be extended by mutual agreement – only enables the member state to demand a decision from the European Commission within two months on the basis of the information available to it (Art. 7, Para. 7 Procedural Regulation). The law does not lay down any conditions should the European Commission also fail to meet this deadline. In particular, unlike the preliminary procedure, a direct sanction in the form of fictive approval will not be imposed. In such a case the member state could therefore only lodge a complaint of excessive delay with the European Court, under Art. 232, Para. 1 EC Treaty.

118. If under Art. 7, Paras. 2 to 5 Procedural Regulation the European Commission concludes the formal investigation procedure by deciding that state aid is not involved, the aid can be approved without objection (positive decision). The European Commission can also issue a positive decision with conditions attached or declare the aid incompatible with the Common Market (negative decision). In practice negative decisions are the exception. The European Commission only decides not to allow aid for about 2% of the duly notified measures.[126]

5.4.1.2 Aid that is Formally Unlawful

119. In practice it often happens that member states grant aid with breach of the obligation to notify the European Commission under Art. 88, Para. 3 EC Treaty and the ban on execution which it contains. Between 2000 and 2006 the European Commission carried out more than 600 procedures on aid that was formally unlawful in this way.[127] Around 24% of the procedures carried out concerned the Federal Republic of Germany.[128] The number of cases of formally unlawful aid is probably even higher, as the European Commission will not learn of every case of infringement. Under Art. 10, Para. 1 Procedural Regulation the European Commission must examine without delay all the information it receives on apparently unlawful aid, regardless of its origin. Generally the European Commission is informed that there may have been infringement by third parties who have right of communication under Art. 20, Para. 2 of the Procedural Regulation.

120. The procedure for formally unlawful aid is the same as the procedure already described that is applied for duly notified aid (Arts. 10ss. Procedural Regulation). However, there is a crucial difference in that no deadlines are provided for in the procedure for formally unlawful aid.

121. The European Commission cannot order aid that has been given prematurely in breach of Art. 88, Para. 3, Sentence 3 EC Treaty to be recovered, solely on the grounds of formal

---

[126] Commission Report, State Aid Scoreboard, Spring 2007, loc. cit., p. 7.

[127] Loc. cit., p. 4.

[128] The large member states grant formally unlawful aid relatively frequently. Beside Germany with 24%, Italy accounted for 17%, Spain 12%, France 10% and the United Kingdom 9% of the procedures. Cf. Commission Report, State Aid Scoreboard, Spring 2007, loc. cit., pp. 15ss.

illegality. The European Courts also require the aid to be materially incompatible with the Common Market with no possibility of exemption – as under Art. 87, Para. 3 EC Treaty. In the past the European Commission came to the conclusion that formally unlawful aid was also materially inadmissible in about 25% of the cases.[129] The decision that the aid must be recovered, regularly issued in these cases, is addressed to the member state, who under Art. 14, Para. 3 of the Procedural Regulation must demand repayment of the aid "without delay", in accordance with its national law.[130] Objections to repayment are rarely successful.[131]

122. In the past, contrary to Art. 14, Para. 3 Procedural Regulation, recovery of aid was frequently not implemented speedily by member states, the payments were stretched, if they were made at all, over several years.[132] It may be difficult for a member state to obtain return of the aid, for instance if the company has meantime registered insolvency, if the ownership has changed or if a large number of companies have profited from the aid and the benefit consisted of reducing their expenses (for instance through selective tax concessions). In such cases the parties who are obliged to repay and the amount that should be demanded of them can only be determined with considerable expenditure. In only a few member states is the responsibility for implementing the demand for recovery entrusted to a central state authority. In Denmark and Great Britain the national competition authorities are responsible for making the demand. In Germany and most of the other member states, on the other hand, the office that originally granted the aid is responsible for recovery, but it generally does not have the appropriate specialised knowledge. In Germany this problem is lessened as the central department for aid is in the Federal Ministry of Economics and Technology. Beside making the initial notification of individual grants and regulations on aid to the European Commission it has the task of mediating between the European Commission and the various national donors when carrying out aid measures, including any recovery procedures.

123. Another reason why the recovery procedures can take so long is that in most member states – as in Germany – there are no specific regulations on recovery, general procedural law is applied. A recovery procedure will be very protracted if the recipient of the aid appeals to the national courts against the demand for repayment. These legal proceedings can have the effect of postponing the repayment, a possibility which the state authorities cannot prevent.

124. Under German law, for instance, this will be the case if the aid was granted as part of a contract under civil law. According to general principles a repayment demand must also go through the civil courts in such cases, and it cannot be ordered by sovereign administrative act. However, with reference to the effectivity requirement in Community law,[133] the appellate administrative court in Berlin-Brandenburg expressly permitted repayment demands by act of administration for unlawful aid in a decision of 7 November 2005.[134] This decision raises legal

---

[129] Commission Report, State Aid Scoreboard, Spring 2007, loc. cit., p. 5.

[130] Repayment may not be demanded (Art. 14, Para. 1, Sentence 2 Procedural Reg.) if this would infringe a general principle of Community law. Under Art. 14, Para. 2 Procedural Reg. the obligation to repay includes the obligation to pay interest from the date the unlawful aid was made available to the recipient and until it is actually repaid.

[131] For more detail see Sinnaeve, A., in: Heidenhain, M. (ed.), loc. cit., § 34, Nos. 16ss.

[132] Cf. Commission Report, State Aid Scoreboard, Spring 2007, loc. cit., pp. 17ss.

[133] Under the effectivity requirement (effet-utile principle) national legal protection regulations may not make it practically impossible to implement claims under Community law or hinder these excessively.

[134] Appellate Administrative Court of Berlin-Brandenburg, Decision of 7 November 2005, OVG 8 S
cont.

doubts, as a measure by a public authority that involves an obligation – like the issue of an administrative act that must be implemented without delay – may under the principle of the rule of law only be imposed with legal authorisation (the doctrine of legal reservation). A basis in national law is not evident here, and the direct applicability of the regulation in Community law, Art. 14, Para. 3 Procedural Regulation, seems questionable in view of the wording of the regulation.[135] The effectivity requirement in Community law can mean that a national regulation is not applied, but it cannot of itself provide a basis for authorising intervention to impose an obligation. However, the national legislature should create a legal basis for authorisation that will make immediate recovery possible and generally exclude delay through legal proceedings on national level. Otherwise the distortion to competition caused by granting the aid could possibly persist for years. Exclusion of the delaying effect would not be disproportionate, as a decision by the European Commission to obtain recovery must be implemented by member states. Due account should be taken of the concern for legal protection on the part of the recipients of the aid by enabling them to appeal against the European Commission's decision to demand repayment on EU level, before the Community courts.[136]

125. In keeping with its announcement in the SAAP, the European Commission has now issued a Notice to accelerate the implementation of decisions to recover aid. In it the Commission draws attention to the principles elaborated by the Community courts and aims to explain the Commission's practice in demanding repayment.[137] The Notice can be a useful guide for the offices in member states that are responsible for dealing with demands for repayment, but it cannot create a binding set of uniform rules for this. In the view of the Monopolkommission, an EU directive to create uniform minimum standards of legal protection in aid cases before national courts would be helpful, as it would i.a. include rules on the possibilities of legal protection against recovery demands.[138]

93.05, NvwZ 2006, 104-106. In this case the state authority responsible (Bundesanstalt für vereinigungsbedingte Sonderaufgaben – Federal Institute for Special Expenditure related to Reunification) ordered the immediate recovery by act of administration, although the aid had been granted to the beneficiary enterprise (Aker Warnow Werft GmbH) under a contract in civil law. The Berlin-Brandenburg court held the view that owing to the efficiency requirement in Community law a sovereign order was permissible, as only in this way could the obligation imposed by the Commission's decision and in Art. 14, Para.3 Procedural Reg. be fulfilled and repayment be demanded immediately.

[135] Art. 14, Para. 3 Procedural Reg. states: "Without prejudice to any order of the Court of Justice of the European Communities pursuant to Article 185 of the Treaty recovery shall be effected without delay and in accordance with the procedures under the national law of the Member State concerned, provided that they allow the immediate and effective execution of the Commission's decision. To this effect and in the event of a procedure before national courts, the Member States concerned shall take all necessary steps which are available in their respective legal systems, including provisional measures, without prejudice to Community law."

[136] Cf. 5.4.3.

[137] Notice from the Commission – Towards an effective implementation of Commission decisions ordering Member States to recover unlawful and incompatible State aid, OJ EU C 272 of 15 November 2007, p. 4.

[138] This is also recommended in the Study on the Enforcement of State Aid Law at National Level, March 2006, Jones Day, Lovells, Allen & Overy, http://ec.europa.eu/comm/competition/ state_aid/ studies_reports/studies_reports.cfm. The study was commissioned by the General-Directorate for Competition.

5.4.1.3 Comparison with the Antitrust Procedure

126. The procedure in aid control differs in several respects from the procedure used in EU antitrust cases. Private parties – especially the enterprises benefiting from the aid and their competitors – have fewer rights and are subject to considerable restrictions. Only the European Commission and the member state granting the aid are parties to the procedure. Private parties can only participate – apart from the permission to send a communication at any time under Art. 20, Para. 2 Procedural Regulation – when the European Commission has initiated the formal investigation procedure, and here they are limited to handing in written statements.

127. The reverse side of the bilateral structure of the aid procedure is that the European Commission does not have the scope for examination which it has in antitrust law. It cannot oblige enterprises and their associations to give information or carry out a sector-specific study (Arts. 17, 18 of the Antitrust Regulation).[139] As the European Commission has no direct powers to investigate the private market participants affected in an individual case, and who are best informed of conditions in the sectors concerned, it cannot examine the current competition situation to the extent possible under antitrust law. The information problem is made worse because the European Commission must communicate only with the central government of the member state, even if the aid has been planned or given on regional and local level.

128. The law on state aid does contain specific deadlines for Commission procedures on duly notified aid. These deadlines are, however, noticeably longer than those in merger control. While periods of two and 18 months are set for the preliminary and the formal aid control procedures respectively, in merger cases the preliminary procedure may take at most 15 working days, and the main investigation procedure generally at most 105 working days (Art. 10, Paras.1 and 3 Merger Control Regulation).[140] Unlike in merger control (Art. 10, Para. 6 Merger Control Regulation), failure to meet the deadline in the formal procedure in aid control does not involve sanctions on the European Commission, as no fictive approval is gener-ated.[141]

129. A further difference from antitrust law is that owing to the low level of proof required by the European courts to establish most of the facts under Art. 87, Para. 1 EC Treaty, the European Commission is obliged to investigate cases of little relevance. In aid control, unlike antitrust law, the opportunity principle does not apply, as it does for infringements of Arts. 81 and 82 EC Treaty (Art. 11, Para. 1 Reg. 1/2003) nor are there high thresholds for taking up a case, as in merger control (Art. 1, Paras. 2 and 3 Merger Control Regulation). As soon as the ex-amination of the information shows that unlawful aid may have been given the European Commission must continue the procedure, as for notified aid, and reach a decision (cf. Art. 13 in connection with Art. 4 Procedural Regulation). These requirements are only eased by the De Minimis Regulation, which sets a very low threshold (EUR 200,000 within three years),

---

[139] Council Regulation (EC) 1/2003 of 16 December 2002 on the implementation of the rules on competition laid down in Articles 81 and 82 of the Treaty.

[140] Council Regulation (EC) 139/2004 of 20 January 2004 on the control of concentrations between undertakings (the EC Merger Regulation), OJ EU L 24 of 29 January 2004, p. 1.

[141] Aid control procedures that are concluded in the preliminary phase last on average 5.2 months, according to information from the General-Directorate on Competition. The cases for which the European Commission initiates a formal investigation procedure, last on average 21.4 months.

and by the block exemption regulations issued for state aid. Reform of the Procedural Regulation is not planned under the present Commissioner for Competition, Neelie Kroes.

130. In the view of the Monopolkommission the state aid control procedure needs to be reformed, and in certain points brought into line with the antitrust procedures. Instead of the legality principle applied so far (Art. 10, Para. 1 Procedural Regulation) the European Commission could be allowed to judge whether to take up a case, as it can under antitrust law. However, the opportunity principle should only be introduced below a certain volume of promotion. This is still to be determined, but it could be set at EUR 1 million for individual aids. That would enable the European Commission to react flexibly and set priorities by concentrating on important cases. Any distortion to competition caused by low amounts of aid is generally less than that caused by larger amounts. However, that may not be the case for small, highly concentrated markets, or markets that are just developing, and intervention by the European Commission may well be needed here. Effective control and assessment could be made possible if EU member states had to send a brief communication and a description of the aid granted and its recipient to the European Commission for aid that does not exceed a certain fixed threshold. If the European Commission did not express any doubts within a period still to be settled (e.g. two months) the aid could be regarded as approved. If the member state fails to fulfil this obligation ex post intervention by the European Commission should still be possible.

131. The discretion allowed to the European Commission over whether to take up a case could be flanked by the introduction of a private action for a declaratory judgement by competitors affected or their associations. The competitors of the recipient of the aid could be given the right to bring an action before the Community courts if the European Commission decides not to carry out a procedure on opportunity grounds. To prevent the European Commission's scope for decision being counteracted and avoid a flood of legal actions the possibility should be considered of allowing the private action only if the competitor's position on the market in question is considerably restricted by the state aid.

132. In addition, the procedural rights in the aid control procedure of the recipients of the aid, their competitors and their associations should be strengthened. The procedure should not remain purely bilateral between the European Commission and the member state concerned, the recipients of the aid should be admitted in the preliminary procedure as a party and the competitors affected (or their associations) as participants. The European Commission should also be allowed direct powers to investigate private parties. That could give it better access to the information it needs to make an economically well-founded estimate of the competitive situation. The efficiency of the Commission's procedure could be increased by introducing both binding and shorter deadlines, with fictive approval to come into force if the deadlines are missed and no decision is taken. However, this would only appear to be appropriate if the member states have duly notified the European Commission of the aid and did not grant it prematurely by infringing the ban on execution in Art. 88, Para. 3, Sentence 3 EC Treaty. The decision not to set deadlines in the procedures for formally unlawful aid – which is already intended – sets an incentive to observe the obligation to report the aid.

5.4.2 *Proceedings before the European Courts*

133. If the European Commission has taken a decision classifying aid as incompatible with the Common Market (a negative decision) the member state in question can appeal against the decision in the European Court of Justice on grounds of invalidity under Art. 230, Para. EC Treaty.

134. An authority within a member state can also appeal against a negative decision by the European Commission on grounds of invalidity. That could happen if a German Federal state, for example, or a municipality wished to grant aid entirely or partly out of its own funds and were prevented by a negative decision by the European Commission. Unlike the member states themselves, their regional subdivisions are not, however, entitled per se to appeal. They must prove that they are directly and individually affected by the negative decision (Art. 230, Para. 4, EC Treaty).

135. The criterion of direct effect is met, according to jurisprudence, if the act of Community law affects the interests or the legal position of the plaintiff, without further executory act, or if the national authorities have no discretionary powers at all in the implementation. That is the case in negative decisions by the European Commission, since, although these are addressed exclusively to the member state, they allow no scope for judgement and must be observed by the regional authorities as well.

136. Persons (natural or legal) who are not the addressees of the act of Community legislation are only individually affected, according to the Plaumann verdict by the European Court of Justice,[142] if the act of legislation affects them owing to certain personal qualities or particular circumstances that mark them out of the group of all other persons, and so individualise them in a similar way as addressee. This condition is regarded as met for a regional authority if it is involved financially in the aid or has autonomous powers in granting or demanding repayment of the aid.[143] Insofar, unlike for cases brought by member states it is not the European Court of Justice that is first competent but the Court of the First Instance (the European Court).

137. The potential recipient of the aid can also have an interest in appealing against a negative decision by the European Commission on grounds of invalidity. He, too, is only empowered to bring the suit if he can show that he is directly and individually affected by the negative decision (Art. 230, Para. 4 EC Treaty). The criterion of individual effect is interpreted narrowly by the Community courts following the Plaumann formula. In this context it is important whether the negative decision was on an individual grant or a general aid scheme.[144]

138. Individual aids are characterised by the fact that they are tied to a specific project or are individualised for the recipient.[145] If the European Commission forbids an individual aid, and the enterprise bringing the lawsuit would have profited from it, the individual effect required by the European courts is regarded as present without further examination.

139. The situation is different in cases where the negative decision is on a general aid scheme. In these cases those entitled to receive aid and the projects promoted are not specified in concrete but defined in general and abstract terms (e.g. a statutory tax concession for the

---

[142] ECJ, Judgement of 15 July 1963, Case. 25/62, Plaumann/Commission, Rec. 1963, 213.

[143] Cf. ECJ, Judgement of 15 December 1999, Verb. Cases T-132/96 and T-143/96, The Free State of Saxony et al./Commission, Rec. 1999, II-3663, No. 91.

[144] Cf. Art. 225, Para. 1 EC Treaty together with Art. 51 of the Protocol on the Statute of the Court, OJ EC C 80 of 10 March 2001, p. 63.

[145] In Art. 1 c) Procedural Regulation "indiviudal aid" is defined as aid "that is not awarded on the basis of an aid scheme and notifiable awards of aid on the basis of an aid scheme."

application of certain environmental standards).[146] Aid schemes are "self-executing", that is, they can be implemented in themselves and they justify direct claims. The individual assignment of the favourable treatment follows later, when concrete aid is granted on the basis of the aid scheme. This aid – if it is covered by the decision to allow the aid – does not have to be reported separately to the European Commission under Art. 88, Para. 3, Sentence 1 EC Treaty. In the case of general aid schemes enterprises that can show that they would have profited from the scheme had the European Commission not taken a negative decision are only regarded as authorised to appeal in exceptional cases.[147] If the aid scheme provides for benefits to enterprises in a specific sector, according to jurisprudence it is not sufficient for the enterprise bringing the suit to belong to the sector in question and to have been directly eligible fo benefit. In the view of the European Court of Justice the aid scheme is only a general legal norm, from the standpoint of the enterprise bringing the suit. Consequently, the conditions in the Plaumann formula outlined above, namely that the plaintiff must be individualised by the decision owing to personal qualities or special circumstances, are not met. This restrictive line is a fortiori applied in cases where the ban by the European Commission is on a horizontal aid scheme, that is intended to benefit enterprises in various sectors.

140. By contrast, in cases where a member state has already implemented an aid scheme in breach of the ban in Art. 88, Para. 3 EC Treaty before the European Commission has issued its final decision, the enterprises benefiting are regarded as individually affected.[148] These enterprises can then appeal against the decision by the European Commission in which the general aid scheme is classified as incompatible with the Common Market, pleading invalidity under Art. 230, Para. 4 EC Treaty. This leads to contradictory assessments.[149] As a result of this jurisprudence, enterprises that have already received aid in breach of Art. 88, Para. 3 EC Treaty are ultimately privileged over enterprises that would be directly entitled to appeal if the European Commission had not raised objection to the duly notified aid scheme.

141. Nor does the Lisbon Treaty provide for improvement in the legal protection against general aid schemes.[150] Art. 265 of the reform treaty, that is intended to replace Art. 230 EC Treaty, does provide for extension of the right to appeal. In future natural and legal persons will be able to appeal against acts of EU legislation that have the character of regulations if they are directly affected and if no implementation measures are required. They do not have to provide separate proof that they are individually affected. However, this condition is not met if the European Commission approves a general aid scheme, as it is issued by the member states themselves and not the EU organs, and further concretising measures are generally needed to execute it, like establishing the entitlement. So even after the Lisbon Treaty comes

---

[146] In Art. 1 d) Procedural Regulation the term an "aid scheme" is defined as any act "on the basis of which, without further implementing measures being required, individual aid awards may be made to undertakings defined within the act in a general and abstract manner and any act on the basis of which aid which is not linked to a specific project may be awarded to one or several undertakings for an indefinite period of time and/or for an indefinite amount."

[147] Cf. ECJ, Judgement of 2 February 1988, Cases 67, 68 and 70/85, Van der Kooy/Commission, Rec. 1988, 219, No. 5.

[148] Cf. ECJ, Judgement of 29 September 2000, Case T-55/99, CETM/Commission, Rec. 2000, II-3207, Nos. 23ss.

[149] Cf. Soltesz, U., in: Heidenhain, M. (ed.), loc. cit., § 43, No. 16.

[150] Lisbon Treaty to Amend the Treaty on the European Union and the Treaty to establish the European Union, signed in Lisbon on 13 December 2007, OJ EU C 306 of 17 December 2007, p. 1.

into force proof of direct effect will be needed for general aid schemes as well, to which ECJ applies the restrictive requirements of the Plaumann formula outlined above.

142. Competitors of the enterprise benefiting from the aid can also appeal on European level if at the end of the preliminary or the formal investigation procedure the European Commission finds that the measure in question is not aid, or if it approves an aid. The decisive hurdle for admission of the competitor's suit is again whether he is individually affected under Art. 230, Para. 4 EC Treaty. The jurisprudence of the European courts on the criterion of individual effect on third parties who can be disadvantaged if aid is granted is not stringent. The requirements vary depending on the phase of the procedure (preliminary or formal investigation) and the form of the aid (individual or general).

143. If the decision by the European Commission is not on an individual aid but on a general aid scheme individual effect on competitors is on principle abnegated, as for appeals by the recipient of the aid with reference to the Plaumann formula. The situation is only different if individual aids have already been granted to competing enterprises on the basis of the aid scheme.[151]

144. If an aid is approved, and if only a preliminary examination has been made, it must be taken into account that the competitor lodging the appeal has had no possibility to participate, as third parties are not admitted at this stage of the procedure. As already shown, parties other than the member state only have the opportunity to exercise their procedural rights, guaranteed also under Art. 88, Para. 2 EC Treaty, by giving a written statement in the formal investigation procedure. At least according to earlier jurisprudence, to prove that a private third party was affected it was sufficient to point out that this party has had no opportunity to exercise its rights as a party involved in procedures by the European Commission as the formal procedure was not opened.[152] To justify involvement in the formal procedure it is sufficient if enterprises' "interests might be affected" (Art. 1 lit. h) Procedural Regulation). Simply potential affection is therefore sufficient, without the necessity to prove actual affection. The jurisprudence outlined here has not so far been expressly abandoned, but in more recent decisions, in addition to the restriction of individual interests, proof has been required from the competitor that his competitive position on the market is negatively affected by the aid.[153] So implicitly the requirements to lodge an appeal are greater than would have been necessary to justify the position of the plaintiff as participant in a formal investigation procedure – a procedure which the European Commission did not instigate. However, no specific degree of restriction (noticeable or considerable) is required for Commission decisions completed in the preliminary procedure.

145. If an individual aid is approved after a formal investigation procedure a competitor of the recipient is to be regarded as individually affected, according to the Cofaz judgement, if he played an active part in the aid procedure, and if his market position will be noticeably

---

[151] Cf. ECJ, Judgement of 5 June 1996, Case T-398/94, Kahn Scheepart/Commission, Rec. 1996, II-477, Nos. 41 and 49.

[152] Cf. ECJ, Judgement of 19 May 1993, Case C198/91, Cook/Commission, Rec. 1993, I-2487, Nos. 20ss.; ECJ, Judgement of 15 June 1993, Case C-225/91, Matra/Commission, Rec. 1993, I-3203, Nos. 14ss.

[153] Cf. ECJ, Judgement of 21 March 2001, C-69/96, Hamburger Hafen-und Lagerhaus/Commission, Rec. 2001, II-1037, Nos. 41ss.

restricted by the aid.[154] As the European Court of Justice explained in its Sniace decision of 22 November 2007, the criterion on active participation is not to be regarded as an essential condition.[155] Unlike situations where the decision by the European Commission that is being contested was taken during the preliminary examination, here the restriction must be shown to be "noticeable" or "considerable". Under which conditions that can be confirmed is not entirely palpable from the jurisprudence. It is clear however that on the one side it is not enough for the enterprise to compete in some way with the recipient of the aid,[156] while on the other side it is enough if the aid in question would have enabled the competing recipient to survive on a market that is characterised by a very limited number of producers, fierce competition and big excess capacities.[157] In the Sniace judgement mentioned above the European Court of Justice agrees with the preceding instance, namely that the existence of direct competition between the enterprises is not sufficient to prove noticeable or considerable restriction of a market position, and so there is no right of appeal.[158]

146. Legal proceedings before the Community courts brought by associations are on principle admitted to a much more liberal extent than in general German case law. Business associations can act in aid cases for the recipient and for his competitors. The scope for associations to bring an action on the grounds that their own interests are restricted is very limited.[159] However, according to the jurisprudence by the European courts, an association is not only empowered to bring an action if it can show that it has an interest in the case, but also if the individual enterprises in the association (or some of them) are in turn authorised to appeal and the association is acting as administrator of the individual interests of its members.[160] An action by an association on behalf of the recipient would appear to be a meaningful and efficient instrument, particularly if the European Commission has not forbidden an individual aid but a general aid scheme from which several members of the association would have profited. Conversely, actions by associations for competitors will mainly be brought if many of the members are affected by aid approved by the European Commission. As already shown, an association that wishes to represent the interests of its members can only bring an action if at least some of the members are themselves authorised to appeal under Art. 230, Para. 4 EC Treaty. As the jurisprudence takes a very restrictive line on actions by private plaintiffs on general aid schemes, actions by associations are also prevented by the hurdle in Art. 230, Para. 2 EC Treaty.

147. The Monopolkommission on principle takes a positive view of the admission of actions

---

[154] Cf. ECJ, Judgement of 28 January 1986, Case 169/84, Cofaz/Commission, Rec. 1986, 391, Nos. 24f.

[155] Cf. ECJ, Judgement of 22 November 2007, Case 260/05, Sniace/Commission, No. 57, http://curia.europa.eu/juris/cgi-bin/form.pl?lang=de.

[156] Cf. ECJ, Judgement of 22 October 1996, Case T-266/94, Skibsvaerftsforeningen/Commission, Rec. 1996, II-1399, Nos. 45ss.

[157] Cf. ECJ, Judgement of 21 October 2004, Case T-36/99, Lenzing/Commission, Rec. 2004.

[158] Cf. ECJ, Judgement of 22 November 2007.

[159] According to the jurisprudence it may be assumed that the association is affected if its position as partner in negotiations is negatively affected by the Commission decision that is contested. That is if the association has considerable rights of co-determination in the national or EU regulations on aid in question. Cf. ECJ, Judgement of 2 February 1988, Cases 67, 68 and 70/85, van der Kooy/Commission, Rec. 1988, 219, No. 15.

[160] Cf. ECJ, Judgement of 10 July 1986, Case 282/85, DEFI/Commission, Rec. 1986, 2469, Note 16; cf. also Soltész, U., in: Heidenhain (ed.), loc. cit., § 45, Nos. 4ss.

by associations, as they can help the efficient implementation of the legislation on aid. In contrast to the jurisprudence by the European Court of Justice, actions against decisions on general aid schemes by the European Commission brought by recipients of aid, their competitors and their associations should be admitted, and in so far the restrictive Plaumann formula should not be applied. This corresponds to the standpoint put forward by the Advocate General Jacobs in his summing up in the Aktionsgemeinschaft case.[161] The only proof required that a potential recipient of the aid is individually affected should be that he would have been directly entitled to benefit had the aid been approved.

148. The same applies to actions brought by competitors against a decision by the European Commission to approve aid, if it can be shown that individual aid will be granted in future on the basis of the scheme and will negatively affect the competitive position of the enterprise. In addition, the criterion of individual restriction should not be made dependent on procedural aspects but – independent of the procedural stage in which the decision by the European Commission was taken – on material restriction.[162] To prove that they are individually affected in the meaning of Art. 230, Para. 4 EC Treaty competitors should not be required to show that their competitive position has actually been restricted as a result of the aid. Such proof of causality will only be possible in very few cases, and it will prevent many from bringing an action. It should be sufficient for a competitor to show substantively that he can be negatively affected by the aid. To simplify the procedure and for legal certainty individual affection should be presumed if the plaintiff can show that he is a direct competitor of the enterprise benefiting from the aid, and if the aid exceeds a certain amountto be specified, e.g. for individual aids EUR 1 million. The existence of concrete and direct competition should generally – in contrast to the view of the European Court of Justice – be regarded as sufficient.

5.4.3 Proceedings before National Courts

149. The legislation on aid envisages not only cases before Community courts, but proceedings before the national courts as well. Beside cases for recovery of the aid,[163] actions brought by competitors are particularly important. To provide legal protection for competitors on national level it must be remembered that the ban on aid in Art. 87, Para. 1 EC Treaty does not have direct effect, according to the jurisprudence by the European courts, that is, it cannot serve as grounds for appeal before national courts or be applied by them. As the grounds for exemption to this ban given in Art. 87, Para. 3 EC Treaty are very broad, the concretisation and unconditionality required to establish direct effect are lacking. The examination of whether aid is compatible with the Common Market is therefore exclusively the responsibility of the European Commission, which is in so far controlled by the European courts. However, under European jurisprudence the national courts have the task of ensuring effective legal

---

[161] Cf. ECJ, Judgement of 13 December 2005, Case C-78/03 P, Commission/Aktionsgemeinschaft, Rec. 2005, I-10737, Nos. 138ss. (summing-up by Advocate General Jacobs).

[162] Cf. Advocate General Jacobs, loc. cit. However, only the procedural aspects should be considered if the European Commission has not opened the formal investigation procedure, and the request to appeal by a third party who has not been able to claim its rights as a party involved under Art. 20, Para. 2 Procedural Reg. should be limited to obliging the European Commission to open the formal investigation procedure.

[163] See above 5.4.1.2.

protection against infringement of the directly applicable disposition of Art. 88, Para. 3 EC Treaty. This is intended to secure the system of preventive aid control by the European Commission and avoid competitive advantages which the beneficiary could derive from aid not granted in the envisaged way.

150. It is generally accepted that a competitor who is affected can appeal for an injunction or for removal of the aid if there is infringement of the obligation to notify in Art. 88, Para. 3 EC Treaty and of the ban on granting aid, by bringing an action against the public donor authority (action by a competitor). He also has the alternative of sending a communication to the European Commission under Art. 20, Para. 2 Procedural Regulation, or he can combine these two methods. Should he bring an action the national courts must examine whether the aid is formally unlawful. Should that be the case the national court to which appeal has been made must, according to jurisprudence by the European Court of Justice, generally order the aid to be repaid, independently of whether it was materially legal and is later approved by the European Commission. If the aid was granted as part of an exchange agreement under civil law, according to jurisprudence by the German Federal Supreme Court the agreement as a whole must be regarded as invalid, as the ban in Art. 88, Para. 3, Sentence 3 EC Treaty has been breached.[164]

151. In its CELF judgement of 12 February 2008 the European Court of Justice expressly stated that the national courts can if necessary order repayment of aid that is formally unlawful even if the European Commission has in the meantime taken the final decision that the aid is materially within the law and compatible with the Common Market.[165] This applies without prejudice to the right of the member state to grant the aid again. In addition, the national courts are obliged to impose on the recipient of the aid to pay interest on the amount for the period of illegality. As the European Court of Justice has convincingly shown, the unjustified advantage to the recipient lies firstly in the fact that he has not paid interest on the aid in question, whereas he would have had to pay interest if he had borrowed the same amount on the market until the decision by the European Commission was issued, and secondly in the improvement of his competitive position against other market participants during the period when the aid was formally unlawful. In its CELF judgement the European Court of Justice also states – without further concretisation – that the national court could also be induceed to approve claims for damages suffered through the (formal) illegality of the aid.

152. The examination to be undertaken by the national courts under Art. 88, Para. 3 EC Treaty can be complex – even if it does not include the examination of material legality. Answering the question whether a measure meets all the criteria of aid in Art. 87, Para. 1 EC Treaty or if it does not need to be notified owing to a block exemption, can be difficult, involving both factual and legal problems. The national courts can, or must, apply to the European Court of Justice for a preliminary decision if there are legal doubts (Art. 234, Paras. 3 and 4 EC Treaty). In addition, the courts may consult the European Commission, question it on its usual practice in classifying a measure as aid and ask for information, like statistics, market studies and economic analyses.[166]

153. The classification of a measure as aid by national courts could in future be made more

---

[164] Cf. BGH, Judgement of 4 April 2003, V ZR 314/02, EuZW 2003, p. 444

[165] Cf. ECJ, Judgement of 12 February 2008, Case C-199/06, CELF.

[166] Notice from the European Commission on cooperation between the Commission and the Courts of Member States on State aid, OJ EC C 312 of 23, November 1995, p. 8.

difficult if – as the Monopolkommission advocates – the criterion of distortion to competition in Art. 87, Para. 1 EC Treaty were to be established, not generally but only with justification based on economic considerations. This could create legal uncertainty. It applies correspondingly to the decision to be made by member states on the question of obligatory notification, as under Art. 88, Para. 3 EC Treaty only those measures are to be reported to the European Commission that are aid in the meaning of Art. 87, Para. 1 EC Treaty, and as thecriterion of distortion of competition is regarded as a component of the concept of aid. However, this could be countered in two ways. Firstly, the low requirements for proof of distortion of competition under Art. 88, Para. 3 EC Treaty could be retained, while more proof could be required from the European Commission under Art. 87, Para. 1 EC Treaty. Secondly, and as an alternative, the concept of aid could be interpreted differently by not regarding the criterion of distortion of competition as essential to qualify a measure as aid. Consequently, only the other criteria listed in Art. 87, Para. 1 EC Treaty, and which justify supranational aid control by the European Commission, would be regarded as reasons for taking up a case, while the criterion of distortion of competition would be interpreted purely as a criterion for intervention, which only the European Commission would have to observe.

154. As well as the actions to stop and remove aid, which are intended to prevent formally unlawful aid from being disbursed or to require its repayment, competitors affected can also sue for damages. They have the possibility of claiming against the member state that has granted the aid and infringed the ban in Art. 88, Para. 3 EC Treaty, in accordance with the principles in the Francovich jurisprudence by the European Court of Justice.[167] In Germany the obligation to pay damages in European law is realised through a claim on official liability under § 839 Civil Code, in conjunction with Art. 34 of the Basic Law. Claims for damages can be made against the public authorities under the following conditions: (1) The regulation in European law that has been infringed is directly applicable and is designed to protect the plaintiff's subjective interests, (2) the infringement is sufficiently qualified, (3) there is a direct causal relation between the infringement and the damage suffered. Competitors will frequently succeed in providing evidence of the first two conditions.[168] However, competitors negatively affected by aid generally fail to make a successful claim for damages on the third condition. Proof that specifically the infringement of the ban in the EC Treaty has caused concrete damage to his enterprise is difficult to provide – without easier conditions provided in legislation.

155. It is unclear whether, if there is infringement of Art. 88, Para. 3 EC Treaty, a competitor can only bring an action against the public donor of the aid, or whether he can also claim on the private enterprise that has benefited from the aid. The clauses in civil law that apply here

---

[167] Cf. ECJ, Judgement of 19 November 1991, Cases C-6/90 and C-9/90, Francovich/Italy, Rec. 1991, 5357ss.

[168] The first condition is fulfilled, as the ban in Art. 88, Para. 3, Sentence 3 EC Treaty is intended to ensure before the European Commission approves aid that no competitive disadvantage will accrue to private third parties and they can exercise their procedural rights in the formal investigation procedure before the European Commission, or before the Community courts. The second condition can also be regarded as fulfilled. Infringement of Community law is sufficiently qualified if the member state clearly and considerably goes beyond the limits of its power to act. That can be assumed on infringement of the obligation to report aid and the ban on granting aid in Art. 88, Para. 3 EC Treaty, as member states have no discretionary powers in this. If it is doubtful whether a measure is aid member states must report the measure to the European Commission, which can take a binding decision.

are §§ 8 and 9 in conjunction with § 3 Unfair Competition Law and §§ 1004, Para. 1, analogous in conjunction with 823, Para. 2 Civil Code. However, these regulations on claims for cessation, removal and damages only apply if the defendant has infringed an obligation. In some opinions this is denied on the grounds that under the wording of the provision the obligation to notify aid and the ban on granting aid in Art. 88, Para. 3 EC Treaty only apply to member states.[169] Others hold the view that the beneficiary should generally be regarded as a liable party as well (§§ 830, 840 Civil Code), sharing responsibility for the infringement of the ban.[170] In support of the latter view it can be said that a market participant who achieves an advantageous position in competition through the receipt of aid is the actual beneficiary of the measure that has to be reported, and that such favouring at the expense of third parties can only be justified if the prescribed procedure is observed. Hence it appears appropriate to interpret the meaning and purpose of Art. 88, Para. 3 EC Treaty as that the beneficiary is a member of the group obliged to notify, and that competitors affected can bring an action directly against him if he infringes that obligation. Accordingly, they can require the beneficiary to cease participation in the granting of unreported aid in future and repay to the public donor aid already granted. However in claims for damages against the beneficiary enterprise the problem arises that it will scarcely be possible to prove damage and causality, since, unlike antitrust law, for instance (§ 33, Para. 3, Sentences 2 to 4 Act against Restraints of Competition) the law does not offer easier conditions.

156. In view of this it is not surprising that, according to a study commissioned by the European Commission, claims for damages by private market participants are extremely rare before the courts of member states, either in the form of claims against a public authority on grounds of official liability, or in the form of cases in civil law against the benefiting enterprise. So far, not a single case is known in which the claim was successful.[171] In regard to actions for an injunction and removal brought by private parties before national courts on grounds of infringement of Art. 88, Para. 3 EC Treaty the study differentiates between the following: (a) a private market participant wishes to defend himself against positive favouring of a competitor and (b) the plaintiff objects to an obligation laid upon him and by which other market participants are not affected (e.g. a selective environmental charge). The latter accounts for the clear majority of claims brought by competitors.[172] This is probably due firstly to the fact that there can be no doubt in such cases that the plaintiff is individually affected, and secondly, the first situation probably presents a greater obstacle, as the enterprise is not directly affected and would like itself to profit from future aid. So competitors have a rational reason not to sue. Actions for injunction and removal are also very rarely brought by competitors in the European courts.

157. In the view of the Monopolkommission, legal protection on national level could be improved by enabling associations to bring actions, similar to their rights in antitrust law (§ 33, Para. 2 Act against Restraints of Competition- GWB). Incorporated associations can claim under antitrust law for injunction and removal under § 33, Para. 1 GWB to promote

---

[169] Schmidt-Kötters, T., in: Heidenhain, M. (ed.), loc. cit., § 58, No. 34.

[170] Cf. Tilmann, W., Schreibauer, M., Rechtsfolgen rechtswidriger nationaler Beihilfen, Gewerblicher Rechtsschutz und Urheberrecht 104, 2002, pp. 212-224, 222.

[171] Study on the Enforcement of State Aid Law at National Level, March 2006, Jones Day, Lovells, Allen & Overy, http://ec.europa.eu/comm/competition/state_aid/studies_reports/studies_reports.cfin, pp. 48ss.

[172] Loc. cit., pp. 33ss.

commercial or independent professional interests (but they cannot claim for damages), if a considerable number of their member enterprises are selling goods or services of the same or related kind on the same market, if they are capable, especially due to their staffing, material and financial situation, of fulfilling their statutory tasks in the pursuit of commercial or independent professional interests, and if the infringement will affect the interests of their members.[173] No doubt an association cannot necessarily be expected to sue enterprises in the same member state, particularly if they are its own members. But the situation is different if the beneficiary is an enterprise in a different member state and is competing with its members who cannot benefit from the – foreign – aid. An action here seems very possible. An incentive to effective private implementation of the law could be created for situations where a large number of enterprises are affected. This could overcome the rational disinterest on the part of the individual competitors in bringing a court action.

158. To improve efficiency and legal certainty the possibilities for legal protection on national level should be regulated as a whole and adjusted to the legislation on aid. Beside excluding the delaying effect of actions for repayment, the admission of associations and easier proof requirements for claims for damages, a special competence could be created to represent legal protection interests in aid cases. It could be regulated analogous to the legislation on public procurements.[174] To ensure a more uniform application of the law within the EU, minimum standards that would apply generally should also be laid down in an EU directive. The Monopolkommission recommends the European Commission to commence the preliminary work for such a package of directives, which could be oriented to the comparable project for the private implementation of Arts. 81 and 82 EC Treaty.[175]

6. Reform Projects by the European Commission – Establishing a More Economic Approach in Aid Control

6.1 The European Commission's State Aid Action Plan

159. The objectives and substance which the European Commission is pursuing in its proposed reforms to European aid control are not identical with those it is pursuing as more economic approach in European antitrust law. In this section the European Commission's reform projects in aid are first discussed in more detail, before the characteristics of a more economic approach in aid are compared with those in antitrust law.

160. Under the Commissioner for Competition Neelie Kroes the European Commission is endeavouring to carry out comprehensive reform of European aid control, and on 7 June 2005 it published the State Aid Action Plan (SAAP).[176] The plan contains a roadmap for the

---

[173] There is a similar model in EC Directive 98/27/EC by the European Parliament and the Council of 19 May 1998 on pleas for injunction to protect consumer interests, but it only covers actions for injunction under consumer law. OJ EC L 166 of 11 June 1998, p. 51.

[174] See 4.3.

[175] Cf. most recently the White Paper "Damages Actions for breach of the EC competition rules", 2 April 2008, COM(2008) 165 final.

[176] European Commission State Aid Action Plan: http://ec.europa.eu/comm/competition/state_aid/reform/reform.cfm.

revision of the rules on aid in secondary law.[177] The Community frameworks, communications and regulations that have applied so far are to be redrafted between 2005 and 2009 in the light of a more economic approach, while the primary law regulations in the EC Treaty (Arts. 87ss.) are retained. The SAAP is conceived as a consultation paper intended to stimulate political debate on reform of European aid policy. Several measures have now been taken to implement the reform concept in the SAAP.

6.1.1 The Contents of the SAAP

161. In the SAAP the European Commission names four principles that are to be pursued in reforming aid legislation:
* less and better targeted state aid
* more efficient procedures, better application of the law, greater predictability and more transparency
* shared responsibility between the European Commission and member states and
* a refined economic approach.[178]

6.1.1.1 Less and Better Targeted State Aid

162. The SAAP takes up the objective formulated by the European Council in the Lisbon Strategy for member states to grant less and better target state aid in the future.[179] The quantitative level of state aid is to be lowered and aid concentrated on the objectives of the Lisbon Strategy (innovation, research and development, investment in human capital and the promotion of new businesses). According to the SAAP the European Commission would like to reduce aid to a minimum that does not serve common interests of the Community. The particularly problematic rescue and restructuring aids should be avoided as far as possible. Aid given by member states should be more horizontal and in contrast to sectoral aid not limited from the start to individual sectors. Aid should be permissible particularly for cases of market failure.

---

[177] In a speech to the European Committee of the German Federal Parliament on 6 July 2006 Neelie Kroes said: "We are overhauling all our rules in order to firmly ground them on rigorous economic analysis and improve the speed, transparency and predictability of their application."

[178] This is the wording in the English SAAP, Item 18.

[179] At a special summit held in Lisbon in March 2000 the heads of state and government of the EU member states (the European Council) agreed on the Lisbon Strategy, the aim of which is to make the EU the most competitive and dynamic knowledge-based economic area in the world within ten years. Productivity and the speed of innovation are to be increased by various political measures. The Lisbon strategy is mainly concerned with innovation and the international competitiveness of the EU, and at a meeting in March 2005 the European Council made an interim assessment. As the growth gap, particularly to the United States, had widened in the past five years no concrete targets were formulated at this meeting. However, a revitalisation of the Lisbon growth targets was decided, for which each member state was to draw up its own reform programme. In its concluding remarks the European Council also discusses national state aid, urging member states to continue to lower the general level of state aid besides conducting an active competition policy. Any market failures must be taken into account. This tendency must involve a redirection of funds towards certain horizontal aims, like research and innovation and investing in human capital. Regional aid should also be reformed as agreed in the Lisbon Strategy to encourage a high level of investment and reduce the gap between regions.

On principle the Monopolkommission welcomes these objectives. However, it points out that the European Commission does not have any fiscal policy competence in aid control under Arts. 87ss. EC Treaty. The supervision of the use of resources by member states is not one of its tasks. So the European regulations on aid cannot be used directly to lower the quantitative level of aid given in member states. Reducing aid and preventing waste of (member) state funds must first and foremost be secured on national level. The focus of future aid control should rather be on ensuring less distortion to competition through aid and on better targeting aid to keep cross-border distortion of competition on the EU internal market as low as possible. In the view of the Monopolkommission such a European competition policy would indirectly lead to a welcome reduction of the volume of aid.

6.1.1.2 More Efficient Procedures, Better Application of the Law, Greater Predictability and More Transparency

163. One of the European Commission's main objectives in the planned reform is to reduce its own work load. It wants to concentrate on the more difficult cases, and for this purpose it intends to extend the area of application of the De Minimis Regulation and pass a uniform block exemption regulation. The aim of reducing the work load was also the background for the new Antitrust Procedure Regulation, in which Art. 81, Para. 3 EC Treaty, that had been interpreted as a preventive ban with the possibility of exemption, was declared a directly applicable legal exception.

6.1.1.3 Responsibility shared between the European Commission and Member States

164. In the SAAP the European Commission urges member states to endeavour to achieve greater efficiency and transparency and a better implementation of aid policy. In particular, more care in notification should be taken to shorten procedures.[180] The European Commission also intends to issue best practices guidelines.

165. The idea of setting up independent authorities in member states to support the European Commission in implementing aid law is also aired in the SAAP.[181] In this the European Commission is building on experience in the last accession process, when controlling authorities in the new member states were responsible for checking state aid.

166. In the view of the Monopolkommission, as already explained, macroeconomic aid control should be carried out on national level by an independent national body.[182] This body could also be required to work closely with the European Commission and support it in the implementation of the European aid rules to protect competition.

6.1.1.4 More Refined Economic Approach

167. The European Commission would also like to "refine" the economic approach in aid control in order to "ensure a proper and more transparent evaluation of the distortions to

---

[180] SAAP, Item 49.

[181] SAAP, Item 51.

[182] Cf. Item 69 in this chapter.

competition and trade associated with state aid measures. This approach can also help investigate the reasons why the market by itself does not deliver the desired objectives of common interest and in consequence evaluate the benefits of state aid measures in reaching these objectives. One key element in that respect is the analysis of market failures".[183]

168. So, according to the SAAP, whether granting state aid for economic policy purposes is justified is to depend in future on whether there is market failure. The possible reasons for market failure named by the European Commission are external effects, public goods, asymmetrical information, lack of coordination and market power.[184] But even if, as the European Commission desires, correcting market failure is to occupy a central place in future, the social, distribution policy and cultural objectives named in the EC Treaty may still justify aid.

169. In assessing compatibility on the justification level, when the positive and negative effects of aid are weighed, the European Commission intends in future to proceed according to a uniform scheme. As explained in more detail in the Community framework for state aid for research, development and innovation, a three-stage balancing test is to be carried out (cf. Table VI.2).[185]

Table VI.2:

The European Commission's Three-Stage Balancing Test

Stage 1
Does the planned aid measure serve an exactly defined purposes of common interest, to remove market failure or a different aim (e.g. regional or social)?

Stage 2
Is the aid instrument likely to achieve the purpose that is in the Community interest, i.e. correct the market failure, or pursue some other aim? a) Is state aid the appropriate means? b) Will it have an incentive effect, i.e. will it change companies' behaviour? c) Is the aid proportionate, i.e. could the same change in behaviour also be achieved with less aid?

Stage 3
Are the disadvantages – especially the distortions to competition and trade – limited, so that the positive consequences of the aid outweigh the negative? How greatly aid distorts competition is to depend on • the criteria by which the beneficiaries are chosen and which charges or conditions are attached to the aid, • the characteristics of the market and the beneficiaries, and • how large the aid will be and what kind of instrument it is.

Source: European Commission

---

[183] SAAP, Items 22 and 23.
[184] On compensating for market failure as a possible reason for granting aid see 2.2 above.
[185] OJ EU C 323 of 30 December 2006, p. 1.

170. The Monopolkommission welcomes the European Commission's intention to typify the compatibility assessment it will undertake on the justification level (Art. 87, Para. 3 EC Treaty). However, the European Commission has neglected to include in the SAAP a more indepth economic analysis of the circumstances requiring aid (Art. 87, Para. 1 EC Treaty). Generally the European Commission only makes the cursory and general examination outlined above in such cases – and particularly when assessing any distortion to competition. This is far less than the standards that have traditionally been applied in EU antitrust law, and which the European Commission now wishes to replace with a more economic approach. A more detailed examination of the initial market structure and competition situation is, as the European Commission proposes, only to be made on justification level in Stage 3 of the balancing test. The test amounts to an examination of proportionality, in which the suitability, necessity and adequacy of a state measure are to be assessed.

171. However, before an examination of proportionality generally a more detailed examination is made of whether the case constitutes an intervention, meaning not intervention in the narrower sense, that is, intervention in a specific subjective legal position, but intervention in the form of restraint of competition on the European internal market. Only if there is such restraint is the European Commission empowered as part of its aid control under Arts. 87ss. EC Treaty to forbid a member state from executing the measure. For, as already shown, the protection of competition on the internal market is the only purpose of the European rules on aid. The Monopolkommission regards it as generally appropriate to assume distortion to competition from certain forms of aid given by member states, and to work with assumptions on other aspects of aid. But as the criteria of selectivity and the restriction of trade between member states are interpreted very broadly, a general assumption is not justified in every case. Hence, in the view of the Monopolkommission, reform to aid legislation should start on the factual level in Art. 87, Para. 1 EC Treaty, especially regarding distortion to competition and trade between member states.

6.2 Implementing the SAAP – Examples

172. Since the SAAP was published in June 2005, a large number of measures have already been taken to implement the reform announced in it.[186] Moreover, the Directorate-General for

---

[186] They include: In services of general economic interest: Decision by the European Commission of 28 November 2005 on the application of Art. 86, Para. 2 EC Treaty to state aid granted as compensation to enterprises entrusted with the provision of certain services of general economic interest (OJ EU L 312 of 29 November 2007, p. 67) and a Community framework for state aid granted as compensation for the provision of public services (OJ EU C 297 of 29 November 2005, p. 4).

In regional aid: Commission Reg. EC 1628/2006 of 24 Oct. 2006 on the application of Arts. 87 and 88 EC Treaty to regional investment aid given by member states (block exemption regulation on regional investment aid, OJ EU L 302 of 1 Nov. 2006, p. 29) and the Guidelines for state aid for regional objectives 20072013 (OJ EU C 54 of 4 March 2006, p. 13). In these Guidelines the European Commission explains under which conditions it will regard aid to promote the economic development of certain disadvantaged areas within the EU as compatible with the common market under Art. 87, Para. 3 a) and c) EC Treaty. So it differentiates between investment aid to large companies, operational aid and investment aid to SMEs domiciled in these disadvantaged areas.

Other examples are: The De Minimis regulation (Commission Reg. 1998/2006 of 15 Dec. 2006 on the application of Arts. 87 and 88 EC Treaty to de minimis aids, OJ EU L 379 of 28 Dec. 2006, p. 5, the
cont.

313

Competition has also taken internal organisational measures to move towards a more economic approach. Like the Merger Task Force the State Aid department has been split up and its staff moved into the existing departments for the various industrial sectors to make use of the knowledge available there. To make the approach to reform taken by the European Commission clearer three different implementation measures will now be discussed in more detail as examples.

6.2.1 Extending the De Minimis Regulation

173. The European Commission had already announced in the State Aid Action Plan that it intended to raise the upper limit for de minimis aid, and the corresponding regulation has now been issued. Before this financial aid that did not exceed the total amount of EUR 100,000 within three years was not regarded as state aid. Under the new De Minimis Regulation this amount is raised to EUR 200,000 and credit guarantees are admitted up to an amount of EUR 1.5 million.

174. However, the regulation only applies to "transparent" aid.[187] An aid is only regarded as transparent if its gross grant equivalent[188] can be calculated exactly in advance without requiring a risk assessment.[189] Such precise calculation is possible for grants, interest grants and limited tax concessions, for example, but it is not possible for capital injections by public authorities. As a consequence of this condition many municipal projects, like those in the form of a public private partnership, cannot benefit from the exemption allowed in the De Minimis Regulation. On the contrary, these projects have to be notified under Art. 88, Para. 3, Sentence 1 EC Treaty, and so they involve heavy transaction costs for the participants. But the transparency criterion has the advantage that the De Minimis Regulation is clear and easy to handle for those applying the law.

175. One possible objection to the De Minimis Regulation is that it sets an absolute threshold that applies to all branches equally. This can cause inappropriate results as the exemption applies independent of the size of the market, the position of the beneficiary on the market and the specific competition situation. Moreover, when a general threshold applies the distortion to competition that an aid might cause cannot be correctly estimated. Nevertheless,

---

Community Guidelines on state aid to promote risk capital investment in small and medium-sized enterprises (OJ EU C 194 of 18 August 2006, p. 2), the communication from the Commission to member states to amend the communication under Art. 93, Para. 1 EC Treaty on the application of Arts. 92 and 93 EC Treaty to short-term export credit insurance (OJ EU C 325 of 22 Dec. 2005, p. 22), Community framework for state aid for research and development and innovation (OJ EU C 323 of 30 Dec. 2006, p. 1) and the Community Guidelines for state environmental protection aid (OJ EU C 82 of 1 April 2008, p. 1).

The European Commission has also put forward several proposals for future regulations, especially a draft general block exemption regulation for state aid.

[187] Art. 2, Para. 4 De Minimis Regulation.

[188] The grant equivalent or the cash value of promotion shows the economic benefit of the measure. It is frequently given in percent of the total project costs (that can be taken into account). The gross grant equivalent differs from the net grant equivalent in that the tax payable on the promotional funds is not taken into account.

[189] Cf. Preamble 12 of the De Minimis Reg.

the Monopolkommission regards the use of a general threshold, below which aid in small amounts is exempt, as a meaningful way to simplify procedures; it increases legal certainty and allows to avoid bureaucracy costs. This eases the work load on the European Commission and enables it to concentrate on difficult cases, where considerable distortion to competition may ensue. However, the new threshold of EUR 200,000 is still very low.

176. The Monopolkommission holds the view that easier exemption conditions should also be introduced for higher volumes of aid. Power to intervene could be granted to the European Commission for aid of an amount to be specified – it could be EUR 1 million.[190] For aid below that threshold it could arguably be assumed that there is no noticeable distortion to competition under Art. 87, Para. 1 EC Treaty. However, this assumption should only apply if the aid is also tied to particular activities, if the intensity[191] is relatively low (not more than 30%) and the grant is given in an open and transparent procedure.[192]

6.2.2 Draft of a General Block Exemption Regulation

177. In order to reduce the number of aids requiring notification the European Commission is also increasingly using block exemption regulations. These are directly applicable rules and their correct use can be examined before the national courts – for instance in cases brought by a competitor of the beneficiary. The European Commission announced in the SAAP that the former block exemption regulations would be consolidated, replaced by a uniform regulation on block exemption, and extended to include more areas. It has now published the draft of a general block exemption regulation,[193] which provides for the possibility of exemption for almost every economic sector and, if it is implemented, will cover a wide range of aid cases. In future member states would no longer be obliged to report to the European Commission aid that is covered by this regulation and meets its requirements, nor would they have to wait for the Commission's approval before granting the aid. They could put their aid measures into practice without delay.

178. The five block exemption regulations issued so far (for aid to small and medium-size enterprises or SMEs,[194] for research and development by SMEs, employment, training and regional promotion) are to be integrated in the general block exemption regulation, which is also to include new groups of aid: environmental protection, risk capital, and research and development aid for large companies.

---

[190] See 1015ss. above.

[191] Aid intensity is the share of the promotion in the total expenditure on the project.

[192] See 1106ss. Below.

[193] 193 Request for comment on the draft general block exemption regulation for state aid, OJ EU C 210 of 8 September 2007, p. 14.

[194] SMEs are defined as follows in Annex 1 of Commission Regulation (EC) 70/2001 of 12 January 2001 on the application of Articles 87 and 88 EC Treaty to state aid to small and medium-sized enterprises, OJ EU L 10 of 13 January 2001, p. 33: SMEs are enterprises that employ fewer than 250 persons and have an annual turnover of at most EUR 40 million or an annual balance sheet total at most EUR 27 million and which meet the criterion of independence defined in Para. 3. Should it be necessary to distinguish between small and medium-sized enterprises, a small enterprise is one which employs fewer than 50 persons and has an annual turnover of at most 7 million or an annual balance sheet total of at most EUR 5 million and which meets the criterion of independence defined in Para. 3.

– 60 –

179. The maximum permissible intensities of aid for the various groups and the eligible costs are defined in more detail in the draft. With the level of permissible aid intensity as the share a member state may contribute to the (recognised) total costs of a project the European Commission shows how high it sets the risk of distortion to competition in each category of aid, and the expected benefit of the aid to the general community. The greater the aid intensity, the less restraint of competition is feared. Fixing the intensity of the aid thus involves weighing – albeit generally and roughly – the positive and negative effects of the aid. According to the draft regulation, for general training measures, for example, in which transferable qualifications are acquired, a higher intensity is permitted (65%) than for specific training measures that will primarily benefit the company providing the training (35%). Moreover, in several places the draft envisages favourable treatment for SMEs.[195] If an aid meets the conditions named in the draft and does not exceed the intensity specified for its group it is to be assumed compatible with the common market. Beside these conditions for assumption the draft also contains conditions that set higher requirements for those applying the law. For aids to large companies, for example, it must be shown positively that the aid will have an incentive effect. That will not be the case if the recipient would carry out the project to be promoted under market conditions, also without the aid.

180. An incentive effect is assumed for aid to SMEs if the company concerned applies for aid to the member state before starting to implement the project or embark on the activity to be promoted (Art. 8, Para. 2 of the draft regulation). In the case of aid to large companies the member state must check (Art. 8, Para. 3 of the draft) whether the recipient has analysed the viability of the project or the activities to be promoted with and without the aid in an internal paper. The recipient company must carry out this analysis ex ante using quantitative and qualitative indicators. The member state must check the analysis and include it in the records.

181. The Monopolkommission regards it as positive that the former block exemption regulations on aid are to be grouped into a single regulation to improve transparency and legal certainty. In the view of the Monopolkommission block exemption regulations can make an important contribution to simplifying procedures. However, they can only fulfil that purpose if the conditions for exemption are formulated clearly and implementing them is not complicated. Providing the positive proof of the incentive effect envisaged in the draft for aid to large companies, on the other hand, will be costly and time-consuming. Large companies will certainly draw up a business plan before applying for aid, and for this they will already have made a detailed analysis, weighing one alternative against another. However, the requirement for authorities in the member state to check the analysis in detail will involve considerable bureaucratic expenditure and it hardly seems efficient, as the office granting the

---

[195] For instance, under the draft regulation investment and employment aids, aid for early adjustment to future Community norms and aids for the use of consultancy services are only to be exempt if granted to SMEs. For groups of aid in which on principle large companies could also profit from the exemption, higher intensity figures are envisaged for SMEs. Finally, easier conditions of proof are to apply for SMEs (Art. 8, Para. 2 draft reg.). The European Commission classifies SMEs as particularly deserving of promotion, as they play a decisive role in creating jobs and are one of the pillars of social stability and economic dynamic. So the European Commission expects positive external effects to come from promoting SMEs. It also assumes that SMEs are typically disadvantaged owing to market failure. They often have difficulty in raising risk capital or loans, owing to the unwillingness to bear these risks frequently found on certain financial markets and because SMEs can offer less security.

aid is responsible for control. So in the view of the Monopolkommission the proposed provision should not be included in a directly applicable block exemption regulation.

6.2.3   The Community Framework for Research, Development and Innovation

182. The Community framework for research, development and innovation (R&D&I) of 22 November 2006 can be taken as a typical example of how the European Commission envisages to realise the aims specified in the SAAP, especially the more economic approach. Unlike the previous regulation it includes innovation projects as well as research and development. This Community framework only applies to those aid measures that are not already exempt from the notification requirement in Art. 88, Para. 3, Sentence 1 EC Treaty under the De Minimis regulation or a block exemption. In the R&D&I framework the European Commission also touches upon the question of the model for European aid control.[196] The legitimate aim of R&D&I aids is economic efficiency. Without explaining why the main concern here is not consumers' welfare, as it is in the other areas of competition policy, the European Commission mentions the general welfare as the determinant model only in passing.

183. In the R&D&I Community framework the European Commission envisages two test procedures of differing intensity: firstly, a faster procedure in which legal assumptions will also play a part, then a very elaborate test procedure, in which concrete application of the threestage balancing test will be made adjusted to the R&D&I field. A detailed assessment is to be undertaken if the aid exceeds certain upper limits laid down in Chapter 7 of the Community framework. These thresholds will differ depending on the kind of aid and the activity pro-moted.[197] The framework also contains special instructions for appraising the incentive effect.

184. In Chapter 5 of the R&D&I Community framework the European Commission first defines various categories of aid for which it sets concrete conditions and the permissible aid

---

[196] Fig. 1.1, Para. 3 of the Community framework states "The objective is through State aid to enhance economic efficiency (Footnote 3) and thereby, contribute to sustainable growth and jobs. Therefore, State aid for R&D&I shall be compatible if the aid can be expected to lead to additional R&D&I and if the distortion of competition is not considered to be contrary to the common interest, which the Commission equates for the purposes of this framework with economic efficiency. The aim of this framework is to ensure this objective and in particular to make it easier for Member States to better target the aid to the relevant market failures." Footnote 3 adds to this: "In economics, the term 'efficiency' (or 'economic efficiency') refers to the extent to which total welfare is optimised in a particular market or in the economy at large. Additional R&D&I increases economic efficiency by shifting market demand towards new or improved products, processes or services, which is equivalent to a decrease in the quality adjusted price of these goods."

[197] According to 7.1 of the R&D&I Community framework the following thresholds will be determinant:
   – in case of project aid and feasibility studies
   – for projects mainly in basic research: EUR 20 million per enterprise and project/feasibility study;
   – for projects chiefly in industrial research EUR 10 million per company and project/feasibility study;
   – for all other projects: EUR 7.5 million per enterprise and project/feasibility study;
   – for process or organisational innovation in the services sector: EUR 5 million per enterprise and project;
   – for innovation clusters: EUR 5 million per cluster.

in-tensity.[198] The further from the market the promoted activity is the higher may the state aid's share in the project be (100% in basic research, 50% in industrial research and 25% in experimental research). These limits are based on the correct assumption that harmful distortion to competition on product markets is more likely the more the planned investment is concerned with developing new or changing products or processes.

185. In Chapter 6 of the R&D&I Community framework the European Commission then discusses the criterion of the incentive effect, which it regards as of crucial importance. For certain types of aid, namely project aid for large companies, project aid for SMEs above EUR 7.5 million, aid for process and organisational innovation in the services sector and aid for innovation clusters the member state notifying the aid must provide concrete proof of the incentive effect. In such cases, and regardless of whether the threshold named in Chapter 7 for that specific activity has been exceeded or not, the member states must present to the European Commission an ex ante assessment of the increased R&D&I activity, based on a comparison of the situation without the aid with the situation after it was granted. As possible indicators the European Commission names increase in the size of the project, increase in its range, acceleration of the process and increase in total expenditure on R&D&I.[199]

186. If the aid fulfils the criteria in Chapter 5, does not exceed the threshold for the promoted activity laid down in Chapter 7[200] and the incentive effect can be shown in accordance with the procedure described in Chapter 6, no further examination will be made. It will be assumed that the three-stage balancing test would yield a positive result. As the European Commission thus relies on thresholds and not on market shares, for instance, the assumption will be made independently of the size of the market and the market position of the beneficiary.

187. If the threshold laid down for that activity is exceeded the three-stage balancing test is to be carried out for the individual case and in accordance with the procedure described in more detail in Chapter 7.

In Stage 1 the member state must first prove a justified common interest. Under the R&D&I Community framework aid can only be justified if the aim is to remove market failure.[201] Other social or distribution policy aims are not accepted by the European Commission as areas to which the framework applies. It holds the view that the forms of market failure

---

[198] Aid intensity is the level of gross aid expressed in percent of the eligible costs of the project. All the amounts entered are amounts before tax or other charges. If aid is not given in the form of a grant the level of the aid will be determined by its grant equivalent (Fig. 2.2 c) R& D&I Community Framework).

[199] If the threshold named in Ch. 7 has not been exceeded the European Commission would like to assume as a general rule that the planned aid will have an incentive effect, if significant changes can be shown in at least one of these factors, taking into account normal behaviour in the sector in question. Otherwise more stringent proof requirements apply.

[200] The criteria include
. • project aid and feasibility studies for which the aid is given to an SME and the amount per SME and project is below EUR 7.5 million (project aid plus aid for the feasibility study),
. • aid for the cost of commercial patents to be borne by SMEs,
. • aid for young innovative enterprises,
. • aid for innovation consultancy and for services in support of innovation, and
   • aid to lease highly skilled personnel.

[201] Cf. 1.3.2 RDI Community framework.

conceivable in the field of research, development and innovation are knowledge spillover, imperfect and asymmetrical information and lack of coordination and networking. It is not enough to claim that these are evident, the member state must provide proof of why there is a specific market failure in a particular case.

In Stage 2 then the European Commission is to examine whether the aid is an appropriate instrument, if there is an incentive effect and if the aid is proportionate. A measure is regarded as an appropriate instrument if the member state has considered other measures and estimated their consequences, and has (demonstrably) reached the conclusion that granting an aid with selective effect will have advantages. In this context the European Commission allows member states scope for estimates. But for the incentive effect it requires definite proof. This involves extremely complex and expensive analysis, which goes beyond the requirements named in Chapter 6. Calculating the incentive effect is, according to statements by the European Commission, the most important condition for the analysis of a state R&D&I aid in the balancing test.[202] By contrast, for its examination of proportionality the European Commission only requires member states to provide concrete evidence of in how far an open selection procedure has been held and whether the aid will exceed the stipulated minimum amount.

Finally, in Stage 3 of the test possible distortion to competition and trade are analysed and weighed against the positive effects of the aid (removal of the market failure). As distortion to competition that can be caused by an R&D&I aid the European Commission names: Reducing the dynamic innovation incentives for competitors by stronger presence of the favoured enterprise on the product markets (displacement effect); in this context the European Commission wishes to take into account the amount of the aid,[203] the market proximity/type of aid,[204] the method of granting the aid,[205] any possible barriers to exit,[206] the competition incentives for a future market,[207] the product differentiation and the intensity of competition.[208]

- Creating or maintaining market power; the European Commission announces that the level of entry barriers,[209] the buyer power[210] and the selection process will be in

---

[202] Cf. 7.3.3 RDI Community framework.

[203] In the view of the European Commission considerable displacement effects are more likely from particularly large amounts of aid (measured by total private R&D expenditure in the sector concerned).

[204] With increasing market proximity of R&D activity promoted by state aid the likelihood of considerable displacement effects grows, according to estimates by the European Commission.

[205] Aid granted on the basis of objective criteria is assessed more positively by the European Commission.

[206] The European Commission argues that competitors will be more inclined to maintain their investment, or even increase it, if the barriers to abandoning the innovation process are high. That can be the case if much of the earlier investment expenditure by the competitor is tied into a particular RDI technology.

[207] In the view of the European Commission RDI aids can induce competitors of the beneficiary to decide not to compete on a future market, as the advantages brought by the aid (in degree of technical advance or time advantage) make it less profitable for him to enter the market.

[208] If the product innovation is directed to developing more differentiated products (e.g. in relation to certain trademarks, norms, techniques or consumer groups) competitors will generally be less strongly affected, in the view of the European Commission. The same applies when many effective competitors are active on the market.

[209] The European Commission explains that the barriers to access for newcomers in the RDI field can be high. Here it includes legal barriers (especially intellectual property rights), size and association

cont.

– 64 –

corporated in its examination.[211] It explains that it is unlikely that competitive concerns due to market power will arise on a market on which every beneficiary has a share of less than 25% and the market concentration is below an HHI of 2000.[212]

• Maintaining inefficient market structures; the European Commission wishes to examine whether the aid is being granted on markets with excess capacities, for shrinking economic sectors or in sensitive sectors.

188. It is to be welcomed that the European Commission has expressly typified the distortions of competition that R&D&I aid can cause and expressly named the criteria for assessment in a Community framework. The examination of the negative effects in Stage 3 of the test requires a detailed analysis of the competition on the basis of a concrete definition of the materially and geographically relevant market. In this competition analysis the European Commission studies various market characteristics (the position of the beneficiary company in the relevant market, the level of market shares and market concentration, barriers to market entry, the degree of product differentiation and excess capacities on the market) and the characteristics of the aid (the method of granting it,[213] the amount, the type of aid and the market proximity of the activity promoted).

189. In view of the fact that the justification in Art. 87, Para. 3 EC Treaty is very broadly formulated the Monopolkommission regards it as positive that the European Commission intends to concretise the procedure for its examination in more detail and adjust it to the particular features of R&D&I aid. This will increase the transparency and economic foundation of the European Commission's decisions on aid in the R&D&I field over earlier practice. A critical view can be taken of the fact that in its examination of compatibility in Stage 3 of the balancing test the European Commission does not examine the competition situation on the factual level (Art. 87, Para. 1 EC Treaty) but only on the justification level. In contrast to the concept followed by the European Commission and current practice, the cross-border distortion of competition should be established on the factual level with well-founded economic data , before the European Commission examines in its compatibility test the suitability and necessity of an aid for the economic and distribution policy aims it is intended to serve.

190. In the view of the Monopolkommission criticism can also be levelled at the fact that the European Commission accords the incentive effect a central position compared with the other

---

advantages, barriers to access to networks and infrastructures and other strategic barriers to market access or growth.

[210] The market power of a company can be limited by the market position of its customers, according to the European Commission. The presence of big customers can mean that a strong market position is of less importance if it can be assumed that the customers will try to ensure that there is sufficient competition in the market.

[211] In the view of the European Commission aid is questionable if it enables companies with a strong market position to influence the selection process, e.g. if they have the right to recommend companies in the selection process or can influence the research path in such a way that alternative paths are unjustifiably disadvantaged.

[212] HHI is the abbreviation for Herfindahl-Hirschmann Index, which describes the sum of squared market shares of companies on the market in question.

[213] Aid granted as part of a broad aid programme or in an open selection procedure is ceteris paribus less distorting than targeted ad hoc measures for individual firms.

points examined, describing it as the most important condition in its balancing test.[214] In the view of the Monopolkommission this criterion should not be overvalued compared with other issues in the test, nor should such elaborate and complex proof be required as is envisaged in Chapter 7 of the R&D&I Community framework. Although aid should on principle only be given if it creates an incentive to change behaviour, as otherwise windfall gains will ensue, in regard to competition simply the non-existence of an incentive effect is not proof of restraint of competition. If the aid does not change behaviour in relation to the project promoted that means that without the aid the beneficiary enterprise would not have made any other price or quantity decisions on the markets in question, and in so far would not have caused any distortion of competition. Admittedly, conversely it cannot be concluded from the lack of an incentive effect that there is no distortion of competition, as an enterprise can in the long term view use the resources made available to it through the aid, and which improve his operating result, to achieve a competitive advantage – on neighbouring markets, for instance. But the incentive effect is not a suitable a criterion for the balancing test which the European Commission conducts to protect cross-frontier competition.

191. If the functioning of a certain market is seriously restricted undistorted competition will not produce efficient allocative results. However, in its compatibility examination the European Commission should look more closely at in how far the market failure in question can be specifically and effectively removed by the aid, and whether milder means are clearly available that will be less distorting of competition. For even if there is market failure this does not automatically mean that the situation can be improved by state intervention. There is, rather, a risk that aid will fail to have the desired effect owing to erroneous estimates by the state, and that the competition will be changed for the worse. The European Commission should therefore also examine whether there are several market failures and the competition situation is likely to be worsened by the state intervention (second best problem) – if only one market failure is being targeted with the aid.

6.3 The Characteristics of the More Economic Approach in Aid Control

6.3.1 The Origins of the More Economic Approach in EU Competition Law

192. In introducing a more economic approach the European Commission was initially only aiming gradually to change the focus of its competition regulations on companies (antitrust law).[215] This is the origin of the new reform approach by the European Commission, which operates on several levels and issues:
- what the main aim and model should be,
- how to typify law, respectively guidelines (soft law/policy), and
- what economic knowledge and methods should form the basis of individual decisions.

So the concept of the more economic approach is complex and its realisation in competition law is conceivable in various forms. There is no generally valid definition. In this chapter the approach pursued specifically by the European Commission as a more economic approach

---

[214] Cf. 7.3.3 R&D&I Community framework.

[215] The term "antitrust law" is used in this chapter in a broad sense and also covers abuse and merger control.

will be characterised in greater detail. The aims pursued by the European Commission in antitrust law can be summarised as follows:

- Directing the competition rules to protecting consumer welfare
- The importance of the effects of the behaviour or transactions in question on the market outcome (effects-based approach)
- Carrying out a comprehensive analysis of difficult individual cases (instead of undifferentiated per-se rules)
- Admission of the efficiency objection throughout, and
- The use of new economic models, knowledge and quantitative methods.

193. The more economic approach which the European Commission wishes to adopt in antitrust law is the subject of numerous scientific studies and controversial discussions. The Monopolkommission will not enter into these arguments in this chapter, instead it will assess the opportunities and risks of applying a more economic approach in aid control. However, in order to clarify the common factors and differences between the more economic approach desired by the European Commission in antitrust law on the one side and aid control on the other, the characteristics of the two reform concepts will be compared.

6.3.2 Characteristics of the More Economic approach desired by the European Commission in State Aid Control compared with that in Antitrust Law

6.3.2.1 The Model

Antitrust Law

194. Securing a competitive market structure and protecting the freedom of competition are the traditional aims of German competition law, which for decades has also influenced European competition law. According to this model competition as such is in itself a good worth protecting. This interpretation, formed by ordo-liberal ideas, is based on the assumption that protecting competition will in the long term and indirectly also benefit the end-user, and it is based on whether the behaviour in question entails restriction of action by competitors and market participants on up-or downstream market stages. In this approach securing freedom has independent weight. It has two aspects, firstly, protection of individual freedom of economic action, and secondly, protection of the market economy order in civil law from the dangers that can ensue if interest groups try to obtain privileges through the political process.

195. In adopting a more economic approach the European Commission would like to establish a model in EU antitrust law in which economic results will be of particular importance. The efficiency of the market results are to form the main parameter. It must be stressed that models are not descriptive but normative. As the European Commission is clearly not aiming to change the bases in primary law through the European legislature it must orient the discussion it is conducting over the model to the existing legislation and its requirements. Hence the discussion can at most aim for a different interpretation of the existing regulations and features of the law (such as restraints of competition in Art. 81, Para. 1 EC Treaty), whereby the European courts will take the final and binding decision on these interpretations. The European Commission intends to put the main focus on the protection of consumers (consumer welfare standard). Competition is thus not to be protected for its own sake or as an institution, it is to be used as a means of achieving that objective.[216]

196. Establishing a standard of consumer welfare is not uncontroversial. Some authors, like the European Commission, are in favour of a more economic approach in which efficiency would be the model for competition policy. Nevertheless, they are not in favour of a consumer welfare standard, preferring a total welfare standard, which beside the benefit to the consumer would also include the advantages to producers.[217]

197. In explanation of the European Commission's decision not, as is usual in economics, to make the total welfare standard its model but the consumer welfare standard, it is pointed out that in the relation between the competition authority and the enterprise notifying aid there is asymmetry of information, moreover consumers lack the possibility and incentive to lobby which financially strong companies have.[218] Hence asymmetry must deliberately be introduced, and the competition authorities need to take more account of the benefit to consumers than of the profits to producers. The fact that this approach is easier to handle in industrial economics and analytical studies may have helped to make it more widely used. The new accentuation by the European Commission was probably also largely influenced by competition practice in the United States, where the consumer welfare standard has long been the basic model.[219]

198. The European Court of Justice, which is responsible in the final instance for interpreting the European legislation, commented on the question of the determinant purpose of pro-

---

[216] In a speech at the 13th International Conference on Antitrust Law on 27 March 2007 in Munich, "Consumer Welfare and Efficiency – New Guiding Principles of Competition Policy?" Director-General Philip Lowe commented on the model question as follows: "Ladies and Gentlemen, my overall message is short and simple. Yes, consumer welfare and efficiency are the new guiding principles of EU competition policy. Whilst the competitive process is important as an instrument, and whilst in many instances the distortion of the process leads to consumer harm, its protection is not an aim in itself. The ultimate aim is the protection of consumer welfare, as an outcome of the competitive process. And believe me that as head of the competition authority charged with protecting consumer welfare, I am at least as concerned about false negatives, i.e under-enforcement, as I am about false positives, i.e. over-enforcement. I am therefore committed to make the new rules work in practice." http://ec/europa.eu/competition/speeches/text/sp2007_02_en.pdf.

[217] Cf. Schmidtchen: Der "more economic approach" in der Wettbewerbspolitik, Wirtschaft und Wettbewerb 56, 2006, pp. 6-17, 6s.

[218] Cf. Röller, L.-H., Neven, D.J., Consumer Surplus vs. Welfare Standard in a Political Economy, Model of Merger Control, International Journal of Industrial Organization 23, 2005, pp. 829-848; Heidhues, P., Lagerlöf, J., On the Desirability of an Efficiency Defense in Merger Control, International Journal of Industrial Organization 23, 2005, pp. 803-827.

[219] Some economists are against using economic efficiency in the sense of the welfare approach and instead want freedom of competition to be the model. However, they also want to see the effects for consumers used as the main criterion for the application of competition rules. Promoting the freedom of one market participant always means restricting the freedom of another. The freedom of entrepreneurial decision for companies with a strong market position should accordingly also be protected, and must be weighed against the freedom of competition for each competitor or the opposite market side. Consumer interests are accordingly a suitable indicator of whose freedom of competition deserves greater protection in any individual case. Cf. Hellwig, M., Effizienz oder Wettbewerbsfreiheit, Zur normativen Grundlegung der Wettbewerbspolitik, Preprint 2006/20, Max-Planck-Institut zur Erforschung von Gemeinschaftsgütern, Bonn, August 2006, pp. 2ss. http://www.coll.mpg.de/pdf_dat/2006_20online/pdf.

tection, and the model to be used, in its judgement on the British Airways case of 15 March 2007. It pointed out that Art. 82 EC Treaty does not only refer to behaviour that can directly harm consumers but also to behaviour that can cause them harm through intervention in the structure of existing competition, as referred to in Art. 3, Para. 1 g) EC Treaty.[220] So the ECJ is not against the protection of consumers as an aim of competition law, indeed, it expressly acknowledges that aim by stating that Art. 82 EC Treaty not only refers to behaviour that can be directly disadvantageous to consumers. Nevertheless it stresses that intervention in the structure can be sufficient to establish infringement of competition. So it follows the traditional structure-oriented approach, which is still the determinant approach in German competition law. Hence direct harm to consumers' interests is not an essential condition for intervention under European competition law, and the ECJ is not in favour of exclusive use of the consumer welfare standard.

State Aid Law

199. The State Aid Action Plan does not contain any information on the question of which model is determinant in EU aid control. As already shown, in discussing the question of the model the existing legal framework conditions in the EC Treaty must be observed. In the new R&D&I Community framework the European Commission mentions casually that in European aid control – unlike other areas of competition policy – it is not consumer welfare but the total welfare standard that should be determinant, as beside the benefit to consumers it also includes the benefit to producers.

200. The Chief Economists' Team at the Directorate-General for Competition suggested in a study that in the field of aid a standard of consumer welfare should be used, but one in which – unlike EU antitrust law – the interests of taxpayers would also be taken into account.[221] In a further study commissioned by the European Commission as part of its planned aid reform, the authors argue that both the interests of consumers and the interests of competitors in making a profit should be taken into account.[222]

201. Independent of how one sees the new model used by the European Commission in European antitrust law, a pure and exclusive consumer welfare standard should not be used in aid control. A simple transfer of this approach, in which the direct effects for consumers on the product markets in question is the main criterion, would entail the risk of an inaccurate and over-positive assessment of aids. In the short-term view aids can initially result in lower prices. That will certainly be the case if the aid granted leads to a reduction in variable costs or the entry to the market of other companies. At first sight allocative gains in welfare could generally be expected on the relevant product markets.[223]

202. However, that would be to ignore the fact that aid – which would have to be financed through taxation, which in turn causes welfare losses – can in the medium and long term lead to restraint of competition, which will result in over-pricing and ultimately leave consumers worse

---

[220] ECJ, Judgement of 15 March 2007, Case C-95/04, No. 106.
[221] Cf. Friederiszick, H.W., Röller, L.-H., Verouden, V., loc. cit, pp. 39ss.
[222] Cf. Nitsche, R., Heidhues, P., Study on methods to analyse the impact of State aid on competition, European Economy, Economic Papers No. 244, February 2006, pp. 5ss. http://ec.europa.eu/economy_finance/publications/economic_papers/2006/economicpaper244/en/htm.
[223] That is, unless perfect competition is assumed, which is unrealistic.

off. Aid to established companies can frighten efficient newcomers away from the market. Moreover, inefficient firms can acquire market shares at the expense of more efficient firms that have not received promotional funding. Moreover, aid can became a habit of mind and reduce cost pressure (soft budget constraint), leading to inefficient production. For companies have less incentive to produce efficiently and to invest if they can assume that the state will come to their assistance if they find themselves in financial straits (for instance to preserve jobs). Moreover, continuous aid can cause distortion in the economy as a whole, as it permanently changes price relations and causes misallocation of resources. The Monopolkommission therefore welcomes the fact that the European Commission evidently does not intend to establish a consumer welfare standard in aid control in the form which it approves in antitrust law.[224]

203. As already shown, under Art. 87, Paras. 1 and 2 and Art. 3, Para. 1 g) EC Treaty the protection of competition on the European internal market is the determinant aim of European aid control. The European Commission does not have fiscal policy competence under Arts. 87ss. EC Treaty. Hence in aid control it should concentrate on preventing negative effects of aid on cross-border competition on the European internal market, in keeping with its statutory obligation, or reducing these to the unavoidable level. To assess whether an aid is causing restraint of competition the short-term price trend on the relevant product markets, which consumers see as a result of the aid, should be one of several factors to be taken into account. To what extent the aid is likely to have negative effects on the other market participants – on the same market stage, upstream and downstream and on neighbouring markets – and to intervene across frontiers in the functioning of markets is also of considerable importance.

6.3.2.2 The Effects-Based Approach

Antitrust Law

204. In its introduction of the consumer welfare standard as model the European Commission is reorienting European competition law to the more economic approach in antitrust law. Its aim is to establish an effects-based approach in contrast to the traditional structure-oriented or form-based approach.[225] The main concern of the form-based approach is to secure a competition structure that functions, and risk in the abstract is enough to justify intervention by the competition authorities. It is generally easier to prove infringement in regard to structural features than if the effects-based approach is used, where the concrete effects of a measure are determinant. To justify a ban in the effects-based approach more information must be used than hitherto in critical individual cases.

---

[224] 224 In an experts discussion between members of the Monopolkommission and representatives of the General-Directorate on Competition on 10 April 2008 in Bonn the latter confirmed that the European Commission does not intend to adopt the consumer welfare standard applied in antitrust law in aid law. "Even leaving equity considerations aside, State aid assessment focuses on the effect of the aid on rivals and on the competitive process rather than measuring the direct effect on consumers. Such a focus is justified by the fact that if efficient rivals are weakened by aid measures, effective competition may be hindered with the result that allocative efficiency is reduced in the long run."

[225] Cf. Albers, M. (member of DG Competition), Der more economic approach bei Verdrängungsmissbräuchen: Zum Stand der Überlegungen der Europäischen Kommission, pp. 2s.; http://ec.europa.eu/comm/competition/antitrust/art82/index.html.

205. The effects-based approach is evident in the formulation of recent secondary law and in the guidelines in which the European Commission explains the basic principles of its own application of the law and in so far binds itself (soft law).[226] The European Commission intends the effects-based approach to play a major role in practice in individual cases. Hence the effects on the market result are to be examined comprehensively in difficult cases, using industrial economics models and quantitative analyses. In accordance with the consumer welfare standard the determinant factor is to be whether the effect could be of advantage to consumers, whereby the actual and probable effects are to be considered.[227] So in assessing a merger, for instance, what matters is how prices are expected to develop following the merger. Changes in market structures or the form of competition are to be important in so far as they enable statements to be made on the consequences for consumers.[228]

State Aid Law

206. Neither the State Aid Action Plan nor the implementation measures taken to date provide for the European Commission to examine the economic effects on competition more closely on the factual level, i.e. Art. 87, Para. 1 EC Treaty. In practice so far, only a general economic examination has been made in regard to cross-frontier trade and distortion to competition under Art. 87, Para. 1 EC Treaty, without a more precise delineation of the market. This practice is not being changed. In the past it has also been supported by the European courts. Hence the economic proof required of the European Commission by the courts in aid law differs fundamentally from the requirements set by the ban in the antitrust rules, Art. 81 and 82 EC Treaty and Art. 2, Para. 3 of the Merger Control Regulation.

207. Accordingly, in future, too, in order to prove restraint of cross-frontier competition and trade by state aid (Art. 87, Para. 1 EC Treaty) the European Commission need neither take due account of the requirements of the effects-based approach, which it is now applying in antitrust law, nor meet the requirements that have traditionally been determinant in antitrust law under the form-based approach.

208. A study of the market situation and the effects of state aid on competition is only to be made as part of the examination of compatibility under Art. 87, Para. 3 EC Treaty, to be more precise on Stage 3 of the balancing test outlined above. In many cases, however, this test will never be made. For if an aid does not pass one of the preceding stages of the balancing test – because it is either not intended to remove a market failure (Stage 1) or not suitable or necessary for this (Stage 2) – the test will be stopped. Accordingly in future, too, cases will be conceivable in which the European Commission forbids an aid without examining its negative effects on competition in the EU internal market. That would appear to be problematic, as the European Commission is only legitimised to exercise aid control following the protective goals of Arts. 87ss. EC Treaty, if competition in the European internal market would be restricted by the aid.

---

[226] One example is in the Guidelines on the assessment of horizontal mergers (OJ EU C 31 of 5 February 2004, p. 5), and the comments on non-coordinated effects (unilateral effects) in Nos. 24ss.

[227] Cf. Albers, M., loc. cit., p. 2.

[228] Cf. European Commission, Guidelines on vertical restraints, OJ EU C 291 of 13 October 2000, p. 1, here § 3, No. 7; Guidelines on the assessment of horizontal mergers, loc. cit., Nos. 8s. and DG Competition discussion paper on the application of Article 82 of the Treaty to exclusionary abuses, December 2005, No. 4, http://ec.europa.eu/comm/competition/antitrust/art82/index.html.

6.3.2.3 Individual Case Analysis instead of Per Se Rules

Antitrust law

209. The European Commission intends in future to examine the effects of aid on the market in especially critical individual cases. This will form part of an exact and complex individual case analysis, which should enable the European Commission to take economically efficient decisions. So in such cases it will not rely on generalising risk factors and applying per-se rules. It is characteristic of the latter that behaviour or restriction of action defined in concrete terms are classified per se as either impermissible or permissible under competition law. Per-se rules have the advantage that the outcome of the procedure is generally easier to forecast for those involved, and this can increase legal certainty. However, the European Commission does not intend generally to cease to rely on assumptions and per se rules in future, an exact and elaborate consideration will only be made of difficult cases. In merger control, for instance, a low number of competition cases will be affected. The European Commission is also aiming to revise the per-se rules used to date and formulate more differentiated economic rules.

State Aid Law

210. The European Commission is not pursuing the aim of ceasing altogether to use per-se rules and assumptions in future European aid control, either. Rather, as already shown, in its reform it has increased the area of application of the De Minimis Regulation and raised the upper limit for exempt aid. The rules in this regulation are clear and easy to handle. Moreover, the European Commission has also proposed a general block exemption that should free more aid than hitherto from obligatory notification and create a uniform legal framework.

211. Should an aid meet neither the requirements of the De Minimis Regulation nor a block exemption regulation it must be notified under Art. 88, Para.3, Sentence 1 EC Treaty and it will be examined by the European Commission. The principles of this balancing test are concretised in guidelines and Community frameworks. It is typical of the guidelines published since the reform that they provide for two different kinds of procedure – firstly a faster procedure, in which legal assumptions are also used, and a more detailed procedure for difficult cases and large projects, in which an exact economic analysis is to be made, using the balancing test outlined above. As the first cases where the new R&D&I framework was used show, this involves an examination that is much more complex and elaborate than the test used so far on compatibility level. As the European Commission has so far only used the more economic approach on the justification level (Art. 87, Para. 3 EC Treaty) and not on the factual level (Art. 87, Para. 1 EC Treaty), it is not the European Commission but the member state that bears the onus of proof. If a detailed test is carried out the member state responsible for providing proof – and as a secondary instance the beneficiary enterprise – will incur considerable expenditure to convince the European Commission that the aid is compatible, as they must provide a large amount of information. This is one of the main differences from antitrust law, where the more economic approach has created more stringent proof requirements for the European Commission. The structure of aid control which the European Commission is endeavouring to achieve can be shown in the form of Table VI.3 below.

Table VI.3:

The Structure of the Aid Test

De Minimis Regulation
• no obligatory notification • criteria that are easy to handle • directly applicable by member states

General Block **Exemption**
• directly applicable by member states • more stringent requirements to apply the law (proof of incentive effect) • no obligatory notification

Test in Individual Cases

• Obligatory notification
• Conceivable variants, where envisaged in guidelines:
  a) faster test procedure, in which assumptions are (also) applied
  b) elaborate test procedure with balancing test actually performed.

Source: Monopolkommission

6.3.2.4 Taking Proven Efficiency Advantages into Account

Antitrust law

212. In applying the more economic approach in antitrust law the European Commission intends to enable efficiency advantages to be taken into account throughout. The EC Treaty expressly provides for consideration of efficiency advantages, that is, possible welfare gains, in Art. 81, Para. 3 EC Treaty, if consumers participate appropriately.[229] Art. 82 EC Treaty does not contain a corresponding clause. In its British Airways judgement of 15 March 2007 the ECJ first established the disadvantageous displacement effect of British Airways' discount and premium arrangement, and then expressly permitted efficiency advantages as an objection under Art. 82 EC Treaty.[230] In this regard, and unlike the question of the model, the British airways judgement is a success for the European Commission's more economic approach.

---

[229] Under Art. 81, Para. 3 EC Treaty an agreement can be exempt from the ban on cartels if it "contributes to improving the production or distribution of goods or to promoting technical or economic progress, while allowing consumers a fair share of the resulting benefit, and which does not: a) impose on the undertaking concerned restrictions which are not indispensable to the attainment of these objectives or b) afford such undertakings the possibility of eliminating competition in respect of a substantial part of the products in question." The onus of proof that the conditions for exemption are met under Art. 81, Para. 3 EC Treaty is on the enterprises that claim under this rule (Art. 2, Sentence 2 Regulation 1/2003).

[230] ECJ, Judgement of 15 March 2007, Case C 95/04, British Airways, No. 86.

This jurisprudence is based on the assumption that market behaviour can have a dual effect, that is, it can restrict competition and promote welfare.[231]

Efficiency advantages have been important in merger control since the reform carried out in 2004 to introduce a more economic approach.[232] As the European Commission states in its guidelines for horizontal mergers, it takes all the proven efficiency advantages into account in its overall assessment of a merger. These must benefit consumers, be specific to the merger and be provable.

State Aid Law

213. The European Commission will not admit an objection of efficiency in aid control identical to that in the antitrust competition rules. Nor would it be possible there, as the parties that may cause restriction of competition are not companies but sovereign states. However, the criterion of market failure can be described as a kind of efficiency objection in state aid. For the fact of market failure, which is to play a central role in future in the examination of compatibility under Art. 87, Para. 3 EC Treaty, is given, in the European Commission's definition, if the market is not producing an economically efficient result. Moreover, the member states – as always under Art. 87, Para. 3 EC Treaty – are responsible for proving that there is sufficient market failure in the meaning of the three-stage balancing test. As the onus of proving market failure is on the member states, and it is not easy to produce that proof, the more economic approach which the European Commission wishes to apply in competition law may not automatically result in a more positive assessment of aids and excessive awarding practice. On the contrary, more restrictive aid control is to be expected.

6.3.2.5 Economic Analysis Methods

Antitrust Law

214. In the more economic approach which it wishes to adopt the European Commission will make greater use of industrial economic models and quantitative analyses in its decision-making. It will rely on the Herfindahl-Hirschman Index (HHI), which has long been used in US merger control to establish the degree of concentration on a market before and after a merger.[233] The European Commission uses price correlation analyses, shock analysis[234] and in

---

[231] By contrast, the European Advisory Group on Competition Policy (EAGCP), a body of independent experts who advise the General-Directorate for Competition, have proposed that any pro-competition effects should be examined in all cases by the European Commission as part of its abuse control, and always taken into consideration. Cf. European Advisory Group on Competition Policy (EAGCP, Gual, J., Hellwig, M., Perrot, A., Rey, P., Schmidt, K., Stenbacka, R.), An Economic Approach to Article 82, EAGCP, http://www.europa.eu.int/comm/competition/publications/studies/eagcp_july_21_05.pdf.

[232] Cf. Merger Control Regulation, No. 29, and the statements by the European Commission in the guidelines for horizontal mergers Nos. 76-88 and in the guidelines for non-horizontal mergers (Guidelines for the merger of enterprises linked vertically or in conglomerates, No. 53).

[233] The HHI shows the sum of squared market shares for companies on the market in question.

[234] Past events and shocks on the market in question (like the introduction of a new product) are used to assess the market, cf. Schwalbe, U., Zimmer, D., Kartellrecht und Ökonomie, Frankfurt a.M. 2006, pp. 133.

particular the hypothetical monopoly test (SSNIP test, small but significant non-transitory increase in price)[235] to define a market materially and geographically.[236] It also uses simulation models directly to obtain the effects of a merger on prices, quantities and welfare, especially for mergers of producers of differentiated goods.[237]

State Aid Law

215. If a detailed examination of compatibility is made on the justification level the European Commission intends in future to carry out complex economic analyses, which it has not used before. They will be used particularly to assess the criterion of the incentive effect. Unlike under the antitrust prohibitions, in state aid control the European Commission does not intend to apply new economic methods on the factual level (Art. 87, Para. 1 EC Treaty). Initially, only the cursory examination will be made, which is still very much less than the standard applied in EU antitrust law in the form-based approach that precedes the more economic approach.

7. Proposals by the Monopolkommission

7.1 The Economic Approach under Art. 87 EC Treaty

216. The Monopolkommission is in favour of a more economic interpretation of distortion to competition under the ban in Art. 87, Para. 1 EC Treaty. It recommends that the objective likelihood of an aid noticeably distorting competition should be examined under Art. 87, Para. 1 EC Treaty, as is the practice under the antitrust rule in Art. 81, Para. 1 EC Treaty.

217. Under the ban in Art. 87, Para. 1 EC Treaty so far an in-depth economic analysis has only been made on "favouring", and in the private investor test, which is determinant here. Distortion to competition is not generally subject to a more differentiated economic assessment, the European Commission only makes a general sector-specific examination, which is clearly less than the standards traditionally applied in EU antitrust law, where the European Commission now wishes to replace it with the more economic approach. Nor is "noticeable" distortion to competition required as an unwritten rule in aid control, as it is under the antitrust rule in Art. 81 EC Treaty. No change to this practice is envisaged, in either the State Aid Action Plan or the

---

[235] This test examines whether the customers of the parties to a merger will react to an assumed small but permanent increase in relative prices (between 5% and 10%) for the products and areas under consideration by switching to easily available substitutes or not. If the substitution is so great that a price increase would not be profitable due to the fall in sales, other products will be included in the materially and geographically relevant market until a slight permanent increase in price would yield profits. For more detail cf. Schwalbe, U., Zimmer, D., loc. cit., pp. 104s.

[236] For more detail see Christiansen, A.: Der "more economic approach" in der EU Fusionskontrolle, Zeitschrift für Wirtschaftspolitik 55, 2006, pp. 150-174, 153, and Brinker, I., Praktische Probleme der Marktabgrenzung aus rechtlicher Sicht, in: Schwarze, J. (ed.): Recht und Ökonomie im europäischen Wettbewerbsrecht, Baden-Baden 2006, pp. 41-52, 47s.

[237] For more detail cf. Schwalbe, U., Zimmer, D. loc. cit., pp. 211s. and Monopolkommission, Hauptgutachten 2004/2005, loc. cit., Item 684. See also No. 29 of the Guidelines on horizontal mergers by the European Commission on the calculation of possible unilateral (one-sided) effects of a merger.

implementation measures to date. The European Commission's more economic approach only starts on the justification level, where the member state is responsible for providing proof. On this level the European Commission examines whether an aid can be approved as an exception (Art. 87, Para. 3 EC Treaty). That is not convincing, as the European ban on aid only takes effect and justifies intervention by the European Commission as the controlling body if a risk of distortion to competition on the internal market has been established (Art. 3, Para. 1 g) EC Treaty). In the view of the Monopolkommission the objective likelihood of an aid noticeably distorting competition should be examined under Art. 87, Para. 1 EC Treaty. This should be combined with a restriction of the area of application of aid control by the European Commission, and should be flanked by the introduction of complementary aid control on national level and by private right of appeal.[238]

218. In regard to the restriction of trade between member states in Art. 87, Para. 1 EC Treaty it should be an unwritten rule – as it is in antitrust law – that the restriction must be "noticeable". This will avoid the area of application of Art. 87, Para. 1 EC Treaty also being extended to matters of less importance between member states and of only local focus. That would appear to be appropriate as aid control, like antitrust law, is designed to protect competition on the internal market (Art. 3, Para. 1 g) EC Treaty). So only if there is proven risk of negative cross-frontier effects can aid control give rise to a ban on European level.

219. The following remarks contain suggestions from the Monopolkommission on how these aims can be achieved. In general, it does appear to be appropriate to assume that certain aids will cause noticeable distortion of competition. However, as the concept of "favouring" (selectivity) in Art. 87, Para. 1 EC Treaty is very broadly interpreted a general assumption does not appear to be justified in every situation. Measures can also be classified as aid if they benefit all the companies in a region or all of a certain size. The same applies to measures that are horizontal in effect and benefit companies in very different branches.

220. Distortion to competition can be assumed for rescue aid to companies in financial difficulties. The danger of inefficient promotion at the expense of more efficient competitors must be regarded as particularly great here. The same applies to aid to benefit sectors with considerable excess capacities (restructuring aids). These aids can help to maintain inefficient market structures, and a closer examination should be made on the justification level to establish whether the measure is permissible by way of exception, owing to market failure (failure to adjust) or for non-economic reasons (especially social considerations).

221. The Monopolkommission recommends carrying out a test of noticeability under Art. 87, Para. 1 EC Treaty for all the other forms of aid. Elements of the "significant impact test" (SIT) could be used here. The European Commission had intended to introduce this in 2003, in order to be able to concentrate more on the more difficult cases of distortion to competition in future.[239] But it was not introduced owing to opposition from member states, who could not

---

[238] See 4.3 and 7.4 for more detail.

[239] The SIT presented a new concept for the assessment of low amounts of state aid and of certain aids with limited effects on trade within the Community. Ultimately it consisted of two different tests, the LASA test and the LET test. Aid control would not to be carried out if the measures met the criteria of both these tests. In the LASA (limited amount of state aid test) test, as under the De Minimis Regulation, a low level of aid would be determinant. Some further conditions would also be set. The test was to be made independent of the sector and include the following criteria:

cont.

reach agreement, particularly on the positive list in the test, which names certain branches to be fixed in advance and where noticeable cross-frontier effects are to be regarded as unlikely.

222. In the view of the Monopolkommission the objection that could be raised to the positive list is that it would be an inflexible instrument and might have omissions. It could be more meaningful to set the following conditions, analogous to the SIT proposed by the European Commission:

- the aid should not be limited from the start to a specific enterprise or a specific sector,
- the aid granted to an individual enterprise within a period of three years would not exceed EUR 1 million,
- the aid would be activity-related, and its intensity, that is the share of the promotion in the total expenditure on a project, would not be more than 30%, and
- the aid would be given in an open procedure. That means that under general rules on aid it must be available to all the enterprises that meet certain criteria, and that individual aids must be given in a transparent tender procedure.

223. In addition, market shares and the resultant degree of concentration should be used as instruments in aid control to help identify distortion to competition. Analogous to the values which the European Commission has named in its guidelines for the assessment of horizontal mergers, a threshold of 25% for a market share and an HHI of 1000 could serve as orientation.[240]

224. In the case of aid to established companies with a strong market position there is a risk that they will be able to extend their advantage over their competitors. Entry to the market will also be made more difficult for newcomers and displacement practices facilitated. The greater the market concentration, the more likely is it that the competition will be distorted by aid to established companies, as in a tight oligopoly the decision of each market participant

---

. • The aid must be directly intended for the eligible costs of a defined aim that is in the Community interest (e.g. R&D, environmental protection).

. • The aid intensity, that is the share of the promotion in the total costs of the project, must be no more than 30%.

. • Maximally EUR 1 million would be granted to any single enterprise within three years.

. • The aid must be entered in a national register.

 • A maximum upper limit would be fixed for the total amount of aid granted under the LASA test by each member state and must not be exceeded.

Under these conditions the LASA test would allow the assumption that an aid would have only limited effects on competition and trade and so that aid control by the European Commission would not be necessary.

The LET (limited effect on trade) test, unlike the LASA test, did not envisage an upper limit and also covered larger amounts of aid. Its key features were:

. • A positive list would be drawn up of certain branches to be fixed in advance and where significant cross-frontier effects would be unlikely, e.g. branches without intensive competition on Community level.

. • The aid must be given in an open procedure. Under general, abstract rules the aid must be available to all companies that meet certain criteria, and individual aid must be given in a transparent tender.

 • The aid intensity must not exceed 30%.

[240] Cf. European Commission, Guidelines for the assessment of horizontal mergers, OJ EU C 31 of 5 February 2004, here p. 7, Nos. 18s.

influences the decisions of others. In this case actual distortion to competition can be assumed. Moreover, the political incentives to grant aid that will distort competition are particularly great here.

225. Conversely, the European Commission could be obliged to provide more reasons if the shares of the company benefiting are relatively low on the markets on which it is operating, or if the market is characterised by low concentration.

226. The degree of selectivity of the measure in question could also serve as a filter.[241] If the aid in question is highly selective, distortion to competition can be assumed. But if the measure is not very selective, e.g. because all the companies of a certain size category or within a certain region are to benefit, the European Commission would be obliged to examine the threat of distortion to competition from the aid more closely, and give reasons for this.

227. Should none of the above factors lead to a clear result the European Commission must clarify whether the measure will cause noticeable cross-frontier restriction of trade in a more detailed examination. Several factors need to be taken into account concerning both the aid and the way it will be given (aid criteria), as well as the relevant markets, the foreseeable effects on competition and the market position of the enterprise benefiting (market criteria). The aid criteria to be considered are the amount of the aid, its size in relation to the costs of the activity promoted (aid intensity) and the way it will be given. Here it is relevant whether the aid will be given only once or repeatedly, and whether an open and transparent procedure has taken place. Market criteria are whether there are excess capacities, the market share of the company benefiting, the market concentration, the distance in market share to the nearest competitor, the level of the barriers to market entry (high sunk costs), the degree of the company's vertical integration, the degree of product differentiation and the price development to be expected as a result of the aid.

228. The investigation outlined above presumes that, instead of a general sector-specific examination, the European Commission will define the markets in question materially and geographically in future in aid procedures as well, as it does under antitrust law, and establish the market position of the beneficiary. A specific delineation of the market with identification of the market share of the beneficiary, however, is only possible if the individual enterprise benefiting and the project to be promoted are already clear. But the ban on aid in Art. 87, Para. 1 EC Treaty not only covers aid of this kind, it also covers general aid schemes. In the case of aid with horizontal objectives it is frequently not fixed which companies in which sectors will benefit and which markets specifically will be affected. In that case the examination should be limited to establishing whether the state measure is likely to cause noticeable intervention in the market and affect the competition process in the EU internal market.

229. It must be remembered that the European courts are ultimately responsible for interpreting the ban on aid and the distortion to competition which it contains, and that traditionally they have set very low requirements for establishing that criterion. This problem could be solved by legal clarification. However, it is also conceivable that a change in the practice of applying the law would suffice, and the European courts could move away from

---

[241] This is suggested by the British Office of Fair Trading in its response to the European Commission's State Aid Action Plan of September 2005, http://www.oft.gov.uk/shared_oft/reports/oft_response_to_consultations/oft820.pdf.

their traditional jurisprudence. The judgement by the ECJ on the Le Levant case of 22 February 2006 could be taken as an indication of this, for the Court expressly admonished the European Commission for not making a more detailed examination of distortion to competition in the negative decision against which appeal was made.[242]

230. If these more stringent requirements to identify distortion of competition are to be applied in future it could be objected that this could make it more difficult for member states to assess whether a measure should be notified under Art. 88, Para. 3 EC Treaty or not. This could be countered by retaining the low requirements in Art. 88, Para. 3 EC Treaty and only laying upon the European Commission a more stringent obligation under Art. 87, Para. EC Treaty.

7.2 The More Economic Approach on the Justification Level (Art. 87, Para. 3 EC Treaty)

231. The justification grounds given in Art. 87, Para. 3 EC Treaty are very broadly formulated and they allow the European Commission considerable scope for discretion. In view of this it is welcome that the European Commission has concretised the condition for decisions under these discretionary powers in more detail as part of its more economic approach, by introducing a three-stage test. The more economic approach the European Commission would like to introduce in aid control will thus provide greater transparency and legal certainty.

232. In the balancing test the European Commission will focus on the criterion of market failure as the possible ground for justifying aid.[243] In this connection it must be asked whether a closer examination should be made of whether there is market failure, by way of exception, and the aid is the appropriate and necessary means of correcting it, on the factual level, in considering distortion to competition under Art. 87, Para. 1 EC Treaty. For should that be the case the competition situation will generally not be worsened, the aim is rather to improve the framework conditions for competition. However, in many cases where – presumed – market failure is to be removed there is a risk of state failure owing to erroneous prognoses, with consequent deterioration in the current competition situation (second-best problem). In view of the threat of over-optimal state intervention it would appear appropriate for the onus of proving a specific market failure to be on member states, and so a detailed examination would only be made on the justification level, which is the current practice by the European Commission. Accordingly, distortion to competition could be affirmed on factual level if the aid is likely to intervene noticeably in the cross-border competition process, and steer the behaviour of market participants and their investment decisions into a very different direction. So the criterion of market failure would have a function on the justification level comparable with the objection of efficiency in the European ban on cartels (Art. 81, Para. 3 EC Treaty).

233. A critical view can be taken of the fact that the European Commission sees the incentive effect as the main condition of its new balancing test. Aid should certainly only be granted if it will have an incentive effect, that is, change behaviour by the enterprise benefiting, as otherwise there would not be an additional economic benefit and public funds would be

---

[242] ECJ, Judgement of 22 February 2006, Case T 34/02, Le Levant/Commission, Rec. 2006, II-267, No. 127.

[243] Non-economic aims of general interest (e.g. regional coherence) can also be grounds for justification.

wasted. The powers of the European Commission in aid control are, however, limited to the protection of cross-border competition. In contrast to the draft regulation by the European Commission the incentive effect should not be included in a uniform, directly applicable block exemption regulation, either.[244]

7.3 An Efficient Procedural Design

234. As shown in 5.4 in the view of the Monopolkommission the efficiency of the aid control procedure could be increased by bringing it into line with the European antitrust procedure.[245] In this context the procedural rights of competitors and the recipients of state aid should be strengthened, the European Commission's powers to investigate companies improved and shorter, binding deadlines for approval introduced. Instead of the legality principle in force to date (Art. 10, Para. 1 Procedural Regulation) the European Commission should also be granted discretion over whether to take up a case, as it has in antitrust law, if the aid does not exceed a volume still to be determined. That would enable the European Commission to set priorities and concentrate on important cases. The discretionary powers should be flanked by the introduction of the right of private parties to bring an action for a declaratory judgement.

235. The Monopolkommission recommends allowing appeals by the recipient of the aid, competitors affected and their associations before the Community courts, on general aid regulations as well. In addition, competitors should be able to obtain legal protection on European level more easily.[246]

236. Legal protection on national level should be regulated as a whole and take account of the requirements in aid law.[247] In this connection especially a right of appeal should be introduced for associations, analogous to German antitrust law (§ 33, Para. 2 Act Against Restraints of Competition, GWB). The suspensive effect of lawsuits when recovery of the aid is ordered should also be excluded and an efficient legal protection system created, comparable to the rules on public procurements (§§ 104ss. GWB).

7.4 Complementary Aid Control on National Level

237. As well as negative consequences for competition in allocative, productive and dynamic regard, the award of state aid can involve considerable costs for the economy as a whole. State aid involves financing costs or other opportunity costs, and it causes loss of welfare, partly through the necessary taxation in other areas and partly through erroneous prognoses and free riding. While the competence of the European Commission in European aid control is limited to protecting cross-border competition, the member states must take account of all the economic costs in awarding state aid and weigh these against the expected benefit.

238. If European aid control is reduced to protecting cross-frontier competition as described above, its area of application will be limited compared with the European Commission's

---

[244] Cf. 181.
[245] Cf. 130ss.
[246] 246 Cf. 146ss.
[247] Cf. 158.

administrative practice to date. In the view of the Monopolkommission it is then absolutely essential to create at the same time effective complementary control mechanisms on national level. Otherwise there is a risk that owing to insufficient density of control aid would be granted on an inefficiently high and economically harmful level.

239. In the view of the Monopolkommission national aid programmes should be subject to regular success control, and in serious cases, where the individual aid or the aid programme exceeds an as yet unspecified volume, ex ante macroeconomic control should be carried out by an independent national body. Moreover, aid should on principle be given in an open and transparent procedure. Aid designed right from the start for individual companies or a specific branch should be forbidden, and only permitted in exceptional cases after national ex ante control. As well as a time limit on aid programmes and digressive long-term promotion, state aid that exceeds a specific volume should be made known in advance by the public authority awarding it on a central Internet website. In particular, the subjective rights of potential recipients of aid, competitors affected and their associations should be upheld and an efficient system of legal protection created analogous to the law on public procurements (§§ 104ss. GWB).

240. The proposals by the Monopolkommission to reduce European aid control and build up national aid control are intended as a package that should only be implemented as a whole.

7.5 Summary of the Recommendations

241. The Monopolkommission believes that in the aid control procedure – as under Art. 81, Para. 1 EC Treaty – an examination should be made on the factual level of Art. 87, Para. 1 EC Treaty of the objective likelihood that an aid will noticeably distort competition and restrict trade between member states. Unlike antitrust law it is not an unwritten rule that an aid measure must have noticeable effects. Consequently, the area of application of aid control also covers cases of mainly local importance. In regard to distortion of competition the European Commission has so far generally only made an overall sectoral examination which is clearly less than the standard which is traditionally applied in EU antitrust law, where the European Commission would now like to supplement it with flexible economic criteria in a more economic approach. The European Commission's envisaged reform, with a more detailed examination of the initial structural situation on the market and the competitive situation to be made only on the justification level (Art. 87, Para. 3 EC Treaty), does not appear convincing, as the European ban on aid will only fulfil its purpose of protection if there is a threat of distortion of competition on the internal market and it has been appropriately identified.

242. In the view of the Monopolkommission it is entirely appropriate to assume distortion of competition from certain forms of aid granted by member states (for instance rescue and restructuring aids). But as the principle of favouring named in Art. 87, Para. 1 EC Treaty is very broadly interpreted a general assumption does not appear justified in every situation. In the view of the Monopolkommission a noticeability test that can be refuted should be introduced, with simplified exemption allowed on the basis of various criteria for aid below a threshold still to be specified (e.g. EUR 1 million). Should neither the noticeability test nor other assumptions yield the required result the European Commission should clarify in a more detailed assessment whether the measure will cause distortion to cross-border competition. In this regard several factors must be taken into account, affecting both the aid and the way it is granted (the aid criteria) and the relevant markets, the foreseeable effects on competition and the market position of the beneficiary enterprise (market criteria).

243. The procedure used in aid control should, in the view of the Monopolkommission, be reformed and in certain points brought into line with European antitrust procedures. In this connection the procedural rights of competitors and recipients of aid should be strengthened, the powers of the European Commission to investigate companies improved and shorter, binding deadlines for approval introduced. It should be considered replacing the current legality principle with discretion for the European Commission over whether to take up a case, as it has in antitrust law, if an aid does not exceed a certain volume. That would enable the European Commission to set priorities and concentrate on important cases. The discretionary powers could be flanked with the introduction of private right of appeal for a declaratory judgement.

The Monopolkommission also recommends admitting suits by recipients of aid, competitors affected and their associations before the Community courts, on general aid regulations as well. In addition, competitors should be able to obtain legal protection on European level more easily. Legal protection on national level should be regulated as a whole, and take due account of the requirements of aid law. In particular, right of appeal for associations should be introduced analogous to German antitrust law (§ 33, Para. 2 GWB). The minimum standards to be introduced for this in member states could be the subject of an EU directive. In addition, the suspensive effect of lawsuits in recovery cases could be excluded and an efficient system of legal protection created, similar to that in the law on public procurements (§§ 104ss. GWB).

244. If European aid control is reduced to the protection of cross-border competition its area of application will be limited compared with the previous administrative practice by the European Commission. In the view of the Monopolkommission it is necessary to create effective complementary control mechanisms on national level at the same time.[248]

245. Finally, the aid (subsidies) given by the EU itself and which, unlike the aid given by member states, does not come under the area of application of Arts. 87ss. EC Treaty, should be subject to more detailed examination. It should be considered extending control of EU subsidies to a new independent European supervisory authority, that could act free of political influence. Beside any EU-related measures the EU and member states should work more on international level for the introduction of a better system of control within the WTO framework.

---

[248] See 7.4.

INDEX

INTERNATIONAL COMPETITION LAW SERIES

1. Ignacio De Leon, *Latin American Competition Law and Policy: A Policy in Search of Identity*, 2001 (ISBN 90-411-1542-0).
2. Wim Dejonghe & Wouter Van de Voorde (eds), *M & A in Belgium*, 2001 (ISBN 90-411-1594-3).
3. Yang-Ching Chao, Gee San, Changfa Lo & Jiming Ho (eds), *International and Comparative Competition Law and Policies*, 2001 (ISBN 90-411-1643-5).
4. Martin Mendelsohn & Stephen Rose, *Guide to the EC Block Exemption for Vertical Agreements*, 2002 (ISBN 90-411-9813-X).
5. Clifford A. Jones & Mitsuo Matsushita (eds), *Competition Policy in the Global Trading System: Perspectives from the EU, Japan and the USA*, 2002 (ISBN 90-411-1758-X).
6. Christian Koenig, Andreas Bartosch, Jens-Daniel Braun & Marion Romes (eds), *EC Competition and Telecommunications Law*. Second Edition, 2009 (ISBN 978-90-411-2564-4).
7. Jürgen Basedow (ed.), *Limits and Control of Competition with a View to International Harmonization*, 2002 (ISBN 90-411-1967-1).
8. Maureen Brunt, *Economic Essays on Australian and New Zealand Competition Law*, 2003 (ISBN 90-411-1991-4).
9. Ky P. Ewing, Jr., *Competition Rules for the 21st Century: Principles from America's Experience*, Second Edition, 2006 (ISBN 90-411-2477-2).
10. Joseph Wilson, *Globalization and the Limits of National Merger Control Laws*, 2003 (ISBN 90-411-1996-5).
11. Peter Verloop & Valérie Landes (eds), *Merger Control in Europe: EU, Member States and Accession States*, Fourth Edition, 2003 (ISBN 90-411-2056-4).
12. Themistoklis K. Giannakopoulos, *Safeguarding Companies' Rights in Competition and Anti-dumping/Anti-subsidies Proceedings*, 2004 (ISBN 90-411-2254-0).
13. Marjorie Holmes & Lesley Davey (eds), *A Practical Guide to National Competition Rules across Europe*, Second Edition, 2007 (ISBN 978-90-411-2607-8).
14. Sigrid Stroux, *US and EU Oligopoly Control*, 2004 (ISBN 90-411-2296-6).
15. Tzong-Leh Hwang and Chiyuan Chen (eds), *The Future Development of Competition Framework*, 2004 (ISBN 90-411-2305-9).
16. Phedon Nicolaides, Mihalis Kekelekis and Maria Kleis, *State Aid Policy in the European Community: Principles and Practice*, Second Edition, 2008 (ISBN 978-90-411-2754-9).
17. Doris Hildebrand, *Economic Analyses of Vertical Agreements: A Self-Assessment*, 2005 (ISBN 90-411-2328-8).
18. Frauke Henning-Bodewig, *Unfair Competition Law: European Union and Member States*, 2005 (ISBN 90-411-2329-6).
19. Duarte Brito & Margarida Catalão-Lopes, *Mergers and Acquisitions: The Industrial Organization Perspective*, 2006 (ISBN 90-411-2451-9).

20. Nikos Th. Nikolinakos, *EU Competition Law and Regulation in the Converging Telecommunications, Media and IT Sectors*, 2006 (ISBN 90-411-2469-1).
21. Mihalis Kekelekis, *The EC Merger Control Regulation: Rights of Defence. A Critical Analysis of DG COMP Practice and Community Courts' Jurisprudence*, 2006 (ISBN 90-411-2553-1).
22. Mark R. Joelson, *An International Antitrust Primer: A Guide to the Operation of United States, European Union and Other Key Competition Laws in the Global Economy*, Third Edition, 2006 (ISBN 90-411-2468-3).
23. Themistoklis K. Giannakopoulos, *A Concise Guide to the EU Anti-dumping/ Anti-subsidies Procedures*, 2006 (ISBN 90-411-2464-0).
24. George Cumming, Brad Spitz & Ruth Janal, *Civil Procedure Used for Enforcement of EC Competition Law by the English, French and German Civil Courts*, 2007 (ISBN 978-90-411-2471-5).
25. Jürgen Basedow (ed.), *Private Enforcement of EC Competition Law*, 2007 (ISBN 978-90-411-2613-9).
26. Jung Wook Cho, *Innovation and Competition in the Digital Network Economy: A Legal and Economic Assessment on Multi-tying Practices and Network Effects*, 2007 (ISBN 978-90-411-2574-3).
27. Akira Inoue, *Japanese Antitrust Law Manual: Law, Cases and Interpretation of the Japanese Antimonopoly Act*, 2007 (ISBN 978-90-411-2627-6).
28. René Barents, *Directory of EC Case Law on Competition*, 2007 (ISBN 978-90-411-2656-6).
29. Paul F. Nemitz (ed.), *The Effective Application of EU State Aid Procedures: The Role of National Law and Practice*, 2007 (ISBN 978-90-411-2657-3).
30. Jurian Langer, *Tying and Bundling as a Leveraging Concern under EC Competition Law*, 2007 (ISBN 978-90-411-2575-0).
31. Abel M. Mateus & Teresa Moreira (eds), *Competition Law and Economics – Advances in Competition Policy and Antitrust Enforcement*, 2007 (ISBN 978-90-411-2632-0).
32. Alberto Santa Maria, *Competition and State Aid: An Analysis of the EC Practice*, 2007 (ISBN 978-90-411-2617-7).
33. Barry J. Rodger (ed.), *Article 234 and Competition Law: An Analysis*, 2007 (ISBN 978-90-411-2605-4).
34. Alla Pozdnakova, *Liner Shipping and EU Competition Law*, 2008 (ISBN 978-90-411-2717-4).
35. Milena Stoyanova, *Competition Problems in Liberalized Telecommunications: Regulatory Solutions to Promote Effective Competition*, 2008 (ISBN 978-90-411-2736-5).
36. *EC State Aid Law/Le Droit des Aides d'Etat dans la CE. Liber Amicorum Francisco Santaolalla Gadea*, 2008 (ISBN 978-90-411-2774-7).
37. René Barents, *Directory of EC Case Law on State Aids*, 2008 (ISBN 978-90-411-2732-7).
38. Ignacio De Leon, *An Institutional Assessment of Antitrust Policy: The Latin American Experience*, 2009 (ISBN 978-90-411-2478-4).

39. Doris Hildebrand, *The Role of Economic Analysis in the EC Competition Rules*, Third Edition, 2009 (ISBN 978-90-411-2513-2).
40. Eugène Buttigieg, *Competition Law: Safeguarding the Consumer Interest. A Comparative Analysis of US Antitrust Law and EC Competition Law*, 2009 (ISBN 978-90-411-3119-5).
41. Ioannis Lianos & Ioannis Kokkoris (eds), *The Reform of EC Competition Law: New Challenges,* 2010 (ISBN 978-90-411-2692-4).
42. George Cumming & Mirjam Freudenthal, *Civil Procedure in EU Competition Cases before the English and Dutch Courts*, 2010 (ISBN 978-90-411-3192-8).
43. A.E. Rodriguez & Ashok Menon, *The Limits of Competition Policy: The Short-comings of Antitrust in Developing and Reforming Economies*, 2010 (ISBN 978-90-411-3177-5).
44. Mika Oinonen, *Does EU Merger Control Discriminate against Small Market Companies? Diagnosing the Argument with Conclusions*, 2010 (ISBN 978-90-411-3261-1).
45. Eirik Østerud, *Identifying Exclusionary Abuses by Dominant Undertakings under EU Competition Law: The Spectrum of Tests*, 2010 (ISBN 978-90-411-3271-0).
46. Marco Botta, *Merger Control Regimes in Emerging Economies: A Case Study on Brazil and Argentina*, 2011 (ISBN 978-90-411-3402-8).
47. Jürgen Basedow & Wolfgang Wurmnest (eds), *Structure and Effects in EU Competition Law: Studies on Exclusionary Conduct and State Aid*, 2011 (ISBN 978-90-411-3174-4).